LOAN RISK

Strategies and Analytical Techniques for Commercial Bankers

MANAGEMENT

Morton Glantz

PROBUS PUBLISHING COMPANY
Chicago, Illinois
Cambridge, England

BANKLINE ™

ISBN 1-55738-384-7

Printed in the United States of America

BB

CTV/BJS

1 2 3 4 5 6 7 8 9 0

Dedication

To my wife Maryann and daughter Felise, a continuous source of love, patience, and inspiration.

To my students for enriching my life.

And to my dear friends at Misr Iran Development Bank, Cairo, Egypt who, in equal measure, returned knowledge and wisdom.

Table of Contents

Preface

Unlike Mark Twain's cat, who once sat on a hot stove lid and would never again sit even on a warm one, bankers should "always be careful to get from an experience just the wisdom that is in it." No more, no less!

Credit officers need a sense of caution in a liberal credit environment—but they also need the courage and wisdom to take reasonable lending opportunities when the bank credit market is gun-shy. Banks are in the business of risk taking.

In *Loan Risk Management*, I steer you through the current jungle of modern corporate finance and credit technology step-by-step. The book can best be used as a textbook and a workbook, but the casual browser will also get full value from his or her investment. I've divided it into seven sections to separate material into more digestible chunks for the textbook reader. The commuter or casual reader will be able to easily select specific topics to update his lending knowledge.

Loan Risk Management will be helpful to accounting, finance, and credit novices and to experienced analysts as well. Readers need no prior business background beyond a basic, maybe even rusty, familiarity with a financial statement, but even the weathered analyst will find the material far from humdrum.

Portions of the book are quantitative and somewhat challenging, but so are the issues facing today's bankers, accountants and corporate managers. Credit competence in the '90s dictates that they must anticipate, not react. They must be perceptive, forward looking, and well informed on corporate finance and credit analytics. Futhermore, they must review credit exposures constantly.

In today's lending environment, what you don't know hurts you badly, so the only way to success is to assume "reasonable" risks—risks that are controlled within defined parameters of credit analysis and are within your financial resources and credit competence.

Acknowledgments

I am first and foremost indebted to William M. Glasgow, my excellent editor and researcher at large. The quality and direction of this project would have been far more difficult, if not impossible, without his devotion, creativity, and enthusiasm.

Since this book is a synthesis, I am indebted to the hundreds of practitioners who have created the body of credit knowledge contained in it and the writers who have made direct contributions. I have acknowledged every source I have been able to identify, but some writers and sources may have been missed unintentionally.

In addition, I wish to offer a special word of thanks to Rob Gaddis, a valuation expert at Price Waterhouse. I called on Rob for his insight and awareness of recent developments in finance and I want to thank him and his firm for allowing me to draw on his expertise and resources, and for overseeing the writing of this book.

A number of colleagues have also provided expertise as well as encouragement and support. I wish to particularly thank Victor Borun, Kevin McMann, Claude Marvin, and Tom Kennedy.

In the course of preparing the manuscript, I had the cooperation of a number of other professionals and I wish to take this opportunity to express my gratitude. Several persons were unusually helpful to me, and I must record my special debt to them: Thomas Carlson, Eric Weissman, Andrew Robertson, Jeffrey Bottari, Peter Overmier, Bert Kaminski, Maura Howard, Joe Cardon, Anthony Mollo, Susan Berliner, and Morton H. Scheer. David Langer, a computer consultant *par excellence*, deserves special thanks for his advice and counsel.

The editorial and production staff at Probus Publishing could not have been more helpful. Gene Grennan, especially, provided encouragement and attention to detail that improved the quality of this book.

I am deeply indebted to my students at the Fordham Graduate School of Business and Adelphi University Graduate School of Business, who have given me valuable assistance. I have used the material several times in graduate classes and have asked for written suggestions for improvements. Many of the latter proved most perceptive, and they have all been taken into account in the final version.

Section I

Fundamental Concepts of Credit

CHAPTER One

Introduction to Credit Risk Management

Credit Risk Management Today

Instead of going into extensive detail about the evolution of commercial credit, I'll get right to my central point:

■ ■ ■

Simply put, banks are in the business of making loans, and it is the credit officer's responsibility to pursue that business by making sound credit decisions.

■ ■ ■

This requires more judgment than technical skill. Reviewing financial statements may yield preliminary findings, but these fail to assess the numerous variables that must be weighed. The loan officer must understand the information, not merely crunch the numbers.

Further, unless credit analysis standards are clearly defined, valuable time and effort are wasted, not to mention the bot-tom-line consequences of reaching the wrong decision.

If a loan officer determines that the borrowing firm's expectations exceed its repayment ability, does this mean all possible repayment sources are exhausted? Since the key is to increase profitability through sound credit judgment, the analyst must always evaluate repayment potential from all alternative sources.

In turn, if the bank is confident of repayment based on the additional findings, the appropriate pricing considerations are issued and monitored. The net effect is future profits for the bank due to a meticulous credit investigation. Otherwise the loan will probably be lost to a better prepared competitor.

Since lenders are in the business of taking risk, why are banks so concerned about losing money? Briefly stated, a bank can never price an individual loan at a loss even if the probability of default decreases. For example, if the bank's net interest margin is 4 percent annually, it would take 25 years to recoup 100 percent of the loss, not including related overhead costs.

Why do banks bother lending if they cannot afford to lose money? They assume risk because loan income is necessary to produce earnings and cover costs.

Thus, the core of credit analysis is evaluating the borrower's ability to repay debt. Critical risk assumptions play a major role in finalizing lending decisions. To calculate risk, comprehensive information is needed. Further, you must understand *how much* information is enough. In other words, identifying what is and is not significant is critical to reliable credit judgment.

One way to do this is to assign a risk rating (above average, average and below average) to all facts. "Weights of importance" will then be assigned to details regardless of a positive or negative rating.

A system or model must be employed in making credit decisions, weighing all available alternatives, and eventually identifying and selecting the best course of action.

The credit model "PRISM" does exactly that. Each letter of PRISM covers qualitative and quantitative issues in assessing the borrower's financial strength. This lets the loan officer achieve equilibrium between repayment and risk. The basic **PRISM** components are:

> **P**erspective
> **R**epayment
> **I**ntention
> **S**afeguards
> **M**anagement

Let's place these components in the context of some pertinent questions:

What is the **perspective** relating to risk/reward?

Is the borrower capable of making **repayment?**

What is the **intention** of the loan?

What **safeguards** does the bank have against default?

Who are the **management** staff running the borrowing company?

For PRISM to be effective, the model must be followed step-by-step. Each question or component must be thoroughly analyzed and interpreted before the next is considered. This is essential to determining, at the conclusion of each step, which of the four following situations exists:

1. There is no material barrier to proceeding to the next PRISM component.

2. Specific problems exist and must be addressed in the remaining PRISM components.

3. There are strong indications that lending is undesirable and the process should be stopped.

4. The lender has been thrown off course, leading almost inevitably to incorrect credit decisions.

In other words, each succeeding component feeds off previous information to develop a trustworthy opinion.

Moreover, it's necessary to re-arrange the PRISM components and questions into a more logical, if less easily remembered, sequence. This sequence more closely follows a logical approach to credit-related decision making. Let's first look at the PRISM model in this order, then review a case study showing how the model might work with a hypothetical firm.

Management

Who are the **management** staff running the company? Evaluating **management** introduces the lender to the borrower, focusing primarily on the qualitative issues that help bankers overview the firm's past, present and future business objectives. The reason **management** is examined first is elementary: bankers want to familiarize themselves with the company and its players. By doing so, a confidence level is established and will eventually be the springboard to future key assumptions.

Establishing rapport with management is part of sound credit pratice. It is helpful to consider that you are lending money to people who, presumably, will ensure repayment.

The importance of the analyst's recording all information and proceeding to further analysis can't be overemphasized.

Management is divided into four categories:

- Business operations
- Management/Administration
- Bank relationship(s)
- Financial reporting

While each category is important in its own right, the order after business operations is of less importance. However, deductive reasoning is critical. **Management**, when analyzed properly, will flag any inconsistencies a company is experiencing or will experience in the future. For example, say a company manufactures and distributes perishable goods using a LIFO inventory system. Although management follows this strategy for tax purposes, the loan officer is alerted to possible inventory problems due to product obsolescence or spoilage if turnover is slow.

Business Operations

Certain characteristics contribute significantly to a firm's general image. These emerge from a number of factors: the number of years it has existed, its reputation and performance record, and its ability to repay debt.

It's obvious that the longer a company has been in business, with current management, the better. To a bank this indicates that the borrower has established staying power with its customers and vendors and, more important, its banks. It also nets out all actions taken by management to build a reputation. There is no stronger recommendation than one earned from peers and customers.

Performance builds reputation and past performance frequently foreshadows future performance. Although this is not always true, it is a working rule used confidently by many credit analysts.

Next is the firm's debt repayment record. This is critical to the overall risk assessment and can easily kill a loan if record of repayment is poor or spotty.

Another critical determinant in assessing methods of operation is the viability of the business. The most efficient and effective way of measuring viability is through the use of a select group of financial ratios. Although these ratios serve only as initial indicators, they will help the loan officer to develop sound opinions as to the borrower's health and strength. Further examination into the quality of the numbers on the financial statements will clarify the company's true status. The financial ratios used include:

1. **Gross Profit Margin (Gross Profit/Net Sales):** Indicates if a firm is suffering from structural or temporary problems as a result of its

inability to pass on manufacturing costs to the customer. How much gross profit is the company making per every dollar in sales?

2. **SG&A Expenses / Sales:** How well does management control discretionary costs in relation to sales? Are funds wasted or well spent for the good of the company?

3. **Net Margin (Net Income/Net Sales):** Relates profits to sales. What is considered a good profit margin will depend upon the industry. Low profit margins usually signify rising costs with lower than proportionate increases in revenue.

4. **Return on Equity or Return on Net Worth (Reported Income/Equity):** Furnishes the analyst with the per dollar yield on investment to the equity holder. If the ROE has been 3 percent over the last 5 years versus a risk-free rate of 4 percent, and the owner isn't taking in large salaries, why is the firm in business?

Management/Administration

The administration section concentrates on the corporate hierarchy: who are the key players in the game, and what contributions have they made to the company? By preparing a brief biographical summary of each executive, the lender becomes better equipped to consolidate management philosophy with business operations, and perhaps is better prepared to communicate with management. The human factor in decision making can have some of the most significant and unpredictable consequences for a firm. That is why consideration of **management** is given a priority position in all credit decisions.

Evaluating management is broken down into two parts: management's success and management's determination to repay. In measuring management's success, the best proof of success is obtained by reviewing corporate leadership through good times and bad. Success depends on management's assumption of an active role now and in the future, especially if growth and expansion are anticipated. This is why it is in the bank's best interest to develop a perspective of the borrower's present and future aspirations. By doing so, it can be determined if management's goals are realistically based on the economic conditions affecting the industry.

How do lending officers determine if management will repay the loan? Words like *integrity* and *character* come to mind immediately. If management makes assurances to pay, any events leading to cash flow problems will in all probability not lead to serious collection problems. Although management promises to pay, reliability can only be determined by past action. If possible, inquiries should be made of competitors, vendors, past financial relationships of both prospective customers and key members of the management team. Since the majority of information will come from management, the lender must have confidence in the information obtained. If thorough analysis diagnoses otherwise, the lender may be taking a gamble rather than a calculated risk.

Bank Relationship

Bank relationship follows one of two paths, depending on whether the company is an existing customer or applying for credit for the first time. This does not mean that the amount of research performed is more or less. The nature of the current relationship simply indicates what direction the loan officer follows in obtaining data. If there is an existing relationship, the affiliation should be researched to determine how solid it has been. Obviously, a loyal customer who pays off credit obligations on a timely basis has a stronger relationship with the bank than one that doesn't.

It is also imperative, and basic, that the analyst verify that the bank maintains operating accounts for the potential borrower. This is critical because the bank does not want to lose one relationship as a result of not properly servicing the other relationship. If the customer is denied credit and takes his business elsewhere, the bank incurs opportunity costs to replace the customer's account balance with borrowed funds at the going rate of interest. As a result, the bank not only loses the loan but also the company's operating balances this year as well as the present value of all future balances.

Also, the loan officer can examine the operating accounts' balance history to gain insight on the dynamics (perhaps seasonal) of the prospective borrower's funding needs. Also after a loan is made, the operating accounts can be early warning sources that liquidy difficulities are being experienced.

If the client is seeking to establish credit with you for the first time, duration and strength of prior relationships with other banks and vendors must be thoroughly examined. This can easily be done by obtaining business credit reports that provide a credit history.

Financial Reporting

As implied previously, the information supplied to the creditor by the client is the foundation for making sound credit decisions. Therefore, the creditor must confirm the competency of the accounting firm which conducts the audits and prepares the loan applicant's financial statements.

Knowing the accounting firm by reputation or having dealt directly with it before is a definite plus. All accounting information supplied to the creditor should comply with Generally Accepted Accounting Principles (GAAP). The applicant's financial reporting style (i.e., what it expenses, what it capitalizes) liberal or conservative, will indicate how accurately it depicts the firm's financial health and strength.

Intention (Purpose)

What is the **intention** of the loan? As a general rule, the **intention** or purpose of every loan should be the basis of its repayment. The last thing a prudent banker wants to do is liquidate a debtor's holdings to collect an unsound loan. It's preferable to explore the economic need for the loan from the outset and to develop critical assumptions as to its advisability and chances for liquidation.

In regard to loan duration, short-term loans are often most desirable in terms of liquidity. Debt to fund noncurrent assets traditionally carries greater risk. As liquidity diminishes, remuneration must come from nonasset conversion sources, extending the length and increasing the uncertainty of the loan.

A loan's intention or purpose generally falls into three broad categories:

a. To replace or support assets

b. To replace or support creditors

c. To replace or support equity

Classifications A and B can either be short-term or long-term in nature. Classification C is long-term. By evaluating the quality of the numbers in the borrower's financial statements, loan officers will be able to develop a hypothesis identifying the reason credit is requested. Is it for the reason the company stated? If not, why?

How will the intention affect the loan officer's judgment in extending credit? Replacement or support of assets on a short-term basis usually signals that the company is seasonal. In turn, loans are necessary to support high points in the cycle. If, on the other hand, the debt is long term, fixed assets are being purchased for either retooling or expansion.

Short-term loans to replace or support credit may indicate problems paying suppliers and other creditors. This usually indicates cash flow problems as a result of the firm's inability to convert assets and pay off creditors. Long-term requests for credit will replace creditors with better terms and lower interest rates.

Replacing or supporting equity short-term or long-term equates to restructuring strategies as simple as a stock buyback or as complex as LBOs and acquisitions. By replacing equity with debt, the company's equity is "taken off" the market. This substitution or relationship of debt for equity is better known as leverage. Of the three possibilities, this is the most risky purpose from a bank's standpoint. It is also the most profitable. By financing equity and replacing it with debt, the firm takes on greater risk of default. But with this greater risk, the greater possibility of reward is offered for the investor.

Repayment

Is the company capable of making **repayment**? Of all the converging PRISM components, this is most important. Since **intention (purpose)** determines **repayment** source, some basic definitions of risk

must be addressed. The ultimate risk characteristics are either: the inability of cash flows to meet necessary outflows (cash insolvency) or the inability of cash flows to meet necessary outflows on schedule (cash inadequacy).

While the result of cash insolvency would be a loss for the bank, cash inadequacy simply means slow repayment. But cash inadequacy can also cause a loss due to opportunity costs for the bank.

Firms have two sources of cash available to satisfy short-term and long-term credit obligations: (1) internally, from business operations and (2) externally, from new debt or equity. The relationship between these two sources in conjunction with the length of the loan will signal the soundness or fragility of the company's **repayment** capabilities.

Internal sources of short-term repayments, usually seasonal loans, are supported through the company's efforts to generate funds from the conversion of assets. This is best illustrated by a firm's conversion/contraction scenario. Under normal circumstances, a company will borrow money in order to support its manufacturing operation. This process increases assets and liabilities accordingly, thus expanding the company's balance sheet. The conversion cycle generates cash flow through the sale of inventory, thereby increasing accounts receivable. Once accounts receivable is converted to cash, the balance sheet contracts as the company retires its debt. As can be readily ascertained, the completion of the conversion cycle signals the contraction of the balance sheet. More important, the conversion of assets is the primary source of repayment to satisfy debt. In many cases, a company does not even have to make a profit to pay off its debt. Thus, the primary source of pay-

Exhibit 1.1

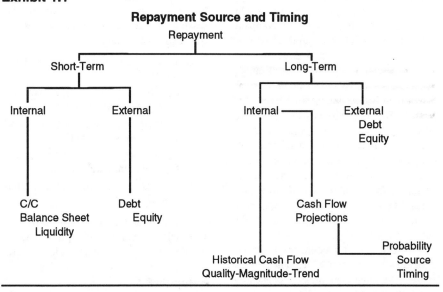

Repayment Source and Timing

Repayment

Short-Term — Long-Term

Internal — External (Short-Term)

Internal — External Debt Equity (Long-Term)

C/C
Balance Sheet
Liquidity

Debt
Equity

Cash Flow
Projections

Probability
Source
Timing

Historical Cash Flow
Quality-Magnitude-Trend

ment of a seasonal or short-term loan is the balance sheet.

If the balance sheet doesn't fully convert, a company will seek external sources of repayment to cover debt. This is done through the firm's ability to either issue debt or obtain an equity injection. From a debt standpoint, is the company strong enough to borrow funds from other banks to replace its current credit? If not, can the owner of the company "inject" more money into the business by floating a stock issue?

The internal repayment for long-term credits is a dichotomy of historical and projected cash flow. Historical cash flow analysis provides a track record of the company's past performance. The main question to be answered is: Does the company have the cash flow to support fixed asset investment(s)? This can be determined by breaking down the historical cash flow into three areas: quality, magnitude, and trend.

The quality of historical cash flow is analyzed by looking at the firm's gross operating cash flow (net income plus non-cash charges less non-cash credits). If the gross operating cash flows primarily comprise non-cash items such as depreciation, deferred taxes or asset write-downs—with a relatively small amount shown as income—the quality of the operating cash flow may be insufficient to repay credit. As stated earlier, profits and the sale of assets play a major role in retiring debt requirements, so it is imperative that the bank analyst identify what accounts for the firm's cash flow.

The magnitude of historical cash flow relative to growth plans will help to identify the external financing requirements facing the firm. The smaller the cash flow, the greater the debt load required to support long-term growth plans. If, for example, the income statement is not producing enough cash flow to service its loans year after year, the firm is in jeopardy of defaulting on its loans and going bankrupt. Astute loan officers should question why funds are being funneled into a company in the first place if it can't produce a decent level of profits to pay back debt.

Historical cash flow trends enable the creditor to determine if the firm's cash flows support the decision to go for growth. This is decided by evaluating the company's viability. A healthy company will be able to contribute a good part of its expansion funding from internally generated funds. On the other hand, a company suffering from declining cash flow performance can only satisfy expansion plans with an infusion of cash in the form of debt.

Cash flow projections use historical cash flow as a jumping off point into the future. The three main areas of concentration both now and in the future are:

- Sales growth performance
- Margins
- Company asset management

This in turn will assist the loan officer in reviewing financing sources and financing ability in terms of:

- The source of repayment
- The probability of repayment
- The timing of repayment

External repayment for long-term credit is financed by issuing debt and/or equity. Debt capacity is measured by looking at the firm's leverage. The higher the debt to equity ratio, the more leveraged the company. What is the company's debt to equity ratio in relation to the industry average? For example, if the company is already highly leveraged compared to the rest of its industry, what is the probability that credit obligations will be satisfied? These questions can be answered by assessing the criteria for bringing in additional sources of funds:

- What is the company's comfort level for debt?
- Can interest payments be covered through company profits?
- Does the company possess good quality assets to attract debt?
- Is the company's ability to generate future earnings well defined?
- What is the company's overall reputation?

A thorough exploration of each question will formulate an opinion as to whether or not additional debt is possible.

Safeguards

What safeguards or protection does the bank have against default? As mentioned earlier, all loans involve a certain level of risk; some more than others. If a bank is to extend credit to a firm, the level of risk determines the amount of safeguards the bank requires. Safeguards can either be internal, external, or a combination of both. Internal safeguards monitor the company's financial statements evaluating repayment while collateral, personal guarantees, and loan covenants provide external protection. Although external safeguards are used all the time, they are the weaker form of safeguards for the lending institution. It cannot be stressed enough that the key to approving or not approving a loan comes from the company's ability to repay the loan while at the same time providing the bank with safeguards against default. Refer to the Repayment/Safeguards matrix on the following page.

Exhibit 1.2

Repayment/Safeguard Matrix

	Short Term	Long Term
Repayment	Bal Sheet	Cash Flow
Safeguard	Cash Flow	Bal Sheet

The repayment/safeguards matrix may bewilder any analyst applying its principles for the first time. But examination and implementation will show it makes perfect sense.

Short-term loans require payments to be secured on the strength of the balance sheet because the bank wants to make sure the company has the ability to convert inventory into cash to pay down debt. Safeguards evolve based on the soundness of the company and its ability to support cash flow with future profits. As long as there are no structural problems with the company, the bank is protected.

Long-term debt is associated with permanent growth and the purchase of fixed assets. Repayment/safeguards for long-term credit are the exact opposite of those for short-term credit. Repayment is guaranteed based on the company's ability to generate a steady cash flow from investments in fixed assets over time. In turn, the strength of the firm's fiscal balance sheet will determine how well the bank is protected from default.

External safeguards can come from a variety of sources. Listed below a few of these sources:

■ Collateral
■ Guarantees
■ Covenants

Perspective

What is the **perspective** relating to risk/reward? **Perspective** is a three-level process:

1. Risk/Reward
2. Operating and financing strategies that improve performance and maximize value
3. Decision and pricing

First Level: Risk/Reward

Perspective requires the analyst to marshal together all the salient points developed in the previous four sections and zero in on the overall risk/reward framework. This is a complicated set of processes requiring the summarization of all risk-adjusted information in the same way a lawyer prepares closing arguments for a case. Once all the facts have been presented, the analyst renders a final verdict.

Second Level: Operating and Financial Strategies

Management worth its salt strives to maximize shareholder value by striking a balance among money management, operating, investment, financing and dividend decisions. Today's decisions affect tomorrow's cash flow and levels of risk. Given your PRISM analysis, what financing and operating decisions would you like management to make that combine to maximize shareholder value, minimize the cost of capital, and keep the bond rating or credit grade from declining.

Third Level: The Decision

No matter what the pricing possibilities, you must be ready to apply all the PRISM components to the final decision, no matter how painful that may be in light of existing relationships.

■   ■   ■

CASE STUDY
Rose Jelly Corporation

It's now time to review a case study applying PRISM principles to a loan request from the hypothetical Rose Jelly Corporation. Let's set the scenario:

Situation: It is March, 1993. As vice president of a bank, you have been approached by Rose Jelly Corporation's vice president/finance, who is seeking a $500,000 increase to $2,000,000 in an existing unsecured line of credit. In light of attractive compensating balances and a relationship dating from 1968, the company has requested that pricing on the line be maintained at the prime rate. You have the fiscal audited statements dated 6/30/92 for review and must make a determination.

RJC's Business: Dating back to 1895, Rose Jelly Corporation manufactures and distributes boxed candy through approximately 300 company owned retail stores and some 2,000 franchised dealers including 30 department stores. Sales are concentrated in the Northeast with recent expansion into the South and West. The primary selling season extends from Christmas through Valentine's Day to Easter. Rose receives 30-day terms from its suppliers while extending the same terms to its franchised dealers. Inventory is protected by refrigeration with buildups liquidated through special sales.

Management: Howard Rose II succeeded his father as Chairman and President two years ago. At the same time Malcolm Singer, whose entire business career has been in the candy field, left a competitor to become RJC's vice president/ finance & operations. Your bank maintains operating accounts for members of the Rose family.

Financial Reporting: A Big Six accounting firm prepared the 6/30/92 fiscal report and gave a standard short form opinion. Inventory cost is on an FIFO basis and the company uses straight line depreciation for both tax and reporting purposes.

BANKING RELATIONSHIP

Account Opened:	1968
Loan Arrangement:	$1,500,000 line, reaffirmed 9/23/92
Rate:	Prime Rate
Fee:	Not Applicable
12 Mos. Avg. Outstanding:	$1,229,000
12 Mos. Affil. Outstanding:	0
Borrowing High Point:	$2,000,000
Last Cleanup:	4/7/92 to 6/25/92
Current Outstanding:	$1,500,000
12 Mos. Avg. Balances:	$464,000
12 Mos. Affil. Balances:	$200,000

Other Banks: Your National Bank is the company's only bank. Since 1969, we have been lending on an unsecured basis under a $1,500,000 line.

ROSE JELLY MONTHLY BORROWINGS
($000's Omitted)

	J	F	M	A	M	J	J	A	S	O	N	D
1990							1,250	1,750	1,750	1,750	1,750	1,750
1991	$1,000	1,000	500	500	0	500	500	1,000	1,500	1,500	1,500	1,500
1982	$1,000	$1,000	500	500	0	500	1,000	1,000	1,500	1,750	2,000	2,000
1993	$1,500	1,500	1,500									

Cleanup 1991: 4/21 6/10
1992: 4/7 6/25

Romino Securities Corporation: Romino is a holding company which owns a 63 percent interest in Rose Jelly and maintains a non-borrowing relationship with the bank. Balances in recent years have averaged $100,000. The most recent fiscal yearend statement of Romino, dated 12/31/92, shows a tangible net worth of $28 million with operations consistently profitable. Rose Jelly Corporation's credit file contains a memorandum, dated 5/11/90, which states that the bank expects Romino to maintain Rose's working capital at $3 million. Attached to the memo is Romino's keepwell agreement to this effect, as Romino would not commit to a guaranty.

Exhibit I

ROSE JELLY CORPORATION
INCOME STATEMENT
($000's Omitted in Dollar Amounts)

	6/30/90	% Sales	6/30/91	% Sales	6/30/92	% Sales
Gross Sales	$17,994	100.1	$18,379	100.1	$18,386	100.3
Less						
Returns & Allowances	18	.1	20	.1	54	.3
Net Sales	17,976	100.0	18,359	100.0	18,332	100.0
Cost of Goods Sold	14,022	78.0	14,596	79.5	15.032	82.0
Gross Profit	**$3,954**	**22.0**	**$3,763**	**20.5**	**$3,300**	**18.0**
S&A Expenses	3.728	20.7	3,238	17.6	3,094	16.9
Operating Profit	$ 226	1.3	$ 525	2.9	$ 206	1.1
Depreciation & Amort.	410	2.3	391	2.1	$ 384	2.1
Interest Expense	54	.3	49	.3	69	.4
Other Income (Expenses)	(28)	.2	34	(.2)	22	(.1)
Net Income (Loss)	**$(266)**	**(1.5)**	**$ 119**	**.7**	**$(225)**	**(1.3)**

Exhibit II

CANDY AND CONFECTIONERY INDUSTRY
Average Results 1992

	% Sales
Gross Profit Margin:	22.0
Operating expenses/Sales:	20.2
Net Margin (Adjusted):	0.9
Return on Equity (Adjusted):	4.5

Exhibit III

ROSE JELLY CORPORATION
BALANCE SHEET
($000's Omitted)

ASSETS	6/30/88	6/30/89	6/30/90	6/30/91	6/30/92
Cash	$710	$802	$841	$ 750	$ 626
Accts. Receivable (Net)	392	383	404	432	472
Inventories	2,879	4,160	3,365	4,067	4,577
Other Current Assets	314	102	84	216	188
Current Assets	**$4,295**	**$5,447**	**$4,694**	**$5,465**	**$5,863**
Property					
Plant, Equip. (Net)	2,667	2,347	2,105	1,935	1,870
Intangibles	58	0	0	40	40
Other Assets	737	851	699	713	681
Total Assets	**$7,757**	**$8,645**	**$7,498**	**$8,153**	**$8,454**
LIABILITIES & EQUITY					
Notes Payable	$0	$1,000	$0	$500	$500
Accounts Payable	541	223	324	583	995
Taxes & Accruals	836	789	821	613	741
Current Portion L/T Debts	14	13	15	16	15
Current Liabilities	**$1,391**	**$2,025**	**$1,160**	**$1,712**	**$2,251**
Non-Current Liabilities	146	133	117	101	88
Total Liabilities	**$1,537**	**$2,158**	**$1,277**	**$1,813**	**$2,339**
Capital Stock	1,400	1,400	1,400	1,400	1,400
Paid in Capital	290	290	290	290	290
Retained Eqrnings	4,530	4,797	4,531	4,650	4,425
Total Equity	**$6,220**	**$6,487**	**$6,221**	**$6,340**	**$6,115**
Liabilities and Equity	**$7,757**	**$8,645**	**$7,498**	**$8,153**	**$8,454**

Exhibit IV

ROSE JELLY CORPORATION
ACCOUNTS RECEIVABLE AGING SCHEDULE

	6/30/90	%	6/30/91	%	6/30/92	%
Less than 30 Days	$154,328	38.2	$152,928	35.4	$139,712	29.6
30–59 Days	145,036	35.9	164,592	38.1	199,184	42.2
60–80 Days	93,324	23.1	103,248	23.9	120,360	25.5
90 Days and Over	11,312	2.8	11,232	2.6	12,744	2.7
Total Net Receivables	$404,000	100.0	$432,000	100.0	$472,000	100.0
Provision for Doubtful Accounts	40,000	9.9	35,000	8.1	41,000	8.7
	$444,000		$467,000		$513,000	

Exhibit V

ROSE JELLY CORPORATION
KEY RATIOS
($000's Omitted in Dollar Amounts)

Year (6/30)	Working Capital	Current Ratio	Quick Ratio	Inventory Turnover	Net Worth	Debt/ Worth	Interest Expense	Net Profit
1988	$2,904	3.08x	0.8x	5.4x	$6,220	25%	N/A	$(546)
1989	3,422	2.69	0.6	5.1	6,487	33	N/A	(30)
1990	3,534	4.05	1.1	4.2	6,221	21	$ 54	(266)
1991	3,753	3.19	0.7	3.6	6,340	29	49	119
1992	3,610	2.60	0.5	3.3	6,115	38	69	(225)
Industry Avg. 1992		1.60	.5	4.6		120		

Exhibit VI

ROSE JELLY CORPORATION
WORKING CAPITAL SCHEDULE
($000's Omitted in Dollar Amounts)

Sources of Funds	1988	1989	1990	1991	1992
Net Income (Loss)	$(546)	$268*	$(266)	$119	$(225)
Amortization of Deferred Changes	565	437	410	391	384
Disposals	60	60	60	0	0
Gain (Loss) on Disposals and Abandonment of Equip. & Sales of Leashold	N/A	N/A	34	36	21
Decrease in Misc. Assets	14	(117)	92	(12)	29
Total	$93	$648	$330	$534	$209
Uses of Funds					
Cash Dividends	$140	$0	$0	$0	$0
Capital Expenditures	164	117	201	245	368
Decrease in Long Term Debt	14	13	17	16	14
Increase in Other Assets	0	0	0	54	(32)
Total	$318	$130	$218	$315	$350
Net Change in Working Capital	$ (225)	$ 518	$ 112	$ 219	$ (141)
Working Capital	$2,904	$3,422	$3,534	$3,753	$3,612
Volume/Working Capital	6.1:1	5.2:1	5.1:1	4.9:1	5.1:1
Volume/Fixed Assets	6.7:1	7.6:1	8.5:1	9.5:1	9.8:1

Handwritten annotation: "Depreciation Expense"

* Includes nonrecurring gains from sale of real estate of $244M and adjustment of prior years' federal income taxes of $54M; excluding these items there was a $30M loss.

■　■　■

Now, you've read the banking background and statements and formed some broad impressions and you're ready to examine details of the company's method of operation. Remember, each type of business has its own set of idiosyncrasies. For instance, Rose may be sensitive to new products, competitors, interest rates and disposable income problems. Also, how well has the firm fared in good markets and lean markets, compared to the rest of the industry?

Factors such as these must be taken into account if the borrower's operational and financial needs are to be fully understood.

RJC's business is highly seasonal, with top-of-the-line holiday products selling from Christmas through Valentine's Day to Easter. It is important both to identify the selling season and to realize that seasonal industries are traditionally undercapitalized. If these two elements are factored incorrectly, the firm's level of risk and capacity to repay debt may be misinterpreted.

During the fiscal year, a seasonal company's balance sheet will expand and contract. At the most active part of the season, sales are in close sync with manufacturing while collections are in all probability slow. Based on Rose's previous borrowing patterns, debt and assets increase July through December, expanding the balance sheet. At the least active part of the season, the last of the receivables are **converted** into cash and short-term debt paid off in "cleanup." At this juncture, Rose's balance sheet contracts from January through June as receivables are collected and debt is retired. This conversion of inventory to receivables and receivables to cash for debt retirement is called the the **conversion cycle**.

Rose is asking to expand an unsecured $1.5 million line of credit to $2 million. This immediately raises the questions of "why and why now," since its borrowing needs usually arise between the months of July and December. The firm won't specify what the additional funds are for, so it can be further assumed that the money will increase working capital to support expansion. Only closer examination will ascertain the true need for the funds.

What also comes into play in conjunction with this type of scenario is exposure to industry risk. Is the company well diversified or does it rely heavily on one or two major industries? It is well documented that from inception, Rose Jelly Corporation has relied on only one industry. Companies in the mature or declining phase of their growth cycle usually seek to invest in rapid growth markets rather than expand in the same industry. That is, of course, unless a new niche or product has been discovered. Is expansion in the same industry the right course of action for Rose?

Over the past three years, Rose's GPM has steadily declined, indicating increased manufacturing costs have not been passed on to the buyer. Whether this problem is permanent and structural or temporary will require a closer audit. Although the company's SG&A expenses have decreased during the same period, those numbers may be misleading. The real question is whether Rose Jelly has too many layers of management or too large a work force to begin with.

Upon reviewing the net margin, additional storm signals go up due to Rose's inability to maintain a string of profitable periods.

Management

Succeeding his father two years ago, Howard Rose II presides as Chairman and President. Malcolm Singer, an executive with extensive experience in the candy field was handpicked by Howard Rose II to fill his vacated position as vice president/finance & operations. RJC has maintained a favorable rating with the bank, based on its ability to meet all short-term obligations. Although the line of succession seems reasonable, profitability ratios discussed in the business operations section identify important weaknesses in the company's current asset management policies.

Both executives are responsible for the current state of affairs, raising questions as to their qualifications and ability to repay the loan.

Rose has been a loyal, sound customer of the bank since 1968. This loyalty will weigh in Rose's favor and figure into the final decision.

The accounting firm used by Rose is a respected, well-known organization that has previously done business with the bank. This reinforces the analyst's confidence level in the quality of Rose's financial statements. It also raises an interesting question on the method used to allocate Rose's depreciation expense. A reputable accounting firm would never direct a manufacturer to employ straight-line depreciation for both reporting purposes and tax purposes unless it didn't matter. Accelerated depreciation is the method of choice for a capital-intensive company in the jelly business because it defers taxes. This would enable Rose to earn additional income by investing the cash retained as a result of delaying tax payments to the future. This methodology immediately sparks additional questions as to Rose's viability.

The initial assumption surrounding the request for an extended line of credit points to Rose's working capital needs for expansion plans in the South and West. It is important to note that when lines of credit are used to infuse working capital, the needs must be seasonal or cyclical; current outstandings should be "self-liquidated" through the conversion cycle. It is usually inappropriate to underwrite permanent working capital or other long-term requirements under open lines of credit. Financing long-term (permanent) assets with short-term credit inhibits working capital expansion.

Other problems begin to surface. First and foremost is the time of year in relation to the level of assets and liabilities on the balance sheet. Theoretically, Rose's balance sheet should contract in March since it is in the least active part of the season. At this juncture, the last of the receivables should be converted into cash to pay off all maturing obligations. In other words, Rose should be in a liquid position to retire debt obligations. Unfortunately, this is not the situation.

Repayment

The primary source of payment for a seasonal loan is balance sheet liquidity. Liquidity can be measured by reviewing the liquidity and activity ratios:

Current Ratio (Current assets/Current liabilities): Most commonly used measure of short-term solvency, providing a rough indication of a firm's ability to satisfy its short-term debt. It is imperative to look behind the numbers to seek the true quality of the current assets regardless of the answer calculated.

Quick Ratio or Acid Test (Current Assets less Inventory/Current Liabilities): A more conservative means of determining a company's liquidity because it measures its ability to pay off all short-term debt without relying on the sale of inventory. Using only the most liquid assets, it is a more accurate ratio than the current ratio.

Inventory Turnover: Reliable tool for calculating how well management controls inventory. Although Rose's current ratio is better than the industry standard, it is a misleading gauge as a result of critical assumptions pertaining to the quality of its assets. The magnitude of current assets over current liabilities is meaningless in light of the quality of inventory (not worth its stated book value because it needs to be liquidated quickly, at low prices) and accounts receivable. In addition, the current ratio reveals a steady downward trend for the past three years. This also indicates problems at Rose Jelly.

The quick ratio, preferred by many analysts, is on a par with the industry but also is on the decline. In all likelihood, if Rose does business as usual next year, the ratio will continue to deteriorate toward the land of no return.

Reviewing the inventory turnover ratio presents all the proof needed to substantitate the hypothesis made in the previous section.

A declining turnover ratio and continued build-up of perishable stock indicate management's inability to fully master the production process and accurately project sales. So Rose is sitting on excessive, deteriorating, and perhaps unsalable stock, representing an unproductive investment. To magnify the problem, the inventory policy Rose Jelly currently uses will continue to ship out only stale merchandise to its customers while freshly produced candy will grow old sitting in the warehouse.

From an external repayment viewpoint, another bank will not bring in debt if RJC can't convert its balance sheet. And an equity infusion is unlikely because nobody is going to buy RJC stock.

Safeguards (Protection)

The primary source of **internal** safeguards in a seasonal loan is cash flow. Based on the information available, cash flow can be conceptualized by using Rose's working capital schedule (Exhibit VI) on the proxy. There is no evidence of company profits being available to retire short-term debt if it were carried over the next few years, or restructured into a five-year term loan. At the very least, Rose has structural problems and the bank has a weak repayment and safeguards blueprint.

Perspective

As a family-run business since 1895, Rose Jelly Corporation has proven staying power in the confectionery industry and the endorsement of its competitors. The banking relationship, dating back to 1968, has been strong with various family members maintaining operating accounts. The company maintains excellent balances and employs a top-notch, highly respected accounting firm to handle its books.

Unfortunately, those are the only positive, risk-adjusted factors that can be cited in Rose's behalf.

From the outset, the key to this case revolves around the time of year the request for credit is made. From a seasonable standpoint, it is evident Rose should be liquid in March. During the company's clean-up period, the balance sheet contracts as the last of the short-term debt is retired. Anytime a seasonal company in this phase is holding a high surplus of inventory, and has collection problems and limited cash, it's very unlikely the balance sheet will contract anytime soon. So the conversion cycle, or lack of one, has Rose frozen inextricably in the expansion stage.

This scenario exposes the real culprit in Rose's predicament: inventory management policies.

From the decline in the gross profit margin, it is evident that RJC cannot pass on its increased manufacturing costs to the buyer. Goods are either produced with machines or labor. What factors uncovered to this point indicate whether Rose is machine- or labor-intensive? Decreasing capital expenditures are a good indication of reduced operating leverage, and often results in an increase in variable labor costs.

Thus, lower operating leverage results in higher costs that must be passed on to the buyer. Marginal price increases over competitive levels might not affect sales at first. But if prices get too high—which is the case with Rose—the product is priced out of the market and sales disappear. Compound this with poor forecasting and inventory control and you have a real mess on your hands. Compare RJC's pricing policies to its major competitors:

Year	Selling Price Rose Jelly Corp.	Selling Price Competitors
1987	$ 7.50	$7.50
1988	8.25	8.00
1989	9.65	8.25
1990	10.26	8.49
1991	12.98	9.20
1992	14.50	9.35

Clearly, as RJC discovered ruefully and too late, consumers are price sensitive.

The business already holds $1.5 million of the bank's money. Extending the requested credit would require the bank to put in another $500 thousand.

The Decision: The opportunity costs of losing a portion of the loan extended, losing a customer and replacing operating balances are cheaper than extending Rose's line of credit and taking the additional hit. Rose can't be turned around at this stage of the game. You should probably take the loss and run.

The New Credit Culture: What's Ahead

In subsequent chapters we will review other important new developments in credit management. We'll examine new methods like multivariate ratio analysis. Does the borrower earn a fair return? Can the firm withstand downturns? Does it have the financial flexibility to attract additional creditors and investors? Is management adroit in its efforts to upgrade weak operations, reinforce strong ones, pursue profitable opportunities, and push the value of common stock to the highest possible levels?

Bank reform legislation and new federal guidelines require that banks identify the impact loan diversification (or lack of it) has on their loan portfolios. We will learn to use the latest models and techniques so you can evaluate portfolio risk. A diversified loan portfolio minimizes the riskiness and profit volatility of a bank without sacrificing returns.

Cash flow, one of this book's prime focal points, is credit's most powerful analytical tool. Cash flow raises questions about the ways firms generate and absorb cash, with unresolved issues forming the basis of a discussion with management.

Future cash flows are critical; projections need to be completed, refined, and calculated with the right tools. We learn to assimilate new developments in spreadsheet design, including simulation and formal projection methods. Projections are not intended to predict the future perfectly, but to see how the borrower will perform under a variety of situations. This is especially true for rapid growth or highly leveraged companies, since the cash flows of these borrowers are particularly uncertain. Furthermore, since rapid growth firms operate in a risky phase of their business lives, we examine their unique credit risks that are often difficult to analyze.

Valuation methods are also important to validate projections used in loan proposals, identify leveraged buyout and restructuring opportunities, analyze the market value of the borrowers' capital structure, and find values in partnership buy-outs.

How does loan pricing fit into the new credit culture? We learn that pricing should be consistent and generate income that fairly compensates a bank for credit risk and exposure. Along with traditional approaches, we study option pricing techniques to help find marginal rate increases corresponding to various risk levels.

How will the new credit culture deal with lending to small business? To encourage banks to make loans to small businesses, President Clinton's documentation exemption program allows *qualifying* banks to form baskets of loans exempt from examiner scrutiny. What this means is that if you learn to recognize red flags early and keep sound fundamentals of lending in mind, you can comfortably assign credits of small to medium sized businesses to the documentation exemption program. You can then focus on obtaining financials and other documentation on your larger credits—and not be overly concerned when a statement from a long-time borrower is six months late.

Finally, we come to credit risk grading: tying it all together. Risk assessment and management are the key skills of a successful bank. The credit risk rating system provides a common language and uniform framework for discussing and assessing risk. The system will enable you to evaluate and track risk on individual transactions on a continuing basis. And, most important, it provides a channel for tracking and managing risk within your bank's overall portfolio.

CHAPTER Two

Accounting Issues in Credit Analysis: Let the Lender Beware

Financial statement window-dressing can make debt ratios appear acceptable, promoting the illusion that borrowers can handle more debt without incurring inappropriate levels of financial risk. Unfortunately, some investors, bankers, and economists aren't sophisticated enough to see through off-balance sheet borrowing tactics.

Banks sometimes don't know that a company seeking a loan is already up to its neck in debt or thinly capitalized. If, for instance, companies borrow in excess of their "true" debt capacity, they may stretch their resources, neglect necessary investments as factors of production and R & D, and become more vulnerable in economic turndowns.

Alternatively, loan covenants—requiring specific working capital and debt ratios—may influence borrowers to window-dress their financials, pushing debt off the balance sheet. Often, loan covenants draw a thin line between compliance and violation when they specify leverage ratios that must be maintained to prevent term loan default. Permissive loan covenants are often structured to allow borrowers to sign lease agreements or engage in project finance activities that, under certain circumstances, push obligations off the financial statements. However, smart bankers insist that certain types of off balance sheet obligations be considered the equivalent of balance sheet debt in their debt covenants.

That's a noble objective, and realizing it involves identifying, interpreting, and resolving accounting precepts advancing in all directions—conservative, liberal—and, alas, a window-dress. Accounting issues, the Achilles' heel of bankers, take on a more congenial hue when understood, recognized, and properly diagnosed. (See Exhibit 2.1.)

Exhibit 2.1

Accounting Magic

Company B's Profits are higher because of:

	Company A	Use of FIFO	Straight Line Depreciation	Deferred Research over 5 yrs.	Reduced Pension Funding	Stock Options Incentives	Capitalized Interest	Company B
Sales in unit	3,000,000							3,000,000
Price per unit	14.00							14
Sales	42,000,000							42,000,000
Cost of goods sold	(23,560,000)							(23,560,000)
Selling and administration expenses	(9,415,000)							(9,415,000)
LIFO inventory reserve	(4,000,000)	4,000,000						
Depreciation expense	(940,000)		235,000					(705,000)
Research costs	(450,000)			360,000				(90,000)
Pension costs	(55,000)				41,250			(13,750)
Interest	(20,000)						4,000	(16,000)
Officers compensation:								
Base salaries	(430,000)							(430,000)
Bonuses	(600,000)					600,000		
Total costs and expenses	(39,470,000)	4,000,000	235,000	360,000	41,250	600,000	4,000	(34,229,750)
Profit before taxes	2,530,000	4,000,000	235,000	360,000	41,250	600,000	4,000	7,766,250
Income taxes	(860,200)	(1,360,000)	(79,900)	(122,400)	(14,025)	(204,000)	(1,360)	(2,640,525)
Net profit	1,669,800							5,125,725

All in conformance with generally accepted accounting principles.

Contingencies: Overview

A contingency exists when the company stands to gain or lose because of a past transaction or event. The amount of gain or loss is "contingent," that is, dependent on the ultimate outcome of a pending transaction/event. For example, a customer falls in a department store and files a lawsuit. The store owners are now in a contingency situation due to the injury. The amount of loss (if any) will be determined in the future by settlement or court verdict.

Financial Accounting Standards Board Statement No.5, "Accounting for Contingencies." Under FASB Statement No. 5, an estimated contingency loss must be charged against net income as soon as the loss becomes probable and estimable. Now that the use of prior period adjustments has been extremely narrowed by FASB Statement No. 16 (Prior Period Adjustments) almost all such loss accruals must be charged against current income. Firms cannot provide reserves for future losses through yearly income statement adjustments to prevent the earnings volatility that results from guesswork. Accrual of contingency losses is prohibited unless it is probable that an asset has been impaired or a liability has been incurred. The loss must be estimable.

Classification of Contingencies

1. Probable—likely to materialize

2. Reasonably Possible—halfway between probable and remote

3. Remote—slight chance of materializing

To review: While some contingencies are disclosed in footnotes, certain balance sheet ratios should be recalculated in figuring possible losses. Also, remember that the risk of accounting loss from financial instruments includes the possibility a loss may occur from the failure of another party to live up to a contact (credit risk), from future changes in market prices making a financial instrument less valuable (market risk), or the risk of physical loss.

Likewise, a financial instrument has off-balance sheet risk if the risk of loss exceeds the amount recognized as an asset, or if the obligation exceeds the amount recognized in the financial statements.

General Loss Contingencies

General loss contingencies may arise from risk of exposure to:

1. Product warranties or defects

2. Pending or threatened litigation

3. Risk of catastrophe, i.e., losses

4. Direct guarantees (guarantor makes payment to creditor if debtor fails to pay)

5. Claims and assessments

6. Pre-acquisition contingencies

Financial Instruments with Off-Balance Sheet Risk

While corporate executives claim off-balance sheet financing instruments are used to mitigate risks, these instruments can function as speculative tools. Borrowers experiencing difficulty may use instruments to improve results not attainable through operating activities.

Some examples of off-balance sheet instruments are:

1. Recourse obligations on receivables or bills receivable (B/Rs) sold

2. Interest rate and currency swaps, caps, and floors

3. Loan commitments and options written on securities and/or futures contracts

4. Obligations arising from financial instruments sold short

5. Synthetic asset swap which might result in an unwind if the bond goes into default

6. Obligations to repurchase securities sold

My banking experience includes a customer who suffered a major, unanticipated loss from derivative instrument speculation during the 1987 market crash. The loss probably couldn't have been foreseen, but the bank had not even been informed by the client that such large sale speculative investment activity was taking place

General Loss Contingencies

Product warranties or defects. A warranty (product guarantee) is a promise—for a specific time period—made by a seller to a buyer to make good on a deficiency of quantity, quality, or performance. Warranties can result in significant future cash outlays by the seller and should be identified as an indefinite possible liability by both banker and accountant.

Litigation Contingencies

Publicly traded companies are required to disclose litigation contingencies when eventual loss from a lawsuit is possible. Studies done on the classification of pre-disposition years (those predating court adjudication or settlement) showed that 47.6 percent of surveyed companies showed unsatisfactory disclosure.

There was either no mention of litigation in the financial statement or it was not accompanied by a strong disclaimer of liability. Resulting legal action could include antitrust, patent infringement, fraud or misrepresentation, breach of contract, or other noninsurable suits.

Contingency losses, which may be explosive and destroy a profitable company (for example, A. H. Robbins), should be put on the balance sheet. Bankers should always ask what impact the possible loss would have on the company's cash flow and can its financial structure and liquidity sustain the loss? Calculate debt/equity. If within industry norm, does the firm appear capable of handling it?

Environmental Contingencies

Environmental protection laws pose many dangers for the unwary lender and borrower. To avoid potentially unlimited liability that can result from a violation, prudent bankers should be familiar with industry environmental guidelines and be sure that environmental risks are reflected in "real value" terms on the financial statement. Some possible environmental trouble spots include:

1. Transportation of hazardous substances

2. Real property contamination

3. Disposition of hazardous substances

4. Manufacturing processes that involve use, creation, or disposition of hazardous waste

Bankers should do on-site visual inspections of clients and question financial statements for non-disclosure if they find:

1. Paint, petroleum or chemicals stored

2. Signs of spillage or stains on the floor or surrounding grounds

3. Dead vegetation or underground storage tanks on the property

4. Equipment used to transport hazardous materials

5. Pipes leading to waterways

If a serious environmental condition exists, the lender should estimate the cost of the cleanup and the firm's ability to absorb the contingency in its financial statements. Obviously, if the risk is unduly high or the cost of extensive cleanup is disproportionate to the expected profit, the bank should pass on credit commitment.

Anytime a current or prospective client uses potentially hazardous materials in production, the banker should closely scrutinize its handling and asses the potential impact on the proposed credit structure; i.e., loss in event of mishandling, impact on potential collateral, etc.

By following this excellent checklist, the Secured Financing Subsidiary of a large bank guarantees that environmental contingencies are reflected on financial statements:

1. Are any toxic, hazardous, or regulated materials (for example, used machine oil) handled at any stage of the production process?

2. Does the borrower have an EPA plan? If so, what is it?

3. If the client has storage tanks, when were they last inspected for environmental impact purposes?

4. Are there paint shops on the property?

5. Before the current owner, what was the property used for and how long has our client been there?

6. Are there any past or present EPA violations against the property? If so, what are they?

7. How close are waterways to the property (including underground waterways)?

8. What kind of process or processes are being done on the property?

9. Does our prospective client stock drums of inflammable solvents or fluids and where on the property are they located?

10. What is happening on adjoining properties? Any environmental risk?

11. Have locally sourced springs been tested?

Risk of Catastrophic Losses

Two criteria must be met before a company can classify a gain or loss as extraordinary:

- *Unusual*—an event unrelated to the typical activities of the business

- *Nonrecurring*—one that management does not expect to occur again

Natural disasters meet the definition of unusual, but they must also meet the criteria of nonrecurring. For example, a flood in Phoenix would be classified extraordinary, while a corn farmer hit by drought in Kansas could not classify the loss as nonrecurring. The two criteria must be considered against the firm's geographical location and type of business.

Direct and Indirect Guarantees

In direct guarantees the guarantor will pay the creditor if the debtor fails to do so. In indirect guarantees the guarantor agrees to transfer funds to the debtor if a specified event occurs. Indirect guarantees connect directly from the guarantor to debtor but benefit the creditor indirectly.

FASB 5 requires the type and amount of the guarantee to be disclosed in the financial statements. Examples of the types of guarantee contingencies which must be disclosed include guarantees to repurchase receivables, obligations of banks under letters of credit or "standby credit," guarantees of the indebtedness of others, and unconditional obligations to make payments. They must be disclosed even if they have only a remote possibility of materializing.

Financial Instruments with Off-Balance Sheet Risk

The market crash of 1987 suddenly revealed some good-sized, sophisticated companies that had taken inordinately large (beyond the size required for risk management), derivative positions that resulted in significant losses. Under extraordinary circumstances, these derivative positions can weaken a credit. It is important that lenders know about these positions.

Recourse Obligations on Receivables or B/Rs Sold

A widely used method to finance small, high-ticket items (notably furs and fine jewelry) is the presentation of bills receivable (B/Rs) or notes receivable for dis-

count, or as security to demand loans. A B/R is an unconditional written order requiring the person to whom it is addressed to pay on demand, or at a fixed future time, a certain sum of money. It proves indebtedness for the sale of goods by the bank's customer. B/Rs are endorsed over to the bank with *full recourse* to the bank's customer. These are off balance sheet contingencies and should be returned to the balance sheet with an amount equal to the expected loss.

Securitization of Assets

A company exposes its general creditors to additional risk when it securitizes its assets. If the firm goes bankrupt, some of its most creditworthy assets will be tied up in a corporation or trust accountable to different creditors. These creditors face little risk in case of bankruptcy, because their assets can be quickly liquidated. However, they receive a lower return on their investments. In addition, if these creditors liquidate the securitized assets, the company will be further away from recovery and its general creditors will be at even greater risk. Other risks, beside credit/default, include maturity mismatch and prepayment volatility.

(Sidenote: Bankers and investors can reduce contingency risks by using computer software containing models and structural and analytical data for asset securitizations. These should include commercial loan securitizations, whole-loan and senior-subordinated securities, and home equity loans.)[1]

Futures Contracts

A commodity used for production, such as copper, may be purchased for current or

---

1   Ron Unz, "New Software Can Provide Risk Models," *American Banker,* August 25, 1992 v157 n164 p12A(1)

future delivery. Investing in commodities futures refers to the buying or selling of a contract for future delivery. In the case of a purchase contract, the buyer agrees to accept a specific commodity that meets a specified quality in a specified month. In the case of a sale, the seller agrees to deliver the specified commodity during the designated month. Hedging against unexpected increases in raw material costs is a wise move; speculating in commodity futures with the bank's money may not be.

Management may *purchase a contract* for future delivery. This is known as a long position in which the firm will profit if the price of the commodity, say copper, rises. Management may also *enter into a contract* for future delivery (short position). These long and short positions run parallel to the long and short positions in security markets.

The intended purpose of this type of hedging is to enable manufacturers to lock in a profit margin on orders received but no yet manufactured.

An adverse raw materials price change can elimate a manufacturer's profit on an order if he is unhedged and is not in a position to pass the price increase on to the customer.

Pensions

Pension expense is the amount management should invest at year's end to cover future pension payments for this additional year's service. Accounting records reflect management's best guess as to real pension costs. Accountants try to measure the cost of these retirement benefits at the time the employee earns them, rather than when the employee actually receives them. A number of pension assumptions must be compiled to come up with the required numbers. These include:

- Projected interest earnings for invested funds
- Life expectancy figures for employees after retirement
- Salary of employee at retirement
- Average years of service at retirement

Beware of Unfunded Projected Benefit Obligation. This liability indicates that pension investments fall short of future pension benefits. Borrowers who continuously underfund current pension expense, or incorporate unrealistic assumptions in their pension plan, could find themselves eventually forced to make up the difference.

Discretionary Items

Many of a business firm's expenditures are, to varying degrees, discretionary, that is, within management's control. These include:

- Repair and maintenance of equipment
- Research and development
- Marketing and advertising expenses
- Introduction of new product lines
- Acquisition and divestiture of operating units

Management can choose to skip maintenance repairs to improve earnings, but underinvestment can erode the long-term viability of the business.

Research and Development

In its Statement of Financial Accounting Standards No. 2, "Accounting for Research and Development Costs" October 1974, FASB concluded that "all research and development costs encompassed by this Statement shall be charged to expense when incurred." The Board followed a reasoning process in which the following preliminary premises were accepted as true:

1. Since R & D expenses are often incurred with small probability of success, there is a high degree of uncertainty of future benefits.

2. There is a lack of causal relationship between expenditures and benefits.

3. R & D does not meet the accounting concept of an asset.

4. Revenue and expenses must be matched.

5. The resulting information is relevant for investment and credit decisions.

To avoid problems associated with over-valuing R & D expenditures, all costs associated with the acquisition of assets shall be expensed where/when it is probable that the asset will turn out to be worth less than its cost. This "conservative" approach is consistent with the ruling on when to expense R & D.

Inventory

Before the financials of one borrower can be compared to another, lenders have to understand the effect different inventory accounting methods have on the income statement and balance sheet. Many companies that use Last In/First Out (LIFO) report lower earnings than companies using First In/First Out (FIFO) or weighted average in an inflationary environment. The LIFO company's tax burden is often less

than under FIFO and it will have much better cash flow than companies using other inventory methods. From the viewpoint of shareholder value, all else being equal, it is better to report lower earnings and pay less tax.

Again, LIFO gives a firm lower earnings and a tax advantage during inflationary periods when prices are rising. LIFO reports lower earnings than companies using FIFO or weighted average, but will generate higher cash flows and produce greater shareholder value because of lower taxes. Why then do companies use FIFO since they may pay millions more in taxes? FIFO increases reported earnings, even at the expense of their after-tax cash flow.

Here's a story about a large firm that played with FIFO and LIFO and got caught! Years back, a major corporation switched from LIFO to FIFO after three consecutive years of substantial losses. The switch in accounting unlocked a huge inventory cushion producing the first profits in years. As a result, the credit files were full of praise for the company's "turnaround." While management celebrated at the fanciest restaurant in town, a management trainee assigned to complete the company's credit review approached me cautiously. "I know the account officer knows a lot more than me, but don't profits look a little fishy to you?" A light flashed YES and I immediately took the trainee out to lunch to crack a few lobster claws *on the bank.* We had our own well-deserved celebration.

Issues on the Income Statement

Revenues, cash received for merchandise sold or services rendered, are generally recorded at the time of sale or completion of service. However, two conditions must be met before revenue can be recorded. First, the earnings process must be substantially complete, and, second, collectibility of the revenue must be able to be estimated. The earnings process is not substantially complete if:

1. Seller and buyer have not agreed on price

2. Buyer does not have to pay seller until merchandise is resold

3. If the merchandise is stolen or physically destroyed, buyer does not have to pay seller

4. Buyer and seller are related parties, that is, intercompany transactions

5. Seller must continue to provide substantial performance or services to the buyer or aid in reselling the product. If, however, substantial performance has occurred and collectibility of revenue can be estimated, sale of the product or service can be recorded.

If collectibility cannot be estimated, accountants use either the installment or cost recovery method to record revenue as customers make payments. Firms record revenues only as customers send checks.

Under long-term contract arrangements, revenue may be recorded over the life of the contract. For example, the construction industry records revenue on major long-term contracts as the work is performed rather than when the sale is consummated. The percentage of completion method is based on construction costs, estimates of final price, and the stage of completion.

Discontinued Operations

When Manufacturers Hanover Trust sold its headquarters complex for a huge profit, the accountants correctly separated the gain from the bank's operating income. Companies may undertake financial transactions that represent a completely separate line of endeavor (for example, this gain on the sale of a major asset) and no longer contribute to earnings and then separate these earnings.

Gains and losses, the difference between book value and selling price, are included as well. Gains/losses on the sale of business units are nonrecurring and nonoperating, but bear in mind that firms sometimes sell assets to window-dress the income statement during poor performing years. Segregating operating from non-operating income permits analysts to focus on business units that will contribute to future earnings growth.

Capitalized Interest

FASB Statement No. 34 requires that the interest incurred on debt capital for certain assets be capitalized. The qualifying assets are, in the main, self-constructed capital assets and assets held "for sale or lease that are constructed or otherwise produced as discrete projects (i.e., ships or real estate developments)."

The argument is that equity and debt disbursements are costs of doing business and should be treated like any other costs. Since interest is the cost of using funds for specified time periods, interest cost should be charged to assets (projects) in proportion to the funds used. Public utilities which tie up funds including interest costs during construction are, in reality, timing cash inflows and outflows. The capitalized interest flows through the income statement when the plant is completed and produces revenue.

Interest costs of funds used during production is an element of product cost and should be assigned to products in the same way that depreciation on plant and equipment is assigned.

We will now go on to a review of elemental financial statements and demonstrate how they can best be used in credit analysis.

CHAPTER *Three*

Elemental Financial Statements

Since ratio analysis employs data from the borrowing firm's financial statements, we'll review a case study involving the statements of a large manufacturer, the Gem Furniture Company, Inc. I think that you will find our example is indeed a "gem" because it shows you how to use basic financial statements to learn a great deal about a firm's creditworthiness:

The Second City Bank's new loan analysis program recently alerted Susan V. Toms, vice president and loan officer, to the deteriorating financial position of Gem Furniture Company.

The bank requires quarterly financial reports—balance sheets and income statements—from its major loan customers. This is fed into the computer, which then calculates the key ratios for each customer, charts trends in these ratios, and compares the statistics of each company with the average ratios and trends of other firms in the same industry.

If any ratio of any company is significantly lower than the industry average, the computer notes this fact. If the terms of a loan require that certain ratios be maintained at specified minimums, and these minimums are not being met, the computer notes the deficiency.

Three months earlier Toms had noted that some of Gem's ratios were trending toward dipping below its industry's averages. Toms had sent a copy of the computer report with a note voicing concern to Moe Zarchen, president of Gem Furniture. Zarchen had acknowledged receipt of the material but had taken no action to correct the situation.

Gem had developed an innovative therapeutic mattress and bed combination for treating backache and related problems. Zarchen felt that the new product promised to turn the company around. However, management decided to scrap the project when simulation analysis revealed it as too risky in the firm's present condition.

The first financial analysis indicated that some problems were developing, but no ratio was below the level specified in the loan agreement between the bank and Gem Furniture. However, the recent analysis, based on the latest financial and industry comparatives, showed the firm's liquidity below the position specified in the loan agreement. According to the loan agreement, the bank could legally call upon the company for immediate payment of the entire bank loan, and if payment was not forthcoming within ten days, the bank could force Gem Furniture into bankruptcy. Toms had no intention of actually enforcing the contract to that extent, but she did intend to use the provision to prompt Gem Furniture to take some decisive action to improve its financial condition.

Gem Furniture was formed in 1936 and manufactures a full line of stylish wooden tables. Until recently, the company was quite successful. In 1986, Moe Zarchen became president, following the death of Jack Lewis, the sole surviving founder. Gem's financial condition had deteriorated during the final years of Lewis's control. However, the firm's owners felt that Gem's prospects were promising—provided capable management was retained. A key concern of the owners was the lack of financial planning, as well as management's "fire fighting" approach, which had come to characterize the firm's operations.

Seasonal working capital needs were financed primarily by loans from Second City, and the current line of credit permits the company to borrow to $55,000,000. In accordance with standard banking practices, however, the loan agreement requires that the bank loan be repaid in full at some time during the year, in this case by February, 1992.

When Zarchen received a copy of Toms's latest computer analysis and her blunt statement insisting on immediate repayment of the entire loan unless the firm demonstrated how the financial picture could be improved, he began trying to determine what could be done. He rapidly concluded that the present level of sales could not be continued without increasing the loan from $55,000,000 to $65,000,000, since payments of $8,000,000 for construction of a plant addition would have to be made in January 1992.

Even though Gem furniture had been a good customer of the Second City Bank for over 50 years, Toms began to question whether the bank would continue to supply the present line of credit, let alone increase outstandings.

Sections of the computer output are highlighted in Exhibit 3.1.

Gem's Balance Sheet

The balance sheet is a statement of assets, liabilities, and stockholders equity at the close of business on the date indicated. The balance sheet represents a given point in time in a company's life cycle. The left side of the balance sheet represents all items owned by the business that have a monetary value. The right side reports liabilities and equity, which represent the claims of the creditors and owners (stockholders) against the firm's assets. Both sides must always be in balance. Since the claims of creditors take preference over those of owners or stockholders, the interest of the latter is determined by subtracting the liabilities from the assets. Another common way of stating the balance sheet equation, therefore, is assets minus liabilities equals stockholders equity $(A - L = E)$.

Following are a series of definitions explaining the different line items contained on a typical balance sheet.

Assets

Current assets represent cash and other assets or resources which are reasonably ex-

pected to be realized in cash or sold or consumed during the normal operating cycle of the business—typically less than one year. These assets are mostly working assets in the sense that they are in a constant cycle of being converted into cash. Inventories, when sold on credit terms, convert

---

Exhibit 3.1

Gem Furniture
Company Balance Sheet
Year Ended December 31 ($ Thousands)

Assets	1989	1990	1991
Current Assets			
Cash and cash items	$15,445	$12,007	$11,717
Accounts and notes receivable, net	51,793	55,886	88,571
Inventories	56,801	99,087	139,976
Current Assets	124,039	166,980	240,264
Property, plant & equipment	53,282	60,301	68,621
Accumulated Depreciation	(8,989)	(13,961)	(20,082)
Net Fixed Assets	44,294	46,340	48,539
Total Assets	**$168,333**	**$213,320**	**$288,803**
Liabilities and Equities			
Current Liabilities			
Short-term loans	$10,062	$15,800	$55,198
Accounts payable	20,292	31,518	59,995
Accruals	10,328	15,300	21,994
Current Liabilities	40,682	62,618	137,187
Long-term bank loans	19,125	28,688	28,688
Mortgage	8,606	7,803	7,018
Long-term debt	27,731	36,491	35,706
Total Liabilities	**68,413**	**99,109**	**172,893**
Common stock (no par value)	68,807	69,807	69,807
Retained Earnings	30,113	44,404	46,103
Stockholders Equity	99,920	114,221	115,910
Total Liabilities and Equity	**$168,333**	**$213,320**	**$288,803**

into accounts receivable; receivables when collected turn into cash; cash is then used to pay the supplier or bank that financed inventory as well as the production costs that began the operating cycle.

Cash and Cash Items

Cash represents bills and coins in the till and on deposit at the bank. Cash and marketable securities should be combined, since marketable securities represent near transaction cash rather than term investments. If Gem had disclosed restricted cash, the bank's computer would footnote the item or list it separately. Examples of restricted cash include cash held in a collateral trust account or cash held by a foreign subsidiary not available to pay the firm's debt. The inclusion of funds other than those freely available for withdrawal to meet current obligations results in an overstatement of both the working capital and current ratio position of the company. It is also important to note that cash transferred into the U.S. from foreign subsidiaries may also be subject to a heavy foreign tax.

Accounts Receivable

Receivables represent amounts due from trade customers within the period of one year or less on open accounts known to be collectible. Customers are usually granted credit terms of 30 days. The amount due from customers of Gem Furniture is $98,210. Some of Gem's customers will fail to pay. To reflect expected receipts, the total is net, after a provision for doubtful accounts. Failure to exclude bad debt and to provide for an adequate allowance for doubtful accounts and notes receivable overstates assets and current earnings.

Notes receivable represent a contingency until honored by the maker at date of maturity. Gem may be able to discount its notes at the bank. Since the endorser is liable if the maker refuses payment at maturity, disclosure of this information will help you appraise the firm's current asset position and its ability to pay short-term debt. If Gem's balance sheet had listed Receivables from Affiliates, Officers, or Subsidiaries, the bank would have considered these amounts as non-current assets. Advances to subsidiaries or management may represent funds transferred out of the core business.

Inventories

Inventory represents assets held for sale in the ordinary course of business. Inventory consists of raw materials used in production, work in process, goods in process of manufacture, and finished goods ready for shipment. Inventory is normally reflected in the financial statements at cost or market, whichever is lower. The general tendency in times of rising prices is for inventory values on the balance sheet to be less than replacement costs. We should break out inventory components which are material or change significantly.

Property, Plant, and Equipment

Property, Plant, and Equipment represent assets not intended for sale over the normal course of business. However, these assets are considered essential to the production, distribution or warehousing activities of the company. This asset category includes land, buildings, structures, machinery, and equipment. These items are shown at aggregate cost under a single figure with a single aggregate deduction of allowances for depreciation and depletion.

All of these items added together produce the figure listed on Gem Furniture's balance sheet as total assets.

Liabilities and Equities

Current liabilities include all obligations that are owed within one year. The classification is intended to include obligations for items which have been entered into during the operating cycle. Examples include payables incurred for the purchase of materials and supplies like lumber to be used in the production of furniture, or in providing services to be offered for sale; and debts which arise from operations directly related to the operating cycle, such as wages incurred but not yet paid. Other current liabilities, whose ordinary liquidation is expected to occur within a year, include short-term debt and current maturities of long-term obligations.

Short-Term Loans

Short-term credit in the form of bank loans, for example, may be either unsecured or secured. Unsecured debt includes all debt whose "security" is the firm's cash-generating ability.

Accounts Payable

Accounts Payable are incurred when a firm purchases goods or services on credit from suppliers. It is analogous to a consumer's charge account. By accepting cash payments at some future date rather than immediately following the sale, the supplier assumes the role of a lender. Nearly every firm uses trade credit to finance inventory.

Accruals

Gem Furniture also owes salaries and wages, interest on funds borrowed, fees to accountants and attorneys, pension contri-

butions, insurance premiums and similar items. To the extent that the amounts owed and not recorded on the books are unpaid at the financial statement date, these items are grouped as a total under accruals. Income tax payable is usually stated separately because of the amount and importance of the tax factor.

Long-Term Liabilities

The category "long-term liabilities" is used to include all obligations not classified as current. The most important items included are notes and bonds payable with maturities of over one year. Notes and bonds are normally valued at face value. Of all the methods to raise long-term capital, long-term debt is the most widely used.

Long-Term Bank Loans

Long-term obligations must be retired after the current fiscal year. Such obligations may include bonds that are outstanding and long-term bank loans. In the financial statements, a breakdown of the various debt issues may be footnoted after the body of the financial statement. If subordinated debt appeared on Gem Furniture's financial, the bank's computer would include it under capital funds. Subordinated Debt is junior to senior creditors in the event of asset liquidation.

Stockholders Equity

Common Stock: All corporations issue common stock. It is the first security to be issued and the last to be retired. Common stock represents the chief ownership of the company and has the greatest voting rights. Common stockholders have the last claim on earnings. Gem's common stockholders also stand to benefit the most from the success and profits reported by the firm. Other stakeholders, such as bondholders, have fixed claims and do not participate in earnings over and above such claims.

Retained Earnings

Retained earnings delineate profits, income, and various adjustments from the date of incorporation after deducting dividends and transfers to capital stock accounts. Retained earnings accumulate as the firm earns profits and reinvests them into productive assets.

Now let's take a look at Gem's income statement in Exhibit 3.2.

The Income Statement

Net Sales

The first item on the income statement is usually gross sales or operating revenues. If other sources than sales of merchandise are important (such as commissions earned or rents received), disclosure of the amount from each of these sources is essential. (Ten percent or more of the combined total for either source is considered significant under Rule 5-03 of S.E.C. Regulation SX). Lenders usually distinguish between sales and extraneous income like interest income, equity earnings and other revenue not related to the primary business.

Cost of Goods Sold

At Gem the cost of goods sold represents costs involved in manufacturing furniture; these costs are critical to the company's operation. Production costs consist of raw material, labor and overhead. For example, lumber is a direct materials cost while carpenters' wages represent a direct labor cost. Overhead costs, while not traceable to finished goods, are usually significant and need to be controlled. Examples of overhead costs are plant rent and depreciation, maintenance and repair.

A reasonably detailed disclosure of the composition of cost of goods sold, including opening and closing inventories, together with an explanation of the basis used in inventory valuation is essential to any informative analysis of the production cycle. A rapid rate of change in cost of goods sold relative to sales means that production costs cannot be passed along to consumers, and thus the firm faces a structural problem in its operations.

Cost and Expenses

Selling, General & Administrative Expenses

For the most part these expenses are controllable and may vary with gross sales (variable expenses) or be a fixed component regardless of sales levels. Selling expenses include salaries and other expenses of the sales department. General and administrative expenses include salaries of Gem's officers and other administrative employees, research and development costs, insurance, and rent allocated to operations.

Earnings Before Interest and Taxes (EBIT)

Earnings before interest and taxes (EBIT) is a measure of the strength of the firm's operations, or the cash generated from operations. Cash generated from operations includes earnings, as well as other non-cash expenses, such as depreciation.

Less Interest Expense

Interest expense is the cost of borrowed funds, whether the borrowing is for short-term purposes or long-term purposes. Bor-

Exhibit 3.2

Gem Furniture Company
Income Statement
Year Ended December 31 ($ Millions)

	1989	1990	1991
Net Sales	$512,693	$553,675	$586,895
Cost of goods sold	405,803	450,394	499,928
Depreciation expense	4,781	4,973	6,120
Gross profit	**102,109**	**93,308**	**80,847**
Costs and expenses:			
Selling, admin. & general expenses	38,369	46,034	50,643
Miscellaneous expenses	6,082	10,672	17,174
Total costs and expenses	44,451	56,706	67,817
Earnings before interest and taxes (EBIT)	57,658	41,602	13,030
Less Interest expense:			
Interest on ST loans	956	1,682	5,469
Interest on LT loans	1,913	2,869	2,869
Interest on mortgage	779	707	636
Total interest expense	3,648	5,258	8,974
Earnings before taxes	54,010	36,343	4,056
Income taxes	26,068	17,589	2,091
Net Income	27,942	18,755	1,965
Dividends on stock	7,060	4,464	266
Additions to retained earnings	$20,882	$14,291	$1,699

rowing funds to finance the company's operations or capital purchases imposes a burden on the company, as the loan plus interest on the borrowed funds, will be repaid from cash generated from operations.

Income Taxes

Corporations are taxed on profits at the federal and in some cases at state and local levels. U.S. corporations pay taxes on earnings at a statutory rate of 34 percent of their pretax profit.

Net Income

Net income is the profit generated by the company's selling activities less all applicable expenses for production, sales expense, general and administrative expense, interest and taxes.

At this point, having been introduced to the general concepts of balance sheet and income statement composition, and to the Gem Company, we'll go on to Chapter Four where we'll meet Gem again in the context of ratio analysis.

CHAPTER *Four*

Ratio Analysis

Ratios emerged at the beginning of the twentieth century from studies of the credit relationships businesses had with each other and with lenders.

In 1919, the first comprehensive system of ratio analysis was introduced, primarily representing the creditors' viewpoint. Ratio analysis helps creditors evaluate a company's financial strengths and weaknesses, flagging any irregularities that may affect repayment of debt.

Today, to examine potential credit serviceability, asset managers analyze internal operations in much the same way. But ratios don't tell the whole story; they offer clues, not answers. It's unreasonable to expect that the calculation of one ratio or a group of ratios will automatically yield critical information about a complex corporation. Analysts must interpret, compare and look behind the numbers in order to form conclusions about a company's well-being.

Ratios provide the tools to measure the extent, trend and quality of a company's financial statements and cash flow, as well as the extent and nature of its liabilities. We

can track a firm's historical performance, evaluate its present position, and obtain a relative value to compare with industry averages to provide answers to the following basic questions:

Does the company earn a fair return? Can it withstand downturns? Does it have the financial flexibility to attract additional creditors and investors? Is management adroit in its efforts to upgrade weak operations, reinforce strong ones, pursue profitable opportunities, and push the value of common stock to the highest possible levels?

In this chapter, we'll cover ratios comprehensively, from their limitations to the descriptions of specific ratios and their uses. We'll be using financial data from the Gem Furniture company described in the previous chapter to illustrate our points.

Limitations of Ratios

Consideration of ratios requires an extensive number of caveats, most of them based on the fact that accurate ratio analysis necessitates comparable results between the standard and the ratio itself in order for the information to be usable.

∎ The ratios in this chapter apply to manufacturers, wholesalers, retailers and service companies. Divergent asset quality and capital structure make it necessary to employ other ratios to analyze banks, utilities and finance companies.

∎ Ratios concentrate on the past.

∎ Some firms "window-dress" their financial statements to make them attractive to credit analysts. For example, a firm might sell its corporate aircraft for cash just before issuing a quarterly statement.

∎ Benchmarks or industry leaders are better targets for high-level performance. Match firms against the solid performers rather than the average ones.

∎ The lack of quality and availability of data usually diminishes the usefulness of ratios.

∎ Ratios come from raw numbers derived from accounting data. Generally Accepted Accounting Principles (GAAP) allow for flexibility and therefore, varied interpretation. Different accounting methods distort inter-company comparison. Consider the impact of using different methods for:

1. **Revenue Recognition:** Certain types of companies, such as contractors, may recognize revenue on a percentage of completion method for major projects to closely match the timing of costs and profits earned.

2. **Inventory Valuation:** LIFO vs. FIFO

3. **Depreciation:** Even under GAAP, there is considerable latitude for depreciation schedules for various asset classes. Firms with large capital equipment requirements may benefit from accelerating depreciation to minimize taxes.

4. **Bad Debts:** Although GAAP requires companies to establish a reserve account or provision for doubtful accounts, there is room for interpretation on what percentage of problem accounts should be recognized or when a bad debt should be charged off. The banking industry presented a good example of this in 1991. Federal regulators viewed the banks as under-reserved with respect to potential problem loans, particularly in real estate. The regulators encouraged banks to make huge additions to their reserves resulting in large losses for the banks.

5. **Capitalization of Costs:** GAAP allows computer software companies to capitalize certain developmental costs over the expected life of the software. This technique can significantly affect a company's perceived profitability and cash flow.

6. **Pension Fund Costs:** You should be familiar with all the pension assumptions that combine to make up pension costs. The major problem for lenders are unfunded pension costs.

7. **Cost versus Equity Accounting for Investments:** How an investment (for example, in another company) is recognized on the balance sheet can greatly impact

the financial statements. Investments at cost remain on the balance sheet at the lower of cost or market. Provided that the value of the investment does not depreciate below cost, there will be no change in the carrying value of the investment. Under the equity method of accounting for investments, the company is required to reflect its percentage share of the profit or losses from the investment in each period. Suppose Company A owns 35 percent of Company B. Company A is required to report 35 percent of Company B's profit or loss in each period on Company A's financial statements, though these are non-cash events to Company A.

8. **Seasonality and Differing Fiscal Years**: Differences in business flow and accounting periods can obviously hinder inter-company ratio analysis.

9. **Major Mergers and Acquisitions:** Plans to divest subsidiaries or acquire new business units will have a material effect on future performance. Smart bankers will ask for details and use information supplied by the borrower to construct proforma consolidated statements as if the divestiture or acquisition occurred during the last fiscal.

Peer Group or Industry Comparisons

Comparative ratio analysis can be extremely informative. Under certain circumstances, we might question the validity of comparative ratios, especially when we compare a firm's ratios to industry norms without knowing its history. Also, keep in mind the performances of the rest of the industry and suitable industrial averages against which the firm will be benchmarked. We begin to question comparative ratio analysis when a firm's position or business cycle differs from that of the rest of the industry. This often creates an illusion of poor or exaggerated ratios.

For example, a firm with a high current or quick ratio may be viewed as liquid (able to convert current assets into cash quickly and meet expenses) but the high ratio may be due to inefficient resource usage.

We might find it difficult to compare a diversified firm's financial statement to industry averages. We are not really comparing "like numbers." The firm's ratios may be composed of figures from many industries. Before jumping to conclusions about quality, magnitude and ratio trends, judge each company individually, using insightful benchmark matches. Is the ratio composed of the *right stuff*?

A comparison of IBM with Cray Research, for example, would not easily yield accurate information. IBM is so much larger than Cray that the two firms have separate and diverse financial statements while both are in the same industry. Consider Electric Boat. It has a few very expensive submarines listed on its balance sheet and could greatly influence comparisons if it disposed of one submarine just before or after the end of a fiscal period.

Differing assets lead to different levels of quality in the ratios. Look at R.J. Reynolds with its numerous diverse divisions and product lines. If you use only consolidated data, you miss how its differing product lines contribute to profitability and risk.

In the highly volatile capital markets industry, we might find it hard to establish a meaningful set of comparative industry averages. Here, the varying methods of classifying assets and liabilities add up to a comparison quandary.

Companies specializing in niche markets pose still another problem. The Concord Jet, for example, is the sole company in its market, so there is no other firm to compare it to.

One area of benchmark comparisons where ratio analysis simply falls short is the seasonal business. Because the flows and contractions of seasonal businesses do not always coincide, lenders might find it hard to peg an industry average. This will, of course, depend on whether we calculated ratios before or after the peak season.

You get the idea. Ratios, to be useful, have to compare like against like. Beware of differences and distortions caused by size, volatility, diversity, seasonality, geography, patents, litigation, foreign ownership, varied accounting procedures, the newness of an industry and a host of other differentiating factors.

Comparative ratios are guides. We should know enough about an industry to select the appropriate benchmark. If you feel comfortable with averages check to see if the firm's ratios fall beyond one standard deviation of the median. We should all talk to people familiar with the industry. Accountants, consultants, suppliers and industry specialists provide first-rate information.

Ratio Trends

Are financial trends consistent with the past, or do ratios show us an altering pattern established within the firm's operating and financial strategies? Industry comparisons correlate trends, thus helping us vali-

date the financial strength of borrowers. Loan officers can regretfully furnish myriad examples of cases where loans went bad because they missed the trends.

Take the seasonal amusement park operators who historically were cash rich in summer season but needed to borrow in the winter to pay expenses. The pattern in the financial statements would be to examine the expansion and contraction in the balance sheet. A newly assigned account officer notices that the company's loan is fully extended in August and begins to ask questions. The answer—the borrower diverted cash normally used to repay the bank loan into a new enterprise, and thus couldn't repay the debt.

Identifying Financial Ratios

There are several types of financial ratios, each relating to a different area of corporate operation: liquidity, activity, profitability, leverage, growth, and valuation.

Liquidity Ratios

The first financial consideration taken into account by lenders is a firm's liquidity. Liquidity ratios measure the quality and capability of current assets to meet maturing short-term obligations. Essentially, lenders weigh seasonal cash conversion loans against short-term resources to determine if these loans will be satisfied. Acceptable liquidity levels depend on economic and industry conditions, and the predictability of cash flow. Firms that consistently meet their short-term commitments ultimately increase their options for obtaining additional debt financing. On the other hand, companies unable to generate enough cash flow to satisfy short-term debt, can do little else until they rectify the problem.

Current Ratios. The current ratio is the most commonly used measure of short-term solvency since it indicates, roughly, a firm's ability to service current debt. To calculate the ratio, current assets are divided by current liabilities. The result obtained will identify how much a company has in current assets for every $1.00 in current liabilities. Here we go back to our illustration, Gem Furniture. Its current ratio at year-end 1991 is shown below.

Current Ratio = Current Assets/Current Liabilities = $240,264/$137,187 = 1.75

1989	1990	1991	Industry Average
3.05	2.67	1.75	2.50

Generally speaking, one would surmise that the higher the ratio comparative to industry averages, the greater the "comfort zone" between short-term resources and short-term obligations. This assumption can prove incorrect on two counts. First, a company with a rapid conversion cycle (aka current assets turnover) usually requires a lower current ratio as compared to one with a sluggish conversion cycle. Secondly, the allocation and quality of current assets is of great importance in determining acceptable ratio levels.

If we analyze Gem's current ratio over the last three years, current assets have decreased in value from $3.05 to $1.75 for every $1.00 in current liabilities. From a lender's perspective, this precipitous drop below the industry average causes immediate concern unless Gem is now converting assets at a faster pace than the industry average. Closer examination of the balance sheet proves that this is not the case. The first and most obvious problem is the rising levels of inventory stock. Creditors will question whether Gem is holding old, obsolete or unsalable stock worth stated value. Secondly, an expanding accounts receivable base signals a lengthening aging schedule with possible bad debt exposure. This leads us to believe that Gem does not have the cash flow necessary to cover short-term debt because current assets may not be worth their stated value.

What if Gem is able to convert its current assets close to book value? If this is so, 57% of Gem's current assets must be liquidated to pay off current creditors in full. Since cash and accounts receivable only make up 42% of the current assets needed, inventory will have to be sold to make up the difference. This conclusion is supported by the quick ratio.

Quick Ratio (aka Acid Test). The quick ratio is a more conservative measure of a company's liquidity because it measures a firm's ability to pay off all short-term obligations without relying on the sale of inventory. Since the quick ratio isolates the most liquid assets, it is more accurate than the current ratio. This can be of particular importance if inventory is a large portion of current assets.

Quick Ratio = Cash and Accounts Receivable/Current Liabilities = $11,717 + $88,571/$137,187 = 0.73

1989	1990	1991	Industry Average
1.65	1.08	0.73	1.00

Gem's quick ratio has declined during the past three years. Usually, if any value is one or less, the company can't pay off its current liabilities without selling inventory. At a time when its financial performance is deteriorating, Gem would have to rely on selling inventory at a loss (i.e., future sales) to pay existing obligations. The steep decline shows that Gem must sell inventory to pay bills at a time when its financial performance is deteriorating. The quality of that inventory and the timing of such sales become critically important.

Net Working Capital (aka risk). Returning to the current ratio for one moment, closer inspection reveals it as another way of expressing a company's net working capital position. Current assets minus current liabilities measure the amount of money that would be left over if a firm liquidates its current assets at face value.

Net Working Capital = Current Assets – Current Liabilities = $240,264 – $137,187 = $103,077

Net working capital is a good indicator of a company's health. The dollar value of net working capital equals the capital structure less long-term assets. This suggests that when a large amount of current assets are covered by long-term debt, it is more than likely that the firm will not have any short-term debt problems. Gem is currently financing 57 percent of its current assets with short-term debt. As stated earlier, the same percentage must be liquidated to satisfy all short-term creditors in full. Both ratios complement one another, and will be directly affected by the actual value of Gem's current assets.

Cash Flow versus Current Liabilities Ratio. On an ongoing basis, current liabilities must either be renewed or refunded. If a firm is unable to refund a liability, creditors will stall renewing it. As a refresher, cash flow is net income plus depreciation and other noncash expenses.

CF vs. CL Ratio = Cash Flow/Current Liabilities

The higher the ratio, the greater the chances are that the firm will be able to renew its current debt or pay off a portion of it.

Activity Ratios

Activity ratios, also called asset management ratios, assume an equilibrium between assets and sales which determines how efficiently a firm utilizes its resources. Lenders pay close attention to this group of ratios because the success or failure of a company's asset management policies directly affects business relations. We recognize five intrinsic benchmarks of asset efficiency: the average collection period, inventory turnover, fixed asset turnover, total asset turnover, and working capital turnover.

Average Collection Period (ACP). The Average Collection Period calculates the time it takes to convert accounts receivable into cash. ACP factors can be external or internal. For example, economic fluctuations affecting a specific business sector will justify the number of days every company needs to collect payments. Alternatively, if only one company is affected in the industry, internal problems exist.

Average Collection Period = (Accts Receivables/Sales) × 365 = $88,571/$586,895 × 365 = 55

1989	1990	1991	Industry Average
37	37	55	32

A shorter ACP usually suggests that accounts receivable is a high-quality asset that enhances cash flow. On the other hand, the increase in Gem's ACP over the last three years supports the liquidity ratios conclusion that a cash flow problem exists. In order to determine the extent of the problem, an aging schedule must be analyzed. The aging schedule will confirm if a company is having serious collection problems that may result in lost revenues and higher bad debt expenses. The latter scenario may also suggest stale inventory and a host of other financial woes. However, we should look more carefully at the causes of an increase in the ACP before concluding that something is amiss. For example, an increasing ACP may be a sign that a company is taking advantage of operating leverage and creating an asset that will generate profits.

If the ACP is lengthening, Susan Toms at Second City must first rule out external causes. For instance, if Gem management explains that the firm's receivables have slowed because of a sluggish economy, Susan can easily check that explanation by looking at the ACP of a benchmark company or at the industry average. If the industry average is 32 days but the borrower's collection period is averaging 55 days, the borrower's explanation is incomplete. A lender then might want to look for problem areas.

For example, if an increase in the ACP follows an earlier increase in inventory turnover, there may be a problem. In such a case an increased ACP may reflect the borrower's exchanging one bad asset (stale inventory) for another (low-quality receivables). This scenario is pertinent for businesses with perishable inventory. If the increased ACP is not connected to inventory problems or external factors, there may be another explanation—rooted in the relationship between a firm's operating leverage and its credit standards.

The Cost of Acceptance and Rejection

First, we should understand that the factors influencing the Average Collection Period include discounts, terms, collection policy, and credit standards. The last of these factors, the credit standards a firm uses, is usually difficult to figure out. Yet, whether these standards should be strict or liberal is usually influenced by the variables contained in one simple model: acceptance versus rejection cost.

The Cost of Acceptance

Equation 1. Acceptance Cost = (probability of default associated with the new order × the incremental cost of producing and selling an additional unit) + (the cash tied up in receivables × the number of days between the sale and the collection of the receivable/365 days × the cost of funds) + (clerical, investigation, and collection costs associated with the new order).

The Cost of Rejection

Equation 2. Rejection Cost = probability of non-default × the incremental profit from the sale of an additional unit.

In the first equation, the incremental cost of production is the major cost consideration. Thus if the incremental cost of production is low, the acceptance cost will most likely be low. Similarly, a low incremental production cost shows a high incremental profit and, a high cost for rejection of a credit sale.

Example: Acceptance versus Rejection Costs

Assume Gem's competitor, Robert Furniture Mfg. Corp., can take on new business from XYZ Inc. by selling bedroom sets worth $100,000 expected to generate a marginal profit of $40,000. Credit Investigation indicates the probability of payment is 96%. It costs $60,000 to manufacture the order and sell it. Payment is expected to be received in 45 days. The cost of funds is estimated to be 15%. Clerical, investigation and collection costs of a comparable order are $200. Should the corporation accept or reject the order?

Acceptance Costs = (.04)($60,000) + ($100,000)(45/365)(.15) + $200 = $4450

Rejection Costs = (.96)($40,000) = $38,400

The order will be accepted because it costs more to reject it than to accept it. The spread between acceptance and rejection costs is substantial, reinforcing the decision to accept the order.

What would keep the incremental cost of production low? Consider the idea of operating leverage. Once a firm generates sales volume to cover fixed production costs, the incremental profitability of additional units sold increases. For instance, consider the ferryboat company that has a scheduled departure with one vacant space. It costs the ferry company almost nothing to fill that space with one additional car. Thus, it might think twice before rejecting a credit sale for that space because the customer might not meet its credit standards. The ferry company has "liberalized its credit standards" because its incremental cost of production is low, or, to put it another way, its operating leverage is high.

Although it may not be immediately obvious, a firm's capital expenditure policy may influence its accounts receivables management. Thus, if Gem had been making substantial and profitable investments in capital expenditures, which would have the effect of lowering its production costs, it may well translate into more liberal credit standards and thus increase the ACP.

A Smaller Role for Credit Investigation

By setting equations 1 and 2 equal to each other (accomplished in the Excel template illustrated on the next page), it is possible to solve for the probability of default. For instance, if it is still advantageous for a firm to accept a credit sale even when the probability of a default is as high as 30 percent, that firm may de-emphasize the role of credit investigation in credit decision making.

A shocking notion? Not really. The key here is that the potential for profit from the sale of an additional unit is so much greater than the potential for loss that the maintenance of extremely strict credit standards may reflect poor management of accounts receivable. Besides, it reflects poor utilization of fixed assets in the sense that the firm invested in fixed assets to create a certain operating leverage but then didn't reap the full benefit of its investment. The most important point is rather than panic at the increasing ACP we might get behind the number and consider whether the increase represents a smart move by the borrower.

However, Gem's 55-day ACP versus the industry norm of 32 days is totally unsatisfactory. The management of accounts receivable should be scrutinized. Poor control of the receivables is affecting the company's liquidity position and its earnings power. In the first instance, the collectibility of a large portion of the accounts is questionable, which directly affects Gem's ability to meet its maturing obligation of short-term debt. The second matter, earnings power, could be noticeably improved. For instance, if the firm had an ACP of 32, substantial cash would be released for debt

	A	B	C	D	E	F	G	
Acceptance versus Rejection Costs Model								1
	A	B	C	D	E	F	G	2
Input Screen							Enter Costs Below	3
								4
Acceptance Costs								5
								6
Clerical Cost Associated with Opening Account							$30	7
Credit Investigation Cost							$40	8
Collection Costs							$130	9
Dollars Tied-up in Receivables (Sale Price)							$100,000	10
Probability of Non-Payment							4.00%	11
Incremental Cost of Production and Selling							$60,000	12
Average Time in Days between Sale and Payment							45	13
Cost of Funds							15.00%	14
								15
Rejection Costs								16
								17
Incremental Profit from Sale							$40,000	18
Probability of Non-Payment							96.00%	19
								20
Output Screen								21
								22
Acceptance Cost			$4,449					23
								24
Rejection Cost			$38,4,00					25
								26
Accept/Reject Credit:			ACCEPT CREDIT					27
								28
Probability B/E			0.380					29
								30
								31
								32
								33
Output Screen Formulas:								34
Acceptance Cost		equal ➡	(G11*G12) + (+ G10* (G13/365)*G14) + SUM (G7:G9)					35
Rejection Cost		equal ➡	G18*G19					36
Accept/Reject Credit: = IF (D25>D23, "ACCEPT CREDIT", "REJECT CREDIT")								37
Probability B/E = (G18/ (G18 + G12) − ((G10 *G13*G14) / 365)/(G18 + G12) − (G8 + G9) /(G18+ G12))								38

repayments, thereby reducing interest expense and improving net profits.

Bad Debt Expense/Sales measures overall accounts receivable quality. Follow the procedure below:

- Ask your customer for specific client information
- Divide the bad debt expense by sales

Compare the ratio to other years to see if collectibility is consistent or if an up or down trend is developing. Increasing trend in bad debt expense to sales may point to lax credit screening, or reflect the poor financial condition of its customers.

Inventory Turnover measures the number of times the level of inventory likely to be found on the balance sheet at any one time is sold during the fiscal year, showing how well management controls inventory. By comparing the turnover ratio to the industry standard, a company can assess if they are carrying excessive levels of stock. Optimal inventory control is essential to a firm's game plan. Proficient asset managers know that exorbitant inventory levels represent unproductive investments with a low or zero rate of return. While all activity ratios employ sales as the numerator, inventory turnover sometimes uses the cost of goods sold. This alternative is suitable because inventories are carried at cost. However, since sources of comparative ratios like Robert Morris Assoc. or Dun & Bradstreet measure inventory turnover with sales, you should too.

Inventory Turnover (Cost) = Cost of Goods Sold/Inventory = $499,928/ $139,976 = 3.6
Inventory Turnover (Sales) = Sales/Inventory = $586,895 / $139,976 = 4.2

1989	1990	1991	Industry Average
7.1	4.5	3.6	5.7
9.0	5.6	4.2	7.0

The diminishing turnover rate for the last three years verifies that Gem is holding old, obsolete and possibly unsalable inventory stock not worth its stated value. This reinforces our faith in the liquidity ratios, confirming two assumptions made earlier: First, that the excessive level of merchandise on hand is the main source of Gem's cash flow problem, and second, short-term obligations cannot be fully satisfied without selling off inventory. Since lenders are unwilling to service Gem with additional credit, current assets financed by long-term debt will have to be converted to cover the company's short-term credit crunch. After inventory has been restated, Gem's long-term debt shortfall will reflect the difference between the stated book value of inventory and the revised book value of inventory.

Looking at the opposite extreme, an appreciably large turnover rate comparative to industry standards also suggests problems. Frequent stock-outs, which lead to lost sales, are the result of management's inability to accurately project sales patterns or fully master the production process. The clues are always there if you take the time to look behind the numbers.

As a rule of thumb, high inventory turnover usually suggests good inventory management. Good inventory control starts with fundamental understanding of the three stages of inventory: Raw materials (RM), work-in-process (WIP) and finished goods (FG).

Raw materials leverage is based on anticipated production, the seasonality of the business and the reliability of suppliers. If raw materials are highly salable and commodity-like, this stage is often closer to cash than work-in-process inventory.

A buildup of raw material usually indicates speculative activity in anticipation of price increases or shortages. Work-in-process is defined as the length of the production cycle. Factors that directly affect WIP include the grade of the equipment, engineering techniques and the maintenance of highly skilled workers. Exorbitant work-in-process inventory depicts production slowdowns and/or manufacturing inefficiencies.

Finished goods involves coordinating the sales effort. Salability of finished goods depends generally on the type of business operation. If there is a problem in this area, review sales strategy to find out why potential customers don't want to buy the firm's product. This will spotlight which inventory stage needs fine tuning.

Economic Order Quantity (EOQ)

Inventory management's primary responsibility is to regulate the investment in inventory. By successfully maintaining a high level of inventory control, firms have more flexibility in planning capital investments and increasing profitability. This has two dimensions: how much to order and how often to do it. Properly employed, EOQ is a powerful inventory tool capable of measuring the optimal order quantity for inventory. Requirements for putting this cost control tool into effect include reliable sales forecasting techniques, accurate knowledge of variable ordering and carrying costs, and the expenditures related to safety stock.

Because the EOQ model is calculated exclusively by variable inventory costs, let us take a moment to identify them. Carrying costs fluctuate with the

level of inventory and frequency of orders. Examples include: storage, handling costs, insurance, cost of capital, and most important, obsolescence. Textbook carrying cost expenses range from 20–25 percent of inventory value. Ordering costs are associated with the acquisition of inventory. Examples include: clerical costs associated with ordering, shipping and handling, and overhead related to the purchasing department. Our last variable cost, safety stock, serves as a kind of insurance policy or buffer against greater-than-expected demand or problems related to the ordering and delivery of goods.

The Fixed Asset Turnover Directing the firm's capital equipment policies is central to management's goal of maximizing shareholder's wealth. Fixed assets decrease cash flow. As a result, cash generated by productive assets must offset initial investment outflows, producing a positive net present value. In other words, what this ratio really represents is cash flow.

Fixed Asset Turnover = Sales / Net Fixed Assets = \$586,895 / \$48,539 =12.09

1989	1990	1991	Industry Average
11.6	12.0	12.1	12.0

Let's review the cues suggesting management is operating fixed assets efficiently. A large ratio may suggest that:

- Efficient use of property plant and equipment has resulted in a high level of operating capacity
- Merger and divestment activity has changed the composition and size of fixed assets on the consolidated balance sheet

■ Plant capacity has increased, utilizing more of the machines already in place

■ Management has planned expansion carefully, using up-to-date capital budgeting techniques

■ Fixed assets not required to maintain a degree of operating leverage and production efficiency were divested

On the other hand, management may have allowed plant facilities to wear down. Is a large fixed asset ratio good or bad? Susan Toms will likely decompose the elements that produced a high turnover rate by analyzing Gem's cash flows and multivariate ratios. If operations are amiss she'll notice that:

■ Cash flow reveals a deferred tax runoff

■ Depreciation expense (related to older machinery) is consistently greater than capital expenditures (related to replacement costs). Gem's unfilled orders (backlogs) increased

■ Work-in-process inventory increases due to production slowdowns

■ Reduced operating leverage developed with additional labor channeled to production

■ Gross profit margin eroded significantly

Working Capital Turnover. Working capital is, within its broad definition, the excess of current assets over current liabilities. It is cash and the other more liquid assets that are expected to be consumed or converted into cash within the accounting period over obligations due within one year. Working capital is a general measure of liquidity and represents the margin of protection short-term creditors look for behind the primary source of payment; the conversion of current assets. Knowledge of the mechanics of working capital (and certainly cash flow) will provide a lender with the insight to quickly distinguish between temporary or structural problems.

Working Capital Turnover = Sales/Working Capital = $586,895 / 103,077 = 5.7

1989	1990	1991	Industry Average
6.2	5.3	5.7	4.5

A cash flow analysis is more refined than a working capital analysis and should always be the focal point for analyzing bank loans with maturities beyond one year. Preparing a working capital analysis, however, when used to protect a short-term creditor consumes less time than a cash flow analysis. Working capital analysis also eliminates captions (all those current items) that clutter and obscure the analysis of short-term loan protection.

However, a working capital analysis including analysis of the working capital turnover does not take into consideration the composition of current accounts. While a firm's working capital may be growing, its liquidity may actually be decreasing. For example, the working capital reconciliation may indicate working capital is increasing, but this may be a buildup of stale or otherwise unsalable inventory and slow receivables. Consider the case of an East Coast commercial sprinkler wholesaler who believed that the construction boom in California was worth pursuing. After he purchased inventory and a West Coast warehouse, recession hit California and he could not convert the inventory to cash. So he couldn't pay off the bank and his firm was liquidated.

A simple but powerful working capital derivation, presented in the chapter dealing with seasonal loans, crystallizes important signals provided by the funds flow. The flow of funds solution to working capital changes uncovers a firm's dominant, long-lasting operating and financing strategies.

The Average Settlement Period The Accounts Payable Turnover Ratio calculates how many times trade payables turn over in one year.

Average Payment Period = Accounts Payable/Avg Purchases Per Day

The lower the ratio, the shorter the time between purchase and payment. If for example, Gem's payables turned over more slowly than the industry average, it can be surmised that they are disputing invoices, received extended terms, deliberately expanded their trade credit or are experiencing cash flow problems.

The Average Settlement Period or Day's Payables ratio yields the average length of time trade payables is outstanding.

Accounts Payable Turnover = Cost of Goods Sold/Accounts Payable

Average Settlement Period (ASP) = (Accounts Payable / Cost of Good Sold) x 365 = $59,995 / $499,928 x 365 = 44 days

1989	1990	1991	Industry Average
18	26	44	35

The above ratio measures the use of trade debt by providing the number of days a firm takes to pay suppliers. You can compare *The Average Settlement Period* to terms offered to customers and peers. Ideally, only inventory purchases should be in the numerator, but this figure is usually unavailable.

Profitability Ratios

Although a company's ultimate goal is to maximize shareholder wealth, profitability is a traditional benchmark for assessing success. Profitability ratios reveal a great deal about corporate policies and decisions— about management's ability to control expenses, improve profitability, and withstand downturns. In other words, these ratios give the final answers pertaining to managerial effectiveness on corporate investments and sales. Here we focus on the quality, trend and magnitude of earnings.

The Gross Profit Margin measures the profitability of the production process, revealing through the firm's pricing policy if management has successfully passed on increased production costs to consumers. Are pricing and production decisions on the money? Are raw material costs adequately controlled, along with the labor/machine amalgam? Do production policies and methods measure up to peer standards? Gross profit margin is a powerful tool that can answer these questions by assessing temporary (short-term) or structural (long-term) problems.

Gross Profit = Net Sales – CGS

(Net Sales = Gross Sales – Returns, Allowances, Discounts)

Cost of Goods Sold = Beginning Inventory + Purchases + Factory Labor + Labor + Factory Depreciation + Freight In – Ending Inventory

Gross Profit Margin = Gross Profit/Net Sales = $80,847 / $586,895 = 13.8%

1989	1990	1991	Industry Average
20.0%	17.8%	13.8%	18.0%

The consequence of a deteriorating gross profit margin as in Gem's case, can be the result of either a pricing policy that is too low, production costs that are too high or a combination of both. Gross profit troubles can usually be traced back to asset management policies and objectives which define the desirable degree of operating leverage based on projected sales levels now and in the future. Operating leverage, in its simplest form, implies that for every small increase in sales, large increases in net operating income will result.

Let's take a closer look behind Gem's numbers and build a case. We know for certain that poor inventory control is the culprit responsible for the excessive purchases of raw materials. Referring back to previous ratio analyses, the inventory turnover and the liquidity ratios isolate this problem. It is also very likely that some of these raw materials have been converted to the next stages of inventory. This in turn has generated unnecessary labor and overhead costs for products with no demand. As a result, the cost of goods sold has increased without a proportionate increase in revenue, putting the squeeze on gross profits.

Additional investigation also reveals that over the past three years depreciation expenses (for older equipment) have been consistently greater than capital expenditures (replacement costs). This is usually an indication that management is allowing the plant facilities to wear down. Gem's short-sightedness on long-term capital improvements (fixed assets) tells us that it will eventually run the risk of reducing profitability as product demand increases. This statement sounds totally contradictory, but it is true.

As product demand grows, variable costs, such as labor, disproportionately increase the cost of the manufacturing process. In a highly competitive marketplace, Gem will come to realize that, like Rose Jelly Corporation, it will be extremely difficult, if not impossible, to pass this additional cost on to the consumer. As a result, profit margins are squeezed one way or another due to excessive manufacturing costs or decreased demand as a result of higher prices. By investing in fixed assets for the long haul, a company will produce products at minimal cost, thereby improving the GPM.

Selling, General and Administration Expenses/Sales. We want to see if management holds down unnecessary marketing, entertainment, salaries and administrative expenses. However, some increases are justified; outlays for advertising, promotion, and research expenditures may actually increase shareholder value.

Selling, General, Administration plus Miscellaneous Expenses/Net Sales =
$50,643 + $17,174 / $586,895 = 11.6%

1989	1990	1991	Industry Average
8.7	10.2	11.6	4.1

We should ask if Gem's operating expenses are further contributing to the problem. Gem's operating expenses relative to sales are worse than the industry.

Effective Tax Rate The provision for income taxes excludes excise, social security and sales taxes. You may want to compare this rate to the statutory tax rate and to the prior year's effective tax rate. We should not stop short of looking at the specific expenses contributing to this gap.

Effective Tax Rate = Income x Expense / Pre-Tax Income = $2,091 / $4056 = 51%

1989	1990	1991
48.3%	48.4%	51%

The nature and magnitude of the permanent differences which cause variances between effective and statutory rates should be examined, e.g.: intercorporate dividends, differing foreign tax rates, depletion allowances.

The Net Margin. This ratio measures the percentage of each sales dollar remaining after all expenses and taxes have been deducted. What is considered a good profit margin will depend upon the industry. For example, a low profit margin might be acceptable for a grocery store, whereas it would be unwelcome for a jewelry store.

Net Margin = Net Income / Net Sales = $1,965 / $586,895 = 0.3%

1989	1990	1991	Industry Average
5.5%	3.4%	0.3%	2.90%

Gem's low profit margins reflect rising costs with lower than proportionate increases in revenue.

Return on Net Worth. This is the final criterion for measuring profitability. It provides the per dollar yield on investment to the equity holder. This return should be examined in relation to the firm's financial leverage. When a loss has been incurred, the ratio is meaningless. High profits reflect greater capability of cash inflows per sales volume. If the ratio is consistent, greater sales should provide greater cash inflows and assist in financing growth. A high ratio could indicate highly leveraged financials.

Return on Net Worth = Reported Net Income / Average Net Worth = $1,965 / $115,910 = 1.7%

1989	1990	1991	Industry Average
28.0%	16.4%	1.7%	17.5%

The firm's return on common stock is low relative to the industry and trended down since 1989. The level of this return can be expressed as a function of Gem's return on assets, and the company's capital structure. These two factors represent the key determinants of the return on stockholders equity. Gem's low return on common ensues from the extremely low return on assets.

Return on Total Assets. Also called Return on Investment or ROI, this ratio measures how effectively a company employs its total assets.

Return on Total Assets = Reported Net Income/Total Assets = $1,965 / $288,803 = 0.7%

1989	1990	1991	Industry Average
16.6%	8.8%	0.7%	8.8%

Although this ratio does calculate the profitability of assets, it does not take into account the company's asset composition or the debt to equity mix. However, a comparison of this return with the return on net worth indicates the effect of financial leverage on the stockholder's return.

In 1991 Gem's asset turnover dipped significantly below the industry, indicating that Gem employed more assets per dollar of sales than the industry average. The decline in this ratio shows that the firm is becoming increasingly less efficient in its asset utilization. With fixed assets turnover marginally above average, Gem's problem clearly lies in its current asset management policies and long-term strategic planning. This is corroborated by accelerated current assets and modestly increasing fixed assets.

The Dividend Payout Ratio This ratio quantifies the percentage of earnings paid out in dividends. It should be examined in conjunction with leverage and industry characteristics.

Dividend Payout Ratio = Total Cash Dividends/Net Income = $266 / $1965 = 13.5%

1989	1990	1991	Industry Average
25.3%	23.8%	13.5%	27%

Dividends also play a role in determining the debt to equity ratio of a business. Leverage will increase if a high dividend payout rate is accompanied by substantial debt infusions. Because dividends represent a use of cash, dividends should only be distributed when debt levels are acceptable.

Excessive dividend distribution caused a closely held company serving the entertainment industry to experience financial difficulties. The company had been historically very profitable and built a huge liquidity position. It began paying large dividends to its stockholders, occasionally using bank loans to do so. When recession hit the industry, the company lacked the liquidity to survive.

Leverage Ratios

Capital is nothing more than the resources necessary to achieve an objective. There are three reasons for a firm to raise capital: to purchase an asset, pay an expense or make an investment. There are two broad classifications of capital: debt and equity. Debt refers to the money that belongs to another organization, while equity is the owner's money. Firms increase financial leverage by raising the proportion of debt to equity.

Leverage is a powerful factor in determining the health of a company. Unlike activity and profitability ratios, financial leverage is not something management necessarily wants to maximize, even when doing so might increase return on assets or provide greater tax shelters. Instead, the challenge of financial leverage is to strike a prudent balance between the benefits of debt and the costs of risk. Management is obviously concerned with the level of indebtedness since it recognizes the attention paid to it by all classes of investors.

We are interested in the amount of leverage borrowers employ because it indicates the firm's risk exposure in meeting interest and principal payments. The more indebtedness present, the higher the probability that the firm will be unable to satisfy the claims of all its creditors. A firm heavily financed by debt offers creditors less protection in the event of financial distress.

Shareholders pay close attention to debt levels because creditor claims must be satisfied before earnings are distributed.

Financial leverage influences the rate of return owners expect on investments. As leverage increases, the potential for profits or losses grow. This equates to the risk/reward theory which states: the greater the risk, the greater the potential for reward or loss. Therefore, the opportunity to improve return on equity is balanced by the risk involved in assuming more debt. Cash flows can be improved with the proper application of leverage.

Debt to Equity and Debt to Total Assets Ratios determines the relative use of borrowed funds. The appropriate debt ratio for a company will vary depending on its industry. It is not uncommon for businesses with extremely liquid assets, such as banks, to have ratios up to 900%. Manufacturing companies like Gem, on the other hand, tend to have ratios below 100% due to the illiquidity of their fixed assets and the tangible value of inventory if it has to be sold on short notice.

Regardless of what industry they are in, owners prefer to be leveraged with the highest possible (though prudent) debt ratio in order to maximize their return on investment. For example, assume that XYZ company has $1 million in total assets financed by $750,000 in debt and $250,000 in equity. At year-end, XYZ company turns a profit of $50,000 which generates a return on investment of 20%. If XYZ company had debt to equity structured with $250,000 in debt and $750,000 in equity, the return on investment would only be about 7%.

Total Debt/Stockholders Equity = $172,893/ $115,910 = 149.1%

TotalDebt/TotalAssets = $172,893/ $288,803 = 59.9%

1989	1990	1991	Industry Average
40.6%	46.5%	59.87%	50.0%

Besides identifying the use of borrowed funds, the debt to asset ratio also indicates the proportion of assets owned and the proportion of assets borrowed. The debt to equity range varies strikingly from industry to industry. Financial institutions are able to use financial leverage because assets are liquid. Industrial firms are capitalized with far less debt because of reduced asset quality and the large fixed asset components of industrial firms. We know that the size of financial leverage is influenced by:

- Asset quality (liquidity and turnover ratios)
- Composition of debt (short-term vs. long-term financing)
- Ability to cover interest payments with cash flow (cash flow and fixed charge coverage ratios)
- Market leverage (spreads between market debt to equity and book debt to equity ratios)

In viewing a firm's financial mix, two perspectives are generally taken, the relative participation of creditors in financing the company's assets and the ability of the business to meet cash outflow as a result of management's financing policies. These two criteria, typically measured by the debt to equity or debt to asset relationship, show Gem to be using a relatively large portion of debt to finance its investment decisions. However, this marked deficiency is worsened by inclusion of the more subtle benchmarks of financial leverage. While the relative amount of Gem's debt is close to the industry average, the two leverage ratios are clearly understated. Gem's questionable asset quality, the apparent imbalance between short and long-term financing, and weak interest coverage are benchmarks of the firm's true leverage.

Debt Service

Knowing how much debt can be taken on is probably as vital for corporate survival as any other piece of information. The following ratios measure the ability to service debt or how readily a firm meets the required contractual payments on a scheduled basis. Creditors are interested in debt service ratios because they signal financial difficulty.

Times Interest Earned. This ratio measures how far earnings can decrease without embarrassing the firm because it is unable to pay annual interest costs.

Times Interest Earned = EBIT/Interest = $13,030 / $8,973 = 1.4

1989	1990	1991	Industry Average
15.8	7.9	1.4	7.7

If our borrower's earnings before interest and taxes are 20 times interest, presumably there is a smaller chance that it will not be able to meet the interest payments than firms with identical business risk characteristics whose earnings before interest and taxes is 2 times interest.

Debt Affordability Ratio. The two components of determining debt affordability are a firm's cash inflows and cash outflows. Basically, cash inflows equal operating income + noncash expenses, and cash outflows equal financing costs.

Debt Affordability Ratio = Cash Inflows/Cash Outflows

When the result is less than one, too much debt has been taken on because the inflows can't cover the outflows. In some cases, even if the results are greater than unity there may still be too much debt since coverage of the outflows is tight. In other words, the risk of failure is a real possibility if expenses rise or revenue falls.

Growth Ratios

Growth ratios trend the various areas of the company over time to help in identifying the company tendencies and general economic position. Growth rates can highlight successful and problem areas and allow the firm to act accordingly. Appropriate levels of growth in a company signify that it is maintaining or expanding its position. Good judgment must be used when analyzing these ratios. For instance, growth coming from the inflation influence alone just changes the measuring stick. Important growth ratios to measure include the rate of change in the company's Return on Equity, Return on Assets, and Return on Investments.

Valuation Ratios

Valuation ratios extend beyond historical cost-based analysis to provide a more representative value of corporate growth. Since balance sheet and income statement values may not suggest the full financial position of the company, alternate means are required to obtain an understanding of the company's position. The company's share price will establish the reference since it provides the influence of risk ratios to return ratios. Through an analysis of valuation ratios, such as the price earnings ratio, *book value per share,* and dividend ratio, an indication of the derived value of the company with implied risk is obtained. If market indications are higher than book indications, the market has confidence in the company.

Book Value per Share/Market Range.
This ratio compares the equity market's "view" (market range) of the company to its book net worth per common share. The ratio is a further indicator of financial flexibility. Generally, if a firm's shares trade in excess of book value, the favorable market view could enable the company to raise additional equity. Conversely, a company whose shares trade at a discount (below book value) might have trouble raising equity capital or would be reluctant to do so because of the resulting dilution of stockholders' equity.

Book Value per Share = Common Equity/ Number of Common Shares Outstanding

The market range for the last year is found in the annual report or in the newspaper.

Statistical Analysis of Ratios

Credit analysis, particularly the credit literature, is naive from a statistical point of view—surprising because statistics fit the traditional methods lenders have always used to evaluate their borrower's ratios. Existing databases provide, for many of the ratios studied in this chapter, long lists of industry medians and means. It will be shown how these techniques add a potent dimension to traditional ratios.

Decomposition Analysis

Decomposition analysis derives its strength from the premise that little in business is left to chance. Management is constantly faced with external forces tugging at their firms, and must continuously shift assets and financial resources to counter these forces and preserve cash flow equilibrium. It is the extent, or magnitude of statistical "shifting around" that corroborates decomposition. Equilibrium relationships in business organizations, suggested Baruch Lev, a professor at the University of Chicago and author of *Financial Statement Analysis: A New Approach*, (Prentice Hall, 1974), are usually the result of economic optimality criteria designed to improve efficiency and maximize value. Thus for every level of activity there exist "optimal relationships between labor and capital inputs, inventory and sales, cash and short-term securities, debt and equity capital." Management allocation decisions in the face of external economic and market forces are reflected in financial statements.

Decomposition made it possible to measure the degree of stability firms have been able to sustain in an often volatile marketplace—inherent in the mix and volatility of their financial statements over time. Variations over time in the relationship among financial statements items shadow significant business events, planned and unplanned and are thus crucial to lenders engaged in assessing future performance. Lev studied the implication of decomposition analysis to a wide range of administration and social science areas including economics, sociology, psychology, and accounting. Statistical decomposition of financial statements is especially suited for the analysis of mass data such as large computer files of financial statements.

The application of decomposition analysis to Gem's balance sheet is discussed in Exhibit 4.1.

The instability of assets during 1990/1991 reflects, once again, Gem's serious inventory and accounts receivable problems. That decomposition measures reflect the occurrence of important events is supported by several empirical studies. This point is important—financially dis-

Exhibit 4.1

Application of Decomposition Analysis to
Gem's Balance Sheet

	Absolute Value			Relative Value		
	1989	1990	1991	1989	1990	1991
Cash and cash items	$15,445	$12,007	$11,717	0.092	0.056	0.041
Accounts receivable, net	$51,793	$55,886	$88,571	0.308	0.262	0.307
Inventories	$56,801	$99,087	$139,976	0.337	0.464	0.485
Net Fixed Assets	$44,294	$46,340	$48,539	0.263	0.217	0.168
Total Assets	$168,333	$213,320	$288,803	1.000	1.000	1.000

Lev designates the earlier relative values *by* p_i, $i = 1,.....n$. In Gem's case for 1990, $p1$ (cash) = .056, $p2$ (receivables) = .262, etc., and n = 4. The corresponding values of a latter financial statement is qi, where $q1 = .041$, $q2 = .307$, etc. The asset composition measure is defined by Lev as:

$$I_A = \sum_{i=1}^{n} q_i \log \frac{q_i}{p_i}$$

Gem's decomposition measure for 1990/1991 was calculated as follows:

I_A = .041 log$_e$ .041/.056 + .307 log$_e$ .307/.262 + .485 log$_e$ .385/.464 + .168 log$_e$ .368/.217 = 0.01252 nits

Asset Decomposition Measures (in 10– 4 Nits)

	1984/85	1986/87	1988/89	1990/91
Gem Furniture	352	392	372	125
Industry Average (assumed)	125	165	140	153

tressed firms had, for at least five years before bankruptcy, substantially larger balance sheet decomposition measures (shifts) than those of comparable solvent firms.

Ratio Variability

Lenders are comfortable with the traditional ratio techniques—trends, ratio quality tests, cross-sectional analysis (industry comparison) and the magnitude of the ratios they study; volatility complements conventional methods. The standard deviation is eminently suited to ratios.

Standard Deviation of the Current Ratio

A small standard deviation (measuring the extent of variation around the mean) indicates that management controls liquidity, desirable in short-term lending. Three possibilities exist:

1. Excessive current ratio deviation combined with weak or unstable sales and profit growth. Management likely has failed to control liquidity and performance; the firm may be out of control.

2. Volatile current ratio combined with strong operating performance. Management's operating strategies are the focus, not steadfast liquidity.

3. Tight variation around the mean followed by strong sales and profits; the best of all possible worlds.

Consider the following example, based on two steel companies, Allegheny and Bliss and Laughlin:

Compound Growth Rates: Ten Year Period

	Allegheny	Bliss and Laughlin
Sales	7%	9%
Profits	7%	13%

Ratios and Standard Deviations, same ten year period:

	Allegheny	Bliss and Laughlin
Ratio	Standard Deviation	Standard Deviation
Sales/Inventory	.40	1.08
Avg. Coll. Period	6.28	5.23
Fixed Assets/Net Worth	.06	.25
Current Ratio	.34	.78
Quick Ratio	.23	.45
Debt/Equity	.08	.35
Sales/Working Capital	.30	.60

In almost every case Bliss and Laughlin's ratios were more volatile. However, Bliss and Laughlin's sales and profit growth rates exceeded Allegheny's, a suggestion that management was inclined to trade off stability for growth.

Using Statistical Benchmarks to Improve Ratio Performance

If receivables were reduced to the average level for the industry, this would provide Gem Furniture with about $37,117, calculated as follows:

1. Gem's Average Collection Period as we saw:

Average Collection Period = (Accts Receivable/Sales) × 365 = $88,571/$586,895 × 365 = 55

1989	1990	1991	Industry Average
37	37	55	32

2. Set the average collection period to the industry average; include Gem's sales and solve for Accounts Receivable. We might take our pro forma analysis a step further, by adding a statistical window, the standard deviation. That is, bring Gem's average collection to within one standard deviation of the industry average.

Industry Collection Period 32 = (Accts Receivables / 586,895) × 365; Accounts Receivable = $51,454

Fiscal Accounts Receivable	$88,571
less Pro Forma Accounts Receivable	$51,454
Cash Available to Gem If Collection Time Improved to Industry Average	$37,117

We see identical results below (dollars in thousands):

Industry Mean Average Collection
Period   32
Sales $586,895
Accounts Receivable $88,571

Average Collection Period = Accounts Receivable/Sales × 365

Therefore: Accounts Receivable/Average Collection Period = Sales/365

Thus: Accounts Receivable/Average Collection Period = Daily Sales

Sales $586,895
Divided by Days in Year $1,608
Multiplied by Days to
  Accelerate: (55–32)   23
Cash Inflows: Faster
  Collection Time $36,984
                (allow for rounding errors)
Hurdle Rate   12%
Annual Savings $4,438

If inventories could be reduced to the average level for the industry, this would provide the firm with approximately $52,269 in receivables and/or cash calculated as follows:

1. Gem's Inventory Turnover:

Inventory Turnover (Cost) = Cost of Goods Sold/Inventory = $499,928 /$139,976 = 3.6

1989	1990	1991	Industry Average
7.1	4.5	3.6	5.7

2. Set the Inventory Turnover to the industry average; include Gem's sales and solve for Inventory:

Industry Inventory Turnover (Cost) = Cost of Goods Sold/Inventory = 5.7 = $499,928 / Inventory; Pro Forma Inventory = $87,707

Fiscal Inventory $139,976
less Pro Forma Inventory $87,707
Receivable and Cash Available to Gem
  If Inventory Converted as Fast
  as Industry $52,269

- Download a list of at least fifteen firms in the same industry (identical SIC code).
- Calculate the standard deviation of activity ratios you feel are out of line. The HP-19BII financial calculator and Excel or Lotus make computation easy.
- Review the results with your customer. Establish ratio performance targets, pointing out that activity ratios within one standard deviation of the mean or median represents attainable goals.

SUMMARY

Ratios are only diagnostic tools. Like electrocardiograms measuring changes in the heart's electrical activity, ratios catch irregularities in a business. Just like diagnostic tools in medicine, analysts must interpret, compare and look behind the numbers. Mechanical, unthinking ratio analysis is dangerous—just ask the folks in loan workouts. However, when used intelligently and with good judgment, ratios provide powerful insights into a firm's operations and into the riskiness of cash flows.

CHAPTER Five

Unsecured Seasonal Lending

Credit Analysis of Seasonal Businesses: An Integrated Approach

For many small and medium-sized firms, the essence of seasonal borrowing is an infusion of working capital to support temporary operating activities. This cash conversion cycle (or working capital cycle) is pivotal in the lending process since it marks the transformation of inventory into receivables and receivables into cash. Hypothetically, all short-term debt is repaid at the end of the fiscal period. These credit obligations are satisfied through the conversion of the current assets originally financed by the loan.

In basic terms, the working capital cycle describes the cash flow resulting from a firm employing its current assets. Most companies will finance a large portion of working capital by purchasing raw materials on credit, creating accounts payable and reducing the need for the firm to lay out cash. But this is not nearly enough to support the overall operation.

Commercial banks grant short-term loans with the understanding that loans are retired at the seasonal low point or at the end of the cash conversion cycle. In a sense, banks stipulate that borrowers will "clean up" a working capital line of credit, if even for a short time, to enforce a discipline ensuring that the line doesn't become considered permanent financing. During the fiscal year, a seasonal company's balance sheet goes through expansion and contraction.

At the high point or most active part of the period, debt and assets increase to support seasonal activity, thus expanding the balance sheet. During this phase, sales follow the manufacturing cycle, the result of which is the conversion of inventory into accounts receivable.

At the low point or least active part of the period, the manufacturing cycle has ebbed, leaving the firm with the responsibility of "cleaning up" outstanding short-term debt. This is accomplished through the conversion of accounts receivable to cash. Once all short-term debt has been paid down, the firm's balance sheet will contract back to its normal level. Any excess cash is usually designated for temporary current asset investment next season.

But what actually defines a successful or unsuccessful seasonal cycle? Let's find out.

The Successful Cycle

The typical seasonal company goes through five stages:

1. The Buildup Period: During the buildup period, demand deposits drop, whereas loan balances, trade payables and inventories increase. At this point, the balance sheet begins to expand

2. High Point Period: As a company reaches its high point, inventory, bank debt, and trade payables reach a peak. The need for liquidity bottoms out, and receivables remain low. The balance sheet reaches expansion limits.

3. Conversion Cycle Begins: Inventory decreases and receivables increase as demand accelerates. Payables and bank debt remain steady or decline slightly.

4. Conversion Cycle Intensifies: Shipments accelerate causing inventory to decline quickly and receivables to build further as some receivables convert to cash. Demand deposits rise, but at a slower rate. Payables and short-term loans begin to fall faster as collections are converted into cash. Balance sheet contraction

moves in tandem with cash conversion.

5. Conversion Cycle Subsides: The low point approaches and seasonal demand subsides. Firms ship less merchandise. Inventory is already at low levels and receivables decline quickly, causing deposits to swell. The balance sheet fully contracts to its low point as trade payables and bank debt are retired or cleaned up. After the "traditional 30 day" cleanup has passed, renewed debt replenishes liquidity in preparation for next season.

Let's look at the five stages graphically in Exhibit 5.1.

Defining the Unsuccessful Seasonal Cycle

On the other hand, the typical seasonal company that is unsuccessful will expose problems at some point during the seasonal cycle:

1. The Buildup Period: Demand deposits drop and loan balances, trade payables and inventory increase. The balance sheet starts expanding.

2. High Point Period: As the firm reaches its high point, inventory, bank debt, and trade payables peak. Liquidity requirements abate, receivables remain low, and the balance sheet reaches expansion limits. Still no signs of any problems.

3. Conversion Cycle Fails: Inventory remains at high levels. As a result, receivables and cash are at low levels due to an impeded conversion cycle. A weak cash position makes it impossible to "clean up" payables and bank debt, which remain at high levels.

Exhibit 5.1

Successful Seasonal Cycle

Firm's Selling Season Begins in September

	Jan	Feb	Mar	Apr	May	Jun	Jul	Aug	Sept	Oct	Nov	Dec
Bank and Trade Debt	700	750	800	900	1100	1100	1100	1000	800	700	650	75
Inventory	400	500	580	600	700	950	1050	1000	700	500	300	200
Receivables	300	250	300	225	400	300	250	300	400	1300	600	500
Cash	200	200	200	200	200	200	200	200	200	200	700	200

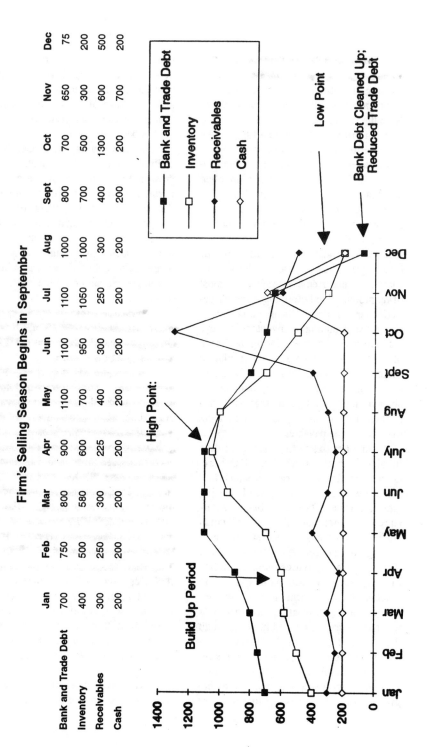

- ■ Bank and Trade Debt
- □ Inventory
- ◆ Receivables
- ◇ Cash

High Point:

Build Up Period

Low Point

Bank Debt Cleaned Up;
Reduced Trade Debt

This phenomenon is further exemplified on the graph in Exhibit 5.2. After reviewing the unsuccessful season, go back and compare it with the successful season. Note the variances.

In order to further understand how seasonal loans work, it is not only important to identify the selling season but also recognize that seasonal industries are often undercapitalized. For example, Acme Toy Company, a manufacturer of beach products and toys, typically receives orders for the bulk of its sales during the winter months. Shipment of these orders follow in the spring just in time for the start of summer. Since Acme manufactures most of its product line before the shipping period, short-term bank loans are necessary to finance its buildup in inventory. As toys are delivered to retailers during the spring months, the firm experiences a buildup in accounts receivable. When the summer season has ended, inventory and receivables decline, and deposits increase. Cash is then used to satisfy short-term bank loans and trade payables.

Another example of seasonal debt involves our old friend Gem Furniture. Gem's small lawn furniture subsidiary closes their books on August 31. During late summer and fall the subsidiary purchases raw materials, the bulk of which are forest products. Now, seasonal borrowing commences. As labor and other manufacturing activities intensify in late fall and early winter, bank borrowing reaches its high point. By late winter, as demand accelerates, the products leave the warehouses and move through the distribution channels. Then inventories start to decrease and accounts receivable increase. By early summer, accounts receivable and bank debt begin running off as cash collections are

made. At the close of the subsidiary's books on August 31, inventories and receivables should be down to an annual low, and all seasonal bank debt cleaned up. Hence, Gem's annual cash conversion cycle has been completed.

Since we are aware of Gem's financial status from previous chapters, let's regress momentarily. In the case of Gem Furniture Company, Susan V. Toms and the Second City Bank are well aware that Gem is highly leveraged financially and not capable of repaying its current credit obligations. In such a case as this, should Susan renew Gem's debt for next season in hopes of full repayment, or cut the bank's losses now?

The two seasonal cycles just discussed are classic examples of self-liquidating loans repaid through the conversion of temporary assets to cash.

This type of scenario would not likely occur if short-term financing was initiated to fund permanent assets. The permanent assets (core assets) of a firm, consisting of both non-seasonal, current, and fixed assets, are considered long-term resources that are necessary to stay in business. Under normal circumstances, long-term assets should be supported by liabilities with the same maturity since a firm with short-term debt tied to long-term assets may not be able to meet its credit obligations, and is probably subject to undue interest rate risk. Repayment of debt related to a permanent balance (or level) of earnings, current assets, as well as fixed assets, can only result from earnings arising from the profitable use of the assets. For most firms, this can only occur over a period of years.

However, some firms will use short-term loans to finance not only temporary

Exhibit 5.2

Unsuccessful Seasonal Cycle

Firm's Selling Season Begins in September

	Jan	Feb	Mar	Apr	May	Jun	Jul	Aug	Sept	Oct	Nov	Dec
Bank and Trade Debt	1000	1000	1000	1000	1000	1000	1000	1000	1000	1000	1000	970
Inventory	400	500	580	600	700	950	1050	1000	1000	950	950	950
Receivables	300	250	300	225	400	300	250	250	300	350	300	325
Cash	200	200	200	200	200	200	200	200	200	200	100	50

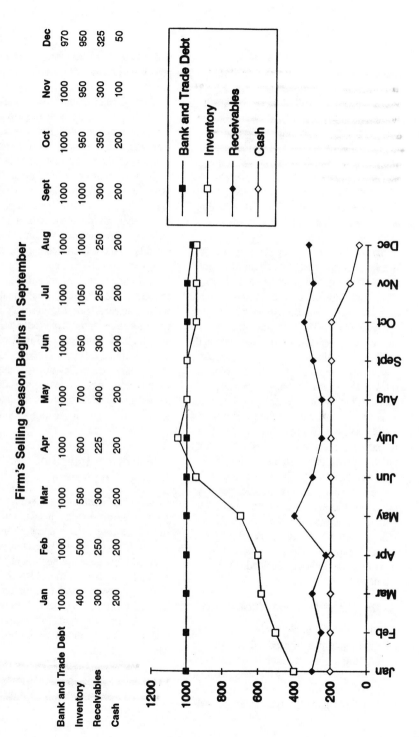

fluctuations in current assets but also permanent current assets. One reason for following such an approach, particularly by larger corporations that have continuous access to short-term credit, is that short-term interest rates tend (with dramatic exceptions) to be lower than long-term interest rates. Thus, short-term financing can be cheaper. Other firms may rely heavily on short-term loans in anticipation of a decline in interest rates. When this decline occurs, they plan to refinance their short-term loans with more appropriate long-term sources of financing. This, of course, is a focus of interest rate speculation, and is often supplemented with hedging.

Let's say the cash conversion cycle of a seasonal business expands beyond a one-year cycle. This indicates that credit support for investments in inventory and receivables will also expand. Also, for purposes of this exercise, the number of days sales is the sum of cash, inventories, and accounts receivable. Using a pipeline as an analogy, the diameter of the pipeline corresponds to the average sales per day. Sufficient days sales must be pushed into the pipeline to fill it before any cash emerges from the other end. The longer the cycle and the greater the average sales per day, the larger the amount of cash required to "fill the pipeline." As the case with any seasonal loan, if inventory blocks the working capital cycle (conversion cycle), reduced cash flow will decidedly jeopardize payment of the loan.

Examples of Seasonal Businesses

Jewelry retailers, book stores, and toy distributors have pronounced sales increases before the holidays. Retail department stores and candy retailers follow a seasonal pattern usually tied to holiday periods. By contrast, garden outlets, sporting goods stores and home lumber dealers generate peak sales during warm spring and summer months.

Swimsuit manufacturers may begin producing swimsuits in the fall to distribute to retailers the following spring. During the manufacturing period, inventories build along with labor and other product costs. In the spring, as swimsuits are sold, these proceeds provide the annual short-term loan cleanup.

Coal and fuel oil dealers build inventories in the summer, running them off steadily in the fall and winter months to a low point by early spring.

Food processors use short-term lines to finance crops grown and shipped at distinctive seasons. Short-term financing supports fertilizer and other production costs, and the harvesting season for distribution and marketing of the crop.

Retail businesses use seasonal loans to support swings in sales activity. Clothing stores anticipate increases in volume in the spring and again in the fall as new lines arrive.

Creating an Image of the Seasonal Borrower

In order to better assess a seasonal company's condition and needs, the lender must go through the process of analyzing its vitality and strength. Employing the methodology does not begin and end once the loan has been approved. Rather, it is an ongoing process used to monitor repayment. Remember, the bank does not want to get caught short suddenly recognizing a bad loan three months after the fiscal statements are finalized.

The *"comfort zone"* a lender looks for is captured, if you will, by creating an image of the company. The rudiments of this image consist of the following techniques:

1. High Point Pro Forma
2. Cash Budgets
3. Trial Balances
4. Break-Even Inventory Analysis
5. Seasonal Ratio Analysis
6. Break-Even Shipments Analysis

High Point Pro Forma

While a cash budget is usually the best source for determining a company's ability to take on additional debt, the High Point Pro Forma (HPPF) is the first technique initiated by the lender on a seasonal loan. HPPF is ranked first because it can immediately indicate if proposed credit line(s) are too burdensome for the borrower. This technique works on the premise that the bank extrapolates the borrower's low point actuals into arbitrary high-point projections. As the company reaches the high point of the conversion cycle, inventory, bank debt, and trade payables peak.

The intention of this exercise is to ascertain if this situation leaves the borrower with low liquidity and high leverage. If anticipated debt levels do place the financial structure at risk, the lender must weigh the risk cost involved. In certain cases, bankers will sometimes require an equity injection (or subordinated debt) to firm up capital.

To better understand how this technique works, let's look at Acme Toy currently renewing its seasonal line of credit.

■ ■ ■

Case Study

Seasonal Techniques—Acme Toy Company Inc.

On August 1, 1994, Acme Toy Co. Inc. requested a reaffirmation of its line at 1st City Bank. Financial managers at Acme Toy have requested an extension in the credit line to $7,500,000. This will give Acme a total of at least $7,200,000 to cover seasonal needs, outlined in the cash budget Acme presented to the bank.

Acme Toy Co., is a medium-sized manufacturer and distributor of beach toys. The company was originally established in 1976 and was primarily a board game manufacturer until 1986 when it began the summer toy line. In 1990 the company introduced their beaded pool cushion. The product has been highly successful and is manufactured in Mexico. Sales are to department and toy stores worldwide. The peak season starts late in March and continues into April and May, when the firm ships for the summer season. Sales are generally made on terms that require payment within sixty days.

The company's largest single customer, Toys 'R' Us, accounted for 20% of sales in 1993 and 14% in 1992. During 1993, the Acme Toy Co. negotiated a $5 million leveraged buyout with 1st City Bank to take the stock private (first payment due in two years). Because of its recent success, the company did not want to disclose financial information, the primary motive behind Acme's desire to keep stock closely held.

While Acme monitors inventory constantly, the firm submits unaudited interim trial balances—on a break-even basis—to the bank. The LBO agreement permits these unaudited statements, although the lenders are concerned about high leverage and may insist on more formal statements in the future. The company's February 28, 1994 fiscal balance sheet (fiscal balance sheets are fully contracted) reveals the following:

**Acme Toy Co. Inc.
Pro Forma Fiscal
February 28, 1994**

Assets

Cash	$1,900
Accounts Receivable	6,300
Fiscal Inventory	1,325
Prepaid Expenses	1,450
Current Assets	$10,975
Net PP&E	$2,555
Other Assets	210
Intangibles	1,000
Total Assets	$14,740

Liabilities and Equity

Accounts Payable	$1,100
Accruals	2,400
Short-Term Debt	1,365
Current Liabilities	$4,865
Long-Term Debt	$5,000
Equity	4,875
Total Liabilities and Equity	$14,740

Pro Forma Solution

1. Enter three columns from left to right on a spread sheet: Fiscal, Adjustment and Pro Forma; translate all existing balance sheet balances into the fiscal column

2. Enter maximum allowable outstanding credit from all banks in the Pro Forma column across Short-Term Bank Debt

3. The difference between fiscal short-term bank debt and maximum exposure represents the drawdown amount. Put this number in the adjustments column across from short-term bank debt

4. Increase Inventory by the same amount

5. Add across and complete the last column.

The step numbers on this page correspond to numbers shown in parenthesis next to the appropriate item on page 72.

Acme Toy Co. Inc.
Pro Forma Fiscal
February 28, 1994

	(1) Fiscal	(1) Adjustments		(1) Pro Forma High Point Fiscal
Cash	1,900		(5)	1,900
Accounts Receivable	6,300		(5)	6,300
Fiscal Inventory	1,325	(4)	6,135	7,460
Prepaid Expenses	1,450			1,450
Current Assets	10,975			17,110
Net PP&E	2,555			2,555
Other Assets	210			210
Intangibles	1,000			1,000
Total Assets	14,740			20,875
Accounts Payable	1,100			1,100
Accruals	2,400		(2)	2,400
Short-Term Debt	1,365	(3)	6,135	7,500
Current Liabilities	4,865			11,000
Long-Term Debt	5,000			5,000
Equity	4,875			4,875
Total Liabilities and Equity	14,740			20,875

Ratio	Historical (Assumed)	Pro Forma 1994
Current	1.3	1.6
Quick	.6	.9
D/E	100% Pre-LBO	328% Post-LBO

It appears Acme's high leverage sends up storm signals. It's time to ask management for a cash budget.

■   ■   ■

Cash Budgets

Probably the best method available to determine exactly when peak requirements for a firm will take place is the Cash Budget. This allows the borrower to initiate the "buildup" period with the full knowledge that funds can be drawn to cover all expenditures. The period of time allotted to compile such a budget is usually dependent on the nature of the firm and the reason for credit. Budgets can range from short periods of time such as monthly, quarterly, semiannually or annually, to long-term strategic plans covering five and ten years, respectively.

Cash budgets are particularly useful planning tools for short-term periods. Implementation of the cash budget assists both the lender and financial manager in deciphering not only the amount required, but also at what stages cash infusions are needed during the season. The element of time is critical since the borrower must validate seasonal credit sources in advance of actual need.

Specifically, cash budgets help lenders analyze seasonal credits in the following way:

- Cash budgets enable the lender to monitor seasonal business activity. For example, if actual cash receipts fall below budget projections, sluggish sales, distribution or product problems may be at fault.

- A cash budget will determine the line of credit. Lenders traditionally establish the line of credit to approximate the largest deficit (financial requirement) disclosed in the budget.

- The cash budget will indicate when repayment is expected. If a firm requests additional funds when loan balances should be decreasing, consider it a storm signal. In all likelihood, it is an indicator that the cash conversion cycle might have failed.

- The cash budget will identify questionable uses of seasonal debt. For example, if the firm suffers losses and the cash budget reveals large dividend payouts, the loan may be targeted to line the pockets of investors rather than supporting seasonal inventory. Also, firms have been known to take seasonal draw downs and advance the funds to subsidiaries or affiliates. Beware of "advances to affiliates" if the account shows up in a cash budget.

- Capital expenditures may represent a large outlay in the budget period. Often, lenders anticipate these outlays by offering borrowers term loans and revolving credit to support capital expansion. In this instance, the cash budget works as a sales tool to drum up additional business for the bank.

- Cash budgets provide a window whereby lenders anticipate cash surpluses. If you plan well ahead of time, these anticipated cash surpluses might be invested in a bank-managed investment account. This presents a valuable sales opportunity for your banks.

Preparing a Cash Budget

The steps involved in formulating a cash budget and completed matrix for Acme Toy Company (see Exhibit 5.3) are as follows:

1. The first step in formulating a cash budget involves setting up a matrix identifying both historical and forecast sales by month. These data are extracted from the firm's sales budget, which projects the expected monthly sales in units and selling price per unit.

2. Next calculate credit sales as a percent of total sales. Acme supplied their projected credit sales for each forecast month.

3. Subtract credit sales from total sales to arrive at cash sales.

4. Next, develop an accounts receivable aging from historical experience and expectations. For example, Acme expects 25% of present month's credit sales will be collected in the current month, 5% of prior month's credit sales to be collected in the current month, and so on.

5. Enter expected collections in the budget you've developed from the aging.

6. Enter total cash inflows.

7. Develop the cash disbursement for purchases schedule following the same method we used to find cash receipts from sales.

8. Enter total cash outflows.

Exhibit 5.3

Acme Toy Company
Cash Budget
March 31, 1994
(in 000's up to decimal point)

Cross Reference		Actual Sales				Forecasted Sales					
		December	January	February	March	April	May	June	July	August	September
(1)	Total Sales	900.00	900.00	1800.00	2250.00	2700.00	3600.00	5400.00	5400.00	2700.00	1800.00
(2)	Credit Sales	45.00	63.00	90.00	180.00	225.00	450.00	1575.00	1575.00	135.00	45.00
(3)	Cash Sales					2475.00	3150.00	3825.00	3825.00	2565.00	1755.00
(4)	Collection										
	First Month (A)					56.25	112.50	393.75	393.75	33.75	11.25
	Second Month (B)					9.00	11.25	22.50	78.75	78.75	6.75
	Third Month (C)					36.90	73.80	92.25	184.50	645.75	645.75
	Fourth Month (D)					5.67	8.10	16.20	20.25	40.50	141.75
(5)	Total Cash Receipts Forecasted from Sales and Collections					2582.82	3355.65	4349.70	4502.25	3363.75	2560.50

(A) Percent of Current Month's Credit Sales	25%
(B) Percent of Prior Month's Credit Sales	5%
(C) Percent of Second Prior Month's Credit Sales	41%
(D) Percent of Third Prior Month's Credit Sales	9%

Total Cash Receipts

Cross Reference		April	May	June	July	August	September
(5)	Total Cash Receipts Forecasted from Sales and Collections	2582.82	3355.65	4349.70	4502.25	3363.75	2560.50
	Cash Dividends Received	45.00			45.00		
	Disposals			540.00			
	Interest	9.00	9.00	9.00	9.00	9.00	9.00
(6)	Total Cash Inflow	2636.82	3364.65	4898.70	4556.25	3372.75	2569.50

Exhibit 5.3 (continued)

Acme Toy Company
Cash Disbursements for Purchases

Cross Reference		Actual Purchases				Forecasted Purchases					
		December	January	February	March	April	May	June	July	August	September
(7)	Total										
	Credit	2700.00	2700.00	1350.00	900.00	900.00	900.00	450.00	225.00	225.00	270.00
	Cash	1800.00	1800.00	1350.00	900.00	900.00	900.00	225.00	45.00	45.00	90.00
						0.00	0.00	225.00	180.00	180.00	180.00
	Payment										
	First Month (A)					225.00	225.00	56.25	11.25	11.25	22.50
	Second Month (B)					558.00	558.00	558.00	139.50	27.90	27.90
	Third Month (C)					148.50	99.00	99.00	99.00	24.75	4.95
	Fourth Month (D)					27.00	20.25	13.50	13.50	13.50	3.38
	Total Cash Disbursements Forecasted from Sales and Purchases					958.50	902.25	951.75	443.25	257.40	238.73

(A) Percent of Current Month's Credit Purchases	25%
(B) Percent of Prior Month's Credit Purchases	62%
(C) Percent of Second Prior Month's Credit Purchases	11%
(D) Percent of Third Prior Month's Credit Purchases	1.5%

Total Cash Disbursements

	April	May	June	July	August	September
Total Cash Disbursements	958.50	902.25	951.75	443.25	257.40	238.73
Selling Expense	765.00	900.00	1080.00	1080.00	540.00	360.00
General and Administration Expense	1350.00	1620.00	1530.00	1350.00	1350.00	1350.00
Taxes: Income	126.00			126.00		
Taxes: Witholding	90.00	90.00	90.00	90.00	90.00	90.00

Exhibit 5.3 (continued)

Acme Toy Company
Cash Disbursements for Purchases
Total Cash Disbursements (continued)

		Forecasted Purchases					
Cross Reference		April	May	June	July	August	September
(8)	Pension	45.00	45.00	45.00		45.00	
	Dividends	63.00			63.00		
	Funded Debt Payments	450.00			450.00		
	Total Cash Outflow	3847.50	3512.25	3696.75	3602.25	2282.40	2038.73

(9) Juxtaposing Total Cash Inflows to Total Cash Outflows

	April	May	June	July	August	September
Total Cash In	2636.82	3364.65	4898.70	4556.25	3372.75	2569.50
Total Cash Out	3847.50	3512.25	3696.75	3602.25	2282.40	2038.73
Net Cash Available	(1,210.68)	(147.60)	1201.95	954.00	1,090.35	530.78
Cumulative Cash Available	(1,210.68)	(1,358.28)	(156.33)	797.67	1,888.02	2,418.80

Thus, Acme Toy Company will require $1,210,680 in cash in April, and $147,600 in May, looking to own its cash and marketable securities account. This assumes that the cash and marketable securities account on March 31, is $900 and the firm needs $900 in cash to operate. It is obvious that the firm does not need a credit line of $7.5 million as requested. A credit line of $1.5 million to 2 million appears to satisfy the requirements of the budget. ATC needs to borrow from outside sources as follows:

		April	May	June	July	August	September
	Net Cash Available	(1,210.68)	(147.60)	1,201.95	954.00	1,090.35	530.78
	Cash Balance Available (Balance March 31)	900.00	(310.68)	(458.28)	743.67	1,697.67	2,788.02
(10)	Cumulative (Financial Needs) Surplus Zero Balance Account	(310.68)	(458.28)	743.67	1,697.67	2,788.02	3,318.80
	Minimum Cash Balance	900.00	900.00	900.00	900.00	900.00	900.00
(11)	Cumulative (Financial Needs) Minimum Balance Account	(1,210.68)	(1,358.28)	(156.33)	797.67	1,888.02	2,418.80

9. Juxtapose total cash inflows with outflows.

10. Complete Cumulative (Financial Needs) Surplus Zero Balance Account Matrix. This schedule assumes that the firm keeps no minimum balance and that all overdrafts will be automatically financed by 1st City Bank.

11. Complete the cash budget assuming Acme requires a minimum $900 transactions cash in their demand deposit account at all times

As the results of the cash budget indicate, Acme Toy Company appears to have peak debt requirements in April and May. Subsequently in June and July, the bank can expect Acme to convert a portion of receivables into cash for the express purpose of cleaning up trade payables and seasonal debt in July. In practice, the cash budget is always extended over the entire season or year to ensure a company's cash surplus is sufficient to cover the seasonal liquidation of debt.

Trial Balance Analysis

By definition, a trial balance provides a preliminary means of verifying whether total debits equal total credits for all general ledger accounts at a given time. This "snapshot or point in time" includes all account balances and ledger activity for assets, liabilities, and owner's equity. Therefore, it can be concluded that a trial balance analysis is used by lending officers as a supplement for audited fiscal statements. Of greater importance to the lender is knowing when to use this method. For example, under circumstances where a company appears to be well situated with bookings,

debt or both, this procedure is not considered a critical or necessary link in the decision making process. However, if the opposite scenario holds true, this technique plays an intricate role in the bank's final credit judgment.

A key component of the trial balance is inventory. As indicated throughout this text, inventory is probably the most crucial component in a company's financial statements (income statement and balance sheet). In the majority of cases where companies employ the periodic inventory method, cost of goods sold and gross profit cannot be calculated with any degree of accuracy, and must be derived. This holds true for profits as well. However, for our purposes, as lenders, a good "ball park" gross profit margin, and derivative profits are all that is needed to track the company's performance at each stage of the accounting cycle..

The last thing a banker wants a month after fiscal close and year-end statements arrive is a whopping loss. Losses are often accompanied by substantial cash drains, causing the borrower to bypass a clean up. In this chapter, we learn to anticipate problems in trial balance figures by the use of analytical techniques.

The suggested procedure is to call the bookkeeper or accountant for account balances at the end of each month. This information is readily obtained from their general ledger software. Information requirements include: sales, returns, purchases, receivables and payables. Bank records will provide demand deposit and loan balances at any point in time. With the information at hand, we can complete enough financial analysis to determine whether or not the company's season shows signs of trouble.

When a periodic inventory system is used, a physical count of units is conducted at the time financial statements are prepared. This equates to beginning inventory being carried in the inventory account. Consequently, estimated profits are either derived using the gross profit method (described later), or a break-even analysis. When a perpetual inventory system is utilized, valuation of merchandise is available at all times, yielding an accurate interim gross profit figure. Thus, profits in all periods are known.

In situations where the company in question does not normally prepare interim statements, the lender can obtain updated balances for current assets and current liabilities using the trial balance general ledger reports. Although there is no substitute for complete financial statements, a year-to-date schedule of receivables, inventory, trade debt, and accruals can provide an excellent monitoring system. This creates additional work for the lender, but it is certainly better than receiving no information at all. Again, the bank cannot afford to lend seasonal credit that becomes a bad loan.

Break-Even Inventory

We derive break-even inventory (BEI) from Acme's trial balance. It is an excellent tool for detecting any liquidity, financial, or operating problems. As illustrated earlier in an unsuccessful seasonal cycle, a failed conversion cycle translates into higher risk for the bank since repayment was expected to be generated from the sale of inventory. During the course of the season, BEI allows the lender to evaluate whether or not the cash conversion cycle has been jeopardized as a result of inventory devalued or written down. This appraisal can come as soon as two or three months into the season if bookings are down in relation to the earlier projections. If this is the case, the value of inventory is sure to be lower than its current book value. Although BEI can be incorporated routinely as part of maintaining loans, it is really only required if the borrower shows storm signals in comparison to the High Point Pro Forma and Cash Budget.

Of the two types of inventory methods, the periodic inventory method is surrounded by more uncertainty since precise inventory values are ascertained during an annual audit. But, while the accountant hasn't actually valued inventory under the periodic method, it is almost certain that management knows if inventory has lost its value or not.

Bankers can compare the results of the BEI with a company's current estimate of inventory at cost or market value—whichever is lower. In the case where break even is greater than management's estimate, inventory may have lost enough value to impair the company's "clean up" at the end of the season. Causes of decreased inventory value include: production problems, stockpiling, canceled orders, poor sales projections or any combination of these.

Example Break-Even Inventory

Acme Toy submitted an eight month trial balance dated March 31, 1994. The figures were cut just before the firm's heavy shipping season (all in thousands).

	03/31/94	03/31/93
Cash	900	650
Sales (Gross)	17,250	15,460
Accruals	3,550	3,200
Purchases	12,600	
Prepaid Expenses	735	
Net Plant and Equipment	2,055	
Discounts on Sales	560	
Intangibles	140	
Fiscal Equity	4,875	
Factory Labor	920	
Freight In	80	
Short-Term Bank Debt	1,600	1,550
Long-Term Debt	5,000	100
Factory Depreciation		
Expense	200	
Officer Salaries	400	250
Returns and		
Allowances	800	760
Other Assets	210	
Fiscal (Beginning)		
Inventory	1,325	
Accounts Receivable	7,100	6,900
Accounts Payable	4,400	4300
Factory Overhead	600	
Administration Expense	1,850	
Selling Expense	3,200	
Estimated Tax Expense	3,000	

Management estimated lower of cost or market inventory: $10,100.

Will the company generate a profit or loss?

Solution

Developing the break-even inventory technique at Acme involves the following steps (see Exhibit 5.4):

1. Set net profit to zero.

2. Next list all expenses below gross profit.

3. Calculate Gross Profit—always equal to expenses when profits are zero.

4. Enter sales, returns and allowances and discounts from the trial balance to derive net sales.

5. Derive break-even cost of goods sold: the difference between net sales and break-even gross profit.

6. Finally, derive break-even inventory, using trial balance and B/E cost of goods sold.

7. Compare actual inventory value to B/E inventory to determine net profit or loss.

Management's estimate of inventory value, $10,100, is greater than the $8,285 inventory break even, leading to a $1,815 profit. The firm's inventory appears to be high quality since operations are clearly profitable. Thus, there is a strong indication that Acme will be liquid enough to satisfy its short-term obligations.

Break-Even Balance Sheet

Cash	900
Accounts Receivable	7,100
Inventory B/E	**8,285
Prepaid Expenses	735
Current Asset	17,020
Net PP&E	2,055
Other Assets	210
Intangibles	140
Total Assets	19,425
Accounts Payable	4,400
Accruals	3,550
Short-Term Debt	1,600
Current Liabilities	9,550
Long-Term Debt	5,000
Fiscal Equity (B/E)	4,875
Total Liabilities and Equity	19,425

**Notice the balance sheet's break-even inventory is the same as the income statement.

Exhibit 5.4

Acme Toy Company
Break-Even Inventory
March 31, 1994

	Steps	Break-Even Income Statement		Break-Even Margins	Actual Income Statement		Actual Margins
Sales	(4)		17,250			17,250	
Returns and Allowances	(4)	(800)			(800)		
Discounts	(4)	(560)	(1,360)		(560)	(1,360)	
Net Sales	(4)		15,890			15,890	
B/E Cost of Goods Sold	(5)		(7,440)				
Actual Cost of Goods Sold						(5,625)	
B/E Gross Profit	(3)		8,450	53.2%			
Actual Gross Profit						10,265	64.6%
Officiers Salaries	(2)		(400)			(400)	
Administration Expenses	(2)		(1,850)			(1,850)	
Selling Expenses	(2)		(3,200)			(3,200)	
Estimated Taxes	(2)		(3,000)			(3,000)	
B/E Profit	(1)		0	0.0%			
Actual Profit						1,815	11.4%

Calculation of Break-Even Inventory

			Calculation of Actual Cost of Goods	
Fisical Inventory		1,325	Fisical Inventory	1,325
Purchases		12,600	Purchases	12,600
Factory Labor		920	Factory Labor	920
Freight In		80	Freight In	80
Depreciation		200	Depreciation	200
Overhead		600	Overhead	600
Less:			Less:	
B/E CGS		(7,440)	Actual Inventory	(10,100)
= B/E Inventory	(6)	8,285	Actual Cost of Goods Sold	5,625

Calculation of Net Profit (7)

Actual Inventory Value	10,100
Less: B/E Inventory	8,285
Net Profit	1,815

Seasonal Ratio Analysis

During the course of the loan, if time is at a premium, the seasonal or self-liquidating loan can be analyzed using relatively simple techniques. The proven ability of a business to expand and contract its balance sheet during seasonal high and low points offers assurance that the process can be safely repeated. Seasonal ratios are analyzed to ensure that borrowers continue to convert assets successfully. The ratios are usually analyzed on a comparative basis and unified in the analysts' report. The ratios are calculated using the break-even inventory trial balance, which is usually in three and/or six month statements.

(Cash + Accounts Receivable)/(Short-Term Bank Debt + Accounts Payables)

1994   (900 + 7100)/(1600+4400) = 1.33

1993   (650 + 6900)/(1550/4300) = 1.29

Near the seasonal low point, cash and receivables should be sufficient to reduce short-term debt and trade payables. Watch for a drop in shipments or slow receivables if the ratio falls below historical levels. Acme's liquidity is on par with the corresponding period last year.

Returns and Allowances/Gross Sales

1994   800/17250 = 4.6%

1993   760/15460 = 4.9%

Increases may be due to large merchandise allowances, defective lines, or a missed season. Contact the borrower to determine if merchandise has been reshipped.

Held over goods are usually written down. Acme's returns are normal—no indication of a missed season or damaged goods.

Short-Term Bank Debt/Accounts Payable

Examine trade inquiries together with the ratio of short-term bank debt to payables. Recall that early stages of the conversion cycle require high debt levels. Suppliers seek credit information *before* shipping raw materials, and flood the bank with inquiries (during the build-up season). Inquiries should reduce dramatically following the high point. Bankers keep a list of all inquiries, recording the date, caller, reason for inquiry, and comments. A high bank to trade debt ratio, off the heels of sizable inquiries, may mean tardy trade debt was transferred to the bank. Acme hasn't shipped heavily yet. Most of their suppliers will not expect payment until summer.

Purchases/Sales

If purchases rise sharply in relation to sales, the firm may be saturated with inventory. The build-up might be a by-product of unwise inventory management, or simply a stockpiling in anticipation of orders.

Break-Even Shipments

The last piece in creating an image of the seasonal borrower is the Break-Even Shipments technique. Developed by the author, this method is exercised during the shipping season to clarify the level of shipments that *must be attained to cover outlays.* Hence, shipments must be sufficient to cover production and operating expenses for both the shipping period and buildup period in the seasonal cycle. If the break even shipment level is unattainable, losses will be incurred. Common sense tells us that if a company struggles to break even during the shipment period, the probability of break even in the buildup period is at best, minimal. The final result of the analysis will also identify the level of sales necessary to reach the break even point.

Shipment figures are readily available since management knows the number of orders they have booked, completed, and placed on the delivery schedule. For example, suppose Acme Toy Company informs the bank of the following:

■ ■ ■

"Bookings are good. $16.5 million was booked for June shipments, and most of the goods are ready to move. We'll probably ship out about 15% over bookings for both June and July. In addition, we estimated our gross profit margin at about 64%, while returns allowances and discounts are expected to continue around 8% of gross sales. Finally, expenses in June will approximate $1.2 million."

■ ■ ■

The problem for many bankers, even bankers who have experience, is "How do I get this information to work for me?" Or "Can it be determined within reasonable bounds whether or not the company will make a profit for a particular month?"

Break-Even Shipments Formula

$$S_b = \frac{E_i}{(G_i)(1 - R_i)}$$

Where S_b = Break-Even Shipments
E_i = Estimated Expenses

G_i= Interim GPM derived from the Break-Even Inventory Technique

R_i = Returns + Allowances + Discount On Sales/Gross Sales

S_b must be compared to S_e, the value of product shipments the company expects to ship over the period being analyzed.

If $S_e > S_b$ then Profits are predicted
If $S_e < S_b$ then Losses are predicted
If $S_e = S_b$ then Break Even

As far as Acme is concerned, can we expect a profit or loss based on the data given?

■ Estimated Gross Profit Margin is 64%.

■ Estimated shipments are $16.5 million.

■ Returns allowances and discounts are expected to continue at 8% of gross sales.

■ Expected expenses for November will approximate $1.2 million.

Solution

$$S_b = \frac{E_i}{(G_i)(1 - R_i)}$$

$$\frac{\$1.2 \text{ million}}{(.64)(1 - .08)}$$

Compare S_b to S_e. Since estimated shipments (S_e) of $16.5 million are above break even of $2.0 million, Acme will be profitable in June. It appears the firm is having a terrific year. Let's hope so. If the year failed, the bank's LBO would be in deep trouble considering the firm's thin capitalization.

Monitoring

If the funding is structured properly, a seasonal loan will monitor itself. In other words, both the borrower and lender should know when the loan will peak (full expansion of balance sheet) and when it will be repaid (full contraction of the balance sheet). Any deviation from the *modus operandi* should trigger an immediate inquiry by the lender. If the company's financial management team is astute, they should already have the answers.

Depending on the financial reporting requirements of a firm, monthly or quarterly financial statements and revised full year estimates should be available to compare with the original projections. All three sets of numbers are analyzed together identifying variances. Any large discrepancies found should be noted and reviewed with the borrower. While the majority of time is spent evaluating the balance sheet, income statements are not completely ignored. It is important to the lender to note if the company is able to generate an operating profit, and if not, why?

Seasonal Loans and the Documentation Exemption Program. Recent initiatives to increase lending to small and medium-sized businesses by improving credit availability and diminishing regulatory scrutiny. Considered part of his economic stimulus package, this policy permits financially sound banks to designate a "basket of loans," which are no longer subject to documentation review. Ergo, examiners are only allowed to measure loans based on the merits of performance, not on what they perceive as inadequate or incomplete financial information.

To ensure accuracy by the loan officer, the implementation of the Document Exemption Program must be interpreted properly. The basic, underlying principle the policy does not suggest is the total elimination of documents considered vital to credit judgment. This raises the question, "What is considered sufficient information to accurately appraise a loan's level of quality?" Let's say, for example, a bank qualifies for the documentation exemption program and decides to designate some of its seasonal loans as documentation exempt. The bank agrees that a good portion of data and reports normally accumulated for this type of loan is no longer necessary. But the lender yet requires financial statement information and projections. Why? Even if the data is limited, lenders still consider it essential to sound credit analysis and prudent banking policy. Realistically, how can a bank make any kind of credit decision if pertinent information is unavailable?

Fortunately, bankers who lend to support seasonal cash conversion cycles and know their clientele, don't require a lot of documentation to confirm quality. This perception falls right in line with the documentation exemption program, since long-time customers with significant net worth are considered likely candidates. An additional factor to take into consideration is that both current loans and new loans will probably be granted documentation exemption. To date, the guidelines have not yet been totally clarified.

As mentioned earlier, lenders must consider what is enough information to perform proper credit analysis on unsecured, seasonal loans. In many instances, small and medium-sized companies may not have the capability *(nor the inclination)* of supplying complete, year-to-date financial information on the spot at a moment's notice.

What Can Go Wrong with a Seasonal Loan?

Storm signals come in all shapes and sizes. Following is a comprehensive list of what the lender should be on the lookout for:

- Slow in-house orders received in comparison to corresponding periods in previous years.
- Factory operating well below capacity.
- Changes in the timeliness in which payables are paid.
- Owners no longer take pride in their business.
- Visits to the business reveal deteriorating general appearance of the premises. For example, stock and equipment has not been properly maintained.
- Loans to or from officers and affiliates.
- The principals do not know the company's condition or direction.
- The lender overestimates the peaks and valleys in the seasonal loan, thereby setting up a seasonal loan that is excessive.
- Inability to clean up bank debt or cleanups affected by rotating bank debt.
- Unusual items in the financial statements.
- Negative trends such as losses or lower gross and net profits, slowness in accounts receivable, and decrease in sales volume.
- Intercompany payables/receivables are not adequately explained.
- Cash balances reduce substantially or are overdrawn and uncollected during normally liquid periods.

- Management fails to take trade discounts because poor inventory turnover.
- Withholding tax liability builds as taxes are used to pay other debt.
- Frequent "down tiering" of financial reporting sparked in an effort to bring on a more accommodating accountant.
- Changes in financial management.
- Totals on receivables and payables aging schedules do not agree with amounts shown on the balance sheet of the same date.
- At the end of the cycle, creditors are not completely paid out. The bank sometimes can be paid out when the borrower leans on the trade. (This often gives bankers a false sense of security, but the company may be unable to borrow from the trade for the next buildup of inventory).
- Sharp reduction in officers' salaries brings a lower standard of living, and might suggest a last ditch effort to save a distressed business. Alternatively, reduced salaries might signal a concerted effort to make headway.
- Erratic interim results signaling a departure from normal and historical seasonal patterns.
- The lender does not allow enough cushion for error. If the seasonal loan is not repaid and there is no other way out but liquidation of the collateral, the lender is taking the collateral at the worst possible time. It is the end of the season, and if the owner cannot sell it, how will a banker?
- Financials are late in an attempt to postpone the bank's awareness of unfavorable information.
- Unwillingness to provide budgets, projections, or interim information.

- Suppliers cut back terms or request COD.

- Change in inventory, followed by an excessive inventory buildup or the retention of obsolete merchandise.

- The borrower changes suppliers frequently, or transient buying results in higher raw material costs.

- Increased inventory to one customer or perilous reliance on one account.

- Changing concentration from a major well-known customer to one of lesser stature often points to a problem with inventory. A good mix of customers is the best defense.

- The lender permits advances on the seasonal loan to fund other purposes, especially payments on the bank's own term debt. Consequently, the term debt is handled as agreed, but the seasonal loan increases. Reaction to a basic problem is delayed.

- Company loses an important supplier or customer.

- Large customer concentrations in receivables and payables. Failure to get satisfactory explanations from the company on these concentrations. Failure to conduct investigations on the creditworthiness of larger receivables.

- The lender finances a highly speculative inventory position in which the owner is trying for a "home run."

- Intangible interpersonal signals such as failure to look you in the eye or letting the condition of the offices deteriorate, and taking longer to return calls.

Defensive Measures

A prudently structured loan should always have a second way out to provide a source of repayment if asset conversion fails.

Once the borrower is in trouble, the lender should ask these questions:

- What caused the problem?

- How long will a turnaround take, if one is possible?

The account officer should prepare a cash budget immediately to pinpoint the inflow and outflow of funds. Loan documentation should be checked to ensure it is current and in order.

If the problem is minor and expected to be temporary, the banker may merely waive this year's cleanup. If the problem is more acute, other steps may have to be taken. The bank may decide to restructure the loan—create a loan to be repaid over months or years from internally generated cash flow (this presumes that future cash flows are expected). The loan agreement, by virtue of its covenants and events of default, will give the bank greater control over the obligation. Loans may also be put on a demand basis, although the effect on the borrower is largely psychological.

Cash Flow. Strong cash flows are crucial! If an established firm has a solid track record, the seasonal lender can look forward to loan reductions despite temporary problems. However, if cash flows diminish, or an eroding gross profit margin cannot be turned around, expect structural problems within the organization.

Equity Injection. Owners may be required to inject equity if profit retention fails to replenish the capital structure, or if assets are poorly utilized. Thoughtful lenders begin an early dialogue with customers if an equity infusion appears justified.

Formula-Based Advances. against confirmed orders, or asset liens may work on a temporary basis.

Seasonal Working Capital Protection: A Second Way Out

Working capital is a general measure of liquidity, representing the margin of protection short-term creditors look for behind the primary source of payment: the conversion of current assets. A lender's knowledge of the mechanics of working capital (and certainly cash flow) will provide him or her with the insight to quickly distinguish between temporary or structural problems. If the current loan can't be cleaned up, as expected, it's important.

Cash Flow versus Working Capital Analysis

A cash flow analysis is more refined than a working capital analysis and should always be the focal point for analyzing bank loans with maturities beyond one year. The preparation of a working capital analysis when used to protect a short-term creditor, is less time-consuming than a cash flow analysis. Working capital analysis also eliminates captions (all those current items) that clutter and obscure the analysis of short-term loan protection.

However, a working capital analysis does not take into consideration the composition of current accounts. While a firm's working capital may be growing, its liquidity may actually be decreasing. For example, the working capital reconciliation may indicate working capital is increasing, but this may be a buildup of stale inventory and slow receivables. Ergo, poor cash flow.

The Mechanics of Working Capital

The simple but powerful working capital derivation crystallizes the flow of funds. A flow of funds solution to working capital changes may reveal the dominant, long-lasting dynamics of a business more effectively than the firm's current account position.

1. $A = L + E$ basic accounting equation

2. $WC = CA - CL$ working capital definition

3. $CA + FA = CL + FL + E$ component parts of (1)

4. $CA - CL = FL + E - FA$ (3) with current accounts moved to left side of equation and non-current accounts to the right.

5. $WC = FL + E - FA$ (2) and (4) are equal and combined

6. $\Delta WC = \Delta FL - \Delta FA + \Delta E$

7. $WC + FA = FL + E$ equation (5) rearranged with FA to the left side

Focusing on **Equation 6** for a moment, the following assessments can be made: increases in non-current liabilities, increases in equity, or reductions in non-current assets represent sources of funds. Decreases in non-current liabilities, decreases in equity, or increases in non-current assets represent uses of working capital.

Equation 7 is the core of working capital analysis. The right side of **Equation 7**, long-term liabilities (generally funded debt) together with equity represents the firm's capital structure (or permanent financing). The capital structure supports not only fixed assets but also the firm's entire working capital position. Suppose you lent money to a business only to find out later that due to structural problems (competitive pressures, eroding gross profit margin, etc.) the company will at best break even. Assuming no new stock is issued, the equity component of the capital structure will not grow.

Since a major ingredient of long-term debt capacity is the expansion of the equity base, the firm may find it difficult to attract additional debt capital. Thus the right side of **Equation 7** will reduce or remain unchanged. Let's also assume capital expenditures are bottlenecked, and a major part of the capital expansion program financed by the bank is sitting on the books. This means that if the fixed asset component (of **Equation 7**) balloons out while the capital structure stagnates or falls, the bank might not have the liquidity protection it thought it had.

On the other hand, suppose the firm generates strong, quality profits—it will prosper and draw on its long-term financing sources. The capital structure will expand. And, if profits are derived from operating leverage promulgated by efficient use of fixed assets, the firm will exhibit strong working capital levels. The increased level of liquidity will certainly flow back to finance innovative product lines, reduce debt levels, help finance acquisitions, and position the balance sheet for lucrative high-yield restructuring, leveraged buyouts, and treasury stock purchases. Thus, **Equation 7** provides a straightforward methodology to working capital (funds) analysis. The equation shows that there are only three factors to examine to ensure that a borrower will generate satisfactory liquidity levels: strong profits, optimal financing strategies and sound, efficient capital projects.

Finally, as with any type of loan (see PRISM), the first priority with seasonal loans is to know the people you are dealing with. If the lender is unfamiliar with the principal, extra time must be spent checking backgrounds and references. Since there are more than normal risks involved with this type of credit, it is imperative to verify all references. Obviously, all responses must be favorable. Lenders must also check other sources in addition to the references furnished by the company. Good sources for cross reference are suppliers, buyers, competitors, and mutual acquaintances. This will give an overall picture of the company in question.

During negotiations, the borrower and bank should agree on the dates by which various documents are to be given to the bank. It is recommended that annual unqualified audits by CPAs acceptable to the bank are received no later than 30–45 days after the customer's fiscal year-end. The audit will include the company's balance sheet, income statement, cash flow statement, and all required footnotes (memo data).

It is also a priority to obtain a cash budget before the season begins. Cash budgets are critical planning tools for short-term periods. Implementation of the cash budget aids both the lender and financial manager in deciphering the amount of cash required, in what stages it is needed during the season and the timing of repayment. Also, seasonal loans must offer a second way out. If your borrower can't clean up seasonal loans, you need to examine three factors to ensure satisfactory long-term liquidity levels. Remember to:

1. Make sure strong profits or cash flow are in the cards and enough profits are retained. Strong cash flows are crucial. If an established firm has a solid track record, the seasonal lender can look forward to loan reductions despite current but temporary problems. However, if cash flows diminish, or an eroding gross profit margin cannot be turned around, expect structural problems.

2. Next, encourage the borrower to finance long term if loans are to be
   used to expand core levels of inventory, accounts receivable and fixed
   assets. This strategy helps working
   capital.

3. Make certain the capital budget program bankrolled by the bank is
   matched by industry standard's internal rates of return.

One last word on loan documentation: if lenders can learn to recognize red
flags early and keep these few fundamentals of seasonal lending in the foreground,
a comfort zone can be established when
assigning the seasonal credits of small to
medium-sized businesses to the Documentation Exemption Program. Bankers can
then focus on obtaining financials and
other documentation on larger credits—
and not be overly concerned when a statement from a long-time seasonal borrower
is six months late.

CHAPTER *Six*

Risk Management of Collateralized Loans

Companies unable to acquire unsecured credit usually fall into one of three categories:

1. They are in the first stage of the business life cycle (new and unproven)

2. Their ability to service unsecured debt is in serious question

3. Their request amounts exceed their unsecured credit limit

Whatever the case, lenders require security to reduce the risk of loss. Credit is considered secured when the lender receives something other than the promise of repayment from the borrower. This involves the pledge of a specific asset or assets by the borrower along with the promise of repayment.

Hence, assets are sometimes pledged as a security if the company's cash flow is unable to service the debt. If a default does occur, the lender has the right, prior to other creditors, to the assets used as security. But, in most cases, banks will not extend secured credit if the borrower's cash flow projections fall short of servicing the debt.

What constitutes appropriate and acceptable collateral for a secured loan? The answer probably depends on whether you're lending or borrowing. Basically, banks always want a margin of safety with a secured loan. A margin of safety is the excess market value of the security interest over the amount of the loan. This protects the bank if its only repayment recourse is to sell the security. The reason for this is elementary. If a borrower defaults on a secured loan and the security is sold by the bank for less than the amount of the loan and interest owed, the secured lender becomes a general or unsecured creditor for the difference.

The last thing a secured lender wants is an unsecured loan balance (or overadvance) since security was required to make the deal in the first place. Therefore, banks will minimize their downside risk by requiring security with a market value well above the amount of the loan. This means that assets pledged must have a durability factor or life span well exceeding the length of the loan. If the borrower balks at the bank's pledge requirements, the firm is more than welcome to shop for a loan elsewhere.

Another important point: If a secured loan is approved pending specific lending agreements, it is vital that the lender review the Uniform Commercial Code before going any further.

The Uniform Commercial Code explains lender protection on security interests. Backtracking for a moment, when a lender requires collateral from the borrower, a security interest in the collateral is acquired. The security interest can include accounts receivable, bills receivable, inventory, or for that matter, any other assets of the borrower. The security interest is finalized with a security agreement signed by both parties and filed with a public office (usually the secretary of state) in the state the collateral is located. This filing gives public notice to all other parties that the lender has a security interest in the collateral highlighted in the security agreement. Before finalizing the loan, it is the lender's responsibility to search public notices to determine if the assets pledged have been used for a loan that is still outstanding. Only the lender with a valid claim has a prior claim on the assets and can use them for collateral.

Now let's get started on secured seasonal lending. For our purposes, secured seasonal lending is broken down into four sections:

1. Accounts Receivable
2. Bills Receivable
3. Inventory
4. Marketable Securities

Loans Secured with Accounts Receivables

Small commercial banks often turn to receivable financing as an alternative to a flat refusal for loan requests in special cases where (1) the bank's lending limit is strained, or (2) the customer does not qualify for an unsecured loan.

Large banks have elaborate networks to handle accounts receivable financing. Small banks can bring in this profitable business as well, as long as they follow guidelines and procedures. The following material covers the ways and means of receivable financing especially from the small-bank perspective.

Assignment of Accounts Receivable

Once rare among smaller banks, because it implied undesirable and unprofitable special handling and affiliated costs, accounts receivable financing is now coming into its own. The introduction of software spreadsheets combined with the growing sophistication of lenders has changed its practicality dramatically.

Receivable financing offers a way to significantly improve the credit picture of seasonal companies that might otherwise find it difficult or impossible to qualify for unsecured lines of credit. Simply stated, receivables financing involves a bank or finance company either advancing funds by purchasing invoices or accounts receivable over a period of time (aka factoring), or by making advances and loans using an assignment on receivables as primary collateral.

Under the terms of a loan agreement, the borrower provides a security interest in all or a portion of accounts receivable. When a loan is secured by receivables on a formula basis, the loan tends to increase as the need for credit grows. Newly created receivables feed into the pool, while reductions flow from payments on account, returns and allowances, bad debts and the charge off of uncollectable past due accounts. Assigned receivables or loans secured by accounts receivable are on a non-notification basis. This means the borrower's customers are not informed that the receivables have been assigned to the bank. Rates are usually quoted as a spread over prime or referenced rate. In addition to charging an interest rate that is usually 2 or 3 percentage points above prime, it is customary to impose a service charge amounting to 1 or 2 percent of the borrower's average loan balance.

Receivable financing is also tailored for firms who overtrade. Take, for example, the seasonal textile manufacturers who spin capital over many times annually. Other factors to consider include:

1. Expansion of volume may often require additional financing as existing bank lines prove inadequate.

2. If the rate of sales increase is significant, cash flow is normally diverted to support inventory requirements, thus making it difficult or financially impracticable to effect an annual cleanup at the end of the season.

3. Loan requirements may fluctuate beyond the norm.

4. The stage of the industry life cycle the company is in. This may provide helpful insight into the financing requirements and dangers involved.

Creditworthiness and the soundness of receivables are the two major factors that determine the exposure taken by the bank. Other considerations include:

1. The credit standing of the borrower's customers.

2. Age and size of the receivable.

3. Merchandise quality.

4. Number of returns due to missed season and/or faulty merchandise.

5. General competitive posture of the borrower.

6. The amount of funds continuously generated in the account.

7. Credit policies.

8. History of receivable charge offs.

The Loan Agreement

Important items usually covered by a loan agreement for accounts receivable financing include:

■ The duration of the lending arrangement.

■ The bank's right to screen the accounts presented by the borrower to determine which are acceptable as security.

■ Terms of collateral eligibility (fit as collateral).

■ The procedure by which accounts held by the bank are to be replaced or the loan reduced, if they become past due.

- The percentage that the bank will loan against the face amount of the receivables.
- The maximum dollar amount of the loan.
- Reports required from the borrower to indicate amounts owed by each customer (also referred to as a Receivable Aging report). As additional sales are made, the borrower may be required to submit copies of invoices or other evidence of shipment.
- The borrower's responsibility to forward directly to the bank payments received on assigned accounts.
- Integration of a lock box account where all customer payments are received and used to reduce outstandings.
- Authorization for the bank to inspect the borrower's books and to verify the receivables through bank internal auditors, or a public accounting firm.
- Terms of any overadvances (amounts lent above level safely collateralized).

Loan Formula Certificate

A loan formula certificate, signed by an official of the company, may be required. This certificate, completed by the customer, shows total receivables, eligible receivables, total inventory, eligible inventory, loan amount outstanding, and the amount of debt that is over or under allowed borrowings. Additional advances may be made if sufficient collateral is available. The debt is to be reduced if it is over the amount allowed as shown by the loan formula certificate.

Exposure Percentage

Except in special circumstances, advances are limited to 75% or 80% of outstanding accounts receivable. This does not include any accounts more than 90 days past due, those which are intercompany or from related businesses, and those which have offsetting payables or prepayments. To derive the exposure percentage:

Divide accounts receivable advances into net collateral. Net collateral represents assigned receivables plus blocked cash accounts, less dilution and 90 days past dues.

Feed these data into a computer and plot them against the borrower's records. Ignore minor differences, but ledger accounts may reveal major discrepancies like unreported receipts.

The Loan Officer's Responsibilities

The loan officer's responsibilities follow designated policies and procedures to ensure the safety and integrity of all receivables assigned in support of the credit. The affairs of the borrower, together with the status of the loan itself should be policed on a regular basis. A recent poll of bank managers indicated that a large number of bank losses in general are attributable to negligence. In addition, Uniform Commercial Code filings should be recorded properly, and state statutes followed with regard to locale and number of filings required to ensure a proper lien.

The Audit: Scope and Details

If a bank decides to take collateral, it requires a judicious and thorough audit of the borrower's financial statements. The bank's auditing staff usually conducts the audit, but if the bank is small, it will sometimes commission the audit outside. If this is the case, the cost of borrowing on the security of accounts receivable tends to be higher than the cost of an unsecured loan.

The following set of steps gives the small bank a basis for analyzing collateral. Keep in mind, collateral protection is one of the smaller links in the analytical chain. Smart lenders dig into financials, cash flows and projections to understand the borrower's business and to come up with an integrated credit picture.

Step #1: Financial Statements

Current information fundamental to a sound audit includes trial balances, interim statements, cash budgets, invoice copies, and ledger computer printouts. In all probability, a trial balance analysis is essential for a thorough audit and holds even more value to the auditor if inventory hasn't been checked by the borrower's accountant (periodic inventory method). If no trial balance is available from the accountant, it is possible to construct a break-even trial balance as we learned in the seasonal lending chapter. In other words, there is no reason to delay, or refrain from, using this critical financial tool.

Step #2: Receivable (Overview)

The next step in the initial audit focuses on the quality of receivables. Since receivable quality is derivative of the character and financial condition of a firm's customers, it is essential to conduct a thorough credit check on each large position.

The three main sources of credit information available are agency reports, banks, and trade debtors. Ratings from these sources are evaluated and recorded on the audit report, then classified as acceptable or not acceptable. Some minor accounts, while not considered prime paper, may be classified as acceptable due to their small size. Other measures of receivable

quality, or lack of it, include: (1) collection period, and (2) proximity to economically depressed areas, diversification, and the balance of the portfolio. If the firm's credit policy is liberal compared to its peers, the bank may find itself with collateral of very little value.

Conversely, if the borrower enjoys a client base consisting of excellent payers, the bank's risk will be negligible. Another point, banks do not like to see receivables heavily concentrated in a few accounts unless they represent customers enjoying solid credit ratings. When receivables are concentrated, the danger of control looms large. For example, the borrower's customer may dictate terms or threaten to cancel orders on the slightest provocation.

Key Points

1. Receivables are to be evaluated very thoroughly. The examination of receivables encompasses both the lassification of accounts and aging.

2. Credit reports and checkings are obtained on the largest accounts. Sources of information include agency reports, banks, trade journals, suppliers, and credit reporting agencies. Information is evaluated and recorded in the audit report. Verify receivables with trade debtors and compute collection periods for each account.

3. Accounts are classified as acceptable or unacceptable.

4. Other measurements of receivable management include: (a) Collection period accounts receivable (365) divided by credit sales, (b) The delinquency ratio: past due receivables divided by credit sales, and (c) The bad debt ratio: write-offs over net receivables.

5. Files of past due accounts are also checked for recent correspondence and collection efforts. Large positions are reviewed carefully.

Step #3: Accounts Receivable Aging

This audit step requires special attention, since the banker examines an aging schedule for a company's largest receivables. The agency code, usually D & B's, is used to approximate the borrower's net worth. Receivables are recorded along with columns measuring the amounts due one through 30 days; 31 through 60 days; 61 through 90 days and accounts over 90 days past due. Each column is then totaled.

Using these data, the level of concentration is measured simply by dividing the sum of the largest accounts receivable into the total of all receivables. The percentage relationship is compared to previous years. Accounts over 90 days are automatically discarded from the net collateral figure.

Aging of Accounts Receivable

No. of Days Outstanding	Amount	Percent
0–30	$45,000	66.3%
30–45	$11,300	16.6%
45–60	$6,500	9.6%
60–90	$3,200	4.7%
90 or more	$1,900	2.8%
Total	$67,900	100.0%

1. Concentration is measured in two ways: (a) Acceptable accounts receivable to total accounts receivable, and (b) Average of the five largest receivables to total receivables.

2. The average size of accounts is calculated to determine expense allocation. The larger the account, the more work—the more the bank should be compensated.

Step #4: Credit and Collection Policies

1. Terms of sale, which vary according to industry, and range from cash before delivery, to extended seasonal dating.

2. Credit approval. Firms having strict policies will have fewer accounts receivable outstanding, and a contracted sales volume.

3. Collection policies. The total of outstanding receivables is related to the collection policy. Policy should be balanced on maintenance of goodwill. Collection policies should be convincing without being harsh.

4. Analyze Average Collection Period trends along side the Inventory Turnover and always include industry benchmark comparisons (see ratios chapter).

Step #5: Analysis of Delinquencies

When a firm borrows on accounts receivable, it can quickly fall into serious difficulty if some of the pledged receivables become delinquent. The problem is apt to be serious if previously pledged receivables are rejected when the borrower has no surplus funds and no other means of raising money. For example, if a company is growing rapidly, running short of cash to support rising inventory levels might be troublesome.

Instead of supplying the borrower with additional funds as new sales are made, the banker may:

1. Substitute new receivables for those no longer acceptable as collateral until the deficiency has been eliminated.

2. If the amount of delinquent receivables is large, the borrower may be faced with the prospect of having to operate for a considerable period of time without receiving any cash from either its customers or its bank.

Step #6: Evaluation of Sales Policies

A detailed analysis of the borrower's sales records is essential during the initial audit. In many instances, valuable information is buried in invoices and cash budgets. Sales analysis will determine if marketing activities are fluid and often uncovers product life cycles important in risk assessment of receivables.

1. Sales analysis enables the lender to probe and discover whether or not the borrower's marketing activities are fluid and, if not, isolate the problem.

2. A detailed analysis of the client's sales record is essential to the initial audit. More than a few companies fail to appreciate the value of sales analysis, not realizing that omitting this often leads to weak forecasting results. Valuable sales information is frequently buried in invoice files.

Step #7: Product Analysis and Product Policies

Analysis of the client's customer sales base should be directed to product planning where specific objectives and policies are outlined. Also, since products have life cycles, it is essential that the product be defined in terms of its life cycle. In the first stage, promotion is essential to pioneer stage acceptance of the product, while the growth stage marks the introduction of competitors. The first phase generally requires large-scale promotion in order to "get the product off the ground," and could bring on a cash drain placing the capital structure and pledged receivables at risk. Product policies should be reviewed and generally include:

- sales volume
- type and number of competitors
- technical opportunity
- patent protection
- raw materials required
- production load
- similarity to major businesses
- effect on other products

Step #8: Inventory

If the audit includes an examination of inventory, determine the amount and condition of the inventory, and the division of inventory as it pertains to raw materials, work-in-progress and finished goods. Merchandise quality is very important in accounts receivable financing because the higher the inventory quality, the fewer the returns and refusals to pay. The ratio returns to gross sales is an effective monitor of inventory quality. Bankers watch this ratio carefully before agreeing to advance against receivables, and they continue to monitor the returns closely after a lending relationship has been established.

Step #9: Analysis of Accounts Payable and Purchases

The status of accounts payable is of major concern to the bank since an absence of diversity here is almost as risky as the concentration factor with regard to receivables. Payables represent purchases and, if payables are slow, the firm's major source of supply could be cut off at any time. If curtailment is initiated during the production phase of the seasonal cycle, goods may not be produced and, conceivably, the company may be put out of business. It is possible to isolate the large payable(s) and derive the Payable Concentration Ratio (large payable over total payable) to determine if there is cause for concern.

A detailed audit of accounts payable should include:

1. Dates of each payable

2. Maturity date

3. Amount

4. Aging. This schedule is comparable to the aging obtained to measure borrower's receivables

5. A listing of large or unusual payables

Step #10: Analysis of Deposits in Cash Account

Analysis of the cash account can often spot unauthorized sales of encumbered assets, withdrawal of funds for personal use, or fraudulent practices, like unauthorized multiple assignments of receivables. Cash position determines if remittances have been diverted. Differences in unreported credits are recorded and explained.

Step #11: Bank Statement Audit

This section of the auditing procedure serves as a reminder to scrutinize the borrower's bank statement:

1. Confirm that collections have been earmarked to reduce loan balances

2. Checks payable to subsidiaries (representing advances) should be watched very closely since they represent a cash drain from the core business. In addition, the principals may be devoting excessive time to an outside venture unrelated to the core business

3. Bank statements and checks are also reviewed for large items, stale or unusual checks

4. Federal, withholding and social security taxes are recorded, and paid checks sighted to verify that remittance to governmental agencies has indeed been made. Nonpayment of taxes easily jeopardizes the bank's collateral position. Paid checks are also reviewed to ensure that subordinated indebtedness remains intact

5. Bank accounts at other financial institutions are examined for updated credit stories. Other banks will probably not make unsecured loans if they find liens against receivables.

Step #12: Pre-Billings

Pre-billing represents the assignment of invoices before goods are actually shipped. The pre-billing audit simply compares invoice and delivery dates. No invoice is to be forwarded to the lender by the client prior to the shipment date. To spot pre-billings, compare the shipment date to the assigned invoice date. Pre-billing practices should obviously be discouraged since no invoice should be forwarded to the lender before shipment.

Step #13: Check for Fraud

All accounts appearing in the general ledger should be of sufficient quality to minimize the risk of fraud. Lenders should be cognizant of two areas of concern regarding deceptive practices because the nature of accounts receivable financing provides opportunities for dubious practices, and a variety of fraud possibilities. Opportunities exist for deceiving lenders. The varieties of fraud include:

1. Assignment of fictitious accounts, accompanied by forged shipping documents

2. Duplicate assignment of the same account

3. Diversion of collections to client's use, otherwise known as personal withdrawals beyond a reasonable amount

4. Failure to report chargebacks (returns and allowances)

5. Submission of false financial information.

6. Forged shipping documents.

Step #14: Record Comparisons

Lenders should compare the borrower's records with the bank's. Comparison of the ledger accounts may reveal credit allowances and/or contra items like bills receivable discounted. Major discrepancies must be noted, explained, and corrected.

Step #15: Subordination Agreements

Advances from principals to their firm usually boost working capital and remain as capital funds unless the subordinations are released by the lender. However, subordination agreements are sometimes circumvented when substantial funds are withdrawn from the business for personal use.

Bills Receivable

One of the most widely used methods of secured financing involving small high-ticket items such as furs or jewelry is bills receivable (B/Rs) or notes receivable for discount. To review, a B/R is an unconditional, written order addressed and signed by the seller requiring the buyer to pay on demand or at a fixed or determinable future date, a certain sum of money to the bearer (the bank).

In other words, bills receivable evidences indebtedness arising out of the sale of goods by the bank's customer in the normal course of business. B/Rs are endorsed over to the bank (with *full recourse* to the seller) in exchange for cash.

When the notes are presented by the seller to the lender, terms must be verified to ensure that the instrument matures within a reasonable time. For example, goods sold on credit represent a time lag between the actual sale and collection date. The lag time is based on the seller's credit terms, discounts offered, credit policy, and overall product demand. In most cases, the closer the note is to maturity, the greater the cash flow, and the lower the borrowing requirement.

Consider the jewelry trade. Three to four months usually passes from the time stones are sold to the date payment is made. If "Joe" jeweler presents B/Rs to the bank, he has the use of cash for three to four months before the note matures.

The next validation process involves checking all endorsements (against bank records) to ensure favorable comparisons with the resolutions on file. Additionally, all parties required to sign negotiable instruments (as indicated on the resolution) must do so. Further, it is important for the lender to always verify the exchange of goods between the buyer and seller. Some people have been known to discount notes signed by "fictitious" makers, and at maturity try to "cover" the paper.

Bills Receivable are financed one of two ways:

- Demand Basis. All the B/Rs are totaled and are used as collateral to cover one loan. The loan is reduced as each B/R is collected.
- Discount Basis. Each B/R represents a separate loan. Each loan is retired when the B/R covering it is collected.

Interest on the note(s) is usually calculated on a "gross" basis. This includes the interest the customer pays for the privilege of having the notes discounted plus the interest the maker agrees to remit to the payee (the bank's customer).

After B/Rs are received, maturity date verified and signatures checked against the resolution on file, the credit department begins a credit check on the maker and carefully checks the instrument(s) securing the loan. Computer programs on software packages such as Excel or dBase can be set up to handle the credit check. The computer can be programmed to sort out the B/Rs by maker, listing the date and maturity of the instrument, and the amount of the note as well as interest due the payee. Brief financial highlights and agency reports may also be programmed into the maker's file.

Financial information is important if the maker represents a substantial exposure or if B/Rs cannot be absorbed by the bank's customer with a comfortable margin of safety. Remember, the B/Rs would ultimately be charged back to the customer under a full recourse agreement if returned uncollected by the maker's bank. A brief bank story is obtained if one has not recently been received.

Agency reports update supplement bank checkings by disclosing changes in management, litigation, and financial condition. In addition, agency reports show if trade payments are handled on a timely basis or if bankruptcy occurred last year. Lastly, a summary of outstanding notes issued by the maker to all customers of the bank should be included. This important information will signal an overexposure if credit limits on the maker are programmed into the computer.

A computer program can also be developed on the customer (the payee presenting the notes). The program might include date and maturity of the instrument, name of the maker, the amount of the transaction, and the reason for recall. If any notes submitted by the borrower indicate potential problems, a pro forma adjustment can be made on the borrower's fiscal statement. For example, the note in question is added back to current assets under the label "Notes Receivable Discounted" with an offsetting entry to "Notes Receivable Discounted Contra" (current liability). This way, the Debt/Equity ratio reflects the contingency in a more conservative light.

When the credit investigation has been completed, the computer files are updated and details of the transaction recorded and analyzed, the notes and supporting data (including the results of the investigation and credit check) are sent to the credit officer. The credit officer should check the following before rendering a decision:

1. Completeness of supporting documentation

2. Verification that the concentration of notes to any one maker is reasonable and not excessive

3. The credit responsibility of each maker.

Acceptable notes are then totaled (including interest), and credited to the customer's account. Unacceptable notes with identifiable problems are usually returned to, and discussed with, the customer. In certain instances, the customer may request the bank to present questionable notes at maturity to the maker's bank for payment.

Loans Secured by Inventories

Inventory pledged as security is second to accounts receivable for secured short-term loans since it also represents a reasonably liquid asset. If a borrower has good credit, the mere existence of quality inventory may be sufficient cause for the lender to advance an unsecured loan. This scenario is even more prevalent if the firm has a stable level of diversified inventory, meaning no single item has an excessively high dollar value.

But if a firm is or questionable risk, the lender may insist on security, which can take the form of a blanket lien against inventory—a lien against all inventories of the borrower. But the borrower is free to sell the inventory that the bank secured as coverage when the loan was made. Additional downside exposure for the bank can also come as a result of rapidly depreciating stock values or severe price markdowns by the borrower in a panic.

Therefore, a blanket lien against inventory really does not provide the bank with enough coverage and control, making it less desirable. If this is the case, what characteristics are important when deciphering whether or not inventory is a viable security? Let's look at three areas: Marketability, Price Stability/Physical Properties, and Inventory Components.

Marketability

Inventory's most important characteristic is its marketability. If inventory can be sold at prices at least equaling its current book value or replacement cost, then its "market value" as a security is greatly enhanced. Inventories consisting of items such as automobile tires, and hardware goods fall into this category.

High-tech inventory, in contrast, is not considered desirable because of looming obsolescence. Also marketability is associated with the inventory's physical properties. A warehouse full of frozen turkeys may be quite marketable, but if the cost of storing and selling the turkeys is high, they may fall short of the mark. Specialty goods like pretzel twisters are not desirable collateral either, since finding buyers for them may be nearly impossible.

Price Stability/Physical Properties

Standardized and staple durables are very desirable as collateral since these items have prices that are not volatile, have ready markets, and no undesirable physical properties.

Perishability will definitely create problems for the inventory seller. What bank will secure a loan with inventory that at best only has downside potential?

Specialized items may also be of questionable use to the bank as collateral if the market is determined to be thin. Items like special-purpose machinery, fresh produce, and advertising materials are not desirable as candidates for inventory liens. Also, very high-ticket items may not be desirable as collateral if storage and transportation expenses are high.

Inventory Components

Of the three components or types of inventory—raw materials, goods in process, finished goods—only raw materials are usually considered security for short-term loans. Common sense dictates that a partially finished product has no real value to anyone. Commodities and products such as grain, cotton, wool, coffee, sugar, logs, lumber, canned foods, baled wood pulp, automobiles, and major appliances tend to be very acceptable as collateral. Partially completed refrigerators offer very little collateral.

Trust Receipts

As mentioned previously, when pledged inventories are left in control of the borrower, there is risk that they will be liquidated before the loan is repaid if the borrower gets into serious financial difficulties. Operating losses often lead to cash flow problems, which in turn lead to slowness in the payment of suppliers and a problem in keeping high-quality inventories in stock. Thus, because of the weakness of the blanket lien, another collateral structure is often used for the trust receipt. A trust receipt is an instrument acknowledging that the borrower holds the goods in trust for the lender. The lien is valid as long as the merchandise is in the borrower's possession and properly identified. When the lender advances funds, the borrower conveys a trust receipt for the goods financed.

The goods can be stored in a public warehouse or held on the borrower's premises. With a trust receipt loan, the borrower receives the merchandise and the lender advances anywhere from 80 percent to 100 percent of its cost. The lender files a lien on the items financed, listing each item along with its description and serial number. The borrower is free to sell the merchandise but is "trusted" to remit to the lender the amount lent (against each item) plus accrued interest—immediately after the sale is completed. The lender then releases the lien on the item. The lender should periodically check the borrower's inventory to ensure that all the required collateral is still in the hands of the borrower.

Inventory financing under trust receipts for retail sale is commonly called "floorplanning." For example, an automobile dealer may arrange seasonal financing for the purchase of new cars on a trust receipt or floor plan basis.

Warehouse Receipts

Like trust receipts, field warehouse financing uses inventory as security. A warehouse receipt loan is an arrangement whereby the bank receives control of the pledged collateral. This arrangement provides the lender with the ultimate degree of security. The costs of warehouse receipt loans are generally higher than those of any other secured lending arrangements. The reason for this is the money paid to the warehousing company (third party) to maintain and guard the inventory collateral. In addition to the interest charge, the borrower must absorb the costs of warehousing by paying the warehouse fee, which is generally between 1 and 3 percent of the amount of the loan.

Terminal Warehouse

A terminal warehouse is located near the borrower and is a central warehouse used to store the merchandise of various customers. A terminal warehouse is used when the secured inventory is easily and cheaply transported. When the goods arrive at the warehouse, the *warehouse official* "checks in" the merchandise, listing each item received on a *warehouse receipt*. Noted on the "check-in" list is the quantity, serial or lot numbers, and the estimated value. Once the official has checked in all the merchandise, he /she forwards the receipt to the lender, who advances a specified percentage of the collateral value to the borrower and files a lien on all the items listed on the receipt.

Field Warehouse

Field warehouse financing represents an economical method of inventory financing in which the "warehouse" is established on the borrower's premises. Under a field warehouse arrangement, the lender hires a reputable field warehousing company to set up a warehouse on the borrower's premises or to lease part of the borrower's warehouse. The warehousing company, as the lender's agent, is responsible for seeing that the collateral is actually in the warehouse. There are instances when warehousing companies fraudulently issue receipts against nonexistent collateral. If this happens, and the borrower defaults on the loan, the lender becomes an unsecured creditor. A number of companies specialize in establishing field warehouses for a fee. The procedures followed by the field warehouse personnel are quite similar to those followed by the terminal warehouse personnel.

Once the collateral is isolated, it is registered in the same manner discussed in the terminal warehouse section. On accepting the warehouse receipt, the lender advances a specified percentage of the collateral value to the borrower and files a lien on the pledged security. A field ware-

house may be a fence around a stock of raw materials located outdoors, a roped-off section of the borrower's warehouse or may actually be a warehouse constructed by the warehousing company on the borrower's premises—a portion of which may have been leased by the warehousing company.

In any case, the warehousing company employs a security official to guard the inventory. The guard or warehouse official is not permitted to release the collateral without authorization from the lender. The secured inventory can only be released with the lender's written approval.

Most warehouse receipts are non-negotiable, but some may be transferred by the lender to other parties. If the lender wants to remove a warehouse receipt loan from its books, it can sell the negotiable receipt to another party who then replaces the original lender in the agreement. In some instances, the ability to transfer a warehouse receipt to another party may be desirable.

For example, a canner of exotic fruits needs major bank financing during the canning season. To get the required seed capital to purchase and process an initial harvest of fruit, the canner can finance approximately 20% of its operations during the season.

As cans are put into boxes and placed in storerooms, the canner realizes that additional funds are needed for labor and raw material to make the cans. Without these funds, operations will come to a grinding halt. A seasonal pattern clearly forms here. At the beginning of the fruit harvest and canning season, cash needs and loan requirements increase and reach a maximum at the end of the canning season. Because of the canner's modest worth and substantial seasonal financing needs, the firm's bank insists on acceptable security. The services of a field warehouse company are obtained and a field warehouse is set up.

The field warehouse company notifies the bank that the canned fruit has been "checked in." At this point, the bank is assured of control over the canned goods and can establish a line of credit under which the canner can draw funds. As the canner receives purchase orders, it sends them to the bank. The bank then authorizes the warehouse custodian to release the boxes of canned fruit associated with the purchase orders.

When the high point of the season is over, the line of credit diminishes as checks from the canner's distributors are received by the canner. This results in a borrowing low point, putting the canner in a low debt position—necessary before a new seasonal buildup occurs.

In certain instances, banks may permit outstanding seasonal loans to the canner to reach an amount many times the amount of the canner's own equity capital. The fruit growers, the canner, the canner's distributors, the field warehouse company, and the bank all join forces in working out a successful distributive process to everyone's advantage. If the runoff of cash isn't enough to retire seasonal loans and the canner's financial structure is sound, the bank will likely carry over the loan(s) until next season. This should give the canner enough time to clean up the debt. The primary consideration for this arrangement is the fact that canned fruit is easily salable.

Negotiable warehouse receipts are used to finance inventories in which trading is active, such as corn, cotton, and wheat. Their major disadvantages are that they are easily transferred, are usually in large denominations, and must be presented to the warehouse operator each time a withdrawal is made. Therefore, banks

prefer the use of nonnegotiable receipts issued in the name of the bank for the simple reason that they provide better control of the pledged inventory.

Lending against Marketable Securities

A loan secured directly or indirectly by any stock or convertible security falls under SEC's Regulation U. Also included are loans used to purchase or carry margin stock. Margin stock may be listed or unlisted, over-the-counter, rights or warrants, mutual fund certificates, or other securities convertible into margin stock.

Suggested Guidelines: Advances against the Market Value of Securities

Collateral	Advance
Stocks listed on major exchanges	70%
Over-the-counter stocks	50%
Listed bonds	80%
Unlisted bonds	function of quality
US Government Securities	90%–95%
Municipal bonds	function of quality
Convertible securities	80% of call value and 50–70% of premium
Mutual funds	70%
Stocks selling below $5	Nominal advance
Stock inactively traded	Nominal advance

Definitions and Points to Keep in Mind

■ Unregistered stock is sold as a block to a private investor and does not fall under the usual regulations. Letter stock cannot be broken up, and is not passed through the market. The security represents a source of funds to the firm, and can be more flexible concerning dividends, since it is off-market and non-voting.

■ Bearer instruments should not secure advances unless the lender is convinced that the securities are owned by the borrower. Proof of ownership must be established by canceled checks, delivery tickets, etc., unless the borrower is well known at the bank.

■ When hypothecated collateral (collateral owned by someone else) secures advances, use extra caution. Hypothecated collateral may cause problems in a liquidation. The best effective way to preserve collateral integrity is to obtain a new hypothecation agreement when the loan is renewed.

■ Stock splits involve the division of capital stock into a larger number of shares. The lender should ensure that additional shares are obtained, since the stock may fall to under-margined levels.

■ Bond quotations should be reviewed regularly. Bond prices are inversely related to interest rates and might fall to under-margined levels during periods of rising interest rates.

Never record securities net of margin debt; rather separate out restricted or control stock and record these separately from fully marketable stock. Determine how much control stock can be sold in a given three-month period and for restricted stock, indicate the date when the restriction expires. If the value of marketable securities is significant, or if you are looking to these securities as a primary or secondary source of repayment, obtain a brokerage statement to substantiate holdings and values.

■ ■ ■

Section II

■ ■ ■

Cash Flow Analysis

■ ■ ■

CHAPTER *Seven*

Cash Flow Analysis: Background and History

Bankers generally consider cash flow a first principle of financial analysis.

Why is it so important? For starters, cash flow statements retrace a firm's financing and investment activities, including how cash has been generated and absorbed over a set time period. What's more, this information identifies major structural flaws within an organization.

Cash flow actually represents management's effectiveness in controlling the receipt and use of cash. From the lender's perspective, it reinforces the evaluation process of companies with analogous business risk and verifies the borrower's ability to service fixed obligations, including principal and interest payments on debt, dividends on preferred stock and lease payments. Another benefit: the cash flow statement reflects the variability of cash flow over time.

Let's illustrate the importance of cash flow. Over a three-year period starting in 1970, retailing giant W. T. Grant reported

$40 million income annually. The lenders and shareholders thought everything was copacetic. Unfortunately, nobody noticed the cash flows from operations. They were declining so precipitously that they reached negative $90 million by the end of the third year. The end result: W. T. Grant went belly-up. Creditors and stockholders took a bath. Why? No one paid any attention to the company's deteriorating operating cash flows reported on the statement of changes in financial position.

W. T. Grant's failure to generate cash internally compounded the need for external financing to the point of collapse. While people admired the profits, few noticed the firm's declining value. Careful cash flow analysis would have revealed financial problems as far back as a decade before bankruptcy.

The W. T. Grant debacle starts to clarify a basic misconception about the correlation between profits and cash flow from operations. For example, Company A and Company B compete in the same in-. dustry. Company A reports net income higher than Company B's. While Company B's operating cash flows marginally exceed profits, Company A's cash flows significantly overshadow profits. Which company is more successful?

The answer is Company B. Why? It successfully converts assets to cash to satisfy cash outflows. Company A, on the other hand, can't cover all its obligations because the income statement produces little cash.

Today's lenders increasingly rely on the Statement of Cash Flows as a measure of corporate performance because it "images" the probability distribution of future cash flows and can be helpful in estimating debt capacity. Sensitivity analysis can accurately calculate the point at which the probability of cash insolvency is equal to risk tolerance accepted by management. Thus, the maximum level of debt is established. This doesn't mean that debt should be increased to this level. It simply measures the effect of debt levels as they pertain to cash insolvency. The greater and more certain the cash flows, the greater the firm's debt capacity.

Cash flow helps assess business problems and judge how well management copes with those problems now and in the future. But, again, no matter how much information comes from financial reporting, there is no substitute for understanding a firm and its management. The cash flow statement's signals can only be detected by a prudent banker fully involved with the company.

The remainder of this chapter covers the varying aspects of cash flow to prepare you for the workshop and analysis you'll find in the next two chapters.

Cash versus Accrual-Based Income

Because a portion of a company's reported net income may consist of accrued revenue, two important questions must be answered:

1. What percentage of net income consists of accrued revenues and expenses?

2. How liberal is the company in recognizing assets like receivables and inventory?

From a bank's viewpoint, a high percentage of a firm's reported net income may consist of accrued revenues. Regardless of bad debt reserves (historically calculated as a percentage of gross sales), these revenues might never materialize into actual cash payments.

For example, a clothing manufacturer may make several large shipments shortly before the end of the fiscal year. The anticipated payment for these goods is booked as a debit to receivables, a credit to revenue, and reflected on the annual income statement. However, if the goods shipped were on consignment, or of poor quality, the customers may return them.

In another scenario, if the goods are acceptable but the customers are marginal credit risks, a substantial portion of the payments may never be realized and must be written off. In both instances, accrued revenue does not translate into actual cash flowing into the company, meaning that revenue is artificially inflated for the fiscal year.

Accounting: Fact or Fiction

Warren Buffet calls net income "white lies." Lee Seidler says "If push came to shove, if a chairman wants a nickel more a share, any good controller knows where to find it." They imply that alternative accounting methods can distort a firm's actual performance. This type of thinking reverts back to the American business disease known as "superficialophobia" or the capricious pressure to blindly deal with only short-term corporate objectives.

Take Prime Motor Inns. In 1989, PMI had a healthy $77 million in income. A year later, the firm filed for bankruptcy. What happened? No cash! A closer look at the 1989 cash flow from operations exposed the Prime Motor Inn's true financial condition—net income came from selling hotels. In other words, the company had negative cash flows from operations.

Crazie Eddy and Penn Central reported huge earnings but went bankrupt. Why? Cash was drained from the business. What about franchise businesses? Franchises book sales after signing a franchise agreement although many franchises don't actually deliver cash. Furthermore, franchises are rarely cash generators initially and will often require steady cash infusions before the business gets on track.

FASB 95/Introduction to Analysis

FASB 95 mandates the cash flow statement as a component of financial statements for business entities. The cash flow statement replaced the Statement of Changes in Financial Position. This development benefits lenders, although for years they have been constructing cash flow statements on their own. A statement of cash flows should provide the lender with the following information about a company:

1. Ability to generate positive future net cash flows

2. Historical external financing requirements

3. Reasons for variances between all outflows and cash produced by the income statement

4. Ability to pay dividends and meet all obligations

By examining changes in individual accounts on a cash flow statement, and how they relate to other transactions, lenders can form impressions of risk. Remember the adage, it's the quality behind the numbers that counts!

Requirements of FASB 95

FASB 95 mandates segregating the borrower's business activities into three classifications: *operating, financing, and investment activities.* The operating activities may be presented using either a direct or indirect presentation. Under either method, a reconciliation of net cash flow from operations to net income is required. Each technique will come up with the exact amount of cash from operations.

The direct method focuses on cash and the impact of cash on the financial condition of the business. By looking carefully at the numbers and comparing the cash based numbers to the accrual results, both quality and quantity of cash flow are determined. The indirect basis starts off with net income, then makes adjustments for non-cash and non-operating revenues, as well as expenses to arrive at an operating cash flow. Most lenders are familiar with the indirect method, since they typically use income statement and balance sheet information to indirectly arrive at operating cash flow. We'll examine both methods and showcase the indirect method in the cash flow workshop.

Indirect Method of Cash Reporting: The Banker's Cash Flow

To fully adapt cash flow to a banker's needs, the FASB 95 format can be aligned more with valuation and credit analysis (Exhibit 7.1). Currently, the statement combines working assets and liabilities with gross operating cash flow items to arrive at net cash flow from operations. Unfortunately, gross operating cash flow, one of the most important categories in credit analysis, is missed.

In simple terms, the power of the income statement provides cash flow for a firm's future growth. There are two ways firms can finance growth: externally and internally . . . remember PRISM? External financing comes from debt and/or equity injections from outside sources. Internal financing is generated from within the business itself.

There are two ways to generate internal cash flow: from the income statement—that is from gross operating cash flow or selling assets. "Can a firm grow by continuously selling off its assets?" As illustrated by Prime Motor Inn, the answer is a resounding No! That leaves only one viable source of internal cash flow—cash generated by the income statement (GOCF).

For purposes of the banker's cash flow, internal cash flow or cash from the income statement is classified as Gross Operating Cash Flow (GOCF). Thus, GOCF is introduced to the FASB 95 cash flow format and is usually compared to cash provided by debt financing activities. This allows the lender to: (1) check for any imbalance in internal versus external financing, and (2) make comparisons in financial leverage trends.

Let's say KVG Company shows its banker $1 million projected GOCF and asset investments (uses of cash) of $20 million. After raising his eyebrows, the banker scrutinizes where the rest of the money will come from. Probably debt. But why is KVG Company borrowing all this money to invest in assets when it can't even generate an internal rate of return (IRR) from internal sources to sufficiently contribute to the company's projected growth? Or why does KVG Company rely so heavily on external sources rather than internal sources?

More important, how long can this continue before KVG Company leverages itself out of business? With no equity injection feasible, the banker walks away from the loan request. Prudent bankers will not issue debt of this magnitude to any company for the purpose of expansion or retooling if it cannot adequately generate funds from internal sources and exhibits weak repayment support.

Another question: "Can GOCF leave the business of distribution to investors?" The answer is no, since GOCF must first cover working capital. Therefore, if the sources of working capital (increases in accounts payable, accruals and other working capital accounts) are greater than the traditional uses of working capital (increases in accounts receivable, inventory and other current assets), cash from the income statement does not have to be diverted to cover working capital and can be redirected to finance investment activities, retire debt and pay dividends. To clarify all this, two new categories are introduced: Operating Cash Needs (increases and decreases in working capital current assets) and Operating Cash Sources (increases and decreases in working capital current liabilities). On the following pages is the revised

Exhibit 7.1

COMPANY X
For the Year Ended December 31, 19X8
(Indirect Method)

Increase (Decrease) In Cash and Cash Equivalents
Cash flows from operating activities:

Net income	3,040	
Adjustments to reconcile net income to net cash provided by operating activities:		
Depreciation and amortization	1,780	
Provision for losses on accounts receivable	800	
Gain on sale of facility	(320)	
Undistributed earnings of affiliate	(100)	
Gross operating cash flow		**5,200**
(Inc.) Dec. in accounts receivable	(860)	
(Inc.) Dec. in inventory	820	
(Inc.) Dec. in prepaid expenses	(100)	
Operating cash needs *		**(140)**
Inc. (Dec.) in accounts payable and accrued expenses	(1,000)	
Inc. (Dec.) in interest and income taxes payable	200	
Inc. (Dec.) in deferred taxes	600	
Inc. (Dec.) in other current liabilities	200	
Inc. (Dec.) other adjustments	400	
Operating cash sources *		**400**
Net cash provided by operating activities		**5,460**
Cash flows from investing activities:		
Proceeds from sale of facility	2,400	
Payment received on note for sale of plant	600	
Capital expenditures	(4,000)	
Payment for purchase of Company S, net of cash acquired	(3700)	
Net cash used In Investing activities		**(4,700)**
Cash flows from financing activities:		
Net borrowings under line of credit agreement	1,200	
Principal payments under capital lease obligation	(500)	
Proceeds from issuance of long-term debt	1,600	
Net cash provided by debt financing activities *		**2,300**
Proceeds from issuance of common stock	2,000	
Dividends Paid	(800)	
Net cash provided by other financing activities		**1,200**
Net Increase In cash and cash equivalents		**4,260**
Cash and cash equivalents at beginning of year	2,400	
Cash and cash equivalents at end of year	6,660	

Exhibit 7.1 (continued)

COMPANY X
For the Year Ended December 31, 19X8
(Indirect Method)

Supplemental disclosures of cash flow information:
Cash paid during the year for:

Interest (net of amount capitalized)	880
Income taxes	1,300

Supplemental schedule of non-cash investing and financing activities:

The Company purchased all of the capital stock of Company S for	$950

In conjunction with the acquisition, liabilities were assumed as follows:

Fair value of assets acquired	6,320
Cash paid for the capital stock	(3,700)
Liabilities assumed	2,520

* Category added to complete Bankers Cash Flow Format

FASB 95 or "Bankers" cash flow format developed by the author:

Direct Method of Reporting Cash (Original—Not Bankers Format)

In contrast to the indirect method, the direct method (see Exhibit 7.2) discloses cash collected from customers and cash paid to suppliers for goods and services as the main source and use of cash. FASB 95 requires enterprises using the direct method of reporting to identify the amount of net cash flow provided from or used by operating activities separately on the statement of cash flows. Principal components of operating cash receipts and operating cash payments include:

- Cash collected from customers (including lessees, licensees) and any similar receipts
- Interest and dividends received
- Other operating cash receipts
- Cash paid to employees and other suppliers of goods or services including insurance, advertising, etc.

- Any other operating cash payments, including interest paid, income taxes paid

The Components of the Indirect Method

To understand the cash flow statement better, let's take a look at each major section individually. Although it comes first on the statement, I'm saving detailed discussion on operating activities until last in this chapter for emphasis and because it leads us more directly into the cash flow workshop.

Investing Activities

The Miller GAAP Guide summarizes Investing Activities as including:

■ ■ ■

Making and collecting loans and acquiring and disposing of debt or equity instruments and property, plant, and equipment and other productive assets; that is, assets held for or used in the

Exhibit 7.2

**Flows from Operations
For the Year Ended December 31, 19X8
(Direct Method)**

Increase (Decrease) In Cash and Cash Equivalents

Cash flows from operating activities:		
Cash received from customers	55,400	
Cash paid to suppliers and employees	(48,000)	
Dividend received from affiliate	80	
Interest received	220	
Interest paid (net of amount capitalized)	(880)	
Income taxes paid	(1,300)	
Insurance proceeds received	60	
Cash paid to settle lawsuit for patent infringement	(120)	
Net cash provided by operating activities		5,460
Cash flows from investing activities:	2,400	
Proceeds from sale of facility	600	
Payment received on note for sale of plant	(4,000)	
Capital expenditures		
Payment for purchase of Company S, net of cash acquired	(3,700)	
Net cash used In Investing activities		(4,700)
Cash flows from financing activities:		
Net borrowings under line of credit agreement	1,200	
Principal payments under capital lease obligation	(500)	
Proceeds from issuance of long-term debt	1,600	
Proceeds from issuance of common stock	2,000	
Dividends paid	(800)	
Net cash provided by other financing activities		$3,500
Net Increase In cash and cash equivalents		4,260
Cash and cash equivalents at beginning of year	2,400	
Cash and cash equivalents at end of year	6,660	
Reconciliation of net income to net cash provided by operating activities:		
Net Income	3,040	
Adjustments to reconcile net income to net cash provided by operating activities:		
Depreciation and amortization	1,780	
Provision for losses on accounts receivable	800	
Gain on sale of facility	(320)	
Undistributed earning of affiliate	(100)	
Payment received on installment note receivable for sale of inventory	400	

Exhibit 7.2 (continued)

Flows from Operations
For the Year Ended December 31, 19X8
(Direct Method)

Decrease in inventory	820
Increase in prepaid expenses	(100)
Decrease in accounts payable and accrued expenses	(1,000)
Increase in interest and income taxes payable	200
Increase in deferred taxes	600
Increase in other current liabilities	200
Net cash provided by operating activities	5,460

production of goods or services by the enterprise (other than materials that are part of the enterprise's inventory).

■ ■ ■

Breaking this broad definition down further, investment activities include advances and repayments to subsidiaries, securities transactions, and investments in long-term revenue producing assets. Cash inflows from investing include proceeds from disposals of equipment and proceeds from the sale of investment securities. Cash outflows include capital expenditures and the purchase of stock of other entities; project financing; capital and operating leases; and master limited partnerships.

Property, Plant, and Equipment

Cash flow relating to PP&E include acquisitions and purchases, capital leases, and proceeds from any disposals of property, plant, or equipment. Non-cash transactions include translation gains and losses, transfers, depreciation, reverse consolidations, and restatements.

Businesses are not usually required to break down property expenditures into categories such as maintenance of existing capacity and expenditures for expansion into new capacity. This would be the ideal disclosure, since maintenance and capital expenditures are nondiscretionary outlays. However, because of the difficulty of subjectively distinguishing expenditures for maintenance from those for expansion, the amounts assigned to the maintenance account would most likely prove unreliable. How, then, can a lender determine whether funds are being allocated for maintenance of existing capacity, replacing rundown equipment or providing expansion (and often discretionary) outlays? The answer lies in the cash flow statement.

Unconsolidated Subsidiaries

Usually, when a company acquires between 20% and 50% of another company's stock, it is called an investment in an unconsolidated subsidiary and is listed as an asset on the acquiring firm's balance sheet. Cash flows from unconsolidated subsidiaries include dividends from subsidiaries, advances and repayments, and acquisition or sale of securities of subsidiaries. Non-cash transactions include equity earnings, translation gains and losses, and consolidations.

Investment Project Cash Flows and Joint Ventures

Investment in joint ventures or other separate entities formed to carry out large projects is referred to as project financing and/or joint ventures. Typically, the new entity borrows funds to build a plant or a project with a guarantee of debt repayment furnished by companies that formed the new entity. Cash flows from the project (or joint ventures) are generally passed (up-streamed) to the owner firms as dividends. Prudent bankers must obtain a full disclosure of the project's future cash flows since construction projects may report non-cash earnings—construction accounting, or equity earnings. Also, cash flow projections may not be useful if most of the borrower's cash streams are hidden in joint ventures and the loan that finances the project is on the borrower's balance sheet. The key question: does the project make sense?

Asset Sales

Asset sales can be positive, as in the case of an unprofitable division sold off to allow management to focus on the firm's core businesses.

Financing Activities

According to the Miller guide, Financing activities include:

Cash flows from financing activities:	
Net borrowings under line of credit agreement	1,200
Principal payments under capital lease obligation	(500)
Proceeds from issuance of long-term debt	1,600
Net cash provided by debt financing activities	2,300
Proceeds from issuance of common stock	**2,000**
Dividends paid	(800)
Net cash provided by equity financing activities	**1,200**

■ ■ ■

Obtaining resources from owners and providing them with a return on, and return of, their investment; borrowing money and repaying amounts borrowed, or otherwise settling the obligation; and obtaining and paying for other resources obtained from creditors on long-term credit.

■ ■ ■

Financing activities include a company's debt and equity infusions. Cash inflows from financing include new equity issues, bonds, mortgages, notes, and other short-term or long-term borrowing. Cash outflows include dividend payments, treasury stock transactions, and repayment of borrowed funds.

Long-Term Debt

Bonds A bond is a financial obligation made by a corporation or government agency. The purchaser of a bond receives periodic interest payments, usually semi-annually, eventually receiving the face value of the bond on the redemption date. The interest payment calculated each period is: the interest rate printed on the bond divided by the number of payments per year, then multiplied by the face value of the bond. For example, a 7% $1000 bond with interest paid semi-annually would pay each six months: $(.07/2)($1,000) = 35.

The semi-annual interest payment is also called the coupon payment. In this case the coupon payment is $35, or 3.5%. The payment amount and the rate on the face value of the bond remain constant. But bonds often sell at prices above or below the face value. A bond selling for an amount greater than the face value (or par) is said to be sold at a premium, while a bond priced below par sells at a discount.

What does this all have to do with cash flow? The key word here is *proceeds* as opposed to increases in long-term debt. Beware of the label "increases in long-term debt." Proceeds and increases are not the same. Proceeds represent the amount a company actually receives from a debt issue, while increases in long-term debt includes amortization of bond discounts. The amortization of a bond discount reduces earnings (a non-cash charge), while the book value of the bond increases. Not a dime comes in or leaves the company, yet debt is adjusted on the financial statement.

Thus, bond discounts are subtracted from debt increases to determine "true" debt increases. The amortization of bond premium is subtracted from long-term debt reductions to determine the "actual" reductions.

Let's consider two short examples:

(#1)Face Value of Bond	$1,000,000
Term	10 years
Interest Paid Annually:	
Coupon Rate	6 %
Market Rate	10%
Solve for Present Value ➡ **$754,217**	

The proceeds of the bond sale in example #1 are $754,217, since the bond sold at a discount below the coupon rate. Each year the unamortized discount of $245,783, a liability against the bond, is amortized. As a result, the debt increases in value on the financial statements, eventually reaching $1,000,000 at maturity. It is important to realize that this is not a cash increase in debt that affects cash flow. Consider the journal entries and the effects of a bond discount on the firm's financial statements as shown:

Cash	$754,217	
Bond Discount	$245,783	
Bonds Payable		$1,000,000

Assume next year a $50,000 discount was amortized:

Amortization of Bond Discount (non-cash expense)	$50,000	
Unamortized Bond Discount		$50,000

Liabilities

Bonds Payable	$1,000,000
Less:	
Unamortized Bond Discount	($195,783)
Net Bonds	$804,217
Debt issue increased	$50,000

Suppose the firm borrowed $300,000 long-term debt in the above example and had no other debt except for the bonds. While the increase in long-term debt is $350,000, proceeds are $300,000.

(#2)Face Value of Bond	$1,000,000
Term	8 years
Interest Paid Annually:	
Coupon Rate	8%
Market Rate	6%
Solve for Present Value ➡ **$1,124,195**	

The proceeds of the bond sale in example #2 are $1,124,195 because, in this case, the bond sold at a premium above the coupon rate. This means the proceeds from the sale are reported as $1,124,195. Each year the unamortized premium of $124,195, a liability, is amortized. In this case, the debt will decrease in value on the financial statements reaching $1,000,000 at maturity:

Cash $1,124,195
  Bond Premium $124,195
  Bonds Payable $1,000,000

Assets	Liabilities
Cash $1,124,195	Bonds
	Payable $1,000,000
	Plus
	Unamortized Bond
	Premium $124,195
	Net Bonds $1,124,195

Assume next year a $13,000 discount was amortized:

Unamortized Bond Premium
(non-cash income) $13,000
  Amortization of Bond
  Premium $13,000

Liabilities
Bonds Payable $1,000,000
Plus:
Umamortized Bond
Premium $111,195
Net Bonds $1,111,195

Debt issue decreased $13,000

Suppose the firm paid off $125,000 in long-term debt in the above example and had no other debt except for the bonds. While reductions in long-term debt are $138,000, the actual cash pay out was $125,000.

As with the first example, it is important to realize that these are really just accounting entries, not a debt reduction or cash decrease in debt that affects cash flow.

How about zero coupon bonds? With this type of bond issue, huge discount amortization greatly increases debt, but no cash transaction is actually made until maturity. Hence, the only time cash flow is affected is at maturity when payment is due to the investors.

Conversion of debt to equity might represent a substantial non-cash transaction. However, conversion will eliminate non-discretionary payments of interest on debt and it will serve to reduce financial leverage. Therefore, conversions should be highlighted in a cash flow analysis. Financing activities include proceeds from issuing preferred and common stock. New common stock takes the form of new issues or stock options. Treasury stock—both purchases and sales—are included in financing activities.

Operating Activities

The Miller GAAP Guide defines operating activities as:

■ ■ ■

All transactions and other events that are not defined as investing or financing activities. Operating activities generally involve producing and delivering goods and providing services. Cash flows from operating activities are generally the cash effects of transactions and other events that enter into the determination of income.

■ ■ ■

Gross Operating Cash Flow

Gross operating cash flow is often the most important line in the cash flow statement— that's what business is all about. It represents net income plus all non-cash charges less all non-cash credits, plus and minus all non-operating transactions. GOCF is the cash generated by the operating income statement which, in turn, is the borrower's main source of internal financing.

Non-cash charges represent reductions in income not requiring cash outlays, such as depreciation and amortization, provision for deferred taxes, amortization of bond discounts, provisions, reserves, and losses in equity investments. Non-cash credits increase earnings without generating cash: equity earnings in unconsolidated investments, amortization of bond premiums, and negative deferred tax provisions. Non-operating charges and earnings such as asset writedowns, restructuring gains/charges and gains and losses on the sale of equipment are adjusted as well, further refining reported earnings.

A typical problem area is unconsolidated entities where cash flow depends on a dividend stream returned by the projects. Since the dividends are not part of income, non-cash profits may be managed by the completed contract/percentage of completion method.

Cash generated from non-recurring credit items may artificially inflate earnings for a period, but cannot be depended upon to provide cash flow to support long-term financing. This category includes gains and losses associated with the sale of business units, judgments awarded to the company, and other "one time" cash inflows.

A few words of review about extraordinary items: A one time extraordinary expense may have little impact on the long-term cash flow of a company. For example, if a firm settles a lawsuit over patent infringement which results in a one-time cash payout, the long-term health of the company may not be affected. That is, if the firm can afford the settlement.

However, what if a pharmaceutical company loses a product liability suit, resulting in a cash settlement and the recall of its best-selling drug? Loss of the product could jeopardize the firm's survival, so a lender must analyze all non-recurring items to decide whether or not they are material to the credit decision.

Net income must be the predominant source of a firm's funds in the long run. In individual years, borrowing or the issuance of capital stock may provide more funds than operations, but operations must provide the funds necessary not only to keep operating but also to repay borrowed capital and pay dividends.

Equity Earnings. Equity earnings appear on the income statement as an increase to net income. These equity earnings end up funneled through to retained earnings (via the income statement), increasing the owners' equity portion of its balance sheet. If another company owns between 20% and 49% of a firm's stock, it has "influence" on the firm as defined by the accountants. Thus, if the firm makes $1,000,000 profit, you take 25% of those profits, $250,000 into your income statement as earnings.

Suppose borrower, Company A, originally invested $1 million in Company B in year zero, obtaining a 25% equity stake. By year 5, the value of this 25% stake may have grown to $2.5 million. The equity earnings from this investment would have been reflected on Company A's income statement over the 5-year period, but cash may not have been received from the investment.

To adjust the income statement, the accountants will pull this non-cash credit out to move closer to true operating cash flow. This may be a prudent investment if the subsidiary is sound and future prospects are bright. However, there is a danger that the subsidiary could be paying out substantial dividends to other investors or maneuvering to siphon funds out of the company. This could lead to an equity investment in a valueless subsidiary.

Deferred Tax Credits. Deferred tax credits may cause earnings to increase, but may not provide cash nor offer a sustainable stream of cash. Deferred tax credits often come about when previous provisions for deferred taxes are reversed.

Operating Cash Needs

Current assets represent more than half the total assets of many businesses. With such a large, relatively volatile cash investment connected to optimizing shareholder value, current assets are deserving of financial management's undivided attention. Hence the term *current asset management*.

Add a level of uncertainty to the picture and current asset management transforms into the maintenance of minimum required balances for each type of asset account and the addition of a safety stock (forecasts are never perfect). Specifically, accounts receivable and inventory levels are critically important to cash flow because they reflect management's marketing abilities and credit policies. Of approximately equal magnitude, together they make up almost 80 percent of current assets and over 30 percent of total assets for manufacturing industries.

Accounts Receivable. Revenue from sales has been reported for the period but cash has not been received. A rise in receivables represents a use of cash and must be financed. A decrease in receivables is associated with cash inflows.

You'll recall that the level of accounts receivable is determined by the volume of credit sales and the average collection period. The average collection period is influenced partly by economic conditions and partly by credit policy variables which current asset management looks to optimize.

Inventory. As previously mentioned, inventory management is a vital component of cash flow cycles. Good inventory control starts with the fundamental understanding of the three stages of inventory: Raw materials (RM), work-in-process (WIP) and finished goods (FG).

Good inventory management translates into good cash flow management. This involves balancing finished goods with financial management's projected sales. Expedient inventory managers believe that with careful planning and open lines of communication within the organization, inventories can be kept at nominal levels. Techniques such as Just-in-Time (JIT) and Economic Order Quantity (EOQ) do just that.

Prepaid Expenses. Prepaid expenses represent a use of cash during the period, but are not expensed until the corresponding service is received in a later period. To show what the actual cash outflow was for the period, the increase in prepaid expenses is subtracted from Cash Flow. Decreases in prepaid items is a source of cash because the prepaid items are now being expensed without an outflow of cash.

Operating Cash Sources

The right side of the balance sheet supports assets. Large increases and decreases in current accounts represent substantial inflows and outflows of cash. Operating cash sources generally include non-interest bearing current liabilities that tend to follow sales increases.

Accounts Payable. Accounts payable represent the purchases of inventory on credit. Increases in accounts payable are a source of cash that delays cash outflows into the future. While the company has use of this cash, it can utilize it for daily needs as well as for investment purposes. Eventual payment to creditors decreases accounts payable converting it into a use of cash. Generally, decreases from one period to the next represent an amount paid to suppliers in excess of purchases expensed.

Another angle to indirectly increasing cash flow is fully utilizing all discounts given by vendors. Normal terms for suppliers are usually 2/10, net 30. If for argument's sake, a borrower at your bank took all the discounts available in a year, its annualized discount savings would amount to 37%.

$$\left(\frac{.02}{(1-.02)} \times \frac{365}{(30-10)} \right)$$

This translates into a cheap source of financing. If a loan officer wants to make points with a firm that has good cash flow and disregards discounts, this technique is a good "bonding" strategy if nothing else because no one else has pointed it out. (Encourage your borrower to draw down lines to take advantage of trade discounts) since it will save the difference between the discount savings and the bank loan rate.

Accruals and Taxes Payable. Increases in accruals and taxes payable represent sources of cash since items such as salaries, taxes and interest are expensed but not paid out. Thus, cash is conserved for a limited period. A decrease in accruals arises from payments in excess of costs expensed. In the current period, therefore, the decrease is subtracted from the cash flow as a use of cash.

Net Cash Provided by Operating Activities

Net cash provided by operating activities or net operating cash flow denotes the cash available from Gross Operating Cash Flow to internally finance a firm's future growth after working capital demands are satisfied. One of the great things about the structure of the cash flow format is how pieces of information surface to formulate powerful insights on company operations. For example—and this deserves repeating—if gross operating cash flow is consistently larger than net cash flow from operations, the traditional sources of working capital, accounts payable and accruals have provided full support to traditional uses of working capital, accounts receivable and inventory. Thus, **precious operating cash income need not be diverted to support working capital** and can be rerouted to finance "growth" strategies like investments in efficient fixed assets and aggressive research and development programs—the lifeblood of optimizing equity and maximizing shareholder value.

Now that the cash flow basics have been reviewed, let's move on to the cash flow workshop. In this section, the nitty gritty of cash flow is fully explored using the indirect method.

CHAPTER Eight

Cash Flow Workshop

Before beginning the cash flow workshop, it is important to consider what distinguishes a source of cash from a use of cash and how each is derived.

We've learned that the cash flow statement originates with the balance sheet, where transactions occurring on a year-to-year basis directly influence its outcome. So working backwards will make it easy to identify all transactions affecting the balance sheet. Let's start with the basic accounting equation:

Assets = Liabilities + Equity

Extrapolating the basic accounting equation further yields:

Cash + Accounts receivable + Inventory + Net-fixed assets + Investments in unconsolidated subsidiaries = Accounts payable + Accruals + Short-term debt + Current portion long-term debt + Long-term debt + Equity

Solving for cash:

Cash = Accounts payable + Accruals + Short-term debt + Current portion long-term debt + Long-term debt + Equity – Accounts receivable – Inventory – Net fixed assets – Investments in unconsolidated subsidiaries

Multiplying both sides of the last equation by delta Δ, the variance between balance sheet accounts from one fiscal year to the next is resolved:

Δ *Cash* = Δ *Accounts payable* + Δ *Accruals* + Δ *Short-term debt* + Δ *Current portion long-term debt* + Δ Long-term debt + Δ Equity – Δ *Accounts receivable* – Δ *Inventory* – Δ *Net-fixed assets* – Δ *Investments in unconsolidated subsidiaries.*

This equation confirms the axiom that changes in cash are governed by the difference between sources and uses of cash on the balance sheet. Note that the assets have negative signs preceding their respective deltas (uses of cash) liabilities and equity deltas (Δ) (sources of cash) are preceded with positive signs. Clarifying this observation further, if Company A manufactures product X, but hasn't paid for the raw materials it used, cash has been conserved. The result is an increase in accounts payable or a source of cash. In turn,

if Company A sells product X to a customer
on terms, no cash is received at the time of
the sale. This results in an increase in accounts receivable or use of cash. The
guidelines to further clarify sources and
uses of cash include:

Sources of Cash:
Decreases in assets (− Δ)
Increases in liabilities (+Δ)
Increases in equity (+ Δ)

Uses of Cash:
Increases in assets (+Δ)
Decreases in liabilities (− Δ)
Decreases in equity (− Δ)

Let's start the workshop by reviewing the five steps necessary to evaluate the
banker's cash flow statement:

Step #1: Review the balance sheet and income statement.

Step #2: Develop the control sheet.

Step #3: Prepare and analyze all reconciliations.

Step #4: Complete the cash flow statement.

Step #5: Develop an analysis.

The first four of these steps will be
covered in this chapter with a review of the
mythical Maryann Corporation. The fifth
step, developing an analysis of Maryann,
needs a chapter of its own.

Step #1: Review Maryann Corporation's 1992 and 1993 Financial Statement

Maryann Corporation
Balance Sheet Fiscal
Year Ending December 31

Assets	1992	1993
Cash	$110	$130
Accounts Receivable	230	280
Inventory	200	220
Current Assets	**$540**	**$630**
Gross Property	620	800
Less: Accumulated Depreciation	(180)	(250)
Net Fixed Assets	440	550
Investment in Unconsolidated Subsidiary	240	410
Total Assets	**$1220**	**$1590**
Accounts Payable	$300	$330
Wages Payable	20	30
Taxes Payable	10	10
Short-Term Debt	100	102
Current Maturities	70	80
Current Liabilities	**$500**	**$552**
Long-Term Debt	$330	$380
Deferred Taxes	25	48
Other Liabilities	15	90
Common Stock	120	170
Paid In Capital	140	200
Retained Earnings	130	180
Treasury Stock	(40)	(30)
Liabilities and Equity	**$1220**	**$1590**

Maryann Corporation
Income Statement Fiscal
Year Ending December 31

	1992	1993
Sales	1,370	1,400
Cost of Goods Sold	(885)	(880)
Gross Profit	**485**	**520**
Depreciation Expense	(84)	(90)
Operating Expenses	(492)	(520)
Operating Profit	**(91)**	**(90)**
(Loss) Gain on Sale of Equip	12	(10)
Equity Earnings in Unconsolidated Subsidiary	201	230
Profit before Taxes	122	130
Current Taxes (A)	2	(27)
Deferred Taxes (B)	45	(23)
Net Profit	**169**	**80**

(A) represents a current tax credit
(B) represents a deferred tax credit

Step # 2: Develop a Control Sheet for Maryann Corporation

The second workshop step is to determine Maryann's year-to-year change in cash. This is accomplished by preparing a control sheet as follows:

1. Calculate the year-to-year balance sheet variances for each account.

2. Determine what is a source and use of cash for each account. For example, Maryann's accounts receivable increased by $50 in 1993, creating a use of cash.

3. Enter the amounts by line item on the control sheet in either the Sources (increase in cash) or Uses (decrease in cash) column.

4. Total both columns to identify the change in cash. The change in the cash account is always equal to the difference between sources and uses of cash. If this does not occur, a mistake has been made and it's back to the drawing board.

The finalized control sheet renders the following results:

Maryann Corporation
Control Sheet
December 31

Assets	Increase	Decrease	
Cash	20		
	Sources	**Uses**	**Further Development**
Accounts Receivable		50	Directly to Cash Flow
Inventory		20	Directly to Cash Flow
Net PPE		110	Fixed Asset Reconciliation
Invest. Uncons. Subs		170	Invest Reconciliation
Liabilities and Equity			
Short-Term Notes	2		Directly to Cash Flow
Accounts Payable	30		Directly to Cash Flow
Accruals	10		Directly to Cash Flow
Current Portion Long-Term Debt	10		Long-Term Debt Reconciliation
Senior Long-Term Debt	50		Long-Term Debt Reconciliation
Deferred Taxes	23		Deferred Tax Reconciliation
Misc. Liabilities	75		Directly Tax Reconciliation
Common Stock	50		Equity Reconciliation
Add. Paid in Capital	60		Equity Reconciliation
Retained Earnings	50		Equity Reconciliation
Treasury Stock	10		Equity Reconciliation
Total	370	350	

Change In			
Balance Sheet Accounts	20		
Proof: Matches with			
Change in Cash	20		Directly to Cash Flow

At this stage of the workshop, the results of the control sheet provide a suitable but limited cash flow profile. Why? Sources and uses of cash are usually net changes, meaning the end result of many different transactions. Thus, reconciliations lie at the core of cash flow analysis. For example, Maryann Corporation has a change in equity from year to year, but until a reconciliation is finalized it is uncertain what portion of equity represents income, currency translations, new equity, dividends and so forth.

Paying particular attention to the *Further Development* column on the control sheet, the "Next Step" for each account is highlighted. Accounts are noted "directly to cash flow" or the appropriate account reconciliation.

The third stage of the workshop, then, is account reconciliation. Since the objective is to move from the control sheet to the final cash flow, all transactions necessary to evaluate risk must be analyzed.

Step #3: Prepare and Analyze All Reconciliations for Maryann Corporation

Net Fixed Asset Reconciliation

Auditors preparing cash flow statements bring together all ledger accounts dealing with fixed assets: capital expenditures, depreciation expense, acquisitions, capital leases, proceeds from disposals of property, unrealized translation gains and losses, and transfers. Proceeds from disposals can be derived by adding the gain or subtracting the loss from book value. Disposals are not left "at book" when proceeds from fixed asset sales are disclosed. Translation gains and losses (FASB 52) earmark currency holding gains and losses. They are included to identify an unrealized fixed asset transaction.

An example of the fixed asset reconciliation follows:

Net PP&E	(prior period)
Less: Depreciation and amortization of net-fixed assets	(current period)
Less: Proceeds from disposals	(current period)
Less: Losses on sale of fixed assets	(current period)
Plus: Gain on sale of fixed assets	(current period)
Plus: Capital expenditures	(current period)
Plus: Acquired fixed assets	(current period)
Plus/(Less): Translation Gains (Losses)	(current period)
= Derived Net PP&E	(current period)
Less: Actual Net PP&E	(current period)
= Increase/Decrease Net PP&E	(current period)

Maryann Corporation Fixed Asset Reconciliation

Property Plant & Equipment	Amount	Information	Source/Use	Category
Beginning Balance	440	Bal Sheet		
Less: Depreciation	(90)	Stmt Cash Flow	Source	Gross Oper. Cash Flow
Less: Disposals	(40)	Stmt Cash Flow	Source	Investment Activities
Plus: Capital Exp	250	Stmt Cash Flow	Use	Investment Activities
Gain/Loss on Disposal	(10)	Stmt Cash Flow	Use/Source	Gross Oper. Cash Flow
Derived Ending Balance	550	Stmt Cash Flow		
Balance Sheet Ending	550	Bal Sheet		
(Inc)Dec Fixed Assets	0	Derived		

Taking a closer look at the fixed asset reconciliation, the sum of the depreciation, disposals, capital expenditures, gain/loss on disposal and (increase)decrease fixed assets transactions equal the change in NFA on the control sheet. Once the banker's cash flow statement is complete, the reasons for doing a reconciliation such as this will be more obvious and meaningful. Another note of interest involves the (increase) decrease in fixed assets. This line item is inserted in the reconciliation as a plug figure, since the results may not be exact. If it is zero, there is no need for it to appear on the final cash flow statement.

Investment Reconciliation

Information can be found in the cash flow statement, income statement, and footnotes. Footnotes usually provide required comprehensive information as follows:

■ Equity investment transactions include equity earnings, dividends from subsidiaries, advances, and repayments, purchase and sale of securities, translation gains/losses, consolidations and deconsolidations. A summary financial statement may be included in the footnotes if equity earnings are relevant.

■ Advances/repayments should be disclosed, if consequential, to track borrowings and funds downstreamed to unconsolidated subsidiaries.

■ Equity earnings are sometimes netted out against dividends. Dividends may be found by subtracting undistributed equity from equity earnings.

■ Project finance activities may also show up in the investment account. Cash flows from contracts (projects and joint ventures) are upstreamed in the form of dividends.

An example of the Investment Reconciliation follows:

Investment in Unconsolidated Subs.	(prior period)
Plus: Equity earnings	(current period)
Less: Cash dividends from subsidiaries	(current period)
Plus: Advances to subsidiaries	(current period)
Less: Repayment of loans	(current period)
Plus: Translation gains (FASB 52)	(current period)
Less: Translation losses (FASB 52)	current period)
= Derived Invest Unconsol Subs.	(current period)
Less: Actual Invest. Unconsol Subs.	(current period)
= Inc/Dec Invest in Unconsol Subs.	(current period)

Maryann Corporation Investment Reconciliation

Category	Amount	Information	Source/ Use	Category
Beginning Balance	240	Balance Sheet		
Plus: Equity Earnings	230	Income Statement*	Use	G. O. C. F.
Div. Received	(140)	Statement Cash Flow	Source	Investment Activities
Plus: Advances	80	Statement Cash Flow	Use	Investment Activities
Derived Ending Balance	410			
Balance Sheet Ending Balance	410			Balance Sheet
(Inc)Dec Investments	0	Derived		

*Information also statement of cash flow and footnotes

Deferred Tax Reconciliation

Tax expense is broken down into two components: current taxes and deferred taxes. Deferred taxes build up from "timing differences" when income/expenses reported on financial statements differ from taxes reported to the IRS. Information on deferred tax is usually found in the tax footnote. Some of the more common factors causing these timing differences include the use of different depreciation methods for financial statement and tax purposes, and recognition of income in different periods for book and tax purposes. If taxable income exceeds book income (this occurs when prepaid cash is booked—such as a subscription), deferred taxes appear as an asset. A negative provision increases income and reduces the deferred tax liability.

An example of the Deferred Tax Reconciliation follows:

Deferred taxes	(prior period)
Plus: Deferred tax provision	(current period)
Less: Deferred tax credits	(current period)
= Derived deferred	(current period)
Less: Actual deferred taxes	(current period)
= Increase/decrease deferred	
taxes	(current period)

The Equity Reconciliation

Comprehensive equity reconciliations are organized in the footnotes of annual corporate reports and the cash flow statement. The equity reconciliation is developed as follows:

- The equity accounts and opening equity balances are spread across the top of the page with total equity the last column on the right.
- Listed down the left column are the various transactions that correspond to their respective equity account. The total for each transaction is recorded in the total equity column.
- After all transactions have been recorded, each column is totalled identifying the ending balance for each equity account. The ending balance should equal the account balances at the end of the year.
- The total equity column should reconcile to the sum of the account balances going across the bottom. This makes the schedule a self-proving system.
- If a transaction does not affect cash flow it will not appear in the cash flow statement. Numbers listed in the total equity column (with the exception of the starting and ending bal-

---

Maryann Corporation Deferred Tax Reconciliation

Deferred Tax Accounts	Amount	Information	Source/Use	Category
Balance sheet beginning balance	25	Bal Sheet		
Provision for deferred taxes	23	Income Stm	Source	Gross Oper. Cash Flow
Derived ending balance	48			
Balance sheet ending balance	48	Bal Sheet	Source	Oth Financing or GOCF
(Inc)Dec deferred taxes	0	Derived		

Deferred tax information is usually found in the tax footnote.

ances) will go on the cash flow statement.

■ Examples of equity transactions include: net income, cash dividends, proceeds from stock sale, exercise of stock options, cumulative translation

adjustments and purchases and sales of treasury stock.

■ Cash transactions affecting equity are carried to the cash flow statement. Equity transfers, like stock dividends, are excluded.

Maryann Corporation Reconciliation of Equity Accounts

Equity Accounts	Common Stock	Paid In Capital	Retained Earnings	Treasury Stock	Total
Beginning Balance	120	140	130	(40)	350
Net Income (Loss)			80		80
Cash Div.			(30)		(30)
Sale of Treasury Stock		60		10	70
Stock Sale	50				50
Ending Balance	170	200	180	(30)	520

Equity Accounts	Total	Source/(Use)	Bankers Cash Flow
Beginning Balance	350		
Net Income (Loss)	80	Source	Gross Operating Cash Flow
Cash Div.	(30)	Use	Financing Activity
Sale of Treasury Stock	70	Source	Financing Activity
Stock Sale	50	Source	Financing Activity

The Long-Term Debt Reconciliation

An example of the Long-Term Debt Reconciliation follows:

Current portion	(prior year)
Plus: non-current portion	(prior year)
Plus: increase in long-term debt	
(current year derived from the issue-by-issue breakdown in the footnotes) less current portion (this year)	
Less: non-current portion	(current year)
= reductions in long-term debt	(current year)

Maryann Corporation Long-Term Debt Reconciliation   Source/(Use)   Bankers Cash Flow

Current Portion Long-Term Debt 1992	70		
Non-Current Long-Term Debt 1992	330		
Plus: New Debt Issue	60	Source	Financing Activity
Less Current Portion Long-Term Debt 1993	(80)		
Less: Non-Current Long-Term Debt 1993	(380)		
= Long-Term Decrease 1993	0	Use	Financing Activity

Other Possible Reconciliations (Absent from Maryann Corporation)

Intangible Reconciliation

Goodwill and intangible reconciliations are required when amortization of goodwill or intangibles are disclosed in the annual report.

An example of the Intangible Reconciliation follows:

Balance sheet beginning balance	(prior year)
Plus: amortization of intangibles	(current year)
Plus: acquired intangibles	(current year)
Derived intangibles	(current year)
Balance sheet ending balance	(current year)
(Inc)/Dec Intangibles	(current year)

Minority Interest Reconciliation

Claims on the parent's income by minority shareholders are recognized as minority interest in earnings (income statement) and minority interest (balance sheet).

An example of the Minority Interest Reconciliation follows:

Balance sheet beginning balance	(prior year)
Flus: Minority interest in earnings	(current year)
Less: Dividends to minority interest	(current year)
Derived minority interest	(current year)
Ending minority interest	(current year)
(Inc)/Dec in minority interest	(current year)

Step # 4: Complete Maryann Cash Flow Statement:

Maryann Corporation
Bankers Cash Flow
12/31/93

Cash Flow Accounts	Amount		Information Transferred From
Net Income	80		Equity reconciliation
Plus/Less: Non-Cash Items			
Depreciation	90		Fixed asset reconciliation
Inc./(Dec.) Deferred Tax	23		Deferred tax reconciliation
Equity Earn.	(230)		Investment reconciliation
Gain/Loss Disposals	10		Fixed asset reconciliation
GROSS OPERATING CASH FLOW		(27)	
(Inc.)/Dec. Net A/R	(50)		Control sheet
(Inc.)/Dec. Inventory	(20)		Control sheet
Operating Cash Needs		(70)	
(Inc)./Dec. Net A/R	30		Control sheet
(Inc.)/Dec. Accruals	10		Control sheet
Operating Cash Sources	40		
Net Cash Provided by Operating Activities		(57)	
Capital Expenditures	(250)		Fixed asset reconciliation
Div. Received from Sub	140		Investment reconciliation
(Advances) Net of Repay	(80)		Investment reconciliation
Cash Received from Sale of Equipment	40		Fixed asset reconciliation
Net Cash Used In Investing Activities		(150)	
Long-Term Debt	60		Long-Term debt reconciliation
Short-Term Debt	2		Control sheet
Cash Flows from Interest-Bearing Debt	62		
Cash Dividends	(30)		Equity reconciliation
Sale Treasury Stock	70		Equity reconciliation
Misc. L/T Liabilities	75		Control sheet
Equity	50		Equity reconciliation
Cash Flows from Equity and Other	165		
Cash Flows from Financing Activities		227	
NET CHANGE IN CASH ITEMS		20	Derived: also matches control sheet

Having completed these four preliminary steps, you're now ready to go on to the next chapter, with its very important focus on cash flow analysis—another indispensable element of today's credit decision making.

CHAPTER Nine

Cash Flow Analysis

Now we come to the fifth and most important step of our cash flow workshop: developing cash flow analysis.

The prime considerations here are how much internal sources can contribute to financing and whether these internal sources are strong enough to cover repayment. Therefore, it is extremely important when reviewing earnings to determine to what extent income is used to fund a firm's operations and growth.

To increase debt financing to fund on-going operations while internally generated cash declines is a clear-cut problem. The result is clearly an accelerating debt/equity ratio and barring any reversal of fortune, this may lead to Chapter 11. Hence, imbalances between debt and equity can be classified as the result of weak internal cash flow.

A less straightforward situation is a business in its rapid growth phase. Although net income may be growing steadily over time, expansion costs might be rising at an even faster rate. Funding increases in receivables, inventories, and capital expenditures might push the firm's

debt/equity ratio perilously high unless new equity is brought in. This is a crash and burn situation: the company crashes because cash has evaporated, and the bank gets burned by losing its investment.

Keep these considerations in mind as you go through the series of fail-safe checklists in this chapter. These lists should be followed to ensure the reliability of your cash flow analysis, and therefore, of your credit judgment. The checklists hint at both definite actions to be taken and specific questions to be answered.

Analysis of Gross Operating Cash Flow

Checklist

☐ Analyze the quality, magnitude, and trend of earnings. When assessing the quality of earnings, evaluate reserves, non-recurring items, cash versus accrual-based income, and cash from operations.

☐ Pay particular attention, in analyzing earnings trends, to income's contribution to overall financing. If income contributes less and less to the firm's financing, there could be a problem.

☐ Also compare gross operating cash flow with new financing. Then check for imbalance in internal versus external financing and compare results with financial leverage trends. Check the composition of gross operating cash flow.

☐ Compare net income to dividends. Are dividends large in proportion to net income?

☐ Watch for large deferred tax credits.

☐ Are liquidity earnings partially offset by dividends from unconsolidated subsidiaries.

Analysis of Operating Cash Uses

Increases in receivables are normal in a growing firm so long as the average collection period remains relatively steady. However, large increases in receivables accompanied by weak operating performance and unaccountable increases in the average collection period should be checked against (1) credit standards, (2) terms of discount offered, and (3) collection policies. Changes in net income should be cross referenced with changes in inventory. If a company suffers losses, have inventory levels increased? This raises the question of why the borrower is stockpiling inventory if it can't be sold off at a profit.

Checklist

☐ If the ACP has increased, why?

☐ If losses are sizable, why isn't the accountant writing down inventory?

Analysis of Operating Cash Sources

A "bulge" in payables may indicate late payments, particularly if the gross operating cash flow is not making an adequate contribution to the financing of the business and if the company is highly leveraged.

Checklist

☐ Does the borrower take advantage of trade discounts and/or have the ability to do so?

☐ Does the borrower's conversion cycle contribute to increased payables balances and late payments?

Analysis of Investment Activities

Net Fixed Assets. A company's assets must be continually replaced and upgraded to ensure efficient operations. For example, if a company fails to maintain its property, plant, and equipment, its aging or outmoded machinery would increasingly experience lengthier downtime and goods produced would have higher levels of defects due to decreasing efficiency. As this situation escalates, the firm will fall behind its competitors from both a technological and opportunity cost standpoint. Worse, its products may be perceived by its customers as being inferior, lower quality or "old-fashioned" compared to its competitors'.

Depreciation expenses consistently exceeding capital expenditures may signal a business in decline and could eventually lead to a decline in earnings and profitability. Capital expenditures represent major non-discretionary outlays. Lenders can decide whether funds are being allocated for maintenance of existing capacity, replacing rundown equipment or providing expansion (and often discretionary) outlays.

Checklist

☐ Check if deferred taxes are running off. Deferred taxes usually increase when capital expenditures accelerate.

☐ Review the borrower's capital budgeting schedule. Focus on project cost, NPVs and IRR.

Unconsolidated Subsidiaries

When analyzing cash flows of unconsolidated subsidiaries, the following points should be observed:

If investment in unconsolidated subsidiaries represents a large item on the balance sheet, lenders should ask for financial statements of the unconsolidated subsidiary—or at least a full financial summary. Equity earnings increases (non-cash) earnings. Taking this one step further, increased earnings flow through to equity. If a bank makes a loan believing the borrower has plenty of debt capacity because of a low debt/equity ratio, it could be in for a big surprise! In this instance, equity is backing "funny money" assets of highly questionable quality.

If the parent company is giving cash advances or transferring other assets to the subsidiary without receiving repayment or cash dividends, this should immediately serve as a "red flag." Lenders need to know if the money they lend to the core business is being diverted to unconsolidated subsidiaries and whether these funds are ever repaid. In extreme cases, the parent company could be left with a balance sheet including debt and a valueless subsidiary.

Checklist

☐ Break out investments in unconsolidated subsidiaries. If the investment change is large and unexplained, it could represent an advance to the subsidiary.

☐ Adequate financial information on unconsolidated subsidiaries generating substantial equities earnings should be available.

Project Cash Flows and Joint Ventures

Once the financial merits of a project have been examined, it must be discerned whether the project's cash flow is reasonably understood. The lender must look at the projected cash flow of the new entity to verify that cash will be available to repay the loan. The loan to the new entity will ultimately be repaid out of the cash flow generated by the project. Therefore, the potential variability of this type of cash flow represents the "level of risk" to the lender. Another factor to be considered is whether the entity represents a major investment for the parent company(s) involved in the project. If so, this will also increase the level of risk to the lender.

Checklist

☐ Is the cost of capital appropriate? If it is artificially low, the NPV of the project will be inflated.

☐ Is the time frame to complete the project realistic, or is it a "pie in the sky" scenario? Projects which take longer to complete than projected will invariably cost more than budgeted.

Analysis of Financing Activities: Debt

Checklist

☐ Examine increases in long-term debt on a specific-issues basis to understand how a firm might plan its future financing. Distinguish between cash debt increases and accounting debt increases. For example, amortization of bond discount results in debt increases, but no cash is involved.

☐ Match decreases in long-term debt against increases in long-term debt. For example, in an expanding business, increases in long-term debt may exceed reductions. As long as leverage is within acceptable levels, the income statement is probably contributing its fair share to the firm's overall financing.

Analysis of Financing Activities: Equity and Other

Checklist

☐ Review dividends to determine whether they are tied to income or are relatively constant. Examined financial leverage to verify that dividends are reasonable in light of future prospects. Remember high leverage plus big dividends usually spells trouble.

☐ If the firm is performing poorly, the company should not be borrowing to finance treasury stock purchases.

■ ■ ■

Cash Flow and Analysis: A Brief Case Study

To illustrate further what we've been talking about in this section, let's return to Gem Furniture Company and its deteriorating financial condition and look at its cash flow statement.

Exhibit 9.1

Gem Furniture Company
Cash Flow
(In thousands)

Cash Flow Accounts	1990	1991
Net Income	18,755	1,965
1965 *Plus/Less: Non-cash items*		
Depreciation	4,973	6,120
GROSS OPERATING CASH FLOW	23,728	8,085
(Inc.)/Dec. Net A/R	(4,093)	(32,685)
(Inc.)/Dec. Inventory	(42,286)	(40,889)
Operating Cash Needs	**(46,379)**	**(73,574)**
(Inc.)/Dec. Net A/P	11,226	28,477
(Inc.)/Dec. Accruals	4,973	6,694
Operating Cash Sources	16,199	35,171
Net Cash Provided by Operating Activities	(6,452)	(30,318)
Capital Expenditures	(7,019)	(8,319)
Net Cash Used in Investing Activities	(7,019)	(8,319)
Long-Term Debt	8,769	0
Long-Term Debt Payments	0	(785)
Short-Term Debt	5,738	39,398
Cash Flows from Inerest Bearing Debt	14,507	38,613
Cash Dividends	(4,764)	(266)
Cash Flows from Equity and Other Financing Activities	290	0
NET CHANGE IN CASH ITEMS	(3,438)	(290)

Reviewing gross operating cash flow, we immediately recognize the amount of cash obtained by Gem as a result of its business operations. Factoring out all non-cash charges, the gross operating cash flow is compared with new financing. In year 1990, the company's gross operating cash flow was $23.7 million and its new debt financing totaled $14.5 million. By 1991, gross operating cash flow had dropped to $8.1 million and new debt financing had risen to $39.4 million. Internal financing was not keeping pace with external financing. It is clear that the company cannot remain viable if this trend continues, since financial leverage would reach a level at which the company would need new debt just to pay the interest on existing debt. Highlighting other factors:

1. Three-quarters of its 1991 gross operating cash flow consisted of depreciation. This emphasizes the fact that the net income of $2.3 million in 1991 was too weak to contribute to the financing of additional assets.

2. Operating cash needs of $73.6 million outpaced gross operating cash flow, drawing all of the cash generated by the income statement to support working capital. This left a net operating cash flow deficit of $30.3 million.

3. The new bank debt of $39.4 million was used to make up the net operating cash flow shortfall. The remainder of new short-term debt financed capital expenditures. This is a traditional mismatch of funds, since equipment purchases should be financed with long-term debt.

4. In spite of the financial pressure placed on the firm and despite its poor operating performance, management elected to pay dividends—another no-no.

Gem is faced with a current asset dilemma which is no surprise because as stated earlier, we uncovered this predicament when discussing ratios. Therefore,

cash flow analysis has added a perspective to the liquidity ratios. Bringing ratio and cash flow together, we must come up with a game plan to present to Gem, not a thrilling prospect since we have, hypothetically, a large investment to protect.

The Merging of Cash Flow and Ratios: Pro Forma Analysis

To develop a sound strategy we undertake pro forma calculations to determine exactly what factors caused operating and financial problems. For example, Gem's cash flow statement in 1991 reveals that accounts receivable and inventory increased by $32.6 million and $40.8 million, respectively. By focusing on either account, we can determine how much of the increase was due to growth and how much is associated with problems relating to current asset management policies.

For purposes of this exercise, we'll address the accounts receivable dilemma: While a growth-related increase in accounts receivable is to be expected given the growth in sales, the increase related to the change in days receivable is potentially ominous. Ratio analysis has revealed that Gem relaxed credit standards to book more sales. As a result, its average collection period increased from 36 days in 1992 to 55 days in 1993. The net effect of a 19-day, or 53%, swing in the conversion cycle is an eye-opener. If collections continue at this rate or worsen, Gem's cash flow drain will continue to be a major burden.

Our pro forma cash flow statement displays the factors, in this case receivables, that contributed to an unhealthy increase in short-term debt.

Had Gem been able to collect as fast as the industry, 32 days, receivables would have been only $51.5 million generating cash of $37.1 million. This would have paid off their entire short-term debt.

By simply reducing Gem's ACP five days to 50 days (Exhibit 9.2), the improved cash flow comparison can be seen in Exhibit 9.3.

Taking it one step further, as should be done by all prudent bankers always, we introduce the "E" formula into the mix. The "E" formula is a powerful equation that distinguishes the projected amount of internal and external financing requisites of a firm (see chapter on projections). This formula melds perfectly with the banker's cash flow statement since unlike FASB 95, it breaks out Gross Operating Cash Flow. We can now compare GOCF with new debt financing, which in turn is linked directly into the "E" formula.

After calculating the "E" formula for Gem's next forecast period, assume we've determined that internal and external financing needs are 5% and 95%, respec-

tively. This means that Gem's GOCF will be diminutive in comparison to the 95% external financing it currently seeks. This is an immediate danger signal since both "E" and leverage are very high. Another point of interest, how would a banker feel about lending to a company that has a poor return on its assets? Over the past three years, Gem Furniture Company's assets have dramatically spiralled 72%, while net profits have declined 93%. Applying the regular cash flow statement won't disclose this information. If this isn't a lock-in to initially determining risk, I don't know what is!

So, the pro forma summary quickly allows us to determine the cash requirements caused by growth (industry or benchmark standard) or cash drain (which in this specific case is accounts receivable). If the reasons for cash flow drain can be identified, corrective measures can be presented to, and put in place by, the borrower.

Exhibit 9.2

Accounts Receivable Pro Forma Analysis
(In thousands)

Gem's ACP = 55 Days   Industry Average = 32 Days

Improve to 50 Days; the firm cannot reach industry efficiency quickly without disrupting its business.

Results

Accounts Receivable 1990	55,886	
Accounts Receivable 1991	88,571	
Source (Use)	**(32,685)**	
Improved Accounts Receivable 1991	72,357	Receivables tied to improvement (50 days)
Source (Use) Based on 50 Day ACP	**(16,471)**	
Cash Flow Saved	16,214	
Original Short-Term Debt	39,398	
Apply improved cash flow to STD	16,214	Cash realized by faster collection (50 days)
Short-Term Debt After Reduction*	23,184	Lower debt requirements due to improved collection

*Accounts receivable collected in 50 days, down from 55 days

Exhibit 9.3

Gem Furniture Company
Improved Cash Flow (Pro Forma)
(5 day reduction in its average collection period)

	Improved	Original
Net Income	1,965	
Plus/Less: Non-cash items		
Depreciation	6,120	
GROSS OPERATING CASH FLOW	8,085	8,085
(Inc.)/Dec. Net A/R	*(16,471)*	*(32,685)*
(Inc.)/Dec. Inventory	(40,889)	
Operating Cash Needs	(57,360)	(73,574)
(Inc.)/Dec. Net A/P	28,477	
(Inc.)/Dec. Accruals	6,694	
Operating Cash Sources	35,171	35,171
Net Cash Provided by Operating Activities	(14,104)	(30,318)
Capital Expenditures	(8,319)	
Net Cash Used in Investing Activities	(8,319)	
Long-Term Debt	(785)	
Short-Term Debt (A)	*23,184*	*39,398*
Cash Flows from Inerest Bearing Debt	22,399	38,613
Cash Dividends	(266)	
Cash Flows from Other Financing Activities	(266)	
NET CHANGE IN CASH ITEMS	(290)	(290)

(A) Cash from improved average collection period applied to short-term debt reduction.

Knowing the nitty-gritty of cash flow, banks will always have the odds in their favor. Observation tells us that cash flow is the very thing management should focus on, but in many cases overlooks. Within the cash flow context, total comprehension of what produces Gross Operating Cash Flow is imperative. The majority of time spent understanding cash flow should be directed toward this area. More important, it is obvious now that prudent bankers need cash flow to evaluate risk and cannot do without it in making credit decisions.

I admit that cash flow is not an easy topic to grasp at first. Many lenders and investors look at a cash flow statement but can neither appreciate the wealth of information it contains nor decipher what the statement says about a company's prospects. In other words, they are staring at the handwriting on the wall but can't interpret or shy away from its warnings. I think we can now read the handwriting and are ready to move on to our next general topic, forecasting.

■■■

Section III

■■■

Forecasting

■■■

CHAPTER Ten

Role and Techniques of Forecasting in Credit Analysis

This two-chapter section is devoted to forecasting, a subject I consider the core of this book and of the credit analyst's job.

The material in this chapter is intended as a brief review of forecasting fundamentals. It's an essential warm-up for the hard-hitting, money-making techniques discussed in detail in the following chapter.

Up to now, we've discussed the formal planning process from the firm's perspective—with good reason. Sound credit analysis zeros in on evaluating the borrower's ability to repay debt, so it's the bank's responsibility to recognize all internal and external factors influencing corporate strategic planning.

All company projections inherently support requests for external financing. Hence, bank projections have become indispensable to credit analysis. The emphasis on bank forecasts became prominent in the 1980s as demand for large sums of

senior debt dramatically increased to fund mergers and acquisitions. These high-risk players represented a new breed of corporate executives who stretched financial leverage to untested limits. With huge amounts of debt offset by depleted equity many firms producing record EBIT also posted after-tax losses.

To better protect their investments, banks developed formal forecasting techniques to improve credit procedures, predict the borrower's financial condition, and identify future funding requirements.

Let's start with a discussion of forecasting factors. Forecasting factors are introduced as variables to determine the "goodness of fit" of the most accurate forecasting technique available. Major points of reference include: the availability, accuracy and accessibility of comprehensive historical data, the pattern of data received, and the length of the forecasting period being evaluated. The magnitude of each factor will enable the banker to assess the speed and accuracy with which the forecast can be completed, as well as the confidence level and cost effectiveness of each technique considered.

Arguably, the availability of comprehensive, historical data is the most important requirement for developing forecasts, particularly when the information will resolve what forecasting method to use. Since different forecasting techniques require various amounts of historical data, the quantity of data available is important.

The next criterion to consider is the accuracy of available information. In some cases, when credit risks are minor, financial statements are strong and the firm operates in non-vacillating surroundings, a forecast in error by as much as 30 percent may be acceptable. In other situations, a forecast in error by one percent might spell disaster for the bank. Based on the accounting and financial methodologies implemented, close attention should be paid to who submitted the information as well as to the information itself.

What about the pattern of information? Whether it discloses measurable trends, seasonal fluctuations, cyclical components, or some combination of these, analysts must identify the flow of historical data being used to generate a forecast as a comparison to the borrowers' projected results.

Forecasts are developed over a time horizon that ranges from days to ten-year plans. In the book *Forecasting: Methods and Applications* by Spyros Makridakis and Steven C. Wheelwright, information needed for planning financial forecasting is broken down into several time horizons. In the immediate term (less than 1 month), sales revenue, production costs, inventory

costs, leading indicators, cash inflows and outflows are required to make a financial forecast. In the short term (1–3 months), total demand, inventory levels, cash flows, short-term borrowing, and prices are required. In the medium term (3 months–2 years), budget allocations and cash flows dominate the information needs for forecasting, while in the long term (2 years or more), sales, investment selection, allocations of resources, capital programs, and other cash flow information is required.

Once alternative forecasting factors and methods have been weighed, development costs associated with each method are considered. The complexity and cost of these techniques vary. Large money center banks and corporations have spent much money to develop in-house forecast models. Creating spreadsheet models on Lotus or Excel is a less costly alternative.

Quantitative and Qualitative Forecasts

Forecasting techniques are not perfectly efficient. This is significant because individual loans affect the type of forecasts required. Since bankers are held accountable for all judgments pertaining to credit analysis, knowledge of both the qualitative and quantitative aspects of all forecasting techniques must be fully understood. In other words, the expertise displayed in constructing and operating forecasting models is as important as deciphering its conclusions.

Qualitative Techniques

Qualitative forecasting is traditionally used when historical data are scarce or not available. It is mentioned because companies may approach lenders with such forecasts.

Take, for example, a firm's introduction of a new product. Since the potential borrower has no historical sales data to manipulate, how are sales predicted? The likely two sources for sales projections are the firm's marketing and sales departments. The marketing department's job is to create a need or demand for the product, while the sales force creates the "buzz" on the street.

Based on findings from both departments, management settles on a first-month sales projection of 130,000 units. This prediction is simply one number or "point" suggested by the borrower. The type of forecast used is known as a point forecast or "best guess" of the future value of the product or variable in question.

Obviously, point forecasts are often in error and so, if used alone, are unreliable.

But what if the firm includes an estimate of how inaccurate its point projection might be? Such an estimate is supplied by a confidence interval forecast. A confidence interval is a range of values calculated so that the value of the forecast variable will be contained in a specified interval (range). If the firm's margin of error is 5 percent, the actual value or projection will be in a 95 percent confidence interval. If the company forecasts sales of 130,000 units in the first projection month with a 95 percent confidence interval, management is 95 percent sure that sales will fall between 120,000 units and 140,000 units.

Although confidence intervals can be constructed with any desired level of confidence, it is customary to construct 95% confidence intervals.

Another mode, *Basic Methods,* provides forecasts without using a formal forecasting technique. For example, one can use inventory for July as the forecast variable for August's inventory forecast—information easily obtained from the general ledger with no cost and very little effort:

$$\text{Inventory}_{t+1} = \text{Inventory}_t(\text{adjustment factor})$$

The current month's inventory value is used as an estimate for next month's inventory after adjusting for seasonality (the seasonal variation may be eliminated if desired). Thus, basic methods are easily obtained, with little or no cost, but are dangerously unreliable.

Other situations in which historical data are not available might involve predicting if and when new technologies will be discovered and adopted, such as a cure for cancer. Qualitative forecasting techniques are also used to predict changes in historical data patterns. Since the use of historical data to predict future events assumes that the pattern will continue, changes in the data pattern cannot be predicted on the basis of historical data. Thus qualitative methods are often used to predict such changes.

Some qualitative forecasting techniques involve subjective curve fitting. A firm introducing a new product will forecast sales over a specific time horizon to determine the capacity and financing requirements needed to produce the product.

Predicting new product sales requires consideration of the product's life cycle as similar to that of a firm's life cycle. During the first stage or start-up, the company will build productive capacity to get into the marketplace. When the first units leave the plant the firm enters into the growth phase as product sales start slowly, spiral rapidly, and then increase at a slower rate. During the third or maturity stage, product sales stabilize, increasing slowly, reaching a peak, and perhaps even decreasing. During the last or declining phase, sales deteriorate at an increasing rate.

When forecasting sales of the product during the growth stage, the borrower may subjectively construct an S-curve to roughly forecast sales during this stage. The company may gather information from other product lines or draw from their sales and marketing staff's expertise to construct the S-curve. In addition, information referencing the economic and industry environment can be used by management to predict how long it will take for the rapid increase in sales to begin, how long this rapid growth will continue, and when sales of the product will begin to stabilize.

are expected to increase at a slower rate. Exponential and logarithmic curves are covered in the chapter on sustainable growth. Forecasters may even decide to use a quadratic curve. Finding the best subjective curve fit is not all that hard, but it does require sound judgment and a fair amount of "gut knowledge."

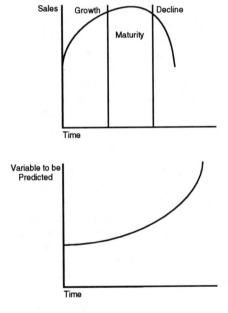

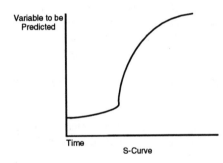

S-Curve

Naturally, one of the biggest problems in using this technique is deciding upon the form of the curve to be used. In predicting a product life cycle, the use of an S curve may be appropriate, but many other functional curves can be substituted. For example, an exponential curve might be suitable when the firm expects that the second stage will be characterized by accelerating growth and management and their lenders make no prediction of when the firm's quickening growth will level off. Other situations might call for the use of a logarithmic curve, for example, when sales

Quantitative Forecast Techniques

Quantitative forecasting methods are grouped into two sections: causal and time series.

The objective is to find a visual lead/lag relationship between the dependent variable and a leading (independent) variable that could subsequently be used in predicting cyclical changes. From a practical point of view, the approach of paired indices can be extremely useful because it provides causal information. It is suggested that the methodologies of multiple regression and econometric modeling can be used to estimate the full explanatory or causal relationships involving the variable(s) being forecast. This can complement time series forecasting if used properly.

Unfortunately, there are problems in applying such explanatory or causal approaches. For example, to predict sales you may decide that GNP and advertising are two factors affecting sales. However, future levels of GNP and advertising must be predicted before sales can be forecast. Thus, even though a perfect relationship may exist between sales and GNP/advertising, it may be of limited forecasting value. The forecasting problem is not necessarily solved by discovering cause and effect relationships.

Time series (easily constructed using available spreadsheet software), the most common forecasting method, encompasses an audit of historical results in an effort to identify a data pattern. Assuming this paradigm will continue indefinitely into the future, the time series forecast technique is calculated by implementing objective mathematical means. In other words, this forecasting model is functional only when future conditions affecting the firm are expected to remain substantially unchanged.

Applied by itself, time series forecasting is an impractical gauge for predicting the impact of changes for a specific lender. For example, if a firm anticipates continued sales growth using its present marketing strategy, it can't account for unexpected events such as fluctuations in consumer demand, industry idiosyncrasies or sensitivity to economic

aberrations. Because of these possibilities the critical (or key) assumptions are initiated. If properly identified and interpreted, the probability of each critical assumption altering a given circumstance can be incorporated into every projection scenario.

When extensive historical data are available, statistical methods are consolidated into the time series forecasting model, assuming that the historical data will contain some sort of stable pattern, such as a trend or seasonal cycle that will continue. With "fairly" accurate data available, patterns will surface for the lender to better judge the direction of a firm. Two examples are: moving averages and exponential smoothing.

Moving Averages

The major objective in using moving averages is to eliminate randomness and to smooth out a time series. This is achieved by averaging several data points together in such a way that positive and negative errors eventually cancel themselves out. The term "moving average" is used because, as each new observation in the series becomes available, the oldest observation is dropped and a new average is computed. The result of calculating the moving average over a set of data points is a new series of numbers with little or no randomness. The ability of moving averages to eliminate randomness is used in time series analysis for two main purposes: a) to eliminate trend; and b) to eliminate seasonality.

Exponential Smoothing

Exponential smoothing methods were developed in the early 1950s. They have become particularly popular among business professionals because they are easy to use, require very little computer time, and need only a few data points to produce future predictions. These smoothing methods are well suited for short or immediate term predictions of a large number of items.

They are suitable for stationary data or when there is a slow growth or decline over time. Exponential smoothing is based on averaging (smoothing) past values of a time series in a decreasing (exponential) manner. In Excel, for example, exponential smoothing averages the smoothed value for the previous period with the actual data for the previous data point. This feature automatically includes all previous periods in the average. You can specify how much to weight the current period.

This chapter has briefly reviewed the background and basic techniques of projection and forecasting. It's just a warm-up for today's more advanced techniques—techniques that make money for the bank and make the credit analyst a valued and well-compensated contributor to the bottom line—techniques you'll find covered in the next chapter.

CHAPTER Eleven

The Real Focus: The Modified Percent of Sales Method

When I state that you can sit with a prospective business borrower and *instantaneously and reliably project financial performance and debt requirements, you may find it hard to believe.*

But the results would be concrete and believable. To start with, you'd save hours of calculation time. Then, you would make money by making the right loans to the right businesses. Your bank would be more successful and so would you!

Well, I am telling you that you can forecast quickly and accurately with a handheld calculator, using the Modified Percent of Sales (MPOS) method.

Note the word "modified." Just plain percent of sales forecasting is not viable because it simply extrapolates historical sales to the future.

The rationale behind MPOS is that most current assets and current liabilities (working capital accounts) tend to vary directly with changes in sales. Whether a firm is restructuring or simply experiencing the prospect of future sales growth, a revision in sales invariably means an adjustment in these assets and liabilities. Therefore, the lender must know the effect a change in sales has on both the balance sheet and income statement before finalizing any projections.

Financial projections are only part of the broader process of assessing a company's strategy. Evaluating the impact of investment, operational, and financing decisions helps formulate financial needs. Financial projections require an accurate account of an organization's current strengths and weaknesses and understanding of future conditions (level of uncertainty). This process involves measuring both internal and external factors (PRISM). To minimize risk, the percent of sales forecasting technique takes into consideration six critical assumptions:

1. Sales
2. Gross profit
3. Accounts receivable
4. Inventory
5. Capital expenditures
6. Operating expenses

By initiating critical assumptions that accurately measure business performance and risk, a loan officer is better able to determine the borrower's ability to satisfy the loan.

Quantifying the critical assumptions, we introduce two equations: the Financial Needs Formula (F) and Projected Percent of Sales Externally Financed Formula (E).

$$(1) \quad F = \frac{A}{S}(\Delta S) + \Delta NFA - \frac{L_1}{S}(\Delta S) - P(S)(1-d) + R$$

The F formula determines the firm's external financing needs. If used in conjunction with the percent of sales method, both techniques will render the same answer.

$$(2) \quad E = \left(\frac{A}{S}^* - \frac{L_1}{S} \right) - \frac{P}{G}(1+G)(1-d) + \frac{R}{\Delta S}$$
* Total Assets

E = Percent of Sales Increase that needs to be externally financed

F = Financial needs (Financing Requirements)

A = Projected Spontaneous Assets

S = Projected Sales

G = Sales Growth Rate

ΔS = Change in Sales

ΔNFA = Change in Net Fixed Assets

L_1 = Spontaneous Liabilities

P = Projected Profit Margin (%)

d = Dividend Payout Rate

R = Scheduled Long-Term Debt Maturities

The E formula identifies the percentage of sales growth requiring external financing. Closely comparing each method, it is evident that the two equations are interconnected. For example, firms with high growth potential are traditionally attractive prospects for lenders. However, a high-growth firm can also be a high-risk firm. Implementing these simple, but effective measures, a bank can quickly assess the risk of lending to a rapidly growing borrower. Although they offer a fast way to quantify whether or not a firm is growing prudently, they are not a substitute for in-depth financial analysis.

To illustrate the modified percent of sales forecasting technique, consider the case study involving Gem Furniture Company. In the ratios chapter, we noted the firm's deteriorating financial condition. A historical analysis three months earlier had revealed that Gem's ratios were in a downward trend, slipping below industry averages despite the fact that the company seemed to be quite successful. While the company had prospered, loans were renewed annually with only cursory analysis.

Let's take a quick snapshot (Exhibit 11.1) of the key conclusions drawn from the ratios chapter.

Accounts receivable average collection period has increased from 18 days to 55 days. This is 23 days higher than the industry average. A review of the company's aging schedule and inventory turnover will likely confirm that the borrower is exchanging one bad asset (unsalable inventory) for another (low-quality receivables).

Exhibit 11.1

Key Ratios: Gem Furniture Company

Balance Sheet	1989	1990	1991	Industry Avg
Current Ratio	3.1x	2.7x	1.8x	2.5x
Quick Ratio	1.7x	1.1x	0.7x	1.0x
Cash/Sales	3.0%	2.2%	2.0%	N/A
Average Collection Period	37	37	55	32
Inventory Turnover	7.1x	4.5x	3.6x	5.7x
Fixed Assets Turnover	11.6x	12.0x	12.1x	12.0x
Accounts Payable/Sales	4.0%	5.7%	10.2%	12.2
Debt/Equity	68.5%	86.8%	149.1%	100%
Income Statement				
Gross Profit Margin	20.09%	17.8%	13.8%	18.0%
Net Profit Margin	5.5%	3.5%	0.3%	2.9%

Accounts payable (as a percentage of sales) reveals an increase from 5.7% to 10.2%. This is worrisome based on the current liquidity problems.

The sharp reduction in both the gross and net profit margin ratios suggest Gem is having problems passing on price increases to its customers.

Gem's seasonal working capital needs were financed by loans from Second City Bank which requires full repayment by February, 1992. Moe Zarchen, Gem president, tells the bank that the present level of sales could not be continued without an increase in the bank loan from $55,000,000 to $65,000,000, since payments of $8,000,000 for construction of a plant addition had to be made in January, 1992.

Well, the inevitable happened and it is now early 1992. Zarchen visited the bank again to push the loan request. He explained that Gem's sales growth was expected to put a strain on working capital and a number of suppliers had recently threatened to put the company on COD for future purchases unless payments were more prompt. When asked how he could reasonably request more money, Zarchen replied that this amount seemed "about right" considering the attempts made to correct the firm's problems.

The bank's loan officer suggested that Zarchen prepare financial forecasts for 1992 through 1996. These projections can be the culmination of intensive, detailed operating plans and budgets, or nothing more than rough projections.

Once the forecasts are reviewed, the bank must assess Gem's financial health and stability as revealed in the financial projections, with major emphasis on financial needs.

Measuring Gem's financial needs means calculating financial leverage (debt/equity ratio). If the firm's financial leverage well exceeds industry averages, the bank will probably not approve the loan. In any case, Gem's business plan must be realistically modified. This is where operating budgets and business plans merge to create a coherent strategy.

To illustrate, Gem has projected annual sales growth of 6%. A decision to reduce its financial needs will entail investigating the following alternative strategies and their impact on the company's external financing requirements:

1. Tighten credit standards and collections so that receivables are 13.8% of sales rather than 15.1%.

2. Improve inventory control. This will decrease inventory to sales to 22.1% from 23.9%, thereby freeing up working capital to be invested in more profitably.

3. Settle for a modest improvement in trade payables so that payables expand to 11.1% of sales rather than 10.21%. This will reduce financing requirements.

4. Tighten expenses not needed to further the interests of the business. In other words, eliminate fat without cutting into the muscle and bone of the operation.

While Second City Bank is aware that these actions reduce financial needs, each strategy has offsetting disadvantages. For example, in make versus buy decisions managers often evaluate the tradeoff between manufacturing key production components and buying the components. Manufacturing often requires an increase in capital expenditures (fixed costs) while buying identical production components from a subcontractor or vendor reduces the gross margin. Thus a make versus. buy decision involves the trade off between fixed asset investments and profit margins.

Without further investigation, the bank cannot say conclusively whether Gem's pro forma operating plan is necessarily better than the original request. If for example, the current ratio is not violating existing loan covenants Zarchen might even try to get the bank to allow for increases in current liabilities through expansion of spontaneous accounts payable and accruals. This strategy would reduce financial needs but increase the ratio of spontaneous liabilities to sales. This is a very unlikely alternative since Gem has already received COD threats from current suppliers.

There is a direct link between the growth of a firm and the financial needs necessary to support current assets. This bares an interesting dilemma for both management and the lender: how much of an investment should be made in current assets and how much should be allocated to short-term and long-term debt?

Our first step involves Gem Furniture's historical financial statments for 1989–91. (See Exhibit 11.2.)

Setting Up the Percent of Sales Method

The asset portion of the balance sheet shows current assets that usually vary proportionately with sales including cash, accounts receivable, prepaid expenses, and inventory.

For instance, if accounts receivable is historically 30 percent of sales, and next year's sales are forecasted to be $100 million, accounts receivable will be projected at $30 million. Fixed assets are normally independent of sales increases. However, while fixed assets are discrete, they can be represented as a percentage of sales if the firm has reached a high level of capacity.

On the right-hand side of the balance sheet, spontaneous liabilities such as ac-

Exhibit 11.2

Gem Furniture Co. Historical

Assets	1989	1990	1991
Cash	$15,445	$12,007	$11,717
Receivables	51,793	55,886	88,571
Inventory	56,801	99,087	139,976
Current Assets	124,039	166,980	240,264
Fixed Assets	44,294	46,340	48,539
Total Assets	**$168,333**	**$213,320**	**$288,803**
Liabilities and Equity			
Short-Term Debt	$9,562	$15,300	$54,698
Payables	20,292	31,518	59,995
Accruals	10,328	15,300	21,994
Current Maturities	500	500	500
Current Liabilities	40,682	62,618	137,187
Long-Term Debt	27,731	36,491	35,706
Total Liabilities	68,413	99,109	172,893
Common Stock	69,807	69,807	69,807
Retained Earnings	30,113	44,404	46,103
Total Liabilities & Equity	**$168,333**	**$213,320**	**$288,803**
Annual Sales	$512,693	$553,675	$586,895
Cost of Goods Sold	405,803	450,394	499,928
Gross Profit	106,890	103,281	86,967
Profit	27,942	18,775	1,965
Dividends	$7,060	$4,464	$266

counts payable and accruals move in tandem with sales and are calculated just as in the accounts receivable example. Interest bearing liabilities such as notes payable, current maturities, and long-term debt are not tied to sales.

Equity, which includes preferred stock, common stock, paid-in-capital, and retained earnings are also isolated from changes in sales. Retained earnings are calculated by deducting the declared dividends from net profits, and adding the balance to previous years retained earnings.

Before we go any further, another important point to make is that the bank must also identify and estimate non-critical variables (not included in this exercise). This is accomplished by extrapolating historical patterns or adjusting historical trends. Examples of non-critical variables include various prepaid assets and other liabilities.

To apply the modified sales percentage method to Gem's 1991 financial statements, the accounts in Exhibit 11.3 have been calculated as a percentage of 1991 sales and will be used as projection assumptions for the company's original five-year strategic plan.

Two outcomes can occur as a result of applying the modified percent of sales method. If liabilities and equity are less than total assets, a cash deficit has occurred. This variance represents the "plug figure" or amount of additional funding required to obtain the predicted sales goals forecasted. This "balancing figure" is entered on the "right side" of the balance sheet below the grand total of liabilities and equity accounts.

However, if the right-hand side of the balance sheet is greater than the left-hand side, the balancing figure is added to current assets as a cash surplus account. This represents funds the firm has available for additional investment, retiring debt, or other expenditures. In Gem's case, let's review the outcome (Exhibit 11.4)—that is, the financial projections Gem submitted to the bank.

As evidenced by the financial needs or "plug" figure, Gem requires additional financing in order to meet expected sales targets in each of the four years projected, if the bank were to go ahead and make the loan.

Variance analysis plays an important role in following Gem's repayment schedule. These data should be updated on a spreadsheet. For example, when the actual numbers are received, they should be logged in next to the projected numbers. You may want to use the statistics program available in spreadsheets like Lotus and Excel to measure the results. If the variance is out of line in relation to peer group companies, the borrower either is trying to fool the bank, is naive about the business or a combination of both. In either case, it's bad news for the lender. It may be a good idea to test the sensitivity of the results to reasonable variations in the sales forecast.

Alternative Strategies

How would the alternative strategies discussed previously in this chapter affect Gem's financial needs (Exhibit 11.5)?

Exhibit 11.3

Projection Assumtpions: Base Case

	1992	1993	1994	1995	1996
Cash	2.0%	2.0%	2.0%	2.0%	2.0%
Receivables	15.1%	15.1%	15.1%	15.1%	15.1%
Inventory	23.9%	23.9%	23.9%	23.9%	23.9%
Fixed Assets	8.3%	8.3%	8.3%	8.3%	8.3%
Accounts Payable	10.2%	10.2%	10.2%	10.2%	10.2%
Accruals	3.7%	3.7%	3.7%	3.7%	3.7%
Sales Growth Rate	6.0%	6.0%	6.0%	6.0%	6.0%
Profit Margin	1.0%	1.0%	1.0%	1.0%	1.0%
Dividend Payout	25.0%	25.0%	25.0%	25.0%	25.0%
Loan Amortization	$500.0	$500.0	$500.0	$500.0	$500.0

Exhibit 11.4

| Gem Furniture Company
Projected Statements
Year Ended December 31 | This exhibit should be read along with Exhibit 11.6 | | | | |

** Note: calculation carried out 5 decimal places to generate projection

INCOME STATEMENT:	1992	1993	1994	1995	1996
Sales ** [Sales 1991 (.06)]	$622,108.7	$659,435.2	$699,001.3	$740,941.4	$785,397.9
Profits [.01 ($622,108.7)]	$6,221.1	$6,594.4	$6,990.0	$7,409.4	$7,854.0
Dividends [.25 ($6,221.1)]	$1,555.3	$1,648.6	$1,747.5	$1,852.4	$1,963.5
BALANCE SHEET					
Cash [.02 ($622,108.7)]	$12,442.2	$13,165.2	$13,955.1	$14,792.4	$15,680.0
Receivables [.151 ($622,108.7)]	$93,885.3	$99,518.4	$105,489.5	$111,818.8	$118,528.0
Inventory [.239 9($622,108.7)]	$148,374.6	$157,277.0	$166,713.7	$176,716.5	$187,319.5
Current Assets	$254,702.0	$269,960.6	$286,158.3	$303,327.8	$321,527.4
Fixed Assets [.083 ($622,108.7)]	$51,451.3	$54,538.4	$57,810.7	$61,279.4	$64,956.1
Total Assets	$306,153.3	$324,499.1	$343,969.0	$364,607.1	$386,483.6
LIABILITIES, FINANCIAL NEEDS AND EQUITY					
Short-Term Debt [not tied to sales]	$54,698.0	$54,698.0	$54,698.0	$54,698.0	$54,698.0
Payables [.102 ($622,108.7)]	$63,567.7	$67,410.4	$71,455.0	$75,742.3	$80,286.8
Accruals [.037 ($622,108.7)]	$23,313.6	$24,712.5	$26,195.2	$27,766.9	$29,432.9
Current Maturity [not tied to sales]	$500.0	$500.0	$500.0	$500.0	$500.0
Current Liabilities	$142,106.3	$147,320.8	$152,848.2	$158,707.2	$164,917.8
Long-Term Debt [not tied to sales]	$35,206.0	$34,706.0	$34,206.0	$33,706.0	$33,206.0
Common Stock [not tied to sales]	$69,807.0	$69,807.0	$69,807.0	$69,807.0	$69,807.0
Retained Earnings [1991 R/E + $6221.1 – $1555.3]	$50,768.8	$55,714.6	$60,957.1	$66,514.2	$72,404.6
Financial Needs ** [Plug]	$8,265.2	$16,950.6	$26,150.7	$35,872.8	$46,148.2
Liabilities and Equity	$306,153.3	$324,499.1	$343,969.0	$364,607.1	$386,483.6

Exhibit 11.5

OUTPUT SCREEN: FINANCIAL PROJECTIONS (thousands)

Gem Furniture Company
Projected Statements
Year Ended December 31

Scenario Two
Tighten Up Assets, Increased Accounts Payable
Strategies to Reduce Financial Needs

INCOME STATEMENT:

	1992	1993	1994	1995	1996
Sales	$622,108.7	$659,435.2	$699,001.3	$740,941.4	$785,397.9
Profits	$6,221.1	$6,594.4	$6,990.0	$7,409.4	$7,854.0
Dividends	$1,555.3	$1,648.6	$1,747.5	$1,852.4	$1,963.5

BALANCE SHEET

	1992	1993	1994	1995	1996
Cash	$12,442.2	$13,165.2	$13,955.1	$14,792.4	$15,680.0
Receivables	$86,108.0	$91,274.5	$96,751.0	$102,556.1	$108,709.4
Inventory	$137,683.4	$145,944.4	$154,701.1	$163,983.1	$173,822.1
Current Assets	$236,233.6	$250,384.1	$265,407.2	$281,331.6	$298,211.5
Fixed Assets	$51,451.3	$54,538.4	$57,810.7	$61,279.4	$64,956.1
Total Assets	$287,685.0	$304,922.6	$323,217.9	$342,611.0	$363,167.7

LIABILITIES, FINANCIAL NEEDS AND EQUITY

	1992	1993	1994	1995	1996
Short-Term Debt	$54,698.0	$54,698.0	$54,698.0	$54,698.0	$54,698.0
Payables	$69,265.7	$73,421.6	$77,826.9	$82,496.6	$87,446.4
Accruals	$23,313.6	$24,712.5	$26,195.2	$27,766.9	$29,432.9
Current Maturity	$500.0	$500.0	$500.0	$500.0	$500.0
Current Liabilities	$147,777.3	$153,332.1	$159,220.1	$165,461.5	$172,077.3
Long-Term Debt	$12,433.0	$11,933.0	$11,433.0	$10,933.0	$10,433.0
Common Stock	$69,807.0	$69,807.0	$69,807.0	$69,807.0	$69,807.0
Retained Earnings [1991 R/E + $6221.1 −$1555.3]	$50,768.8	$55,714.6	$60,957.1	$66,514.2	$72,404.6
Financial Needs **	$6,898.8	$14,135.9	$21,800.7	$29,895.4	$38,445.7
Liabilities and Equity	$287,685.0	$304,922.6	$323,217.9	$342,611.0	$363,167.7

1. Again, tighten up credit standards and collection of accounts receivable so that receivables are 13.8% of sales rather than 15.1%.

2. Improve inventory holding period to 22.1% of sales from 23.9%.

3. Settle for a more modest improvement in trade payables so that payables expand to 11.1% of sales rather than 10.2%.

These strategies reduce financial needs in the first projection period from $8,265.2 to $6,898.8 and cumulative financial needs from $46,148.2 to $38,445.7.

Back to variance analysis: The comparative variance analysis of the hypothetical Kevin's and Bill's furniture companies illustrate this technique:

With average variance −9.3%, standard deviation of 18.8% and correlation of .77, Bill's Furniture results are off target. Kevin's Furniture correlates .99 projected to actual sales (correlation coefficient of 1 is perfect), hitting the mark each month.

Reintroducing the F and E equations, conclusions drawn from the modified percent of sales method can be further analyzed and verified:

$$F = \frac{A}{S}(\Delta S) + \Delta NFA - \frac{L_1}{S}(\Delta S)$$
$$- P(S)(1 - d) + R$$

F	= Financial Needs
A	= Projected Spontaneous Assets
ΔS	= Projected Sales
ΔS	= Change in Sales
G	= Sales Growth Rate
ΔNFA	= Change in Net Fixed Assets

	Kevin's Furniture			Bill's Furniture	Percentage	
	Projection	Actual	Variance	Projection	Actual	Variance
January	1,463	1,475	0.8%	674	450	−33.2%
February	1,545	1,520	−1.6%	694	850	22.5%
March	1,675	1,692	1.0%	776	677	−12.8%
April	1,782	1,775	−0.4%	779	923	18.5%
May	1,983	1,998	0.8%	801	401	−49.9%
June	2,012	1,995	−0.8%	801	900	12.4%
July	1,965	1,945	−1.0%	801	760	−5.1%
August	1,545	1,530	−1.0%	923	830	−10.1%
September	2,097	2,107	0.5%	935	1,100	17.6%
October	2,143	2,134	−0.4%	987	678	−31.1%
November	2,980	3,105	4.2%	1,023	740	−27.7%
December	3,543	3,565	0.6%	1,777	1,546	−13.0%
Total	24,733	24,841		10,971	9,855	
Average			0.2%			−9.3%
Average Deviation						

Correlation	Kevin's Furniture			Correlation Bill's Furniture	
	Column 1	Column 2		Column 1	Column 2
Column 1	1		Column 1	1	
Column 2	0.99	1	Column 2	0.77	1

L$_1$ = Spontaneous Liabilities
P = Projected Profit margin (%)
d = Dividend Payout Rate
R = Scheduled Long-Term Debt
Maturities

F = .4094 (35214) + 2912.3 – .1397 (35214)
– .01 (622109) (1–.25) + 500 = 8244

The results yield exactly the same financial needs as the *Lotus* projected financial statements (The formula's a time saver and money maker. I programmed the E and F formulae into the "solver" of my HP19 II financial calcuator. Note that financial needs generated by our hand-held calculation is very close to the computer based forecast).

By performing sensitivity analysis on the F equation, we can determine the effects on Gem's financial needs when certain variables are adjusted.

The first test involves changes in spontaneous asset levels. Currently, Gem's investment in spontaneous assets is projected at 40.9% of sales. If spontaneous assets levels decrease, the overall effect on financial needs or F will also decrease. For example, trimming A/S to 38% of sales will reduce financing requirements to 7,208.

The second sensitivity variable is spontaneous liabilities. If Gem's spontaneous liabilities are increased from the current level of 14%, F will decrease. For example, by increasing accruals (a source of cash), financial needs will decrease as it approaches or surpasses assets levels.

What would be the overall effect if sales decreased? It makes sense that reduced sales projections require less financing and result in reduced external support. The same theory holds true for the dividend rate. By lowering the dividend payout ratio, additional funds will be funneled back

into the company (retained earnings). With additional internal funds available to support future needs, credit requirements will be lower. Lenders like to see companies that have the ability to support the majority of funding with internal sources.

$$E = \left(\frac{A}{S} - \frac{L_1}{S}\right) - \frac{P}{G}(1 + G)(1 - d) + \frac{R}{\Delta S}$$

E = .492122 – .1397 – .01 /.06 (1 + .06)(1–.25) + .014 = .234
where:
E = Projected Percentage of Sales Growth That Must Be Externally Financed
G = Sales Growth Rate
A/S = Total Assets/Sales

Thus, 23.4% percent of Gem's sales growth will be generated by external financing with 76.6% generated by internal cash flow (.234 × 35213 = 8244, same answer as above).

As the name of the formula suggests, the E equation determines how much of the sales growth requires external financing. The higher the percentage in relation to the debt to equity ratio, the more difficult it will be for lenders to take on the onus of risk.

■　■　■

Probably the most critical test in credit analysis is the comparison of E to financial leverage. If your customer wants financing on a project that results in a very high forecasted E—say 90% against base fiscal leverage—that goes above the industry average . . . watch out.

■　■　■

What if E is set to zero solving for G (the sales growth rate)? This will require Gem to reassess variables to determine how projections can be supported with internal funds only. For example, setting E

Exhibit 11.6   This exhibit is computer generated and is connected to Exhibit 11.4

Deriving Financial Needs Using The "F" and "E" Equations

Gem Furniture Company: Base Case Projection

FINANCIAL NEEDS (F): *(Note: Fixed Assets are Included In A/S)*

F = A/S (ΔS) – L1/S (ΔS) – P(S)(1 – d) + R   [Program this formula into the HP-19BII calculator]

F = .4094 (35214) + 2912.3 –.1397 (35214) –.01 (622109) (1 – .25) + 500 = 8244

The formula yields almost identical financial needs as Gem's financial projections in Exhibit 11.4

	1992	1993	1994	1995	1996
F1 =	8,244.3	8,707.6	9,200.1	9,722.1	10,275.4
F =	**8,244.3**	**16,951.9**	**26,151.9**	**35,874.0**	**46,149.4**

	1992	1993	1994	1995	1996
A/S =	49.2%	49.2%	49.2%	49.2%	49.2%
T =	6.0%	6.0%	6.0%	6.0%	6.0%
L1/S =	14.0%	14.0%	14.0%	14.0%	14.0%
R/ΔS =	1.4%	1.3%	1.3%	1.2%	1.1%
L =	153.9%	158.5%	163.0%	167.5%	171.8%

PERCENT OF SALES EXTERNALLY FINANCED (E):

E = (A/S – L1/S) – (P/G)(1 + G) (1 – d) + R/ΔS   [Program this formula into the HP-19BII calculator]

E = .492122 –.1397 –.01/.06 (1 + .06)(1 – .25) + .014 = .234

	1992	1993	1994	1995	1996
E =	23.4%	23.3%	23.3%	23.2%	23.1%

23.4% of Gem's sales growth will be financed externally.

And so, .23412 (35214) = 8244 which is exactly the financial needs using the "F" formula

	1992	1993	1994	1995	1996
PROOF:	8,244.3	8,707.6	9,200.1	9,722.1	10,275.4
E * ΔS =	8,244.3	16,951.9	26,151.9	35,874.0	46,149.4
CUMULATIVE					

Summary

Method	System	Advantages	"F" First Year	"F" Cumulative
Projected Financial Statements (see Exhibit 11.4)	Computer	Provides forecasted financial statements.	8,265.2	46,149.4
"F" Equation	Financial Calculator	Derives financial need quickly and allows bankers to perform sensitivity analysis.	8,244.3	46,149.4
"E" Equation	Financial Calculator	Used with "F" equation determines if borrower is providing sufficient internally generated funds.	8,244.3	46,149.4

at zero shows that Gem is capable of a 2.1% sales growth rate financed internally.

Critical Assumptions

Critical (or important) assumptions are both quantitative and qualitative. Key areas of concentration include: past performance, expectations about the future, and considerations within the industrial and macroeconomic framework.

It is important to recognize how critical assumptions affect the final credit decision. How does the bank know whether or not Gem is capable of increasing its debt capacity and repaying the loan? Or if Gem is able to manage its current credit situation? What is the risk/reward factor for the bank?

From the standpoint of calculating Gem's projections, only the availability and accuracy of Gem's data has been confirmed. Further evaluation of the company's strengths and weaknesses is needed to assess the "true" quality behind the projections. Consequent insights into sales assumptions and the manner in which the operation is run may shed new light on the whole situation. For example, you may judge that sales projections are too low or that better current asset management policies will generate additional internal cash flows. Whatever the case, the results will give the bank a perspective from which to finalize its credit decision.

Critical Assumption #1: The Sales Forecast

Arguably, projecting sales is the most important, and often the most complex, aspect of strategic planning. Sales projections yield best case (optimistic), most likely (probable) and worst case (conservative) scenarios that define the borrower's feasi-

bility region. Recognizing and substantiating this region will give the lender both upside and downside potential to support the final credit judgment.

Usually, the "most likely" sales assumption is the first selected for validation. If the sales projection seems reasonable given the methodology used by the borrower, the feasibility region based on the extreme points should be in line. Remember, sales is the most important constraint in the forecast mix since it manipulates all other forecasting variables to finalize a projection. In other words, sales must be as accurate a picture of the future as possible.

The belief that projecting sales ranks as the number one priority of financial planning is based on external factors that influence a firm to varying degrees, as well as the integrated effect sales has on an organization. Again, an operating budget is only as accurate as the sales it is based on. Therefore, the point of origin in any financial plan is the sales forecast.

The Economy: Uncontrollable Factors

Generally, forecasting economic trends is broken down into two areas: leading economic indicators and turning point predictions. The first involves continuation of existing conditions (such as housing starts if the borrower is in home construction), or disposable income in a population center of particular interest to a retailer. As with any data gathered, it is also important to look at the quality behind the numbers.

Other External Factors

Other external factors which affect sales include, but are not limited to: industry demand; industry supply; competitor pricing policy; competitor advertising policy; raw material availability; government spending; weather characteristics such as precipitation and temperature. Often thrown into the mix are environmental factors related to the physical environment such as pollution and infrastructure; social variables including laws, health concerns, and of late the very popular life style trends. Consider also:

- Competitive conditions and market share:
  - Fashion and technology
  - Patents
  - Foreign competition (tariffs, quotas, etc.)
  - Supply conditions
  - Barriers to industry entry
- Historical patterns—stable versus cyclical
- Stage in life cycle—growth versus mature market
- Potential mergers, acquisitions or diversification
- Regulatory environment

The Company: Controllable Factors

Controllable variables which affect sales are directly influenced by management decisions and policies. These include: product pricing; change in product mix (diversification); advertising; raw material purchases; production; order backlogs and interim financial statements; finished goods inventory; credit; accounts receivable; and research and development. A strong management team will carry a lot of weight in the decision-making process, and its results are usually reflected in the financial statements during both good economic times and bad.

Critical Assumption #2: Gross Profit

Production standards and the resources necessary to meet production criteria can be established on the basis of sales projected for a specified time. Production requirements are physical unit estimates of output; resources used to manufacture the borrower's product(s) are measured in terms of units of input. Price projections for units of input are necessary so that a monetary value can be consolidated into the forecast to give management a good idea of production expenditure requirements. Thus, the gross profit or gross margin can be calculated (sales less the cost of goods sold). To determine if the borrower's gross margin will be as efficient as possible, review the following criteria:

1. Direct Materials—Part of a firm's finished product. How stable are supply and price in the projection period?

2. Direct Labor—Costs physically traced to the product's creation. What will the company's status be in terms of unions, contract expiration dates, and labor relations history?

3. Manufacturing Overhead—All costs of manufacturing with the exception of direct material and direct labor costs. Are the costs associated with operating the facility compatible with reaching sales goals?

4. Changes in automation, substitution of capital for labor, technology and its effect on costs.

5. Plant Capacity—Is it physically possible to meet expected production requirements with the resources at hand?

6. Operating Leverage—A high degree of operating leverage implies a relatively small change in unit output and sales will result in a larger than proportionate change in net operating income. The ratio of variable costs to fixed costs help determine the degree of operating leverage.

Critical Assumption #3: Accounts Receivable Management

Accounts receivable policy is closely tied to inventory management, since the two are part of the conversion cycle and are the largest current asset accounts. Virtually equal in amount, together they make up almost 80 percent of current assets and over 30 percent of total assets for manufacturing industries.

Critical Assumption #4: Inventory Management

Inventory management is vitally important as part of the overall cycle of cash flows. The Economic Order Quantity is a widely used mathematical model in business and has general applicability beyond inventory (i.e., cash management). Good inventory control starts with the fundamental understanding of the three stages of inventory: Raw materials, work-in-process and finished goods.

Critical Assumption #5: Capital Expenditures

One of the major determinants of business success is today's investment policy. In well-managed firms, the process starts at the strategic level when senior management determines the businesses it will compete against and the means of competition. Operating managers translate these strategic goals into concrete action plans involving specific investment proposals.

Critical Assumption #6: Operating Expenses

This assumption considers expenses deducted from the gross margin to determine a firm's net income or net profit. Operating expenses are basically broken down into selling and administrative expenses. Expenses include advertising, promotion, R & D, career training and administrative overhead.

It is important to see how much they weigh as a percentage of sales, and the impact they have on net profits. Of all the areas in a company, this can be the easiest one to control by maintaining a "low-fat" corporate diet.

Sensitivity Analysis: Adjusting the Critical Assumptions

Computer financial spreadsheets like Excel and Lotus have greatly increased the popularity of using sensitivity analysis in business decisions. Once the basic pro forma forecast is complete, additional trials based on revised assumptions can be spun out in seconds.

However, a well-thought-out sensitivity computation is anything but rote. For example, if you reduce the borrower's sales 10 percent, you should carefully rethink each of the other variables that depend on sales.

Regression

Regression methods are governed by statistics. That is, historical data determine future results. For example, we can plot actual inventory levels associated with year's sales on a scatter diagram. With this information, we can fit a straight line through the data—a line that comes closest to each of the points so that the sum of the squares of the vertical distances from the points to the line be made as small as possible. The technique of calculating this line and its equation is referred to as the method of least squares. Two points that will lie directly on the line are the mean X and Y values. The effect of regression is to minimize the sum of the squared error terms, $e(t)$, between actual and derived data. Regression also gives added consideration to data which significantly deviates from the average because of the effect produced by the squaring of error terms. Excel, Lotus, and other spreadsheet regression programs work by calculating the best fit equation for the straight line as well as the best curve fit that passes through the data. You'll find out how to do this by referring to your Lotus or Excel manuals. Meanwhile, see Exhibit 11.7.

What's New and Advanced

Up to this point in this chapter on forecasting, I've been concentrating on telling you how to make money today with rapid and reliable projections based on the Modified Percentage of Sales concept locking in the F and E equations. Now, we're going to take a look at some of the more advanced techniques which have been emerging and undergoing refinement. We'll review the current status of regression, simulation, and confidence intervals and see what promise they hold. I'll tell you now, the benefits are substantial, just ask any CFO or treasurer of a Fortune 500 company.

Comparison between Percent of Sales and Regression

Regression techniques are limited because regression affecting last year's sales will affect future years' sales to the same extent. Regression techniques such as trend analy-

Exhibit 11.7

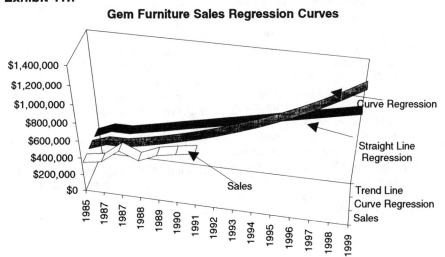

Gem Furniture Sales Regression Curves

sis do not allow the analyst to observe any one variable, or group of variables, and their associated influence on financial needs. As long as such limitations are kept in mind trend analysis provides a widely accepted point of origin from which other key information will ultimately be derived. Modified percent of sales often uses regression techniques as a jumping off point. That is, regression may be thought of as a subset of the larger percent of sales method.

Modified percent of sales requires experience and judgment in developing all critical assumptions. Once all critical assumptions are analyzed, it is the lender's responsibility to arrive at a conclusion regarding the loan request.

This requires zeroing in on all risk-adjusted information in order to determine risk/rewards. Approving a loan based on projection extrapolation alone is dangerous to the future of the bank and your career.

Simulation

Let's examine how to develop a simulation, an elaborate, computer-assisted extension of sensitivity analysis. Simulations have become extremely valuable forecasting tools. Lenders perform simulations easily, using spreadsheet applications like *Crystal Ball* developed by Decisioneering Inc. *Crystal Ball* is a forecasting and risk analysis tool that enhances the decision-making process through the power of simulation. It gives the lender the ability to answer questions such as, "Will the borrower stay under budget if they build this facility?" or, "What are the chances this project will finish on time?" or, "How likely is the firm

to achieve this level of profitability and remain in compliance with term loan covenants?"

Introducing the technique known as "Monte Carlo" simulation, an entire range of results and confidence levels are feasible for any given situation. The principle behind Monte Carlo simulation comprises real world situations involving elements of uncertainty too complex to be solved analytically. It is a simple technique that requires only a random number or a random number generator on a computer. *Crystal Ball* manipulates the Monte Carlo simulation technique to generate random numbers for the assumption cells the decision maker has defined. Using these random numbers, *Crystal Ball* computes the formulas in the forecast cells. This is a continuous process that recalculates each forecast formula over and over again.

In summary, to perform a simulation, a probability distribution is assigned to each uncertain element in the forecast. The distribution describes the possible values the variable could conceivably take on, and it states the probability of each value occurring. The next step is to have the software randomly pick a value for each uncertain variable associated with an assigned probability distribution. The software will generate a set of financials based on the values selected. This creates one *trial*. Performing this step many times produces a large number of trials. The output from a simulation is a table, or a graph, summarizing the results of many trials. For example, the output from a simulation study of Gem Furniture's financial needs for 1992 involving 1,000 trials might be the following shown in Exhibit 11.8.

Exhibit 11.8

Crystal Ball **Summary Analysis**
Varying the profit margin between 0.0% and 2.0%
effect on the firm's financial needs
(see worksheet Exhibit 11.9)

	1992	1993	1994	1995	1996
Mean Financial Needs**	8,293.9	16,639.6	25,775.3	35,474.3	**45,519.2**
Standard Deviation	2,7683.4	4,082.5	5,127.5	6,068.2	**7,033.8**
Range Minimum	3,606.2	7,996.4	12,538.1	18,194.2	**25,856.1**
Range Maximum	12,902.1	25,879	40,115.6	52,299.6	**67,948.3**
5% prob Financial Needs >	12,505.6	23,673.5	34,186.5	45,933.3	**57,284.9**

The range of *Crystal Ball's* software is indicated by the forecast of Gem's financial needs in 1996. (See Exhibit 11.9.)

Varying Gem's profit margin between 2% and 0% (we could have just as easily simulated a profit margin spread between 2% and negative 5%—with dire results!) suggests that there is a 5% chance that Gem's financial needs will exceed $12.5 million in the first projection period, and $57.3 million by 1996. Well, if that kind of borrowing causes risk to break

through the roof we might be looking at a 5% probability of bankruptcy.

Now, let's see how simulation works in a typical situtation as we work through the case study that follows. We'll apply this powerful forecasting technique to Gem Furniture Co. Gem will use Monte Carlo simulation to help decide whether to scrap the project or to proceed to develop and market the innovative product. The project is a multimillion dollar risk.

Traditional forecasting techniques cannot begin to tackle this assignment.

Exhibit 11.9

Simulation Output: 1996
Varying the Profit Margin between 0.0 and 2.0%
effect on the firm's financial needs

Forecast: Financial Needs 1996

Statistics:	Value
Trials	1000
Mean	$45,704.6
Median (approx.)	$45,519.2
Mode (approx.)	$51,742.8
Standard Deviation	$7,033.8
Variance	$49,474,426.8
Skewness	0.04
Kurtosis	2.79
Coeff. of Variability	0.15
Range Minimum	$25,856.1
Range Maximum	$67,948.3
RangeWidth	$42,092.2
Mean Std. Error	$222.43

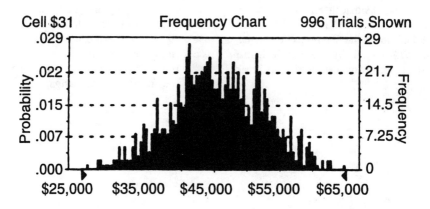

Cell $31   Frequency Chart   996 Trials Shown

Percentiles

Percentile	Value (approx.)
0%	$25,856.0
5%	$34,087.5
25%	$40,995.3
50%	$45,519.2
75%	$50,924.3
95%	$57,284.9
100%	$67,948.3

■   ■   ■

Case Study: Simulation Analysis

Gem's New Project

In an effort to turn the company around, Gem developed an "ingenious" therapeutic bed and mattress. Prototypes could be completed and tested in a number of hospitals and nursing homes within six months. Gem is uncertain whether enough hospitals will approve the product based on preliminary in-house test results projecting a 25% improvement or benefit to patients. Unfamiliar with any health standards, Gem considers 25% only a marginal success.

This venture seems filled with uncertainty although Gem's marketing department feels a simulation is in order. For starters, this undertaking departs from Gem's traditional manufacturing lines. In addition, Gem is uncertain of the product's appeal to its primary customers: the hospitals and nursing homes. Is this a last ditch effort to survive? If this is the case, can Gem expect any financial support?

Gem used *Crystal Ball* to help decide whether to scrap the project or proceed to develop and market the newly designed bed and therapeutic mattress.[1]

Defining Testing Costs: The Uniform Distribution (A)

Year-to-date, Gem Furniture Company has allocated $10,000,000 to research and development specifically for the therapeutic bed and mattress. Further, it expects to spend an additional $3,000,000 to $5,000,000 to test market it. These figures are based on the cost of previous product testing and are considered reasonable. For the variable "testing costs," Gem believes any value between $3,000,000 and $5,000,000 has an equal chance of representing the actual cost of testing. Using Crystal Ball, Gem has chosen the uniform distribution to interpret the testing costs. Uniform distribution describes a situation where all values between the minimum and maximum values have an equal chance of occurrence. The distribution best describes the cost of testing the new product.

Defining Marketing Costs: The Triangular Distribution (B)

Gem's promotion department plans to budget a sizable expenditure to marketing the bed and mattress venture if the proposal is approved by the Health Department. In addition to an extensive advertising campaign, Gem expects to hire and train a large sales force to educate the medical profession on the uses and benefits of its exciting new product. Including sales commissions and advertising costs, Gem Furniture expects to spend between $12,000,000 and $18,000,000; most likely $16,000,000. Gem chooses the triangular distribution to describe marketing costs

---

1 This case study was developed by the author and Decisioneering Inc., the developers of *Crystal Ball* Simulation Software. The case is printed with permission of the developer.

Gem Therapeutic Furniture Project		Suggested Distributions:
Cost (in millions):		
Development Cost of Therapeutic Furniture to Date	$15.000	
Testing Costs	$6.000	Uniform (A)
Marketing Costs	$18.000	Triangular (B)
Total Costs	$39.000	
Drug Test (sample of 100 patients):		
Patients Convalesced	100	Binomial (C)
Health Department Approved if 20 or More Patients Convalesced	TRUE	
Market Study (in millions):		
Persons in U.S. with Orthopedic Disorders Today	40	
Growth Rate in Orthopedic Disorders	2.00%	Custom (D)
Persons with Orthopedic Disorders after One Year	40.8	
Gross Profit on Dosages Sold:		
Market Penetration (New York Market)	8.00%	Normal (E)
Profit Per Customer in Dolars	$12.00	
Gross Profit if Approved (mm)	$39.168	Forecast cell
Net Profit (mm)	$0.168	Forecast cell

since the triangular distribution describes a situation where the firm can estimate the best case, worst case, and most likely scenarios.

Defining Patients Convalesced: The Binomial Distribution (C)

Before the State Health Department will approve the product, Gem Furniture Company must conduct a controlled test on a sample of 100 patients for a period of one year. The Health Department has stipulated that Gem's application will be approved if findings conclude 20 or more patients (20%) improved or benefited from the product. Gem Furniture is very encouraged by their preliminary in-house testing which has disclosed a success rate of around 25% for the same sample size.

For this variable, "patients improved," Gem Furniture only knows that their preliminary testing shows an improvement rate of 25%. The next question is "will the new product meet health standards"? Using *Crystal Ball*, Gem Furniture chooses the binomial distribution to describe the uncertainties in this situation because the Binomial distribution describes the number of successes (25) in a fixed number of trials (100).

Defining Growth Rate: The Custom Distribution (D)

Gem Furniture has projected that 40,000,000 people in the United States are currently afflicted with back ailments and that an additional 0% to 5% will develop this condition during the test year. However, the marketing department has learned that there is a 25% chance that a competing product will be available soon, possibly shrinking Gem's potential market by 5%.

This variable, "growth rate of back problems," cannot be described by any of the standard probability distributions. The uncertainties in this situation require a unique approach. Gem Furniture chose *Crystal Ball*'s custom distribution to represent all the uncertainties surrounding this situation because the custom distribution describes situations that cannot be described using other distribution types.

Defining Market Penetration: The Normal Distribution (E)

The marketing department estimates its company total market share for this product will be normally distributed around a mean value of 8% with a standard deviation of 2%. "Normally distributed" means Gem Furniture expects to see the familiar bell-shaped curve with about 68% of all possible values for market penetration falling between one standard deviation below the mean value and one standard deviation above the mean value, or between 6% and 10%. The low mean value of 870 is a conservative estimate that takes into account some of the problems with the bed and mattress during preliminary testing. In addition, the marketing department estimates a minimum market of 5%, given the interest shown in the product during preliminary testing. Gem Furniture chooses the normal distribution to describe the variable "market penetration."

The president of Gem would like to know the likelihood of achieving a profit on the product.

The forecast charts (Exhibits 11.10 and 11.11) show the certainty range for the forecast. By default, the certainty range includes all values from negative infinity to positive infinity. *Crystal Ball* compares the number of values in the certainty range with the number of values in the entire range to calculate the certainty level. In the upper right corner of the forecast chart, Crystal Ball shows the number of trials. This indicates the number of trials currently being shown in the display range.

Analyzing the Net Profit forecast chart (Exhibit 11.10), it is evident the value range between the end-point grabbers shows a certainty level of 32.6%. That means that Gem can be 32.6% certain of losing money on the project. The chance of making money on the project is 76.4% (100% minus 32.6%). In addition, the firm wanted to know the certainty of achieving a loss below $3 million (Exhibit 11.11). *Crystal Ball* moves the right end point grabber to $3,000 and recalculates the certainty level. Gem can be 43.29% certain of generating results below $3 million.

Exhibit 11.10

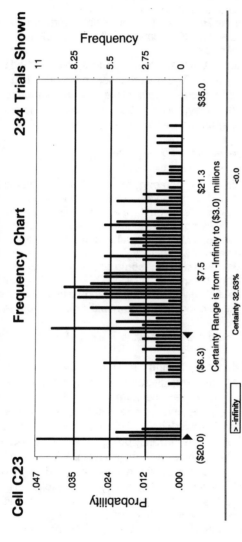

Forecast: Net Profit (MM) Frequency Chart

Cell C23   **Frequency Chart**   **234 Trials Shown**

Certainty Range is from -Infinity to ($3.0) millions

Certainty 32.63%   <0.0

>-Infinity

Forecast: Net Profit (MM)			
Statistic	Value		
Trials	234		
Mean	$3.80	Kurtosis	2.84
Median (approx.)	$4.00	Coeff. of Variability	2.99
Mode (approx.)	($19.70)	Range Minimum	($20.00)
Standard Deviation	$11.40	Range Maximum	$30.50
Variance	$130.80	Range Width	$50.50
Skewness	-0.26	Mean Std. Error	$0.75

Exhibit 11.11

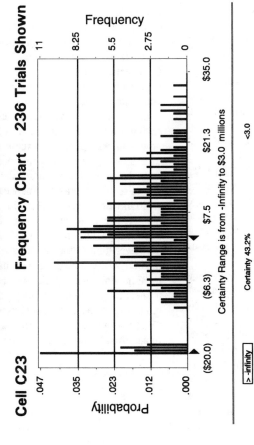

Forecast: Net Profit (MM) Frequency Chart

Cell C23   Frequency Chart   236 Trials Shown

Forecast: Net Profit (MM)			
Statistic	Value		
Trials	236		
Mean	$3.90	Kurtosis	2.87
Median (approx.)	$4.00	Coeff. of Variability	2.96
Mode (approx.)	($19.70)	Range Minimum	($20.00)
Standard Deviation	$11.60	Range Maximum	$32.30
Variance	$133.50	Range Width	$52.30
Skewness	–0.21	Mean Std. Error	$0.75

Since the probabilities of loss fall below a threshold margin, the project was scrapped. In light of Gem's current financial and operating problems, taking on the project would likely increase leverage beyond a tolerable range and would make it very difficult to obtain financing for the project.

■   ■   ■

A Brief Look to the Future

Eric Weissmann, Decisioneering's President, suggests that lenders might establish criteria such as (a) loans that exhibit greater than a 3% chance of default will not be made or (b) financial projections that exhibit an 80% level of certainty will be used.

A very good application for simulation involves helping banks set loan portfolio (concentration) policy. The focus is not *specific* loan risk but risks to a bank's capital caused by portfolio concentrations in particular categories of loans (e.g., large loans, geographically concentrated loans, or industrially concentrated loans). A major accounting firm has done some work in this area, but the jury is still out.

In a nutshell, the principal advantage of simulation over simple sensitivity analysis is that all of the uncertain input variables are allowed to vary at once. The principal disadvantage of simulation, now is that the results may be hard for bankers to interpret. One reason is that few lenders are used to thinking about future events in terms of a range of possible outcomes or probabilities of outcomes. This will change as simulation software becomes an integral part of credit analysis.

Confidence Intervals

Finally, let's develop the notion of confidence intervals a bit more. Suppose your borrower wants a loan to finance the development of additional productive capacity at some future date, and assume also

Crystal Ball establishes that a 95 percent confidence interval for monthly sales one year from now is between 200,000 and 240,000. If current monthly capacity is more than 240,000 units, the upper level of confidence interval, the borrower can be very sure that it need not invest in additional capacity. The bank might respond by saying. "Why borrow now? If you borrow now you will purchase excess capacity. Your loan exposure will increase, eating up more leverage. Furthermore, the internal rate of return generated by new equipment will fall below the cost of capital.

However, if the present monthly productive capacity is less than 200,000 units, the lower limit of the confidence interval, the borrower can be quite sure that investment in additional capacity will be needed to meet future demand for its product. The bank will respect this and perhaps say. "Yes, the purpose of the loan: investment in additional capacity is well founded."

■■■
Section IV

■■■

Advanced Techniques in Credit Risk Management

■■■

CHAPTER Twelve

Risk Management and Sustainable Growth

Expansion is not necessarily a business's most important goal. Obsessed with visions of higher sales, management sometimes neglects the firm's basic financial responsibilities, a potentially fatal course.

A focus on what is, and what is not, a sustainable sales growth rate is necessary. This focus can be provided by a specialized model.

The Sustainable Growth Model is used to decide if the growth rate (in sales) of leveraged, rapid-growth companies is at a level that will strain the capital structure (notably the debt to equity ratio). It helps to identify what portion of growth is fueled through internal and external means, the results of which are set to different degrees of tolerance by manipulating specific variables to determine various levels of risk. This information will provide enough facts to make other inquiries as to the company's capital structure. For example, if the model shows that most of the firm's financing of sales growth will be financed externally, we might question asset productivity.

The sustainable growth rate is calculated by using a formula that incorporates sales, assets, profits, dividends, and financial leverage. This will measure the company's sustainable growth rate compared to the targeted growth rate to find out if the company is growing prudently or straining its capital structure.

Projections are particularly important for leveraged, rapid-growth companies since their cash flows are often volatile and unpredictable. These companies operate in a business phase that is riskier than any other period in their life cycle because their credit risks are unique and difficult to analyze.

The Industry Life Cycle

Start-Up Phase

New firms (and industries) face greater risks and their higher risks require special financing. Their special needs has led to specialized venture capital financing sources. Venture capital companies, including investment banking firms and commercial banks (through special subsidiaries), generally obtain an equity position in firms they finance, but they may also extend debt capital. However, when loans are made, they generally involve higher risk premiums, and are structured with convertibles or warrants or are tied in with the purchase of stock by the investment company. Because risks are so obvious (start-up phase requires initial asset investments in anticipation of sales), venture capital deals are done priced with the appropriate spread over a base rate.

Rapid Growth Phase

Having survived start-up, a firm seems poised for growth. However, the small increment to equity generated by earnings is often too inconsequential to finance the insatiable appetite for new assets required by rapid-growth firms. Creditors advancing funds at relatively low-risk premiums do not often know if loans represent down payments for accelerating credit demands—until the firm explodes; or whether loans can be amortized through internally generated cash flow—the aftereffect of slower growth.

If rapid growth continues for too long, the situation will further deteriorate, and it will become increasingly clear the borrower requires additional equity financing. Unsystematic risk caused by financial leverage will exceed judicious limits, yet the firm may be reluctant to bring in additional outside equity capital because the original owners are unwilling to share control, give up the tax benefits of debt financing, or dilute their ownership.

Mature or Stable Growth Phase

The mature phase of a firm (or industry) life cycle is one in which the growth rates for price, book value, earnings, and dividends are all approximately equal, and are in line with the growth in the general economy, or a broad range of stocks like the S&P Composite. As the firm matures, operating activities throw off more cash at higher levels of sales. The need for growth diminishes enough so that investing activities are reduced. Financing requirements are much lower because the firm generates more cash than it absorbs. The firm easily pays off its debt and raises its dividend payout rate.

Decline Phase

Sales decline and profits may erode as the result of heightened competition or changes in consumer demand. Thus, operating cash flow falls short of working capital requirements and capital expenditures. Balance sheet deflation provides limited cash flow. At this stage the firm should be paying down substantial amounts of debt. In addition, the firm may seek out growth acquisitions to provide a longer lease on life.

Sustainable Growth Assumptions

The standard assumptions of sustainable growth calculation as defined by Robert Higgins are:

1. No equity issues permitted

2. Constant dividend payout

3. Stable financial structure

4. Constant capital output ratio

By withholding equity, we can see how the firm's capital structure looks without new equity and determine if the firm needs additional equity. In addition, the other assumptions, the dividend payout ratio, profit margin, and debt to equity ratio, will also be held constant for the purpose of formulating the sustainable growth model.

The Sustainable Growth Model

Optimal current asset management works on the principle that sales can be optimized with a minimum level of current assets. This strategy assures a firm of having a smooth conversion cycle and strong cash flow. In other words, if the firm is successful, assets will move efficiently, product lines produce sizable profits, and the equity base along with the capital structure strengthens. For companies in the rapid-growth stage of its business cycle, we have seen that this is a very difficult position to attain. Characteristically, companies in the growth phase experience rapid expansion in sales and assets, the most burdensome of which are receivables, inventory, and fixed assets.

Poor asset control is usually blamed on a combination of management inexperience, blind ambition and a manifest destiny attitude. The problems really start to surface when the firm's insatiable appetite for core assets and capital expansion overwhelms modest profit contributions to the equity base. This is recognized by using the standard forecast model illustrated by the following equations and highlighted in the chapter projections:

$$(1) \quad F = \frac{A}{S}(\Delta S) - \frac{L_1}{S}(\Delta S) - P(S)(1 - d)$$

and

$$(2) \quad E = \left(\frac{A}{S} - \frac{L_1}{S}\right) - \frac{P}{G}(1 - G)(1 - d)$$

Δ	=	Change in Sales
A	=	Projected Assets
d	=	Dividend Payout Rate
E	=	Projected Percent of Sales Growth Externally Financed
F	=	Financial Needs (– F = Surplus)
P	=	Net Profit Margin
T	=	Targeted Growth Rate
L^*	=	Equilibrium Leverage
g^*	=	Sustainable Growth Rate
L_1	=	Spontaneous Current Liabilities
G	=	Sales Growth Rate

Consider the historical financial statements of High Risk Inc. for the fiscal period ending 12/31/92. This young growth company is requesting a $50 million loan for plant expansion. The expansion program is needed to raise operating leverage, reduce labor costs, improve production efficiency and increase the gross profit margin. Management presented the following historical and projected financial statements (see Exhibits 12.1 and 12.2) to their bankers in support of their request for a loan.

Exhibit 12.1

High Risk Inc.
Historical Balance Sheet
12/31/92
(In thousands)

		Percent of Sales
Cash	$2,000	.02
Accounts Receivable	4,000	.04
Inventories	54,000	.54
Net Plant and Equipment	60,000	.60
Total Assets	$120,000	1.20
Accounts Payable	$20,000	.2
Accruals	6,000	.06
Long-term debt	44,000	Constant **
Capital Stock	10,000	Constant **
Paid in Capital	10,000	Constant **
Retained Earnings	30,000	Earnings Retention
Total liabilities and equity	$120,000	

**Financing decision; does not vary with sales

High Risk Inc.
Historical Income Statement
12/31/92
(In thousands)

		Percent of Sales
Net Sales	$100,000	1.00
Cost of Goods Sold	75,000	.75
Gross margin	25,000	.25
Expenses (including taxes)	23,000	.23
Net Income	2,000	.02

Assume Projected Sales in 1993 are	$150,000	From this the 1993 projected financial statements can now be derived.

Exhibit 12.2

High Risk Inc.
Projected Balance Sheet
12/31/93
(In thousands)

		Percent of Sales
Cash	$3,000	.02
Accounts Receivable	6,000	.04
Inventories	81,000	.54
Net Plant and Equipment	90,000	.60
Total Assets	$180,000	1.20
Accounts Payable	$30,000	.2
Accruals	9,000	.06
Long-Term Debt	44,000	Constant
Capital Stock	10,000	Constant
Paid in Capital	10,000	Constant
Retained Earnings	*33,000	Constant
Available Capitalization	$136,000	Earnings Retained
Financial Needs	**44,000**	**Derived**
Total Liabilities and Equity	$180,000	

* $30,000 + .02($150,000) − 0 = $33,000

High Risk Inc.
Projected Income Statement
12/31/93
(In thousands)

		Percent of Sales
Net Sales	$150,000	1.00
Cost of Goods Sold	112,500	.75
Gross Margin	37,500	.25
Expenses (including taxes)	34,500	.23
Net Income	3,000	.02

The firm's financial needs can also be derived from:

$$F = \frac{A}{S}(\Delta S) - \frac{L1}{S}(\Delta S) - P\,(S)(1-d);\ \text{Thus:}$$

$$F = 180000/150000(50000) - 39000/150000(50000) - .02(150000)(1-0) = 44000$$

The percent of sales increase that needs to be externally financed can be found by:

$$E = \left(\frac{A}{S} - \frac{L1}{S}\right) - \frac{P}{G}(1+G)(1-d);\ \text{Thus:}$$

$$E = (180000/150000 - 39000/150000) - .02/.5(1+.5)(1-0) = .88.$$

Eighty-eight percent of sales growth must be externally financed. This means that if High Risk were seriously overweight on the debt/equity scales (at fiscal), the projection period adds dangerous weight to leverage due to the imbalance between internal and external financing. Since sales growth is 50% in the first projection period, .88 (50,000) = 44,000, the firm's financial needs. While the "E" formula is efficacious for mature firms, we need a more powerful equation for High Risk Inc. We shall use the sustainable growth model tailored for this specific lending deal.

A firm's financial needs increase if asset efficiency, profits or the retention rate (1– d) decline. On the other hand, reliance on trade credit and/or accruals will reduce external financing requirements. The Sustainable Growth model's powerful logic rests with the notion that the financial structure of a fast growing, highly leveraged firm is already near a fixed saturation point. Increasing leverage beyond that point causes loan risk premiums to skyrocket following the change in unsystematic risk. The Sustainable Growth Rate is estimated:

$$g* = \Delta S/S = \frac{P(1-d)(1+L)}{A/S - P(1-d)(1+L)}$$

We regenerate the *Sustainable Growth Rate* from the *Financial Needs* equation we used to identify High Risk's $44,000 financial needs:

(1) $F = A/S(\Delta S) - L_1/S(\Delta S) - P(S) - (1-d)$

Holding constant A/S, P, L_1 allows us to expand the equation below:

(2) $F = A/S(\Delta S) - L_1/S(\Delta S) - P(S + \Delta S)$
        $(1-d)$

Rearranging terms assuming no equity financing except retained earnings and moving A/S (ΔS) to the left, we have:

(3) $A/S(\Delta S) = F + L_1/S(\Delta S) + P(S + \Delta S)$
$(1-d)$

where A/S (ΔS) = incremental spontaneous assets; $(F + L_1/S (\Delta S)$ = incremental external financing (all debt) and $P(S + \Delta S)(1-d)$ = retained profits.

The diagram below untangles equation (3). If a firm increases assets, A/S (ΔS), management must finance the investment by raising debt, $F + L_1/S (\Delta S)$ and/or by increasing equity, $P(S + \Delta S)(1-d)$:

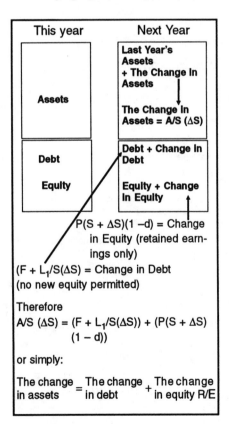

This year	Next Year
Assets	Last Year's Assets + The Change In Assets The Change In Assets = A/S (ΔS)
Debt Equity	Debt + Change In Debt Equity + Change In Equity

P(S + ΔS)(1 –d) = Change in Equity (retained earnings only)

(F + L₁/S(ΔS) = Change in Debt (no new equity permitted)

Therefore
A/S (ΔS) = (F + L₁/S(ΔS)) + (P(S + ΔS) (1 – d))

or simply:

$$\frac{\text{The change}}{\text{in assets}} = \frac{\text{The change}}{\text{in debt}} + \frac{\text{The change}}{\text{in equity R/E}}$$

Simplifying the term $F + L_1/S(\Delta S)$ with the assumption of a stable (or constant) capital structure, we arrive at the obvious:

$$D/E = D/E$$

Multiplying by Δ and dividing by E: $\Delta D = \Delta E$ (D/E) where:

D/E = L, the Debt to Equity ratio is leverage (L); we now substitute:

$$\Delta D = \Delta E(L)$$

From the above, debt increases are followed by proportional increases in equity. Remember, new equity is not allowed while we develop the math. That is ΔE is possible only by retained profits, P (S + ΔS)(1 – d). Since: $\Delta D = \Delta E(L)$, then:

$$\Delta D = P(S + \Delta S)(1 - d)L$$

Setting the above back into equation (3), we obtain:

(4)   A/S (ΔS) = P(S + ΔS)(1 – d)L + P(S + ΔS) (1 –d)

The equation is further simplified by shifting assets to the right side of the equation.

(5)
$$S/\Delta S = \dfrac{P(S + \Delta S)(1 - d)\,L\ +}{A}$$
$$\dfrac{P(S + \Delta S)(1 - d)}{A}$$

= P(S + ΔS)(1 – d)(1 + L)/A
= P (S)(1 –d)(1 + L)/A + P ΔS(1–d)(1 + L)/A

or

ΔS/S = P(S + ΔS)(1 – d)(1 + L)/A
= (P(S)(1 – d)(1 + L))/A + (PΔS)(1– d)(1 + L)/A

Thus:

$\Delta S/S^2$ = P(1 – d)(1 + L)/A + (ΔS/S)(P(1 – d)(1 + L))/A

And finally:

(6) $\Delta S/S = g^* = \dfrac{P(1 - d)(1 + L)}{A/S - P(1 - d)(1 + L)}$

Three Profiles for "L": The Debt/Equity Ratio

The Sustainable Growth Model (g^*) depicts if the company is inundated with additional debt. If the Sustainable Growth Rate (g^*) falls below the Targeted Growth Rate (T), the company may be incapable of achieving its growth objectives due to excessive leverage. This is readily seen in the following three cases:

Profile 1:   Set "L," the debt/equity ratio at maximum levels allowable. The ratio may be set at the industry unsystematic risk maximum, a "bankruptcy" leverage, or simply at the lender's tolerance level.

Profile 2:   Set g^* equal to the targeted growth rate "T" and solve for L* to secure the debt/equity ratio in equilibrium with the borrower's targeted growth rate. The question is, simply: If the borrower continues its growth pattern, how high will leverage climb assuming the firm raises no new equity? **Formula:**

$$T = \dfrac{P(1 - d)(1 + L^*)}{A/S - P(1 - d)(1 + L^*)}$$

Leverage at Growth Equilibrium (**L***): leverage will approach **L*** when the Targeted Growth Rate (**T**) and the Capital Structure are in equilibrium. The model assumes an indefinite growth period.

Profile 3:   Develop a forecast taking the debt/equity ratio in the last year of the forecast period—substituting it into the formula to determine the sustainable growth rate in the firm's residual period.

Example Profile One: Maximum Allowable Leverage

Here we see that the sustainable growth model identifies asset management, dividend payout, operating and leverage imbalance.

High Risk's lenders asked for new projections citing that sales growth of 50% in the first projection period (just examined) was far too optimistic. Consequently, the firm met again with their bankers and presented a set of projections—insisting that while sales were pegged too high, improved manufacturing techniques will boost productivity and increase the net profit margin to 7%.

Ratios were extracted from the new projections including the net profit margin, dividend payout rate, assets to sales, and targeted growth rate. Projections include the plant expansion program related to the loan request (see chart).

Therefore, High Risk Inc. can only sustain a 4% growth rate without raising financial leverage above 150%. However, High Risk's sales growth rate is already targeted at 10%. If the company grows at a higher rate than the sustainable growth rate, the firm's current debt to equity ratio

	High Risk Inc.	Industry Average
Profit margin =	.07	.04
Dividend Payout =	.60	.10
Assets/Sales =	1.80	.70
Maximum allowable debt/equity set by the firm's lenders =	1.50	.80
High Risk targeted at growth rate =	.10	.10

$$g* = \frac{P(1-d)(1+L)}{A/S - P(1-d)(1+L)}$$

$$g* = \frac{.07(1-.6)(1+1.50)}{1.8 - .07(1-.6)(1+1.50)} = .04$$

will without question increase beyond the 150% leverage set by the lenders.

A 10% growth rate will also have a negative affect on cash flow. Poor cash flows may force a high degree of both operating and financial leverage spelling disaster for any company. If a firm has significant operating leverage, it must attain a high level of sales to reach its break-even point. Financial leverage influences profits in much the same way; the higher the leverage, the higher the break-even point for sales and the greater the effect on profits from fluctuations in sales volume. Therefore, if High Risk Inc. has a significant degree of both operating and financial leverage, even minute changes in the level of sales will create wide fluctuations in net income, return-on-equity and earnings per share. This is something they cannot afford to deal with.

The firm's bankers are well aware that without an adequate source of cash, the areas where debt funds are used (debt payments, etc.) run the risk of being in default, putting the bank's investment in jeopardy. High Risk's creditors can determine that an imbalance between internal and external cash flow will occur by comparing the firm's Sustainable Growth Rate to its Targeted Growth Rate.

Example Profile Two : Equilibrium Leverage

Set g* equal to the targeted growth rate "T" and solve for "L" to obtain the debt/equity ratio in equilibrium with the borrower's targeted growth rate.

$$T = \frac{P(1-d)(1+L^*)}{A/S - P(1-d)(1+L^*)}$$

$$.10 = \frac{.07(1-.6)(1+L^*)}{1.8 - .07(1-.6)(1+L^*)}$$

$$L = 4.84$$

Solving for L*, we obtain L* = 4.84. Thus, leverage must increase to 484% for the sales growth rate and financial structure to be in equilibrium. Since the maximum allowable debt/equity set originally by the firm's lenders was 150%, the deal, as presented, will not be approved. While high leverage might provide high returns for shareholders, this is not the bank's major concern. Levels of acceptable leverage are proportional to the quality, magnitude, trend, and reliability of High Risk's projected cash flow. Or, the transaction is at the expense of the lender, who is not being compensated for the additional risk. The characteristics of both the company and its industry, along with specifics of the transaction, are essential when management and their creditors set acceptable or tolerance leverage. Leverage tolerance levels will be governed by sets of very specific factors that decide unsystematic risk.

For example, certain debt structures such as having a layer of mezzanine capital subordinate to other creditor claims might justify a higher tolerance level. If the company is in a very cyclical industry, with rapid technological obsolescence making cash flow more difficult to predict, creditors might set a lower leverage tolerance.

High Risk's profit margin is influenced by the firm's internal performance and its relationship to the industry. Within the analysis, operating trends will be carefully examined, along with the company's position in the industry.

Example Profile Three: Pro Forma Financials

We develop *profile three* solutions by taking the debt/equity ratio in the last year of a forecast period and factoring it into the sustainable growth formula. The forecast period is called a projection horizon, while the firm's remaining life beyond the forecast horizon delineates the residual period. Thus, if the sustainable growth rate falls short of the target growth rate, leverage must increase in the residual period to be in equilibrium with (sales) growth. Assume that a five-year projection yields the following results for High Risk (assume the last year in the projection period is 1997, see chart on the following page):

$$g^* = \frac{(P(1-d)(1+L)}{A/S - P(1-d)(1+L))}$$

$$g^* = \frac{(.07(1-.61)(1+3.30))}{1.8 - .07(1-.61)(1+3.30))} = .069$$

Because the sustainable growth rate, 6.9%, is below the targeted growth rate, 10%, the debt to equity ratio will climb above 330% in the residual period.

Substituting T for G*, solving for L, we have:

Projected Balance Sheet
12/31/97
(In thousands)

Cash	$4,000
Accounts Receivable	18,000
Inventories	123,000
Net Plant and Equipment	173,000
Total Assets	$318,000
Accounts Payable	$96,000
Accruals	40,000
Long-Term Debt	108,000
Capital Stock	10,000
Paid in Capital	10,000
Retain Earnings	54,000
Total Liabilities and Equity	$318,000

Sales	$176,000
Profits	12,400
Dividends	75,000

Profit margin =	.07
Dividend Payout =	.61
Assets/Sales =	1.81
Debt to Equity Ratio in 1987	330%
Targeted Growth Rate	.10

$$g^* = \frac{(P(1-d)(1+L))}{(A/S - P(1-d)(1+L))}$$

$$.10 = \frac{(.07(1-.61)(1+L))}{(1.81 - .07(1-.61)(1+L))}$$

$$L = 503\%$$

To support a 10% growth rate, beyond the 1997 projection period, leverage must climb to 503% (if we assume no common stock issue), well over the 330% debt/equity realized in 1997.

Solving Sustainable Growth Problems

Techniques for solving sustainable growth problems include issuing equity, improving asset management, reducing the dividend payout rate, and increasing the profit margin. Profit pruning, including dissolving unprofitable divisions, is another solution to sustainable growth problems. Also, knowing when the rapid growth phase will end and the mature phase will begin eases potential problems. Once the firm is in the mature phase of its company life cycle, greater amounts of cash will be generated, risk will be decreased, and cash flow will be more predictable.

If selling new equity is not desirable, a firm may cut the dividend payout ratio or simply increase leverage. A cut in the payout ratio increases the sustainable growth rate by increasing the portion of earnings retained in the business, while increasing leverage raises the amount of debt the firm can add for each dollar of retained profits.

As we noted, however, there are limits to the use of debt financing. All firms have a creditor-imposed debt capacity that restricts the amount of leverage the company can use. As leverage increases, the risks carried by owners and creditors rise as do the costs of securing additional capital.

Issuing equity also has its shortcomings including loss of owner diversification, loss of control, public disclosure, and management distraction.

The most conservative solution is to reduce growth to a level compatible with the company's current dividend or financing policies.

When actual growth exceeds sustainable growth, the first step is to find just how long the situation is likely to continue. If High Risk's growth rate is likely to decline in the near term as the firm reaches maturity, the problem is temporary and can probably be solved by increasing leverage to feasible levels. Later, when actual growth falls below the sustainable growth rate, cash is generated, not absorbed, and loans can be repaid.

Improve the Capital/Output Ratio (Assets/Sales)

The assets to sales ratio is an important component of the sustainable growth model. It is positioned in the equation to represent the base (before profit retention) on which an appropriate and sustainable growth rate is calculated. If this rate exceeds a tolerable rate, we know that leverage will increase rapidly. The ratio is largely decided by management as their policies give rise to asset expansion. To analyze the effectiveness, we could easily find a tolerable growth rate (for "g*"), using projected debt levels for "L" to calculate an equilibrium assets to sales ratio. Written covenants should ensure that management is administering the firm's asset portfolio according to sustainable growth guidelines. If not, the problems will easily be detected from the borrower's projections.

As we said, unmanaged growth forces a firm to borrow heavily from external sources because the appetite for funds is enormous—resulting in a rising debt ratio. High debt levels reduce loan protection since it effectively blocks external equity infusions. In addition, as leverage increases within the sustainable growth universe, cash flow needs to be channeled to debt service, cannibalizing operating cash flows. As mentioned previously, a company cannot sustain high financial and operating leverage.

If, on the other hand, a firm's leverage is already too high, rather than using actual leverage in the model, use an industry average debt level and the same tolerable growth rate for g*. The derived equilibrium assets to sales ratio should be compared to the actual ratio of that firm to again decide the appropriateness of asset management policies.

An asset to sales ratio in line with or lower than the industry norm depicts strong asset management practices. We can assume that asset utilization ratios provided in support of the loan agreement are being used efficiently and are growing at a pace which equity capital can support. Firms retire older debt uniformly and regularly, and cash flows are predictable. Credit risk is under control.

The capital output ratio (A/S) is critically important because it examines the levels of assets required to produce a level of sales. In today's ultracompetitive environment, the left side of the balance sheet is managed aggressively to allow for sustainable growth. "Just in Time" inventory is one example of this type of management. Often, JIT requires an expensive investment in technology. For instance, JIT can have point-of-sale scanners transmitting information directly to the supplier, who can then ship additional needed items, eliminating some cost of carrying inventory. Firms not leveraged to the hilt, with strong debt capacity and cash flow, are in a better position to finance sophisticated asset management systems.

However, High Risk is in no position to bargain and may need to make hard decisions to reduce debt levels. For example, the firm may decide to contract out its production assignments to reduce raw materials and work in process inventory. A bitter pill to digest! This activity will reduce profit margins, because goods will cost more to produce.

Increase Profit Margins

Improved profit margins reflect strategic, operating, and financing decisions. Strategies involve critically important decisions: choice of product market areas in which the firm operates; whether to emphasize cost reduction or product differentiation; whether to focus on selected product areas or seek to cover a broad range of potential buyers.

Reduce the Dividend Payout Ratio

Increases in both dividends and financial leverage ratios are potentially alarming because dividends reduce cash flow. On the other hand, profit retention shows a commitment to reinvest in the business rather than satisfy the short-term satisfaction of equity investors through dividend distributions.

Profit Pruning

Higgins reinforced the logic of profit pruning. He said that when a firm spreads its resources across many products, it may not be able to compete effectively in all of them. It is better to sell off marginal operations and plow the proceeds back into the remaining businesses. Profit pruning reduces sustainable growth problems in two ways: It generates cash directly through the sale of marginal businesses, and it reduces actual sales growth by eliminating some sources of the growth. Profit pruning is also available for a single-product company. The firm could prune out slow-paying customers or slow-turning inventory. This lessens sustainable growth problems in three ways: it frees up cash, which can be used to support new growth; it increases asset turnover; and it reduces sales. The

strategy reduces sales because tightening credit terms and reducing inventory selection will drive away some customers.

"The Sermon"

As we saw earlier, g^* is equal to 4%; the company can grow at 4% without increasing leverage over 150%. However, High Risk is forecasting a sales increase of 10%. Since the company is growing at a higher rate than the sustainable growth rate, the firm's current debt to equity ratio exceeds the 150% maximum level set by the firm's lenders. By setting the targeted growth rate at 10%, and solving for "L," the lenders realize that leverage of 484% equates with the firm's 10% growth rate—much too high.

High Risk Inc., like almost all firms, will use their sales growth rate as a major component of long-run financial planning. But in the search for more profit dollars, many managers fail to consider the growth rate the company's financial structure can support. Financial planning establishes guidelines for changes in the firm's financial structure. Therefore, a sure understanding of this firm's financial planning will help to reduce credit risk by structuring a tighter deal.

The sustainable growth model depends on the major elements of the firm's financial planning. High Risk's should include:

- Identification of the firm's financial goals
- Analysis of the differences between these goals and the current financial status of the firm
- Stating the actions needed for the firm to achieve its financial goals

The financial policies that the firm must set for its growth and profitability include:

- The degree of financial leverage it chooses to employ
- The amount of cash thought necessary and appropriate to pay shareholders (dividend policy)
- The investment opportunities the firm elects to take advantage of in the future

Financial plans are not the same for all firms. But, economic assumptions, sales forecast, pro forma statements, asset requirements and financial requirements are some common elements of the financial plan.

High Risk's sales will be influenced by several factors. The prevailing economic conditions at a given time affect separate industries differently. For example, automobiles and home construction contracts would be reduced during a recession, whereas food sales would not be affected as greatly. In analyzing the potential cash flows and credit risks of this firm, the prevailing market conditions will need to be considered first. These are factors that will affect an industry as a whole.

The fact that a firm is an innovator and market leader will reflect market share. Innovative firms with aggressive research and development programs will often gain advantages over competitors. Confirmed orders are good indications of future sales and needed production capacities, but projecting sales is often difficult in emerging industries because the *predictability* horizon is very short.

While growth in leverage ratios also increase the SGR, the composition of High

Risk's debt is also very important. If this emerging company continuously uses short-term debt as a financing mechanism (and is unhedged), it will become overexposed to volatile and rising yield curves. These factors may drastically increase the cost of debt when refinancing/rollover of debt is required. It can also cause overreliance on short-term debt, which reduces the company's financing flexibility. In addition, it may suggest that other creditors are skeptical of the company's future cash flows and may not want the credit exposure of extending long-term debt that may not be repaid. However, it may also suggest management's confidence that liquidity can be sustained principally through profit retention enabling them to search for the lowest cost of capital.

Asset quality should be reviewed with leverage ratios because higher quality assets allow for increased leverage ratios. Regarding debt capacity, an analysis of High Risk's cash flow coverage ratios should be measured and trended over a period to decide if the leveraged company is experiencing any current or near-term problems, covering interest expense and satisfying debt payments.

Also, leveraged companies that continue to increase debt without raising equity capital may prompt questions about the firm's viability if investors have rejected the opportunity to take an equity stake. It may also suggest that the company is not exploring its various capital-raising alternatives, and overreliance on a single financing method may not provide the firm with the least expensive cost of capital.

In High Risk Inc.'s case, the firm's lenders will advise the firm to decrease its debt to equity ratio by injecting new equity. If the firm declines, High Risk could reduce its operating leverage, inventory and debt levels by hiring subcontractors—thus raising the sustainable growth rate to acceptable levels.

High Risk's managers may yet argue that financial leverage greatly affects Earnings Per Share. For example, let's assume that sales and expenses for two firms, High Risk and Low Risk, are identical. Low Risk has little debt. Assume the two firms yield identical EPS. However, a drop in sales would cause the EPS of High Risk to fall lower than its competitor. Conversely, for a given rise in sales, High Risk would yield a greater rise in EPS than that of Low Risk. The greater the amount of financial leverage, the more sensitive is EPS to a change in sales.

A New Strategy: The Solution

Here's how High Risk Inc. decided to proceed, revising its earlier plan by:

1. Not issuing new equity, thus preserving ownership control. Instead subcontractors will produce and ship to High Risk's customers. Sales continue to grow at 10%. But the use of subcontractors will squeeze profit margins because High Risk will absorb higher costs of production

2. Using subcontractors to lower inventory levels and reduce capital spending

3. Consenting to tight control of receivables

4. Reducing dividends

5. Maintaining leverage below the ceiling imposed by the firm's lenders

	Revised Plan	Earlier Plan	Industry Average
Profit margin =	.04	.70	.04
Dividend Payout =	.10	.60	.10
Assets/Sales =	.90	1.80	.70
Maximum allowable debt/equity set by the firm's lenders, the highest leverage in the industry =	1.50	1.50	.80
Targeted a growth rate	.10	.10	.10

Inserting the new assumptions into the model we have:

$$g^* = \frac{(P\,(1-d)\,(1+L))}{(A/S - P(1-d)(1+L))}$$

$$g^* = \frac{(.04\,(1-.1)(1+1.50))}{(.9 - .04\,(1-.1)(1+1.50))} = .11$$

The previous condition was:

$$g^* = \frac{(.07\,(1-.6)(1+1.50))}{(1.8 - .07\,(1-.6)(1+1.50))} = .04$$

The sustainable growth rate is 11%. Thus, High Risk Inc. can grow at 11% a year over the foreseeable future without increasing leverage beyond 150%, the leverage ceiling set by the firm's bankers. Since the firm's 10% targeted growth rate is less than its 11% sustainable growth rate, leverage will fall below the maximum level permitted by the firm's creditors. The model shows us that the firm's cash flow problems were caused by poor asset management combined with an aggressive dividend policy. While profits declined, the sustainable growth rate actually increased.

Exponential Growth Regression Curve and the Sustainable Growth Model

The *Exponential Curve Fit* is an excellent tool for examining rapid or initial growth rates. The key point is: The sustainable growth model's capacity to red flag thinly capitalized financial structures expands in proportion to the *R Square* correlation score of a firm's sales growth rates and the regression curve.

Suppose you owned Mahler Inc., a firm engaged in the manufacture of several prototype parts for a major furniture manufacturer. Sales are exploding. Can you determine what the sales curve is (see Exhibit 12.3)?

The correlation coefficient for the current curve fit is:

R Squared = 0.89 for Mahler

Correlation coefficients close to 1 or −1 indicate an excellent curve fit. The curve fits the data well. The coefficient of correlation, *R Squared*, measures how closely the curve fits the data. If *R squared* is zero, no exponential curve correlation exists between sales growth rates and the curve.

As we saw, industries often grow rapidly at first, then decline with time. Limited resources, competition, or predation cause the slowdown. Populations approaching the saturation point grow along a logarithmic curve. The logarithmic curve illustrates a rapid growth, followed by a gradual decrease in growth rate. After growth and resources balance out, growth may continue at the same rate at which resources increase. When industries grow, they eventually reach the saturation point. From then on, replacements or population growth account for most new sales. Growth rates for industries that have reached this level are nearly straight lines.

Logarithmic Curve Fit–Mahler Unlimited

Is the company's growth pattern exponential or logarithmic (see Exhibit 12.4)?

Logarithmic curves have the form Y = A + B*LN(X)

For the current data, A and B are:

A   − 609.8
B   1075.9

R Squared = 0.608

The logarithmic regression reveals a poor curve fit. Mahler's growth pattern is exponential. This was determined by comparing it to an exponential growth pattern. The 0.89 R Square reveals that the company's growth is a better match to the exponential curve than R Square is to the logarithmic curve. Had growth been logarithmic, sales increases would be expected to slow over time, and the need for additional financing reduced. Thus, creditors *must* ask borrowers: when will the firm's rapid (exponential) growth begin to level off, bringing on slower (logarithmic) expansion rates? If management cannot answer this query with some precision, a sustainable growth problem exists.

Exhibit 12.3

Semiannual Sales Historical and Forecast
Mahler Inc.

Year	Periods	Semiannual Sales
	1	52
1987	2	76
	3	245
1988	4	548
	5	487
1989	6	1,234
	7	998
1990	8	1,123
	9	2,145
1991	10	3,245
	11	3,155
1992	12	4,500

Forecast

	13	9,900
1993	14	11,000
	15	6510

Exponential curves have the form $Y = A*e^{\wedge}(B*X)$
For the current data, A and B are

A	49.20
B	0.44

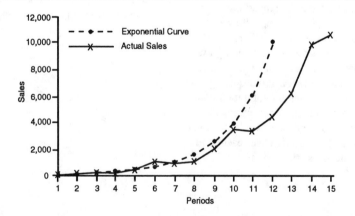

Exhibit 12.4

Logarithmic Regression Curve and the Sustainable Growth Model

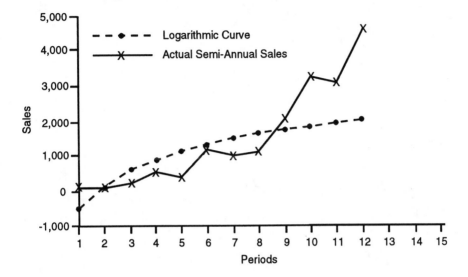

CHAPTER Thirteen

Loan Pricing: A Valuation Approach

The majority of banks have come to realize that returns must be measured by degrees of risk. Loan pricing is no longer viewed as simply an art; it is a science with the power of creating or destroying shareholder value. In today's competitive market, banks are now forced to accept a greater degree of risk and lower returns. If loans are not priced right, banks risk the possibility of underpricing loans or losing business outright. Investment bankers have long used market-based pricing models to refine the pricing of specific transactions.

Competition is forcing bankers to accept more risk, deliver more service, and get paid less and less. Why then, are most good loans overpriced while high-risk credits are underpriced when measured against the market? It seems one group of deal makers—investment bankers—play the risk/reward game under one set of rules and commercial bankers under another.

In any case we need to examine both traditional and mark to market pricing.

Section One: Pros and Cons of Traditional Pricing

Loan pricing must generate income to fairly compensate bankers for credit risk and the exposure assumed by promising future availability of funds:

■ ■ ■

A bank acquires funds through deposits, borrowing, and equity, recognizing the cost of each source and the resulting average cost of funds to the total bank. The funds are allocated to assets, creating an asset mix of earning assets such as loans and nonearning assets such as a bank's premises. The price that customers are charged for the use of an earning asset represents the sum of the cost of the bank's funds, the administrative costs (e.g., salaries, compensation for non-earning assets, and other costs), and a profit objective that compensates the bank for bearing risk. If pricing adequately compensates for these costs and all risks undertaken, bank value is created. Customer value is created if the price is perceived by the customer to be fair, based on the funds and service received.[1]

■ ■ ■

Let's review some basic definitions and concepts associated with the traditional approach to loan pricing before going any further:

Prime Rate. The national prime rate is a loan rate administered by large money market banks. The banks adjust the prime rate to reflect loan conditions and what their most creditworthy customers pay.

LIBOR. Floating rates based on the London Interbank Offering Rate (LIBOR), widely quoted on short-term European money market credits. It influences the overseas lending rates of large U.S. banks, particularly when the spread between U.S. money market base rates and LIBOR favors the latter. Also, access to overseas sources of funds has recently made LIBOR an increasingly popular base rate among borrowers of regional and even smaller banks.

Commitment Fee. When the bank makes a commitment to lend funds or issue a credit facility, the customer is charged a commitment fee. This per annum fee is charged (usually quarterly or at time of interest collection) from acceptance of the commitment until draw down/issuance and on the unused portion of the commitment. A commitment fee is applied to the unused amount of the available portion (the portion which is periodically designated available or the amount the company projects it will need during a specified period). A

lower commitment fee is applied to the unavailable portion.

Commitment fees on the unused portion of the loan are usually assessed in each accounting period (monthly or yearly) by calculating the average usage rate. Because the bank must set aside capital to support the unused credit line, commitment fees should be high enough to generate a desirable return on capital if the credit line is not fully used.

Facility Fee. Charged for making a credit facility available, and is applied to the entire facility regardless of usage. It is frequently used in lieu of balance arrangements and to increase the overall yield.

Prepayment Penalty Fee. Charge if a loan is partially or entirely repaid before the scheduled maturity.

Agent's Fee. Charged by the principal bank in a multi-bank credit for its effort and expense in packaging and servicing a loan. It may be a dollar amount or a percentage of the facility.

Management Fee. Collected by banks designated as managing banks in a syndication.

Miscellaneous Fees. Special financing transactions such as leveraged buyouts, acquisition financing or tax exempt financing often warrant charging fees for the extra costs involved in structuring the deal. Up Front Fees, Arrangement Fees, Closing Fees, and Fees Certain (to be collected whether the loan is closed or not) are common fees collected for complex deals. These flat fees are a percentage of the loan, and can be collected in advance or over the life of the loan.

---

1 Kemp and Pettit, Jr. Excerpted with permission from *The Bankers Magazine*. This excerpt was taken from the original article which appeared in the July/August 1992 issue.

Compensating Balances. Compensating balance requirements obligate the borrower to hold demand deposits or low-interest time deposits as part of a loan agreement. Also, balance requirements are sometimes set on loan commitments. The balance requirement on loans usually require balances to average an agreed upon percentage of the loan amount. Compensating balances in the form of free demand deposits support credit arrangements and contribute to profitability. Deficiency fees are charged retroactively if a balance arrangement is not fulfilled. Deficient balances are treated as borrowed funds and the fee is calculated as interest at the borrowing rate or earnings credit rate.

Compensating balances have been criticized as inefficient pricing because, although they raise the effective borrowing cost, banks must hold idle reserves against the additional deposits and, therefore, cannot fully invest them in earning assets. Among banks that have moved toward unbundled and explicit pricing, balance requirements are thought to obscure the true returns on lending and have been replaced by fees or higher loan rates. Fees in lieu of balances equate compensating balance requirements with fees. At any time a fee in

lieu of balances can be derived, generating income equivalent to earnings from compensating balances. Since balances replace funds which the bank would otherwise purchase they earn income at the lending institution's cost of funds rate. As the cost of funds fluctuates with market interest rates, balances will be worth more when the cost of funds increase and less when the funding cost falls.

Percent of Prime Fee. The value of deposits expressed as a percent of prime fee, line fee or facility fee. Since the prime rate includes a spread over the lenders cost of funds, the percent of prime fee will keep the bankers "whole" despite fluctuations in the cost of funds. Therefore, the primary contribution of customer supplied balances (net of effects of the reserve requirement) is reduced funding costs. As long as the balances are provided at a rate that is less than other funds available from the market, they will reduce funding costs.

The *line facility fee* may undercompensate lenders if interest rates rise, since the fee was calculated on a lower cost of funds. Exhibit 13.1 illustrates and compares the percent of prime fee to the line facility fee:

Exhibit 13.1

$$\text{Percent of Prime Fee} = \frac{(\text{Balance Arrangement})(1 - \text{Reserve Requirement})(\text{Cost of Funds})}{\text{Prime Rate}}$$

Assume
    Balance Requirement = 10%
    Reserve Requirement = 12%
    **Cost of Funds = 8.06%
    Prime Rate = 9.5%
    $100,000 Line of Credit

$$\text{Percent of Prime Fee} = \frac{(.10)(1 - .12)(.0806)}{.095} = .07466$$

Thus, $100,000 (.07466) (.095) = $709.27 fee in lieu of a 10% balance requirement

    Line Facility Fee = (Balance Arrangement)(1 – Reserve Requirement)(Cost of Funds)
    Line Facility Fee = (.10) (1 – .12) (.0806) = .0071 or 71 b.p

Thus, $100,000 (.0071) = $710. The percent of prime fee and line facility yield identical results (at the time of initial calculation).

Cost of funds. The incremental cost of funds rate is the interest rate paid on the liabilities used for funding.[2] This definition is quite narrow, underestimating the true cost of funds rate. Instead, the incremental cost of funds rate should be defined as the total incremental expense incurred in gathering $1 of investable funds. For example, some banks with a significant amount of demand deposits and branch networks might have higher operating costs, deposit insurance costs, and reserve requirements. These costs must be included in the cost of funds.

In addition, operating expenses for the loan should be determined to help bankers figure spread over cost of funds. Yang breaks this down into five expense subcategories:

■ **Direct variable:** Expenses charged to the profit/cost center that are directly associated with the loan. Direct variable expense typically can be easily estimated either from the loan proposal or by the loan department.

■ **Allocated variable:** Allocated expenses are the expenses incurred by other cost centers in support of a product. These expenses can usually be derived from a bank's cost accounting system, which includes variable support expenses for data processing, the customer phone center, and other support departments.

■ **Allocated fixed:** Direct and allocated fixed expenses are calculated according to the total capacity of each operation (cost center) rather than using the fully loaded costs. Otherwise, as volume rises, per-unit fixed costs will be overstated. These

calculations are usually based on an operation research and capacity/unit cost study.

■ **Direct fixed, and Allocated overhead:** Allocated overhead is the portion of the bank's total overhead that should be considered supportive of this particular product.

Some bankers believe that[3] loan pricing must account for risk and assess a cost to the relationship on the basis of risk. A bank's rating system or loan review grades provide a means of classifying loans according to risk, and through the use of these classifications, the likelihood of loss or nonperformance for a given loan can be statistically determined and a cost rate calculated. Ferrari suggests that:

■ ■ ■

Risk should be converted to a cost element and expressed as a percentage of the loan balance. This percentage cost is essentially the risk premium of loan pricing, which must be included in the loan rate to compensate the bank for a given level of risk.

An additional and often ignored cost of risk is risk-related overhead. Riskier loans tend to have higher administrative expenses because of the incremental monitoring and increased involvement of credit administration and supervisory personnel they require. The loan workout department, collection department, and a portion of the legal department can be considered risk-related expenses. Their costs could be apportioned to loans based on their relative risks.

■ ■ ■

While operating expenses factor into the pricing arithmetic, loan pricing in-

---

2   Gilbert Yang, "Capital Profit Consulting," *The Bankers Magazine,* Sept/Oct 1991.

3   Richard Ferrari, *Journal of Commercial Bank Lending,* March 1992.

volves, three essential steps, according to Johnson and Grace.[4]

1. A minimum target or hurdle rate must be estimated. The appropriate hurdle rate incorporates both the funding costs and a specified profit target.

2. Estimate income, expenses and yield associated with the loan.

3. Compare the estimated yield with the target or hurdle rate to determine loan profitability. If the yield is less than the hurdle rate, the loan should be either rejected or restructured so that it meets the target.

Developing Return on Equity/ Return on Assets Pricing Techniques

Pricing loans with specific profit targets in mind first came to light with Return on Equity (ROE) and Return on Assets (ROA) pricing guidelines. The heart of ROE and ROA pricing lies within the *du Pont system* of financial analysis. The du Pont system links productivity, profitability, and financial leverage to determine how business activities interact to produce stockholder's return on equity. To calculate the main ingredients of the du Pont system, the following must be known:

1. **Productivity (Sales/Assets):** What is the level of sales in relation to the asset utilization?

2. **Profitability (Profits/Sales):** Based on sales activity, what is the level of profitability?

3. **Leverage (Equity/Assets):** What is the equity stake in the company? Assets are either owned or funded with debt.

4. **Return on Equity (Profit/Equity):** What return are the owners realizing on profits?

For example, first consider the returns of Company W in Exhibit 13.2:

Exhibit 13.2

			Company W				
Year	Productivity Sales/Assets	x	Profitability Profits/Sales	+	Leverage Equity/Assets	=	Return Profit/Equity
1989	1.75		6.00%		56.00%		18.75%
1990	1.75		5.00%		55.00%		15.91%
1991	1.74		6.00%		54.00%		19.33%
1992	1.76		5.50%		55.00%		17.60%
1993	1.74		6.00%		57.00%		18.32%

Thus:

$$\frac{Sales}{Assets} \times \frac{Profits}{Sales} = \frac{Profits}{Assets}$$

$$\frac{Profits}{Assets} + \frac{Equity}{Assets} = \frac{Profits}{Equity}$$

---

4 *The Bankers Magazine*, May/June 1991.

A reduction in Company W's assets (all other variables remaining constant) increases return on equity. From reviewing each formula, a higher ROE can also be attained by increasing profits. Financial strategies designed to increase leverage tend to produce higher ROE. Now let's compare Company W with Company X in Exhibit 13.3. With the exception of productivity, the two firms are identical.

The consequence is obvious. Company X's asset base has had a direct effect on sales volume, thus lowering ROE. Further activity ratio analysis as discussed in the ratios chapter will help to pinpoint Company X's dilemma. At this point, it should be apparent that if a company experiences decreases in productivity and profitability, ROE may be in trouble.

The DuPont analysis demonstrates how bankers plan asset portfolios, target profit strategies and align high-return products closely with changing markets. For example, by optimizing asset distribution—arranging and syndicating loans, developing fee-based services like cash management, securities processing, corporate trust, foreign exchange and risk management products, bankers improve return on equity. Bank managers are constantly looking for ways to reduce non-interest costs in order to achieve ROE goals. Senior management seeks the optimal liabilities mix, to reduce the cost of funds and risks of debt while still using liabilities to increase the bank's return on equity. Managing leverage is also accomplished by concentrating on risk-based capital ratios in addition to the primary capital base, which includes shareholder equity, and reserve for credit losses.

The criterion for establishing the bank's overall desired ROE, is usually one that the bank feels will attract investors and satisfy shareholders over the long haul. To meet that, "DuPont—generated" pricing is based on *cost plus*. If a deal's cost plus price falls below pricing offered by competitors (the market price), the bank probably has a comparative pricing advantage and could price near cost plus to gain market share or nearer to market to capture a fine profit. Either way, the result will increase ROE since both productivity and profitability will increase. If the bank's loan pricing is below market, the bank could exit the deal, lower costs to improve its competitive advantage, or price above the market and accept the risk that it will lose market share. When all costs in the specific deal's pricing are inclusive, and capital supporting the facility is correctly determined (with the help of a credit risk grading system), banks may find that

Exhibit 13.3

Company X

Year	Productivity x Sales/Assets	Profitability ÷ Profits/Sales	Leverage = Equity/Assets	Return Profit/Equity
1989	1.75	6.00%	56.00%	18.75%
1990	1.55	5.00%	55.00%	14.09%
1991	1.23	6.00%	54.00%	13.67%
1992	1.15	5.50%	55.00%	11.50%

achieving the desired ROE can mean setting a price above the competition. Who said life was easy?

Let's develop a simple but well-defined ROE/ROA spreadsheet using the *Net Borrowed Funds Approach.* In calculating the loan yield, the *Net Borrowed Funds Approach* assumes a company borrows its own funds first and the bank supplies the difference between the deposit and the loan amount. The yield is calculated on the net difference. Presume, in Exhibit 13.4, Second City Bank is pricing an unsecured $1,000,000 line of credit to Picnic Furniture Manufacturing Co., a subsidiary of Gem Furniture Company.

Since the new loan approved by Second City will be priced at a decent spread over prime, there is not much ambiguity about the way ROE and loan rates will vary together. Small increases in price, in this case one percentage point over the "base case," causes considerably larger increases in ROE; small decreases in price cause considerably larger decreases in ROE. The *Sensitivities Multiplier* in Exhibit 13.5 confirms this: a one percentage point increase in the rate charged Picnic Furniture results in a 95% change in ROE.

The effect of bank leverage on ROE explains why some foreign banks enjoy a competitive advantage over U.S. banks since they are able to take their equity/assets ratios below the floors mandated by U.S. regulators. In the example, a foreign bank that has an equity to assets ratio of 3% can price 60 basis points below Second City and still match the 9.75% ROE provided in the base case.

If the borrower provides the bank with healthy profits by purchasing services and numerous bank products, the bank might easily set a profit goal on the entire relationship. For example, Picnic Furniture might purchase a number of products resulting in, say, a 23% overall ROE—well above the 17.8% Second City has targeted under the loan's ROE guideline, providing a good deal of pricing flexibility.

Pricing Errors

Loan pricing that fails as a science will lead to "pricing errors." Authors Kemp and Pettit, offer a few value-hurting hazards of loan pricing:[5]

Meeting the competitor's price. If the loan officer uses competition to justify a lower price, the loan officer either does not understand the risk, has poorly structured the credit to minimize risk, or has ignored the need for an adequate return for the bank. The loan officer must always realize that price is but one element of profitability—it must be considered within the risk/return tradeoff.

Volume is more important than price. Volume does not add value. Profitability that compensates for risk does add value. Loan pricing must cover the costs of the bank's funds acquisition, all location strategies and compensate for risk. All too often, banks and loan officers confuse volume and profitability—they neglect the elements of profitability because they believe that volume is the solution to all problems.

Pricing based on marginal cost. The problem is that the resulting profit is insufficient to cover the costs of the more expensive forms of funding, such as equity. How is the bank going to compensate its bondholders, stockholders, and other stake

---

5   Robert Kemp and Laurence Pettit, Jr. Abstracted with permission from *The Bankers Magazine.* This article originally appeared in the July/August 1992 issue.

Exhibit 13.4

Developing a Simple ROE/ROA Pricing Model

Loan Yield Calculation:	Net Borrowed Funds Basis (Line of Credit (loan) less Balances)
Facility Information	
Borrower:	Picnic Furniture Manufacturing Co.
Lenders:	Second City Bank
Amount:	$1,000,000 Unsecured Line of Credit
Parent:	100% Owned by Gem Furniture
Bank ROA Guideline:	1.25%

Input Screen

Loan Information	
Unsecured Line of Credit (Assumed to be Fully Utilized)	1,000,000
Balances	50,000
Net Borrowed Funds	950,000
Interest Rate: Prime + 1.5%	12.00%
Fees in Lieu of Balances	2.00%
Funding Costs	8.25%
Servicing	3.00%
Loan Loss Expense	1.50%
Taxes	35%
Equity Reserve Requirement (Assumption)	7.00%
Deposit Information	
12-month average balances	50,000
Activity costs as a percent of balances	4.00%

Output Screen

Yield Calculation			
Interest	120,000		Loan × Interest Rate
Fees	20,000		Loan × Fees
Total Loan Revenue		140,000	
Loan Servicing	(30,000)		Loan × Servicing
Loan Loss Expense	(15,000)		Loan × Loan Loss Expense
Annual Activity Costs	(2,000)		12 month average balances ×% Activity Cost
Total Expenses		**(47,000)**	
Income before Funding Costs		93,000	

Exhibit 13.4 (continued)

Output Screen	

Yield Calculation-Net Borrowed Fund Basis

Income before Funding Costs	93,000	
Net Borrowed Funds	(950,000)	Loan Less Balances
Yield	9.79%	Income before Funding Costs/Net Borrowed Funds

Net Income (After Funding Costs)

Net Income before Funding Costs	93,000
Funding Costs	(82,500)
Taxes	(3.675)
Net Income	6,825

Return on Assets Calculation

Loan amount	1,000,000
Net Income	6,825
Return on Assets	0.68%

Return on Equity Calculation

Equity Reserve Requirement	7.00%
Loan amount	1,000,000
Equity Reserve	70,000
Net Income	6,825
Return on Equity	9.75%

Summary: Base Case

Borrower: Picnic Furniture Manufacturing Co.	
Lenders: Second City Bank	
Loan Revenue	140,000
Facility	1,000,000
Net Inome	6,825
Equity Required: 7%	70,000
Bank ROA Guidline	1.25%

Exhibit 13.5

Pricing Strategies	Productivity	X	Profitability	=	Return on Assets	+	Leverage	=	Return on Equity	Sensitivities
	Loan Revenue/ Loan Facility		Net Income/ Loan Revenue		Net Income/ Loan Facility		Equity/Loan Facility		Net Income/ Equity	Multiplier
Base Case	14.00%		4.88%		0.68%		7.00%		*9.75%	0.00%
Increase Funding Costs 25 b.p. to 8.5%	14.00%		3.71%		0.52%		7.00%		7.43%	−23.79%
Increase Loan Loss Expense to 2.0%	14.00%		2.55%		0.36%		7.00%		5.11%	−47.59%
Equity Reserve Requirement	14.00%		4.88%		0.68%		7.50%		9.10%	−6.67%
Raise loan rate to Prime + 2.5% (13%)	15.00%		8.80%		1.33%		7.00%		18.86%	93.43%
Foreign Bank Equity/Assets 3%, pricing 60 b.p. lower	13.40%		2.18%		0.29%		3.00%		9.75%	
Bank ROA Guideline 1.25%					1.25%		7.00%		17.86%	
ROE Shortfall in Percentage Points									8.12	

* rounding

holders? A bank cannot survive in the long run with pricing that is based totally on marginal cost, particularly the marginal cost of a bank's cheapest funds (i.e., demand deposits).

Price can compensate for default risk. Because of competitive pressures, the lure of wider margins from riskier credits is tempting. As loans become more risky, borrowers become less price sensitive. The fact is that no price can compensate a lender for a bad loan.

Stability of price/risk relationships over time. The quickest way to price a loan is to look at the price on the last similar successful deal to the customer. What this practice fails to recognize is that times change. Price relates to the risk in the future, not in the past. Second, risk premiums are not stable in the market. This is true for banks and their customers. In more volatile economic times, it is harder to acquire funds, causing the market to raise the risk premium. In less volatile economic times, funds are easier to acquire, lowering the risk premium. This is easily demonstrated by non-investment grade securities. In good times, it is easy to sell such securities at relatively low yields. In harder, less certain times, the seller of the same security is lucky to find a buyer and typically does so by offering relatively high yields. Price/risk relationships are not stable over time. Loans must be priced to reflect the current and future price/risk relationships created by the customer and the market.

Future pricing can compensate for underpricing current risk. Many loan officers will justify a lower than appropriate price by assuming that future business from the relationship will compensate the bank for today's underperforming loan. Simplifying the logic, the loan officer argues that the bank can overcharge the customer tomorrow because it undercharged the customer today.

Loan risk equal to default risk. Lenders often measure loan risk solely as default risk. Default risk is the risk of nonpayment. Loan risk is more than default risk. The loan risk premium must also cover the uncertainty of late payments and the cost of restructuring due to cyclical or other unforeseen developments, such as the risk of prepayment and the resulting problems with the bank's funds/GAAP management. As the primary earning assets of the bank, loans play a significant role in determining the risk premium assessed on the bank's equity value. Pricing a loan solely on default risk hurts the stockholders of the bank.

Pricing Must Focus on Risk

Looking at pricing from a default opportunity cost perspective, The Globecon Group[6] reported correctly that changes in the lending environment have increased the need for banks to focus more on the way credit is priced.

■ ■ ■

When banks operated in a forgiving credit environment, lending mainly to investment grade credits, default risk was lower and pricing less important. As disintermediation progressed and banks lent to less creditworthy borrowers, the penalty for bad pricing grew—as did the need for rigorous analysis of the risk

---

6 Abstracted with permission from The Globecon Group Limited. This article originally appeared in December 1991 issue of Techniques & Products, part of *The Finance Update Service,* published by the Globecon Group Ltd.

return tradeoff inherent in every deal. Few bankers argue with the need to price properly, but how to do it is a different matter.

■ ■ ■

A Moody's Investors Service study on corporate bond defaults over the last 20 years, reviewed by Globecon, provides just this type of benchmark guidelines on historical default experience by rating category. When combined with assumptions about recovery rates, these default rates can be used to generate prices for loans. Using their proprietary techniques, Globecon priced loans across the credit spectrum comparing these prices to those found in the market. The following exhibit from "The Bankruptcy Code and Violations of Absolute Priority," *Journal of Applied Corporate Finance* (Summer 1991) shows the recoveries by unsecured lenders in thirty bankruptcies. Globecon suggested correctly that the poll supports the notion that recovery rates usually are greater than zero, and creditors generally recover a substantial amount of principal.

Bankruptcy	Recovery by Unsecured Creditors	
AM International	94%	
Anglo Energy	58%	
Bobbie Brooks	100%	
Branch Industries	100%	
Brody	100%	
Combusion	66%	(midpoint)
Crompton Company	20%	
Evans	87%	
Flanigan's	100%	
Garland Corporation	100%	
Goldblatt	24%	
HRT Industries	75%	
Imperial Industries	33%	
KDT Industries	36%	
Lionel Corporation	100%	(maximum)
Manville	100%	(maximum)
Morton Companies	33%	
PennDixie	45%	(plus stock)
Revere Copper	66%	
Richton International	60%	
Salant Corporation	97%	
Saxon Industries	41%	(midpoint)
SpencerCompanies	30%	(plus stock)
Stevcoknit	3%	
Tenna Corporation	0%	
Towle Manufacturing	60%	
White Motor	51%	
Wickes Companies	76%	(midpoint)

Based on historical bond default data that the spread required to compensate investors increases no more than a few basis points in the Aaa to Baa range (the investment grade spectrum), but jumps by over 350 b.p. from Baa to B. Higher risk requires a higher return—a much higher return. Quoting from Globecon:

■ ■ ■

Bank assets used to carry little or no default risk. As long as loans paid a return sufficient to cover overhead and meet earnings objectives, additional pricing margins were unnecessary. This situation changed in the 1980s. The trend towards higher leverage resulted in widespread deterioration of credit quality. Not only did the quality of bank borrowers slip, but disintermediation pressured banks to price more aggressively. Banks were often unable to hike margins enough to offset the dramatically higher risk that accompanies a fall in credit quality to below the Baa level. This dangerous combination—the loss of pricing flexibility at precisely the point where it was needed most—accounts for many of the problems faced by lenders today.

■ ■ ■

Section Two: New Visions

As illustrated in the Globecon Group statement, banks realize the need to properly price loans but seldom take advantage of modern financial techniques to fine tune pricing benchmarks like ROA/ROE. With loan pricing playing such a vital role in building shareholder wealth, why is this so? The penalty for bad pricing continues to grow as does the need for rigorous analysis of the risk/return tradeoff. But no definitive standard has been established. Investment bankers have successfully blazed new trails in the risk/reward game, yet commercial bankers appear to be only treading water. If banks are afraid to explore different pricing techniques, they must do something about it. In such a crucial time, shouldn't the banking industry aggressively move ahead and catch up with the rest of the world? My response is YES!

In today's environment, most financial managers have taken advantage of option pricing. Option pricing is one of the most useful methods available for formulating financial, investment, hedging and operational strategies, and fine tuning benchmark pricing strategies. Let's use a market-based pricing deal to illustrate how it works.

Factoring Volatility Estimates into Loan Pricing

Maryann and Morton Publishing Corp. has been a valued account at 1st Bank since 1925. The firm has grown from a small local publisher to a respected and widely read New England publisher of health, exercise and running books. It produces a suburban weekly under its fully owned Connecticut subsidiary. The suburban operation accounts for one third of the combined business. Both M & M Publishing and the Connecticut operation have loans with 1st Bank (Exhibit 13.6).

Connecticut's loans are unconditionally guaranteed by M & M Publishing. The market value of the company's combined equity is $36 million and the standard deviation (σ) is .35. The standard deviation measures the volatility of what is being examined, and is considered a good measure of the degree of uncertainty involved. Further, it is an excellent tool for estimating the likely divergence of an actual versus expected return from period to period. The greater the volatility, the greater the risk of the expected return. In the meantime, we'll let the computer crunch the numbers:

$$\sigma_j = \left[\sum_{s=1}^{n} (R_j - \bar{R}_j) P_s \right]^{1/2}$$

σ = Standard Deviation

Exhibit 13.6

Maryann & Morton Publishing Corp. and Subsidiary
Loan Schedule

Business	Loan Amount	Years to Maturity	Rate	Amortization
M & M Publishing Co.	$8,000,000	5	8%	None: due at maturity
Connecticut Subsidiary	$4,000,000	5	8%	None: due at maturity

Percentage returns equate to market returns for equity investors, and in any one year, represent the increase in the investor's equity value plus dividends divided by the investor's equity value at the beginning of the year. Getting back to our example, without the Connecticut operations, the standard deviation of percentage returns equals σ = .45. Over the past few years different demographics resulted in a correlation coefficient = –.5 for the firm:

$$\rho_{jk} = Cov(Rj,Rk)/\sigma j \sigma k$$

ρ_{jk} = Correlation Coefficient of company j's return with company k's return

Remember that returns of two diverse business operations tend to be driven by different supply/demand forces, and this leads us to the correlation coefficient. This is a popular tool used to untangle more complicated statistics like the covariance, which is a statistical measure of the relationship between two random variables and how one element moves with respect to the other.

The correlation coefficient simply "rescales" the covariance to facilitate comparisons with the corresponding values for other pairs of random variables.

For example, if the correlation coefficient approaches – 1, M & M and Conn. returns move in opposite directions (diversification). On a scatter diagram, the two returns will have a "perfectly" negative correlation lying precisely on a straight, downward-sloping line. This means one portion of the operation has a relatively high return and the other a relatively low return. In this instance, risk for the bank is considered low.

On the other hand, a correlation coefficient of + 1, suggests that the returns of both operations are perfectly correlated (all eggs in one basket). A scatter diagram would show both returns lying directly on a straight, upward-sloping line. When one portion of the operation has a relatively high return, so will the other. Conversely, a relatively low return for one will be the same for the other. + 1 may involve a degree of risk and uncertainty for the bank.

Lastly, a correlation coefficient of zero suggests that returns are not related. What this means is that the returns of the operations show a pattern that cannot be identified as an upward or downward-sloping line. Hence, the returns are not correlated, meaning when one operation has a relatively high return, the other can have either a relatively high, relatively low or average return. In this case, the level of risk isn't readily identifiable to the bank.

Back to M & M, which opts to sell the Connecticut company. While the suburban weekly is profitable, it recently felt the impact of a decreasing circulation rate base which has contributed to a downward trend in advertising. Thus, management wants to focus on health books, the backbone of the company. If the firm sells its Connecticut subsidiary, the proceeds will be used to beef up M & M. But diversification in both health books and newspaper publishing reduces corporate risk—assuming demand for health books declines due to social, economic or demographic changes. Health books are luxury items historically influenced by discretionary income. As the publishing industry has witnessed, the recent recession has hampered both advertising and circulation revenues, directly affecting the bottom line. The point is, the suburban weekly diversifies total risk by providing a service to different segments of the publishing market. The operation supplies considerable local coverage and gives the paper a competitive advantage over medium-size dailies.

M & M's health book publishing market is subject to the business cycle and changing demographics including a larger ethnic population, the shift of baby boomers into middle age and an increasing elderly population. Like many businesses, health book publishing faces limited market share and competition. As technology progresses, the medium for health awareness changes. Time brings about oscillations in the needs, demands and forms of leisure activities. Thus, this publishing firm has planned operating strategies around a "Darwinian philosophy" in order to survive, and will argue that the strategy pointing to divestment will be "good for the bank."

M & M met with the bank to obtain approval to divest Connecticut as required by the loan covenants. While 1st Bank will likely go along with the request, it wants to be in a position to renegotiate the existing rate on the $12 million loan. M & M may not initially go along with the rate hike citing the long and mutually beneficial business relationship. However, the bank's strategy will be to "convince" management that the increased rate is justified since the "value" of the bank's exposure will decline with the sale of Connecticut. In other words, after the planned Connecticut divestiture, the bank calculates a loan yield under option pricing conditions that leaves it no worse, pricing wise, than before.

Getting back to the correlation coefficient for a moment, the firm's health and popular psychology operations are negatively correlated. By treating the two operations as a portfolio, management determines the risk of the "portfolio." The mean and standard deviation of the percentage returns of the two operations are examined separately and combined. This is accomplished by a formula that yields the standard deviation of a two investment portfolio (two business units).

$$\sigma p = [W_j^2 \, \sigma_j^2 + W_k^2 \, \sigma_k^2 + 2W_j + W_k + Cov_{jk}]^{1/2}$$

σp = The Standard Deviation of a Two Investment Portfolio: Firm J and Firm K

The equation—*standard deviation of a two investment portfolio*—is essential for the bank to determine if a rate increase is justified. For example, if σp = zero before the planned divestiture, the portfolio's standard deviation, or volatility of the combined returns of M & M's two operations (risk) is zero. If, after the divestiture of Connecticut, σp increases, percentage returns are more volatile giving the bank incentive to raise loan rates.

Evaluating the returns of M & M's two business units is accomplished by calculating the covariance, the correlation coefficient and finally the optimal allocation which identifies the point where the variance is at a minimum. These data allow management to graph the portfolio's (that is, the combined business operations) opportunity set and efficiency set. Given a combination of portfolios, the opportunity set provides the minimum variance (or standard deviation) for a given rate of return. The efficiency set represents the locus of all portfolios (business operations) which have the highest return for a given level of risk. Thus, from the efficiency set, M & M's management can see which "portfolio" gives the highest return for the least risk. However, management needs to know the expected rate of return for each project. If they expect more than the portfolio can provide, they will look to alternative investment opportunities. Management has done their homework.

A fundamental aspect of portfolio analysis is that risk inherent in a single asset or business unit contained in a "portfolio" (similar to consolidated financials). This is different from the riskiness of assets held in isolation (financials of unaffiliated individual firms). The covariance of the "portfolio" determines the correlation coefficient.

$$Cov(R_j, R_k) = \rho_{jk}\sigma_j\sigma_k$$

Cov(Ra,Rb) = Covariance of the returns of J with returns of K

Thus, the correlation coefficient, as before:

$$\rho_{jk} = Cov(R_j, R_k)/\sigma_j\sigma_k$$

As we saw earlier, business units with negative covariance returns are inversely correlated and less risky. Zero correlation returns are unrelated, and business units with positive correlation move together with percentage returns of each unit showing a positive covariance.

Again, employing these techniques, management determines the combination of business units (within the portfolio) providing the highest return blended with the least risk. The issue facing M & M Publishing is essentially risk/return. If the firm's business units are compared to a portfolio, then the risk of the firm (or portfolio) can be divided into two parts: unsystematic (unique or company specific risk: credit ratings focus on unsystematic risk) and systematic risk. Systematic risk cannot be eliminated through diversification. This is the risk for which stockholders must be duly compensated. Unsystematic risk is risk that can be eliminated through diversification. Thus, broadly diversified com-

panies, to the limit, are highly correlated with broad-based market indexes, and risk largely arises through stock market movements.

Upon further examination, systematic risk is a function of the firm's covariance of percentage returns with market returns divided by the variance of the market portfolio. The primary—but not the only—risk that counts to the publishing firm's stockholders is unsystematic risk, the risk that is unique to the firm. The Capital Asset Pricing Model (CAPM) relates the firm's systematic risk, beta, to the rate of return which will be required of it in equilibrium.

$$Rj = Rf + (Rm - Rf)\ \beta j$$

Rj	= Stockholders' Required Return
Rf	= Risk Free Rate
Rm	= Market Returns
β	= Firm J's Beta:
β	= 1; Firm J's returns no more or less volatile than market returns
β	> 1; Firm J's returns more volatile than market
β	< 1; Firm J's returns less volatile than market

In other words, according to the capital asset pricing model, returns associated with risky investments are proportional to beta and therefore are in equilibrium with beta. Beta is the measure of systematic risk. A beta of zero should yield a risk free return, while a beta of 1 suggests increased risk. The cost of the publishing firm's equity capital is a direct result of this relationship. For additional information on CAPM see Appendix I following Chapter 15.

Thus, if stockholders own a single line of business-health books, unique risk is very important. But once stockholders diversify into a portfolio (business combinations that add up to the consolidated entity), diversification has done the bulk of its work. The result is reduced corporate (and bank) risk. How will portfolio analysis, then, help M & M's bank determine the market value of debt, shareholder value, and most importantly, the yields required on restructured loans once the firm executes its strategic plan to sell the suburban weekly operation?

Introduction to Option Pricing

The opportunity cost of capital is a weighted average of the cost of equity and debt capital. Further, it is the return on assets that firms must earn to increase shareholder wealth. Therefore, a study of the capital structure of the subsidiary should be undertaken by means of the Option Pricing Model. With estimates of the cost of equity and cost of debt, the capital structures of both the combined firm and M & M on a stand-alone basis, are analyzed to estimate the cost of capital. Option pricing has the ability to calculate the value of equity on combined operations or on a single entity basis. Savings from economies of scale, managerial motives, complementary strengths or technical competence will have an overriding influence upon combined operation.

While the theory looks attractive, the value of combined operations is not easy to quantify. The general methodology for the analysis of divestitures requires a study of the results of breaking up the two organizations. This includes: an estimate of the applicable cost of capital and expected returns, and the application of valuation principles to formulate estimates of the value of the firms separately and combined. If the value of the combined firm is greater than the sum of the two operations

taken separately, then M & M should not divest itself of its subsidiary.

Black and Scholes pointed out that equity in a firm that has debt can be regarded as a call option. When creditors place debt, shareholders receive cash by selling assets to creditors plus a call option. At maturity, if the firm's value exceeds the value of debt, stockholders will exercise their call by paying off the firm's obligation to the bank.

However, if spinning off Connecticut causes M & M to fail, shareholders will not exercise their option. They will walk away as if options were purchased in the market and the stock declined below the exercise price. The bank will end up with the firm's assets, which will be valued below the face amount of debt. In other words, regarding equity in a levered firm as a call option implies that aggressive investments benefit the firm's shareholders at the expense of the bank, even though the value of the firm is unaffected. Why?

Because idiosyncratic risk is independent of the market portfolio.

An increase in this risk will increase the variance of returns for the firm without changing its its expected return. Therefore, the value of the firm will not change.

But, a redistribution of wealth to shareholders away from the bank (as creditors) will occur. The higher variance will increase the value of the call option held by M & M shareholders. Therefore, increasing the riskiness of the firm's production operations increases the value of equity and decreases the value of debt. The risk and expected rate of return of a call option changes daily simply because it is closer to maturity. Sometimes the most important influence on a business "combination" is a consideration not reflected at all in historical quantitative data. The combination may produce a synergistic effect which generates more profits than could be achieved by the sum of the firms operating independently.

■ ■ ■

For example, if the bank lent to a firm with assets consisting of all treasury bills, the yield the bank would expect to receive would be the treasury rate. If the firm sold most of its treasury bills and purchased equipment, the volatility of percentage returns would certainly increase along with shareholder value. The bank recognizes immediately that they could no longer lend at the risk free rate because increased volatility, associated with more aggressive business strategies, has increased risk bringing down the value of debt.

■ ■ ■

While Maryann & Morton Publishing Company's bankers cannot be absolutely certain of the firm's new level of risk, the bank can use the option pricing model to determine the basis point increase the bank should receive on loans planned for restructuring based on new risk estimates the company has assumed.

Now let's assume Black and Scholes' Excel template projection has been developed (see Exhibit 13.7) with the support of simulation software. The results indicate within a 95 percent confidence level that the risk of percentage returns (standard deviation) has increased from 35 percent to 45 percent. Incorporating this information in our option pricing spreadsheet, the yield on the loan (from within the universe of option pricing) increases 120 basis points compensating the bank for the higher level of risk. This translates into the bank receiving a 120 b.p. compensation on the restructured term loan for them to agree to waive the loan covenant restricting divestment activity (if the company's risk level increases from .35 to .45).

Exhibit 13.7

Black and Scholes Excel Template
The Maryann & Morton Publishing Corp. (Consolidated)
Assumption: Low Risk Diversified Business

Standard Deviation	35.00%
Risk Free Rate	8.0%
Combined Debt Years to Maturity	5
Health Book Operation Face Amt. Debt	$8,000,000
Suburban Operation Face Amt. Debt	$4,000,000
Total Face Amount of Combined Debt	$12,000,000
Market Value of the Firm	$36,000,000
Value of Common Stock	$28,089,627
Present Value of Combined Debt	$7,910,373

The Maryann & Morton Publishing Company sells its Connecticut subsidiary, thus increasing the standard deviation of percentage returns to 45%.

Assumption: Higher Risk Concentrated Business

Standard Deviation	**45.00%**	35.00%
Risk Free Rate	8.0%	
Combined Debt Years to Maturity	5	
Health Book Operation Face Amt. Debt	$8,000,000	
Total Face Amount of Debt	$8,000,000	
Market Value of Health Book Operations	$24,000,000	
Value of Common Stock	$18,950,384	
Present Value of Health Operation Debt	$5,049,616	
Pro forma Change in Value Common Stock	**$223,966**	
Pro forma Change in Value Deb (see reconciliation)	**($223,966)**	
Yield to Compensate for Higher Variance (see reconciliation)	**9.2%**	8.0%
b.p. adj. in yield to compensate for higher risk and reduction in debt value	120.3	

Reconciliation 120.3 b.p. Adjustments to Compensate for Increased Risk

The increased risk of the divestment of suburban weekly has raised the market value of equity by	$223,996
Value of equity before divestment of weekly	$28,089,626
Adjustment to reduce firm 1/3 (2/3 * $28,089,626)	18,726,417
Less: value of equity after divestment resulting in greater variance	(18,950,383)
Increase in shareholder value	223,966

The market value of the risky debt on the other hand declined by an equal amount:

Market value of debt as determined by the option pricing model before divestment	$7,910,373
Adjustment (2/3 *7,910,373)	5,273,582
Value of debt with increase in variability to s.d. .45 from .35	5,049,616
Decrease in the value of debt	(223,966)

In conclusion, though risk is on the rise, the bank has agreed to the restructuring and has presented a clear argument for the higher rates (under option pricing conditions). While the volatility of percentage returns has increased, the bank was able to determine the change in volatility and come up with the "right" loan pricing under option pricing conditions. The $4 million loan to Connecticut was repaid from the proceeds of the sale.

Option pricing is not the only way to price a loan and should never be used alone. However, bankers have the capability to incorporate option pricing to their compendium of techniques as the industry moves toward "mark to market" pricing. By estimating the probabilities that shareholders' call options finish "in the money" bankers can determine, under option pricing assumptions, loan yields associated with the volatility of their borrower's percentage returns. For this reason option pricing provides significant insight into the relationship between degrees of risk and the yields bankers ought to receive—enhancing ROA/ROE targeting—and, most of all, bank shareholder value.

Finally, the promised yield to maturity bankers require on the riskier debt can be determined by solving for the discount rate that equates the payoff 5 years from now with the current market value of the debt as produced by the option pricing model. In order to compensate them for increased risk associated with an increase in variability of returns from .35 to .45, bankers would require a yield of 9.269% instead of the 8% required on the lower risk credit. Subtracting the two values gives us around the 120 basis points generated by this template developed by the author.

Pricing Loans with Warrants

Debt instruments structured with a new genre of warrants—modeled with option pricing software—provide bankers with an array of loan pricing opportunities—beyond the banking opportunities associated with hedges and arbitrage.

Equity warrants: An equity warrant is the right to purchase shares of stock at a predetermined price during a specific period. Typically, the warrant exercise period is five years with the exercise price set at a premium over the share price when the warrants are issued. Equity warrants are sought after when stock prices are expected to rise.

American warrants are securities issued by a corporation granting the holder the right to purchase most shares of common stock at a specified price any time before an expiration date. European warrants are exercisable at maturity. Generally, warrants are distributed with debt, and they are used to induce investors to buy a firm's long-term debt at a lower interest rate than would otherwise be required. Keep the following warrant characteristics in mind:

∎ The value of a warrant depends on several variables that relate to the terms of the instrument and the market. Pricing is driven by option pricing models (such as Black-Scholes included in these notes) although volatility is a major uncertain factor.

∎ The exercise price is typically set 10% to 30% above the prevailing market value of the stock. If the share price rises above the exercise price, it would benefit the warrant holder to exercise the option and purchase the stock. Alternatively, warrants could be sold in the marketplace.

Currency warrants are popular when two currencies are volatile against each other and investors expect a change in the underlying relationship. Bonds with currency warrants were introduced in the Euromarket in late 1986, and in the U.S. market in June 1987. Put options on the Deutschmark are in vogue when the Deutschmark is expected to weaken.

Debt warrants appeal to investors expecting falling interest rates since they entitle the holder to buy a fixed-rate bond at a fixed price, usually par, during the exercise period. Debt warrants, usually good for three years, do not have an explicit issue price. Until recently warrants were issued as separate securities, with their issue price. Debt warrants are also desirable when interest rates are expected to fall and bond prices rise.

Commodity warrants have been issued on a wide range of commodities, but the most common are gold warrants. Warrants have been issued on crude oil (when it was expected to continue rising in price), silver, and price indexes of zinc and copper. Silver warrants are attractive when the price of silver is expected to rise.

Embeddos (Embedded Derivatives) Option-linked debt is now commonplace. A new generation of elaborate financing instruments has developed that effectively reduces the cost of capital. Embeddos take advantage of arbitrage opportunities. Embedded derivatives can be stripped from debt instruments and sold for more than cost, resulting in a windfall that reduces financing costs. The price of embedded derivatives is simply the spread between the price of structured embeddo deals and the price of matching straight debt issues.

As in all embeddos, the borrower was not exposed to option risk, since the borrower's position was completely hedged. The cost of funds was reduced due to the arbitrage position associated with the cost of the put and the hedge. Goldman Sachs structured a $20 million one-year issue of silver-linked bull notes in which embeddos were tailored to match investors' needs. Investors in the silver-linked notes desired both an acceptable coupon and (the expectation of) profit in a rising silver market. Bullish silver investors were willing to risk erosion of principal. Since Goldman Sachs is a major silver trader, they easily hedged the open position using the spot, option and commodity swap markets.

In still another deal, Kodak issued three-year debt with embedded gold warrants at a strike price of $460.70 per ounce. The purchase of one bond entitled investors to buy one ounce of gold. If Kodak went to market with this debt stripped of gold linked warrants, the YTM and coupon would be 9% on face and present value of $1,000.

Here are some of the possibilities:

- Gold is a commodity, and price volatility is easily measured. Thus, (using the following Excel Embeddos worksheet), a gold price can be easily determined whereby the cost to Kodak of the embeddo issue exactly matches the cost of a hypothetical straight debt issue.

- If gold falls below the strike price, YTM declines to 4.23% since Kodak would be required to pay only the face amount.

- If gold rises above the strike price, (assuming the issue went to market unhedged), Kodak pays $1,000 face plus the difference between the market and strike price of gold.

The success of the Kodak option linked deal was due to arbitrage. Kodak's cost of the gold hedge was only $12. while the implied purchase price to investors of the attached gold option was $13.80. The spread resulted in a fully hedged reduction in debt cost of 46 b.p.

Kodak Embeddos Worksheet	
Set Strike Price = To Market Gold Price	
Annual Coupon	9.00%
Number of Periods	3
Annual Coupon	$90
Proceeds from Issuance	1,131.8
Liability at Maturity	1,000

Principal Repayment	$1,000
Strike Price	$461
Market Gold Price	$461
Price of Hedge	$120
B/E Yield	4.23%
Strike Price = Market Price	
Cost of Funds	8.54%
Savings in b.p.	46

Valuing Warrants

Assume Phillip Instrument Corporation's investment bankers were sure the firm's

$50 million, 20-year bonds required a coupon of 14% to "get the issue off the ground" and yield to Phillip $1,000 Present Value equal to the face amount of the debt. Assume further that the CFO's strategies called for increasing the firm's cash flow by capping the coupon at 10 3/8.

From the corporation's perspective, the lower coupon reduces cash outlays throughout the life of the debt, without lowering cash inflows at the time of issuance (the result of the lower bond discount). This cash flow deal was part of a general strategic plan that called for expansion objectives within budget.

With this strategy on the table, investment bankers using option pricing determined that *a coupon rate as low as 10 3/8% equates to a required 14% yield,* if financing were structured calling for ten 5-year European warrants linked to each bond. Warrants entitle investors to purchase one share of common stock at a strike price of $38. The stock price traded at $41.

With the help of the HP 19BII financial calculator, the formula value of the detachable warrants outlined in the following example was:

103.75	PMT	10 3/8% × 1000
1,000	FV	the maturity of the bond is 1000
14	I%YR	the yield is 14%
20	N	maturity is in 20 years
PV =	760.24	present value of the bonds, 10 3/8 coupon; 14% yield requirement

Price paid for bonds with warrants = Straight debt

Value of bond + Value of warrants, or $1,000 = $760 + $240 where:

$240 represents the intrinsic value of the warrants.

$760 represents the present value of the bonds at the lower coupon (10 3/8%) discounted back to present value at a 14% effective rate.

While the formula value was derived using the HP, the intrinsic value of the warrants was derived by the investment bankers using the Black-Scholes Option Pricing Model. Ingersoll applied the option model to pricing warrants.[7]

Structuring Debt with Warrants: Anatomy of a Deal

The previous example demonstrates how investment bankers use the option pricing model to structure an optimal debt structure based on a corporation's strategic goals. The question still remains, can bankers use option pricing to negotiate and structure pricing? The Oil And Gas Development Corp. pricing structure serves to illustrate one of many loan pricing issues facing banks and their corporate clients. The following case analysis will demonstrate innovative financial strategies that translated into highly satisfying loan yields.

Price Per Ounce	Yield to Maturity
$300	4.23%
$350	4.23%
$400	4.23%
$450	4.23%
$500	5.37%
$550	6.78%
$600	8.16%
$650	9.49%
$700	10.80%
$750	12.07%
$800	13.32%
$859	14.75%

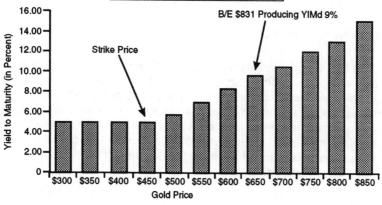

7 Ingersoll, Jonathan. A Contingent-Claims Valuation of Convertible Securities, *Journal of Financial Economics*, May 1977.

■ ■ ■

Case Study

Oil And Gas Development Corp. Structuring Debt
with Warrants

Outline of Terms

Borrowers: Oil And Gas Development Corp. Corporation and its subsidiaries.

Lenders: Oklahoma First Bank.

Facility: Secured $5,500,000 5-year Term Loan.

Purpose: Refinance existing indebtedness to Texas Regional Bank

Rate: LIBOR + 1.5%.

Facility Fee: 2% flat on Oklahoma First Bank's commitment payable upon acceptance by Oil And Gas Development Corp. of the terms outlined herein.

Warrants: 5-year European American warrants for 2,750,000 common shares with an aggregate price of $.50. On a fully diluted basis, the proposed warrant position would represent approximately 18.51% of the common equity. European warrants are exercisable at maturity.

Put: Oklahoma First Bank's right to put warrants to Oil And Gas Development Corp. for $2,000,000 at maturity.

Security: First lien on all Oil And Gas Development Corp. assets including, but not limited to, oil and gas properties, plant and equipment and pipelines.

Maturity: March 31, 1998.

Oil And Gas Development Corp., an Oklahoma corporation, is engaged in the exploration, development and production of oil and gas, primarily in the Southwest. To finance these activities, O & G sponsors its own private placement drilling programs through a network of third-party broker-dealers nationwide. On behalf of these programs, the company performs all services relating to the subject properties from the acquisition of leasehold to the actual marketing production. Income from this process is earned from drilling and operating the wells, and the sale of the hydrocarbon production.

Oil And Gas Development Corp. is traded on NASDAQ. As of 6/30/92, approximately 9.2MM common shares were outstanding, which at the recent bid price of $.50, indicated a market value of $4.6MM. At 6/30/90, the book value of the company was $1.10 per share.

Selected financial information (12/31) is as follows:

Oil And Gas Development Corp.

	12/31/88	12/31/89	12/31/90
Drilling Operations	5,024,000	3,329,000	4,702,000
Oil and Gas Sales	4,698,000	3,944,000	3,407,000
Well Operating Income	1,956,000	1,902,000	1,945,000
Other Income	128,000	119,000	180,000
Total Revenue	11,806,000	9,294,000	10,234,000
Operating Expenses	9,144,000	8,412,000	8,927,000
EBIT	2,662,000	882,000	1,307,000
Net Income (Loss)	184,000	(1,092,000)	(767,500)
Total Assets	27,870,100	27,591,100	28,690,000
Stockholders' Equity	9,805,400	10,711,200	9,943,700

The bank used option pricing to determine the market value of the warrants and the magnitude of the warrant premium. The bank finally settled on a five-year put/call linked debt structure—warrants for 2,750,000 common shares and Oklahoma First Bank's right to put warrants to the company for $2,000,000 at maturity. The three main ingredients served up in the bank's option pricing model were variability of the common stock price, the time remaining prior to expiration and Oklahoma First Bank's yield parameters.

The put/call linked debt feature moves pricing much closer to the risk/reward equilibrium. For example, the interest rate component, plus up front fees equate to a 10.4% loan yield.

Since the company's production is concentrated in oil and gas, any strengthening above certain set prices enhances the value. This will be reflected in the stock price, from which Oklahoma First Bank will directly benefit through its warrant position. If the firm is unable to bring its strategy completely to fruition, Oklahoma

Oil And Gas Development Corporation

Projected Cash Flow

	Actual 1990	Actual 1991	Projected 1992	1993	1994	1995	1996	1997	1998
Net Income	(1,092,000)	(767,500)	(690,750)	(587,138)	(499,067)	(449,160)	(404,244)	(363,820)	(327,438)
Depreciation	1,316,800	1,241,459	1,179,386	1,120,417	1,064,396	1,011,176	960,617	912,586	866,957
Other—Less Expiration	245,247	309,897	300,000	300,000	200,000	100,000	100,000	100,000	0
Deferred Taxes	(549,500)	(371,875)	0	0	0	0	0	0	0
Working Capital Changes	1,989,100	3,367,600	(3,937,880)	0	0	0	0	0	0
Cash Flow from Operations	1,909,647	3,779,600	(3,149,244)	833,279	765,329	662,016	656,373	648,767	539,519
Capital Expenditures	(867,909))	(1,545,900)	(492,300)	(100,000)	(100,000)	(100,000)	(100,000)	(100,000)	(100,000)
Cash Flow from Invest. Act.	867,909	(1,545,900)	(492,300)	(100,000)	(100,000)	(100,000)	(100,000)	(100,000)	(100,000)
Oklahoma First Bank Debt			5,500,000						
Repayment Senior Debt			(500,000)	(1,250,000)	(1,250,000)	(1,000,000)	(1,000,000)	(500,000)	
Borrowing Texas National	130,500	323,700							
Repayment Texas National	(287,700)	(899,300)	(4,500,000)						
Oklahoma FB Front End Fee			(110,000)						
Legal Fees			(150,000)						
Cash Flow from Financing Activities	(157,200)	(575,600)	240,000	(1,250,000)	(1,250,000)	(1,000,000)	(1,000,000)	(500,000)	0
Net Charge in Cash	884,538	1,658,738	(3,401,544)	(516,721)	(584,671)	(437,984)	(443,627)	48,767	439,519
Beginning Cash	2,455,200	3,339,738	4,997,819	1,596,275	1,079,554	494,883	56,899	(386,728)	(337,961)
Ending Cash	3,339,738	4,997,819	1,596,275	1,079,554	494,883	56,899	(386,728)	(337,961)	101,558
Oklahoma FB Facility Begininning			5,500,000	5,000,000	3,750,000	2,500,000	1,500,000	500,000	0
Oklahoma FB Facility Ending			5,000,000	3,750,000	2,500,000	1,500,000	500,000	0	0

	1992	1993	1994	1995	1995	1996
Interest Payments	682,500	612,500	375,000	240,000	120,000	30,000
Principal Payments	500,000	1,250,000	1,250,000	1,000,000	1,000,000	500,000
Fees Paid	110,000					
Loan Servicing Costs	(170,625)	(110,250)	(67,500)	(43,200)	(21,600)	(5,400)
Oklahoma First Outflows	(5,500,000)					
Total Cash Flows	**(4,378,125)**	**1,502,250**	**1,307,500**	**1,196,800**	**1,098,400**	**524,600**
Cumulative Total	(4,378,125)	(2,875,875)	(1,568,375)	(371,575)	726,825	1,251,425
Loan Yield 10.44%						

However, an increase in the stock price to $.60 at loan maturity pushes the yield to 16.49%.

Case Two Fees and Interest, Exercise Call, Stock Price $.60

Stock Price at Maturity	$.60
Exercise Price	$.50
Shares Exercised	2,750,000
Additional Cash Inflow 1996	275,000

	1992	1993	1994	1995	1995	1996
Interest Payments	682,500	612,500	375,000	240,000	120,000	30,000
Principal Payments	500,000	1,250,000	1,250,000	1,000,000	1,000,000	500,000
Fees Paid	110,000					
Loan Servicing Costs	(170,625)	(110,250)	(67,500)	(43,200)	(21,600)	(5,400)
Value of Warrants						275,000
Oklahoma First Outflows	(5,500,000)					
Total Cash Flows	**(4,378,125)**	**1,752,250**	1,557,500	1,196,800	1,098,400	799,600
Cumulative Total	(4,378,125)	(2,625,875)	(1,068,375)	128,425	1,226,825	2,026,425
Loan Yield 16.49						

However, adding the put value of warrants brings the bank's minimum loan yield to 24.01% assuming no upside to the warrants.

Case Three : Fees and Interest, Put Warrants to Company for $2,000,000

Stock Price at Maturity	$.25
Exercise Price	$.50
Shares Exercised	0
Additional Cash Inflow 1996	2,000,000

	1992	1993	1994	1995	1995	1996
Interest Payments	682,500	612,500	375,000	240,000	120,000	30,000
Principal Payments	500,000	1,250,000	1,250,000	1,000,000	1,000,000	500,000
Fees Paid	110,000					
Loan Servicing Costs	(170,625)	(110,250)	(67,500)	(43,200)	(21,600)	(5,400)
Value of Put						2,000,000
Oklahoma First Outflows	(5,500,000)					
Total Cash Flows	**(4,378,125)**	**1,752,250**	**1,557,500**	**1,196,800**	**1,098,400**	**2,524,600**
Cumulative Total	(4,378,125)	(2,625,875)	(1,068,375)	128,425	1,226,825	3,751,425
Loan Yield 24.01						

A rise in the stock price to $1.50 at maturity increases Oklahoma First Bank's loan yield to 26.62%.

Case Three: Fees and Interest, Exercise Call, Stock Price $1.50

Stock Price at Maturity	$1.50
Exercise Price	$.50
Shares Exercised	2,750,000
Additional Cash Inflow 1996	2,750,000

Total Cash Flows	**(4,378,125)**	**1,752,250**	**1,557,500**	**1,196,800**	**1,098,400**	**3,274,600**
Cumulative Total	(4,378,125)	(2,625,875)	(1,068,375)	128,425	1,226,825	4,501,425
Loan Yield 26.62						

First Bank will still be able to supplement its interest/fee return through the put, thus assuring at least a minimum return. On top of excellent yields, the facility is secured with a first lien on all company assets.

■   ■   ■

Conclusion

Based on what was accomplished in the scenario above, doesn't it make sense for a commercial bank to use this type of loan pricing technique? The bank is secured with the company's assets, as well as puts/calls. This is the methodology investment bankers use, and that commercial bankers should use too. Even if a company may be too thinly capitalized, the option pricing model can be used with the Sustainable Growth Model to determine the level of risk and uses of warrants. At this stage, the key catalyst for the bank is convincing the borrower(s) it knows as much as the borrower(s) in each given circumstance. If this is accomplished, companies seeking debt will be more willing to go along with option pricing strategies. Another important point to keep in mind is that if a company does well, it won't mind diluting itself a bit since it: (1) is publicly traded and (2) will receive a greater return. In other words, both the bank and the company have the ability to greatly enhance their profitability using the family of option pricing techniques along with traditional pricing.

The Mathematics of Volatility and Loan Pricing

Assume, hypothetically, a borrower's assets consist mostly of treasuries. If management sold these risk free instruments and purchased productive assets, the firm's earnings would become more volatile. Since equity is a call option, the higher variance increases the value of equity since treasuries pay investors a low yield. The risk of bankruptcy rises and shareholders gain since losses are limited to their original investment. If the bank were funding this fatuous operation, loans lose value on a mark-to-market basis because the borrower's returns become more volatile increasing company specific (unsystematic) risk.

The option pricing model gives us a way to measure the effect volatility has on both debt and equity values. What are options in the basic form? Options allow the holder a right to buy or sell an asset at some predetermined price within a specific period of time. Pure options are instruments created by outsiders such as investment bankers and speculators. These type of options are of greater importance to investors than financial managers. However, except for pure options, financial managers need to understand options to help structure warrants and convertibles. Put options represent the right to sell stock. For example, if you think stock D will fall from its current level of $46.75 over the next five months, you would buy a put option.

Assume that the following information has been obtained on stock D:

1. C = Value of the option

2. S, The standard deviation = .28

3. Rf, The risk free rate = 6.2%

4. T = Days until the option expires = 199

5. S, The stock price now = $46.75

6. X = The exercise price = $45.00

7. $N(d_1)$, the partial derivative with the option's hedged position—to be determined

8. $N(d_2)$, the probabilities that the option will come in the money—to be determined

9. e^{-r_fT} = continuous discounting at the risk free rate for the period the option is exercisable

The option pricing formula is:

$$C = SN(d_1) - Xe^{-r_fT} N(d_2)$$

The heart of option pricing is a statistic called the standard deviation. Digressing momentarily, let's look at two credit applications—The Smith Corp. and The Jones Corp. The firms are homogeneous and boast an average current ratio of 3.0 over 11 years.

	The Smith Corp.	The Jones Corp.
1983	3.2	5.7
1984	3.3	2.3
1985	3.0	3.3
1986	3.2	1.2
1987	3.0	5.0
1988	3.1	0.9
1989	3.1	3.0
1990	3.2	3.0
1991	3.0	1.3
1992	2.0	4.8
1993	2.9	2.0
Average	3.0	3.0
Standard Deviation	0.34	1.56

Jones Corp.'s current ratio deviates or diverges a great deal around the mean (3.0), while Smith Corp.'s ratio is far less volatile. All things equal, you would probably feel more comfortable lending to Smith Corp. If you bought a stock and the stock price was expected to jump all over the place, you would require a higher return to compensate for the risk of capital loss if you had to sell the stock earlier than you originally planned. Also you would be concerned if your customer boasted big profits one year, while suffering huge losses the next. When Standard and Poor or Moody rate a security, a great deal of weight is given to earnings stability.

Returning to the option pricing formula, the standard deviation is a critical variable in $N(d_1)$. To find the value of the option D, the computer will calculate $N(d_1)$, in this case a partial derivative equal to .67401. If the stock price changes 100%, the price of the option changes 67%. From this, a riskless hedge is constructed by buying stock and simultaneously selling "covered" options. The riskless hedge is the reciprocal of $N(d_1)$, $1/.67401 = 1.48366$; we write 148.4 options to hedge against 100 shares of stock D. If lenders hedge foreign currency, or interest rates for their customer, $N(d_1)$ provides the currency or interest rate hedge.

The computer derives $N(d_2)$ = .59661, the probability that the option finishes "in the money" (S X). Thus, e^{-r_fT} = $e^{-.062(199/365)}$ = .966762, represents the present value of $1.00 certain to be received in 199 days, $.9667. However, the $1.00 is anything but certain. If you recall, there is only a .59661 chance of realizing a $1.00 value; the expected present value is therefore = $1.00 (.9667)(.59661) = $.5767. Thus, $Xe^{-r_fT}(d_2)$ = $45(.5767) = $25.95, the expected present value of the exercise price. The stock price adjusts by $N(d_1)$, the reciprocal of the riskless hedge.

$$SN(d_1) = \$46.75(.67401) = \$31.51.$$

Finally, the value of the option:

$$C = SN(d_1) - Xe^{-rT}N(d_2) = \$31.51 - 25.95$$
$$= \$5.56$$

Application of option pricing in corporate finance lies in the insights provided in valuing all securities subject to contingent claims, including warrants, convertibles, and the equity of a levered firm. Equity of a firm with debt can be thought of as a call option. A debt issue is analogous to selling earning assets to creditors who pay for the assets with cash (the loan) plus an implied call option with a striking price equal to the principal plus interest. Since debt is a fixed obligation, the stockholders do well if the firm is successful—the stockholders "buy debt back" at maturity by exercising their call option and paying off the loan plus interest. In this scenario, stockholders pocket a sizeable windfall, since financial leverage rewards owners of a successful business. Should the firm's operating plans cause financial distress, stockholders will not exercise their call, will default on the loan and will hand over the company's assets to creditors.

The Model's Use in Pricing and Valuation Decision: A Pricing Analysis

Jamestown Corporation has outstanding debt of $2,000,000 with First Bank, with five years to maturity. Market value of earning assets are $4,000,000 derived by cash flow valuation techniques. Total risk of the company's percentage returns is .1 (the standard deviation). The risk free rate

is 6%. Using the OPM, we determine the value of debt and equity and the appropriate compensatory loan rate.

Jamestown Corporation

1. S = Value of equity

2. σ, The standard deviation of the firm's returns = .1

3. Rf, The risk free rate = 6%

4. T = Years debt matures = 4

5. V = Value of the firm, combination of the value of debt and the value of equity = $4,000,000

6. D = The face or maturity value of debt = $2,000,000

7. $N(d_1)$, the partial derivative associated with the riskless hedge—to be determined

8. $N(d_2)$, the probabilities that the firm will be financially able to repay the debt at maturity—to be determined.

9. e^{-rT} = continuous discounting factor for the period

The option pricing formula is:

$$S = VN(d_1) - De^{-rT} N(d_2)$$

With $N(d_1)$ and $N(d_2)$ given (by the computer) as 1. The computer solution:

$$S = \$4,000,000(1) - \$2,000,000e^{-.06(5)} = \$2,518,364$$

The value of Debt is:

$$D = \$4,000,000 - \$2,518,364 = \$1,481,636$$

Summary

Jamestown Corporation Assumption:	Low Risk
Standard Deviation in Percent	10.00
Risk Free Rate	6.00%
Days to Expiration	1825
Face Amount of Debt	$2,000,000
Value of Firm	4,000,000
Value of Common Stock	$2,518,364
Value of Debt	$1,481,636
b.p. to Compensate for Increased Risk	0

Now, let's assume Jamestown wants to open a new product line. The company anticipates that the line will increase the volatility of percentage returns from .10 to .35. The computer returns values for $N(d_1)$ and $N(d_2)$:

$$N(d_1) = .9515$$
$$N(d_2) = .81$$

$N(d_2) = .81$ means that a standard deviation of .35 translates into a 19% $(1 - 81\%)$ probability that the new product line will cause the company to fail. Com-

pare this to the earlier calculation that determined that the probability of loan default was zero: $N(d_1) = 1$ and $N(d_2) = 1$ with volatile measured at .10 – the standard deviation. Again $N(d_2) = 1$ means the debt is 100% certain of being paid at maturity. Thus, the value of equity,

$$S = \$4,000,000(.9515) - \$2,000,000$$
$$e^{-.06(5)}.81$$

$$= \$3,806,000 - \$1,200,125$$

$$= \$2,605,875 \approx \$2,606.254.70 \text{ (corrected for rounding)}$$

Under the rules of this version of the option pricing model, we need to adjust the firms value back to $4,000,000 and determine the value of debt. The Value of Debt is:

$$D = \$4,000,000 - \$2,606,254.70 = \$1,393,745.30$$

Values of debt and equity have changed as follows (see chart below):

	Standard Deviation 10%	Standard Deviation 35%	Change In Value
Market value of stock	$2,518,364.10	$2,606,254.70	$87,890.60
Market value of debt	$1,481,635.90	$1,393,745.30	($87,890.60)

The market value of debt has been reduced by $87,890, exactly matching the increase in equity. The firm's value has remained unchanged since wealth has been simply redistributed from one class of investors (the bank) to another (the stockholders). Debt is no longer risk free. At this point the bank needs to recalculate loan rates under option pricing conditions to produce the "right" yield in equilibrium with risk (standard deviation). This part of the calculation is the same as finding the present value of a bond—except now we calculate the yield that equates the obligation's present value and its maturity to face value. The formula is:

Bo $= De^{-rfT}$

Bo — Market value of debt = $1,393,745.30

D = Face value of debt = $2,000,000

e^{-KbT} = continuous discounting factor

Kb = the yield associated with risky debt—to be determined

T = Debt maturity = 5 years

Setting the equation equal to Bo, we have
$1,393,745.30 = $2,000,000e^{-Kb5}$

Solving for Kb and using continuous discounting required by the option pricing model, we arrive at a value of 7.22%, thus:

	Standard Deviation 10%	Standard Deviation 35%	Change	Yield
Stock	$2,518,364.10	$2,606,254.70	$87,890.60	6.00%
Debt	$1,481,635.90	$1,393,745.30	($87,890.60)	7.22%
Basis Point Adjustment Required				122b.p.

In conclusion, the bank requires a 7.22% yield in equilibrium with increased risk. Jamestown Corporation may not initially agree to a rate hike. But by quantifying the tradeoff between risk and pricing, the bank is now in a very strong position to press its arguments. If push came to shove, the bank can at least settle for tighter loan covenants.

CHAPTER *Fourteen*

The Essentials of Interest-Rate Risk Management

A swap is basically an executory contract to exchange interest payments, based on a specified principal amount, over a period of time—floating for fixed and fixed for floating.

Executory contracts imply that one party need perform only if the counterparty performs. Since principal amounts of swaps are not exchanged, they are called "notional" amounts. Swap payments are exchanged monthly, quarterly, or semiannually to match interest payment dates on the underlying funding.

Swaps enable firms to convert effective interest rate on debt from floating to fixed without interfering with the underlying funding. Thus, a company can continue borrowing on a floating basis, but, through a separate agreement, pay the bank a fixed rate in return for receiving a floating rate (e.g., LIBOR, Prime, or Commercial Paper). The floating rate received in the swap offsets the base floating rate index paid on the underlying funding, and the company is left paying a fixed rate, any reserve requirements, and any credit spread over the base floating rate, limiting its exposure.

The swap works because there is a *relative* borrowing rate differential between parties. Both parties gain, despite one probably having an absolute borrowing rate advantage in both the fixed and floating rate markets. The swap arbitrage is driven by the 300–500 basis points spread between credits of varying quality.

Let's illustrate swaps using Doymarn World Construction as a case study:

■ ■ ■

In 1983, Doymarn was fourth worldwide in engineering and construction with a solid reputation as a technical innovator. For fiscal year 1982, Doymarn earned $12.2 million on $1.6 billion in revenue.

First Bank of N.Y. launched a major marketing effort to dislodge Second Bank and Third Bank of California from their lead positions with Doymarn. A break into the Doymarn credit came through a well-known LBO consulting firm known to lending officers at First Bank. The consultants had approached Doymarn's senior management with a proposal to take the company private through an Employee Stock Option Plan (ESOP)-LBO.

The account officers calling on Doymarn at the time proposed aggressive bids to finance the ESOP-LBO; the credit grade was a relatively low-risk 3. The swap was not mentioned in these bids, but Doymarn's management was interested in a series of swaps to hedge against rising interest rates. The projected fiscal year 1983 results were $17.4 million in earnings and $1.4 billion in sales.

First Bank won the bid as co-manager with Third Bank of California. Upon closing in November, 1983, First Bank received a co-manager fee of $650,000. At that time, the established policy was for First Bank's Merchant Banking Group to market the swaps. Group officers outlined the following advantages to Doymarn:

1. The company will be fully protected from rising rates.

2. Future interest flows are certain—important for developing operating strategies and capital budgeting plans.

3. No upfront fees will be required.

4. If the yield curve is inverted when the swap is transacted, the fixed rate will initially be lower than the alternative variable rate (as with any rate-fixing mechanism).

5. If a swap is terminated prior to maturity, and interest rates have risen sufficiently, a gain may be realized (akin to redeeming a bond at a discount).

The second point was particularly pertinent. It made good sense for Doymarn to swap because the ESOP-LBO pushed financial leverage to high levels—approximately $200 million in LIBOR + 2% floating debt. Doymarn's financial managers saw the swap as an excellent hedge against rising rates, and bankers wanted to arrange a swap to lessen similar concerns.

Doymarn's treasurer reviewed the firm's *Investment Opportunity Schedule.* The IOS is important since it compares the expected project returns to the company's marginal cost of capital. This is accomplished by first plotting the returns expected from Doymarn's proposed capital expenditure projects against the cumulative funds required. The result is called an *investment opportunity curve.* Next, incremental weighted costs of capital are combined to determine the company's *marginal cost of capital curve.* Management rejects projects if the investment opportunity curve falls below the marginal cost of capital curve.

What could cause this to happen? For example, unexpected increases in interest rates to K1 produces project losses below the curve. Doymarn establishes rates of return (yields) with relative ease; predicting interest rates is more difficult. Compounding the problem, the company's pro forma post-LBO leverage made it excessively sensitive to unexpected changes in interest rates.

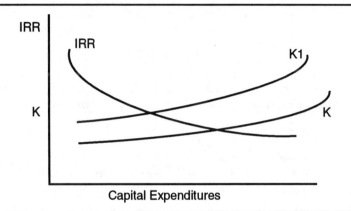

Capital Expenditures

Instead of locking in a fixed rate with a swap, Doymarn could have easily purchased an option on a swap, or a cap. With an option on a swap, the company could pay an upfront premium for the right (not the obligation) to initiate a swap during some definite time period.

Doymarn picks a strike rate, the fixed rate the company pays in a swap if and when it exercises the option.

If rates increase slightly during the option period, the company continues to pay interest on a floating rate basis, letting the option expire unexercised. If rates rise, the company has the right to exercise its option and thereby lock in the fixed strike rate for the remaining life of the loan. The swap option is more flexible than a swap, because it does not commit the company to pay a fixed rate.

An interest rate cap is a widely used agreement which sets an upper limit on a floating rate index on which interest payments are based. The buyer of a cap specifies the index (for example three-month LIBOR) and the "strike" rate (e.g., 8%) of the cap for a specific tenure and dollar amount of protection (e.g., three-year cap on $10 million).

If, on any three-month reset date during the life of the cap the three-month LIBOR is greater than the strike rate on the cap, the issuing bank pays the difference to the owner of the cap. As long as the three-month LIBOR remains below the strike rate on any reset date during the cap's life, no payments are made under the cap. This means the company's effective borrowing cost is equal to the prevailing LIBOR rate plus any reserve requirement and the credit spread. Thus, the borrower absorbs increases in LIBOR only up to the cap's strike rate and no more. The cap is an "asset" which can be sold anytime; the company is not under any obligation once an upfront cap premium is paid. However, the purchase of a cap requires payment of an upfront fee typically higher than the upfront costs of other options-based alternatives, particularly in longer maturities.

A cap is similar to a homeowner's insurance policy. You pay a premium to be protected against fire. If fire doesn't occur, you still win even though you might be momentarily upset because you paid out a premium "but saw nothing for it."

Banks arrange swaps or guaranty performance under a swap agreement. In the former case, the bank brokers the swap and takes an arrangement fee, making no representations about either counterparty's ability to perform. In the latter case, the bank guarantees performance of one or both of the counterparties.

The Doymarn swap facility was guaranteed by First Bank and California Third Bank, each bank sharing the risk and fees. The final deal swapped $75 million of the company's floating debt for fixed rate obligations. The following table represents the end deal.

Amount	Maturity	Pays Japanese Bank	Gty Fee	Pays to Bank	Total
$50MM Tranche	5 Years	12.81%	0.26	+2% over LIBOR	15.07%
$25MM Tranche	3 Years	12.26%	0.21	+2% over LIBOR	14.47%
$75MM Total					

The likely counterparty for Doymarn was a Japanese bank. The counterparty issued a Eurodollar obligation requiring an annual coupon of 12.70%. The Japanese bank had an absolute borrowing advantage in both the fixed and floating markets, but through the swap the Japanese bank's accessed sub-LIBOR money. The following funds-flow illustration is based on the $50 million swap tranche.

Both Doymarn and the Japanese bank now have debt outstanding:

Bank	LIBOR +2	Doymarn	First Bank of N.Y.	Japanese Bank	12.70% Annually	Eurodollar Note
	←					
Debt	LIBOR +2					→
	←					

Doymarn and the Japanese bank swap interest payments through First Bank of N.Y.:

Doymarn	13.07%	First Bank of N.Y	← Libor ←	Japanese Bank
	→		← Libor ←	
	Fixed— Annual		Floating— Semi-Annual	

First Bank of N.Y. in turn distributes the funds according to the swap agreement.

Doymarn	LIBOR	First Bank of N.Y.	12.81	Japanese Bank
	←	26 b.p. Gty. Fee	→	
	LIBOR			
	←			

Counterparties fulfill their respective obligations under the original debt instruments while First Bank of N.Y. splits the 26 basis points guaranty fee with California Third Bank.

Bank	LIBOR +2	Doymarn	First Bank	Japanese	12.70%	Eurodollar
	←		of N.Y.	Bank	Annually	Note
Debt	LIBOR +2				→	
	←					

The effective borrowing costs are outlined below:

Doymarn		**Japanese Bank**	
Pays Annually (12.81% + 0.26%)	− 13.07%	Pays Semi-Annually	− LIBOR
Receives from Japanese Bank	+ LIBOR	Receives	12.81
Pays to Banks	− LIBOR + 2	Pays to Euronote	−12.7
Effective Cost (13.07% + 2)	15.07	Effective Cost	LIBOR −.11

The swap was economically advantageous to all parties since Doymarn could not raise fixed rate money for less than 15.07% fixed.

INTEREST RATE SWAPS: MEASURING RISKS

Don Smith and Keith Brown, two experts in swap risk management, identify two ways of looking at default risk: 1) actual exposure, which is a measure of the loss if the counterparty were to default and is based on the movement in swap market rates between the inception of the agreement and the current date; and 2) potential exposure, which is based on a forecast of how market conditions might change between the present and the swap's maturity date, including in some manner the probability of default by the counterparty.[1]

Smith and Brown suggest that default risk exposure on the most common ("plain vanilla") interest rate swap differs from that on an ordinary bond in three important ways:

1. The swap structure requires no exchange of principal payments at inception or maturity, settling instead on a notional principal used to transform interest rates into cash flows for each settlement period. Thus the principal is not exposed to risk.

---

1 Keith C. Brown and Donald J. Smith, "Default Risk and Innovations in the Design of Interest Rate Swaps." *Journal of Financial Management* V22 N 2 1993.

2. Since swaps are executory contracts, if one party fails to pay the floating rate, the other is not obligated to pay the fixed rate. Smith and Brown intimate that this is why the risk exposure on a swap is considerably less than that on a bond of equivalent face value. Exposure is limited to the difference between the present values of the remaining fixed rate and floating rate cash flows.

3. Default risk exposure is bilateral in that each party must be concerned about the possible default of the other.[2]

Since First Bank and California are acting as guarantors to the interest rate swap, a credit risk is generated in three fundamental ways:

1. If the weaker party (Doymarn) defaults, there is a potential loss to First Bank—at the time of default which is equal to the cost of the bank having to replace the weaker party at then current swap market rate. The default can occur when the counterparty, based on prevailing interest rates, owes funds to First Bank and is unable to meet its obligations.

2. Interest rate differential payments between the Japanese bank and Doymarn are not made on a net basis. For example, payments occur on different settlement dates; First Bank pays floating semiannually (to Doymarn) and receives fixed annually (from Doymarn). This results in additional potential loss above and beyond the replacement value of the swap, should the counterparty default. Doymarn could end up financially distressed after receiving its semiannual payment and not be in a position to remit interest payment when due.

3. Declining interest rates put the bank at risk unless the swap were hedged, which is almost always the case.

Remember, an interest rate swap represents an exchange of interest rates; no principal is exchanged. For example, trading a Ted Williams card for a Joe DiMaggio is analogous to an interest rate swap. You might ask, "What is so risky about trading baseball cards?" Imagine you give me a DiMaggio and I respond by bolting out the door, card in hand, shouting "I forgot Ted Williams, you'll get it in three weeks." (Doymarn receives payment but may go bankrupt before it can pay—or trade the baseball card. I could have easily blazoned, "Give me the Joe DiMaggio now and in ten months I'll trade you for Ted Williams." In ten months, I indeed return with the card, but the market is now flooded with a glut of Ted Williams baseball cards and I trade a worthless card. No matter, you say, First Bank of N.Y. provided a guarantee protecting me from loss in the value of Ted Williams cards.

How will the bank calculate that kind of "intangible" risk, trading baseball cards, interest rates, or anything else for that matter? If the bank made a loan, risk is easily measured; the loan is tangible. The maximum loss lending money is the

2   Ibid.

principal (assuming interest is paid). If the bank lent out $4,000,000 the maximum loss is $4,000,000. Is there a way to calculate the maximum loss the guarantor bank can have on a swap? The answer is yes. The concepts are (1) Fractional Exposure, and (2) Mark to Market.

Fractional Exposure

Fractional exposure represents the maximum loss associated with swap risk—looking past the horizon. It's like taking the concept of swaps and equating it to concepts behind a loan transaction. For example guaranteeing a stream of "X" interest payments is equivalent to making a loan to the borrower of "Y." Let's look at five ways of calculating fractional exposure and evaluate each one.

Method One

When interest rate swaps became a major financial tool in the late '70s and early '80s, banks were not very familiar, or sophisticated in pricing swaps. The first calculation of Fractional Exposure was at best naive, at worst exceptionally conservative: Fractional Exposure was estimated to be equal to 20% of Total Swap.

Amount	Percentage	Fractional Exposure	First Bank Fractional Exposure	California Fractional Exposure
$50MM Tranche				
25MM Tranche				
$75MM	20%	$15MM	$7.5MM	$7.5MM

In the example, the swap risk is $15 Million shared equally by the two banks. If the swap party was General Electric Corp. instead of Doymarn, the calculation would be the same. Obviously, the risks are not.

Method Two

The second method was employed by a number of banks from the middle 1980s until very recently. It is still used by some banks as a "check" but with modifications:

Fractional Exposure = (2% + Netting Factor + (1.6% × original swap tenor)) × notional principal

where:
Netting Factor =

0% in net or favorable non-net settlement swaps

4% where payments are unfavorably semiannual vs. annual

6% where payments are unfavorably quarterly vs. annual

8% where payments are unfavorably monthly vs. annual

Netting Factor	Pay Doymarn	Receive from Doymarn
4%	Semiannual*	Annually
6%	Quarterly	Annually
8%	Monthly	Annually

*Remember the Japanese bank pays Doymarn—**floating**—semiannually while accepting from Doymarn—**fixed**—annually. This mismatch is risk adjusted by the netting factor.

1.6% is a statistical adjustment factor that delineates interest rate volatility in dollars. Swap payments exchanged in Swiss Franc or Yen reduce the benchmark while payments in Australian dollars raise it.

Thus:

$50MM Tranche 5 Years:

Fractional Exposure = (2% + 4% + (1.6% × 5)) × $50MM = $7MM

$25MM Tranche 3 Years

Fractional Exposure = (2% + 4% + (1.6% × 3)) × $25MM = $2.7MM

Total	$9.7MM
First Bank of N.Y. Share	$4.85MM
California Third Bank Share	$4.85MM

Problems with Method Two

(1) If Doymarn had agreed to deposit interest payments (from the Japanese bank) in an escrow account, or if the original swap agreement called for matched payments, the netting factor reduces to zero. (2) The 2% statistical risk factor reflecting average swap risk could easily underestimate Doymarn's fractional exposure. It should be adjusted to reflect the firm's risk. (3) Loan tenure should mirror time remaining instead of original tenure.

Method Three: Econometric Models

By far the best method, econometric models, track historical interest rates, and through simulation find (within a 95 percent confidence level), probabilities that actual exposure is greater than fractional exposure. For example, a 95 percent confidence level intimates a 5% probability that actual exposure exceeds fractional exposure.

Other Techniques Used to Calculate Fractional Exposure

1. In a study by J. Gregg Whittaker, the credit exposure of interest rate swaps was explored to determine if a formula for swap pricing was feasible.[3] As a foundation for his research project, Mr. Whittaker speculated that interest rates follow a log-normal distribution with a volatility of one standard deviation. In conjunction with an options pricing formula to value swaps, the optimum exposure for a 10-year matched pair of swaps (netting factor zero) does not exceed 8 percent of the notional principal.

2. A study by the Federal Reserve Board and the Bank of England was done to evaluate the potential increase in credit exposure of a matched pair of swaps. The findings of the study were used to ascertain the regulatory capital requirements for interest rate swaps. Basically, both organizations formulated a measure of the credit exposure associated with a matched pair of swaps in the same manner that credit exposure is extrapolated off balance sheet loans. To do this, the Monte Carlo simulation technique was employed to estimate the probabilities associated with different potential increases in credit exposure. Interest rates were assumed to follow a log-normal, random walk distribution with the volatility measure equal to the 90th percentile value of changes in interest rates over six-month periods. The Fed and Bank of England discovered that at the 50 percent confidence level, the potential increase in credit exposure was no greater than 0.5 percent of the potential principal of the swap per year. Further, at the 99 percent confidence level, the credit risk exposure was found to be no greater than one percent of the notional principal.[4]

3. Terrence Belton, using a vector auto-regressive model to appraise different Treasury rates, investigated the possible increase in credit swap exposure. His findings indicate that the potential increase in credit exposure of swaps precipitated by rate changes can be sheltered by adding a surcharge of one to five percent of the notional principal to the current exposure for swaps with a maturity of 2 to 12 years.[5]

MARK TO MARKET

Mark to market represents actual loss *today* if the counterparty (Doymarn) failed *today and* (2) interest rates move in the wrong direction as measured *today:*

---

3 "Pricing Interest Rate Swaps in an Option Pricing Framework," working paper RWP 87-02, Federal Reserve Bank of Kansas City, 1977.

4 Refer to C. W. Smith, C. W. Smithson and I. M. Wakeman, "Credit Risk and the Scope of Regulations of Swaps," in Conference on Bank Structure and Competition (Chicago: Federal Reserve Bank of Chicago, 1987) pp. 165–185. Critical analysis of the Federal Reserve and Bank of England study.

5 Terrence Belton "Credit Risk in Interest Rate Swaps," working paper, Board of Governors of the Federal Reserve System, April 1987.

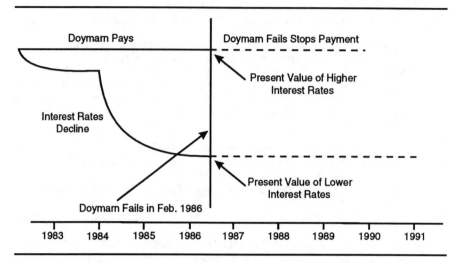

Remember, the bank guarantees Doymarn fixed payments via First Bank of N.Y. (the agent bank) to the Japanese bank. If for any reason payments are not disbursed, First Bank of N.Y. must make good. If you recall, interest rates fell during the period 1983 to 1986. This means that Doymarn is required to pay at the higher rate, provided the firm is still in business. But, Doymarn went bankrupt and liquidated holdings in February of 1986.

This resulted in First Bank having to find an investor willing to pay at the higher rate. Had rates increased between 1983 and 1986, losses would have turned into windfall even if Doymarn defaulted; the bank simply takes the deal over for its own account replacing Doymarn, or finds outside parties.

Through discussions between various swap banks, the conceptual framework was narrowed down to a model that "marked to market" and then "bid the swap." In describing the model, the future credit fees were eliminated. Two generally accepted International Swap Dealers Association brokers were selected by Doymarn and the other two banks. The Doymarn swap looked to the brokered screen quotes from the two swap dealers. By checking these quotes, the banks determined what the spread over treasuries was for various maturities. These averaged together, equal the unwind benchmark cost; this is defined as the maximum unwind loss. Of course, this will not happen unless the investor receives a settlement equal to the present value differential of the streams of interest payments at the two rates. Likewise, bonds paying coupons below the market rate sell at discount, indemnifying investors to the penny for lower coupon payments. Bond paying coupons exceeding the yields investors demand sell at a premium. Similarly, had rates increased between 1983 and 1986, losses turn to windfall even if the weaker party, Doymarn, defaults; the bank simply takes the deal over for its own account replacing Doymarn, or finds outside parties.

A group of four market lending swap banks then had an opportunity to bid on the one year and the three-year tranches. If the winning bid "beats the benchmark," the unwind cost is lower. None of the bids were attractive relative to the benchmark quote. The lead bank, First Bank of N.Y., bought the open bid position for its own account and covered the position with U.S. treasuries. Using this method, the unwind loss (reflecting the market/funding loss) was approximately $8.6 million, shared equally by the two banks.

■ ■ ■

MANAGEMENT OF RISK EXPOSURE

Risk management of swap transactions centers on the assessment of the counterparty's financial stability and condition and its capacity to meet financial responsibilities under the swap agreement. There is no basic difference between the assessment of commonplace credit risk and credit risk associated with interest rate swaps. Observe the following caveats:

■ If the bank is the unfavorable party to a non-net settlement swap (i.e. the bank pays more frequently), consider including a clause in the swap contract giving the bank the right to establish mandatory netted payments if a default or potential default occurs.

■ Borrowers with operating difficulties should not add arbitrage risks. A deteriorating credit should not be dependent on a swap in the hope that the bond market will adjust in favor of the borrower.

■ Reversing swaps—swapping out and back to fixed rates may produce regular funding losses to a company but may reduce the possibilities of a Doymarn recurrence (a funding loss). The swap documentation should provide the bank sufficient flexibility to force a reverse swap without the company's consent if loan covenants are violated.

■ "Collateral-weak" counterparties may agree to post collateral. If collateral values fall below a certain level of the termination exposure, mark to market, the counterparty would be required to post additional collateral to maintain the cover. The failure to produce further collateral may in itself be covered as a default if designated in the swap agreement. Consequently, exposure under the swap on termination can never exceed the value of the collateral posted. For obvious reasons, swap exposure must be consistently monitored.

■ Banks guaranteeing performance under an interest rate swap will lose if the weaker swap party defaults at a time when interest rates have moved adversely. Because interest rates are never static, this solution is impractical because it requires virtually perpetual exchanges of mark to market cash flows. As a more manageable alternative, the counterparties could agree to a strategy in which the renegotiation occurs only on the periodic settlement dates of the swap (i.e., when cash flow exchanges were scheduled to occur anyway).

CHAPTER *Fifteen*

Valuation and Credit Risk: New Developments[1]

Although employed by strategic planners and investment bankers for many purposes, shareholder valuation analysis (SVA) has been largely overlooked in the credit process.

The ultimate purpose of business is to create wealth, and the understanding of how wealth creation is planned and managed is integral to being both a good banker and a good businessperson. Understanding the mechanics of wealth (or value) creation enables the banker to understand and assist customers in achieving their goals and aspirations, while creating value for the bank as well.

Value maximization is broader than "profit maximization." Strategic planning with the goal of maximizing value incorporates the time value of money by considering future cash flow, risk, and going concern assumptions.

- First, funds received this year have more value than funds received one or ten years hence.

- Second, value maximization considers the riskiness of the income stream. For example, the rate of return required on riskless government securities would be lower than the rate of return required on an investment in starting a new business.

- Third, the certainty, quantity and timing of expected future cash flows may vary. Profit figures can vary widely depending upon the accounting presentation and conventions chosen; but there is considerable evidence that financial markets see through differences in accounting

---

1   Rob Gaddis, a manager at Price Waterhouse Valuation Services Group, co-authored this chapter.

procedures that affect reported profit, and gauge underlying true determinants of value.

Approaches to Value

Book Values Reflect the Past

Book values, based on accounting numbers, reflect historical costs. In other words, book values do not consider the future and, therefore, are in most cases not good decision-making references. Accrual accounting reflects prior investments and indicates only a vague approximation of real economic value.

Consider the following example: A company buys a truck and, after depreciating it over a period of time, records it with a zero book value. If the truck is sold, chances are the company will receive greater than zero for the truck if it still runs.

Despite an attempt to match accounting life with economic life, accrual accounting failed to reflect the truck's true value. Accrual accounting is conservative. Consequently, there is often a poor relationship between book and market values. Book value ignores price fluctuations of real assets such as real estate or timberland, as well as intangibles like goodwill, trademarks, franchise licenses and patents, which can be powerful cash-generating assets.

The Market Approach

Under this method value estimation calculations are based on actual prices paid for comparable companies relative to certain accounting and market benchmarks such as earnings, revenue, book value of equity or total market capital. This method of valuation draws on the efficient markets hypothesis: the stock price of publicly traded firms is a composite of all readily available information and the supply and demand effects of educated and rational buyers and sellers. This means that the market continuously values firms, mirroring each value assessment in bids and offers for stock, or outright purchase in a transaction.

One problem with the market approach is the difficulty of locating companies that are truly comparable to a subject company, since most firms in the same industry have different product lines or are diversified to some degree, reducing overall similiarity to the subject company comparability. Alternatively, it is sometimes possible to identify at least a few peers that could be viewed as reasonable comparables for a subject company.

A Coopers & Lybrand manual suggests that the benefit of using the market approach is only as good as:

■ ■ ■

". . . the comparability of the companies from which the analysis is based. The higher the degree of correlation between the operations in the peer group and the subject company, the better the analysis. Some of the more significant attributes used to determine comparability include:"[2]

■ ■ ■

- Type of product produced
- Market segment to which the product is sold
- Geographic area of operation
- Positioning in marketplace
- Influence of buyers/suppliers

---

2   *Coopers & Lybrand Business Acquisitions and Leveraged Buyouts: Solutions for Business*, copyright 1989.

- Growth, historical and projected
- Profitability
- Leverage and Liquidity
- Diversification

Once the peer group has been identified, all of the companies' financials should be examined to allow for comparability. Some of the more important adjustments Coopers & Lybrand identify include:[3]

- Extraordinary and nonrecurring items inventory policy: FIFO vs. LIFO
- Revenue recognition policy
- Non-operating assets
- Excess marketable securities and cash
- Contingent liabilities
- Pension and other post-employment benefits funding and expense policy

Market Approach

Multiples based on industry or peer group analysis include:

Price/Earnings Ratio:

Comparable Company Stock Price
× Subject Company Earnings

Comparable Company Earnings

= Subject Company Stock Price

If the stock should sell at 7 times earnings, and if we assume earnings were $1 million, equity value is $7 million. The simple earnings multiple model may be used where company value is the product of either current or projected earnings multiplied by a P/E ratio. Although there are problems associated with this approach, P/E multiples are popular. To best utilize the price-earnings multiple:

1. Examine past trends of comparable companies for turnover and profit margins similar to your subject company.

2. Adjust earnings of both subject company and comparables for non-sustainable income (i.e., extraordinary income that is unusual in nature, infrequent in occurrence and material in amount).

There are other variations of the multiple method of valuation. These variations include earnings plus interest and taxes (EBIT), cash flow and other multiple calculations.

Commonly used multiples include:

Price	Price	Stock Price
EBITD	EBITDA	Book Equity

Market Capitalization	Price
Book Capitalization	Revenues

Each has its most appropriate use under different circumstances: Price/Earnings is the quickest calculation. The Price to EBITD or EBITDA approaches provide an economically sounder basis for value (cash flow as opposed to net income) but require more data gathering and analysis than P/E. Price/Book and Market Cap/Book Cap are useful if you are examining companies with negative income and cash flow. Price/Revenues is useful if you have no more information than sales figures and/or book equity is negative.

The comparable transactions approach examines specific transactions of comparable companies that have been recently sold, the prices and other relevant information of which may be researched in such published sources as *Mergerstat Review* and the *Corporate Growth Report,*

---

3 Ibid.

among others. The same multiples may be applied as in the market comparable approach. If data on transactions are available on companies comparable to your subject company, these can be used to great advantage. These sources also list private companies and transactions involving subsidiaries or divisions, data for which would be unavailable from any other source.

Market comparables analysis suffers from the difficulty of finding reliable comparable companies and manageability of accrual accounting numbers, and from a hindsight perspective. The market approach to valuation predicts current value purely from historical performance and events, which are largely irrelevant to future benefits a prospective buyer would hope to realize.

An important subset of the reliable comparables dilemma is size bias in using publicly traded companies as comparables—most publicly traded companies are large compared to the vast numbers of small companies which are more likely to be your bank's customers. Small companies are generally riskier than large ones because they can find themselves at a competitive disadvantage against larger companies, and have less access to capital markets and other resources. Business appraisers use techniques such as regression analysis based on studies like the Lynch Jones & Ryan market size survey to adjust market approach results for size differences between comparables and subject companies.

Despite the limitations of market comparables analysis, it is very widely used and it can serve as an excellent benchmark with which to confirm or question values determined by more analytically

rigorous methods, such as the discounted cash flow approach.

Liquidation Valuation Approach

The major assumption here is that value is not based on the firm as a going concern. Normally, there are at least three liquidation values:

- **Orderly liquidation value** is the amount the assets will generate net of any liabilities if disposed of in the normal course of business. Disposal of equipment in the normal course of events is a good example of orderly liquidation value.

- **Not so orderly liquidation based on auction** is associated with a forced sale of company assets at auction prices based on liquidation value.

- **Replacement Value (or cost approach)** represents the amount it would cost a potential buyer to duplicate the firm's assets at current market prices.

Liquidation value should be used when it shows a higher value than discounted cash flow—which means a business is worth more sold off as separate assets rather than run as a going concern. The choice here is between a going concern or a breakup.

Valuation Based on Dividends

This method suggests that the value of equity is driven by dividends. Before the introduction of the Capital Asset Pricing Model, the *dividend valuation method*, known as the *Gordon Dividend Growth Model* was used extensively. The Gordon Model was applied to companies whose earnings and dividends are expected to increase each year.

The presumption implicit to the Gordon Model is that, although expected growth rates vary from company to company, dividend growth, in general, is expected to continue in the foreseeable future at about the same rate as that of the nominal gross national product. On this basis, it is expected that the average or "normal" company will grow at a rate of three to five percent a year, rising if the inflation rate increases.

So if a company's average or normal last dividend (which has already been paid) is D_0, its dividend in any future Year t may be forecasted as $D_t = D_0 (1 + g)^t$, where g is the constant expected rate of growth. For example, Teletron Electronics just paid a dividend of $1.82. If investors expect a 10 percent growth rate, then the estimated dividend one year hence is:

$D_1 = (\$1.82)(1.10) = \$2.00$; D_2 will be $2.20; and the estimated dividend 5 years will be:

$$
\begin{aligned}
Dt &= Do(l + g)t \\
&= \$1.82(1.10)^5 \\
&= \$1.82(1.61) \\
&= \$2.93
\end{aligned}
$$

By using the dividend growth model of estimating future dividends, the current stock value, P_0 can also be determined. By finding the expected future cash flow stream of dividends, the present value of each dividend payment, and then sum these present values, the value of the stock is deciphered. Thus, the intrinsic value of the stock is equal to the present value of the expected future dividends.

If g is constant,

$$
P_0 = \frac{D_0(1 + g)}{ks - g}
$$

ks: Cost of equity capital or the required rate of return.

The equation can be restated as:

$$
P_0 = \frac{D_1}{ks - g}
$$

where D_1 next year's dividend that will grow at a constant rate

Inserting values into the equation, we find the value of this stock to be $33.33:

$$
P_0 = \frac{\$1.82(1.10)}{.16 - .10} = \$2.00/.06 = \$33.33
$$

Weakness of the Constant Growth Models

A few aspects of the Gordon equation require special consideration. First, for the stock to have a meaningful price, the required rate of return (ks) must be greater than the growth rate (g). If ks equals g, the stock price is infinity; ks < g produces a negative shareholder value. Both results are nonsense. Second, it is important to understand the assumptions underlying the Gordon equation, since the model is derived under the assumption that the growth rate in dividends is constant into perpetuity.

The first difficulty is in determining the future growth rate. It must be assumed that this rate will be sustained forever. No company maintains a constant growth rate forever, especially if its current growth rate is high. For example, consider a new company with a current dividend of $1.00 and a growth rate of 20%. Even if one believes that this growth will continue, it cannot last forever. Remember the growth curve of a business cycle? Each phase has a different rate of growth than the other three. Let's say after three years a company's growth rate is expected to come down to a stable 5% per year. The Gordon valuation model is rendered inoperable because the growth rate changed after three years.

Finally, do dividends increase annual returns? It may appear from the preceding equation that the annual return rises when dividends rise. But this may or may not be the case. An increase in dividends draws cash from investments, perhaps compelling management to raise funds through external sources to make the same investments, or to not invest at all. And what about a growth company, (say biotech) that pays a low (or no) dividend because of the necessity to invest for growth? Such a company would be undervalued compared to a mature-industry company paying a high dividend.

Cash Flow Approach (Going Concern)

The Discounted Cash Flow (DCF) valuation approach can provide a "going concern" value; that is, the value driven by a company's future economic productiveness. Although DCF is more precise and economically sound than the other approaches, it is underused.

With DCF the firm's value is calculated by adding the present value of projected cash flows for a specific forecast horizon (projection period) to the present value of the firm beyond the forecast period (residual or terminal value). Thus, shareholder value is determined by discounting the cash flow streams by the subject company's weighted average cost of capital, adding unrealized, and/or non-operating asset values net of the expected value of contingencies, and then subtracting the market value of debt.

To better understand DCF think of the value of a business as the sum of the investments it makes. The value of the firm is then the sum of the values of these individual investments. For example, take one application of valuation, capital budgeting. The principles of business valuation and capital budgeting are almost identical, except in business valuation all assets are considered, not just fixed assets. Understanding how capital budgeting is accomplished leads directly to a deeper understanding of DCF. A review of capital budgeting techniques in Appendix II of this chapter may provide enlightenment.

Finally, financial software is available in various forms, from simple spreadsheets, which require analysts to structure models, to elaborate, pre-programmed systems with a pre-ordained theoretical model structure such as Alcar's *Value Planner* or Chemical Bank's *Financial Analysis System.*

The Four Building Blocks of Valuation

We saw earlier how research and well-thought-out assumptions result in projections that are precise, detailed and offer useful insight into the future. We learned the foundations of critical assumption analysis, and used it to construct a projection and establish a risk profile. Now we'll examine projections on a transcendent plane—how financial forecasts bring corporate strategies to the test in the arena of shareholder value.

The building Blocks of Valuation are broken down into four parts:

1. Establishing a basic procedure for reforming shareholder value analysis.

2. Value driver frameworks.

3. Evaluate the implications of valuation projections.

4. Refine strategies that maximize value.

An Approach to Value

The process starts with the basics by applying what are described as *Value Drivers* and ends by setting up a valuation framework for our old friend Gem Furniture, using Alcar's *Value Planner* software.[4]

1. Establishing a Basic Procedure for Performing Shareholder Value Analysis

In calculating value using shareholder value analysis, we are looking to determine value by estimating the following three "building blocks" of value:

- Cash Flow from Operations
- Long-Term Horizon
- Risk and Time Value of Money

Cash Flow from Operations

By concentrating on forecasting the company's operating cash flow, we can distinguish between the operating and financing decisions of the firm. Once cash flow is estimated, we can then take risk into account, discounting those cash flows by the cost of capital. The definition of cash flow is:

Sales
  – Operating Expenses
  – Depreciation Expense
  – <u>Taxes on Operating Profit</u>
   Operating Profit (after-tax)
  + Depreciation Expense
  – Fixed Capital Investment
  – <u>Incremental Working Capital Investment</u>
  = Operating Cash Flow

The estimation of cash flow obviously involves employing forecast techniques that try to include the best information available to the analyst (e.g.,

management's outlook, third-party industry forecasts, etc.). It's easy to doubt our ability to predict future cash flows, and thus have reservations about the usefulness of a DCF valuation. It's important to keep in mind that value itself is predicated upon investor (or market) expectations. So, the closer the analyst is able to incorporate those expectations into the analysis, the more reliable the resulting value estimate.

When estimating cash flow, it isn't practical to estimate cash flow to infinity for a going-concern enterprise, although, keep in mind that depending on k (the cost of capital), the impact of cash flows after a certain number of years, say 30 or 35, is negligible. Therefore, a simplifying assumption must be made to estimate the value of cash flow generated after the forecast period. Properly done, the value estimate should be equal whether you have forecasted out 35 years or attached a simplified post-forecast calculation of continuing value. Although the value is equal to the present value of a single stream of cash flow, it may be presented as the sum of:

1. The present value of cash flow from a discrete forecast horizon

and

2. The present value of a "residual" value estimate.

As you will see, the length of the forecast horizon affects the overall value conclusion. This presents us with the necessity of developing both an estimate of how long we forecast discrete cash flow for a company (i.e., forecast horizon) and of having to make a simplifying assump-

---

4 Thomas R. Carlson, account manager, The Alcar Group, Inc., is owed a large debt of gratitude. His suggestions and expert insight particularly in the section dealing with value drivers was invaluable.

tion regarding the value of cash flow generated after the end of the forecast horizon (i.e., the residual value).

Choosing the Length of the Forecast Horizon

The length of the forecast horizon is not simply a "convenient" period of time in which management feels comfortable in estimating financial performance (i.e., the typical long-range planning period is three to five years), but a period that is based on the economics of the company and its industry. In general, the main assumption regarding the length of the forecast period is that it should be equal to the length of time that, from the valuation date perspective, the investment community is willing to bet that management can achieve a rate of return on its new investments that exceeds the required rate of return (or cost of capital) for the company or investment. Or, in other words, management is adding value to the company.

So, we will refer to an appropriate time horizon as a company's value growth duration (VGD). As will be demonstrated in the next section on Value Driver analysis, the VGD is as important a measure as any of the key "value drivers" (i.e., sales growth, operating margin, etc.).

It is important to remember that, in forecasting, longer is better. Ten-year forecasts will help you to encompass most VGDs you may encounter, and a simple test of rate of return on new investments, discussed later, will help you to decide whether to lengthen the forecast.

When estimating the appropriate VGD, the analyst should consider the in-

dustry dynamics that will affect the firm's competitive position.[5]

The following is a short list of potential factors that can affect that position and the relevant effect on its VGD (we'll discuss a technique to be referred to as market signals analysis later to estimate what the stock market is estimating a company's specific VGD to be):

Existence of:	Effect on VGD
Proprietary Technologies	Lengthen
Patented Products	Lengthen
Limited Product Life Cycle	Shorten
Established Brands	Lengthen
Extensive Distribution Channels	Lengthen
Industry-Wide Price Competition	Shorten

Residual Value

Once the discrete forecast horizon cash flow have been estimated, a simplifying assumption can be made regarding the cash flow generated after the forecast period. The investment rate of return for new investments made during the VGD is greater than the cost of capital, and will therefore contribute to positive net present value (NPV). In the analysis, the terminal (residual) value is based on the premise that after the forecast period the average rate of return on new investments will equal the cost of capital. Understand that this does not represent a no-growth state. Rather, the implication is that, given competitive forces, the equity investor is not willing to bet that post-forecast period growth will increase shareholder value, since the rate of return (r) on these new investments will be pushed by competition down to a level appropriate to the risk incurred, i.e., the discount rate (cost of capital or WACC). We are not implying anything about future

---

5 Porter provides a detailed methodology to estimate a company's competitive position: refer to *Competitive Strategies: Technique for Analyzing Industries and Competitors*; Michael E. Porter, The Free Press, 1980.

revenue growth, etc., in the r = WACC terminal value calculation.

To capture this assumption mathematically in a simplified fashion, we apply a formula:

$$\text{Continuing Value}_T = \frac{NOPAT_{t+1}(1 - g/r)}{WACC - g}$$

$NOPAT_{t+1}$ = Net Operating Profit after Tax grown to one period after the last forecast period

g = Expected long-term growth rate (most likely, expected inflation rate)

r = Rate of return on new investments (if the forecast period = VGD, then r = WACC)

We refer to this formula as the expanded perpetuity formula.[6]

The figure $NOPAT_{t+1}(1 - g/r)$ is a calculation of cash flow based on the level of investment as a percentage of NOPAT that can support growth (g) given return on investment (r). You can see the origin of the expanded perpetuity formula in the Gordon model. The numerator is a calculation of free cash flow (operating profit after tax minus investment).

Finally, remember to discount the future value of the expanded perpetuity to the present as follows:

(1) Future value of residual value =

$$\frac{\text{Residual Operating Income}}{\text{Weighted Average Cost of Capital}}$$

(2) Present value of residual value =

$$\frac{\text{Future Value of Residual Value}}{(1 + k)^n}$$

where n equals the number of years in the forecast horizon.

For example, assume the projection period for Scott Corporation is five years. Also assume the residual operating income is $2,000,000 and the weighted average cost of capital is 12%. The residual value before discounting is the perpetuity = $16,666,667.

If the $16,666,667 residual value is assumed to be six years hence and the weighted average cost of capital is 12%, the present value of the residual period is:

$16,666,667 / (1 + .12)^6 = $8,443,852

The expanded formula method of calculating residual value is recommended in most instances as it provides a methodology consistent with the shareholder value approach applied during the discrete forecast period. Of course, there may be instances where a more aggressive assumption regarding the value impact from new investments is appropriate. Although one should be cautious in their application, variations of the perpetuity method can be made to accommodate these alternate situations.

Market Signals Analysis

To estimate what the specific value growth duration (VGD) should be for a given company (instead of speaking in relative terms), it is useful to gain insight into what an investor would estimate (or is estimating) the length of the horizon to be. For a publicly traded company, we can use market signals analysis to gain that insight. Having a reasonable handle on a company's (or comparable company's) fore-

---

6 *Valuation: Measuring and Managing the Value of Companies*: Copeland, Koller, Murrin—copyright 1990, McKinsey & Co. Inc., published by John Wiley & Sons.

casted cash flow and risk (i.e., cost of capital), we can "solve" for the known stock price. If our discrete period cash flow forecast is earning rates of returns above the cost of capital, we know that our estimate of value will increase by extending the forecast horizon. This, in essence, delays the time when the residual value assumptions (new investments earning only the cost of capital) will kick in. Privately held companies (or divisions of public companies, for that matter) can estimate their VGDs by performing similar analysis on publicly traded peer companies.

For a private company, the analyst must begin with the forecast management has developed. A simplified calculation of appropriate returns on new investments during the forecast period will provide some guidance towards the believability of management's forecast:

$$r = \frac{NOPAT_t - NOPAT_{t-1}}{CAP\ EX_t - DEP_t + WCI_t}$$

Essentially, this simplified formula says that the growth in dollars of NOPAT (Net Operating Profit After Tax) from year to year will result from returns on new investments from year to year.

Use this formula cautiously. In periods of significant inflation it is less accurate because it ignores the implied investment generated by productive asset appreciation. If management is planning to make positive NPV investments, their projections should show an r which exceeds their cost of capital or WACC. Yet a realistic management forecast probably will not show astronomic returns, and should probably not show r > WACC beyond the value growth duration. The critical analyst

will extend a forecast which shows r > WACC in the last forecast period to the point when r = WACC. The resulting forecast length will represent management's estimate of VGD.

Again, VGD is a measure of market expectations from the perspective of the valuation date. Management will certainly presume that they will, on average, successfully realize returns on new investments which exceed WACC for as long as they are managing their company. After all, it is their job to make positive NPV investment decisions.

The analyst's job is to incorporate a market perspective and apply it as a VGD to the forecast. Investors will not rationally pay a price for a company that can only be justified with the assumption that return on new investments will be greater than WACC forever; that price leaves the investor with inordinate downside prospects in the face of market evidence that the riskiness of the business justifies an expected return of WACC.

2. Value Driver Framework

When estimating shareholder value, it is helpful to think about the three "building blocks" of value (i.e., cash flow, time horizon and risk) in terms of what Rappaport refers to as Value Drivers.[7] Reducing an unnecessarily detailed discounted cash flow analysis to a set of observable value drivers accomplishes two objectives: first, it simplifies the analysis without cutting any corners with regard to the estimation of the key determinants of value, and second, allows for an understanding of the key aspects of a business most responsible for value creation (or value impact). This sec-

---

7 *Creating Shareholder Value: The New Standard for Business Performance*, Alfred Rappaport; The Free Press, 1986.

ond point is important. Knowing which value drivers have the biggest impact on the business' value gives management a basis to formulate strategy to maximize the value of the firm. The seven observable value drivers are:

1. Sales Growth Rate (G)

2. Operating Profit Margin (P)

3. Incremental Working Capital Investment (W)

4. Incremental Fixed Capital Investment (F)

5. Cash Tax Rate (T)

6. Cost of Capital (K)

7. Value Growth Duration (N)

Sales Growth Rate (G)

Sales Growth Rate (G) = (Sales$_t$ – Sales$_{t-1}$) / Sales$_{t-1}$ × 100

Operating Profit Margin (P)

The operating profit margin is composed mostly of the variable and fixed components of cost of sales and selling general and administration expenses.

Taxable Operating Profit =

Operating Profit Margin (P) + Amortization of Good Will

and therefore:

Operating Profit Margin (P) = Taxable Operating Profit/Sales

Incremental Working Capital Investment (W)

The incremental working capital investment required for operations is defined as the increase in total current assets (excluding any marketable securities and other

current assets not necessary to support operations) minus the increase in total current liabilities (excluding debt due and other non-operating obligations).

When this investment is expressed as a percentage of incremental sales, it is referred to as the value driver "W" and is calculated as follows:

$$W = \frac{\text{Increment in Net (operating) Working Capital}}{\text{Increment in Sales}}$$

The reason that incremental working capital investment excludes the increase in marketable securities, current portion of long-term debt and notes payable in calculating cash flow is that those items are financing issues and are not part of the cash required for operations.

Marketable securities are not investments required for operations. Rather, the increase in these investments is the result of a cash surplus generated by operations. They will be added to the equation later. The current portion of long-term debt and notes payable represents sources of financing rather than a direct investment in working capital to support the operations of the firm. They will be subtracted later. Excluding these items from working capital is essential to evaluate investment decisions separately from financing decisions.

Incremental Fixed Capital Investment (F)

The incremental fixed capital investment represents the portion of total capital expenditures necessary to support incremental sales. Value driver "F" is therefore defined as capital expenditures in excess of depreciation expense (and net capitalized interest). Depreciation expense is assumed to approximate the cost of replacing equipment to maintain existing capacity. Net capitalized interest is excluded as it is part of the financing decision, not the investment decision.

"F" is calculated as:

Fixed Capital Investment
– Depreciation Expense
– Net Capitalized Interest
Increment in Sales

Depreciation expense, which is based on historical costs, may understate the cost of replacing existing equipment when that cost has increased due to inflation and regulatory forces (i.e., environmental controls). However, the "F" ratio does account for higher replacement costs because they are captured in the estimate of (total) fixed capital investment.

Consider the following when determining if the historical value of "F%" is a reasonable estimate for a forecast:

1. An assessment of the speed and extent to which increased fixed capital costs can be passed on to customers

2. Whether assets can be used more effectively

3. Whether the number of plants can be reduced without affecting capacity

Cash Tax Rate (T)

As we look to discount forecasted (after-tax) operating cash flows, we must estimate a cash tax on operating profit instead of simply applying an effective tax rate to earnings before tax (EBT). Tax on operating profit represents the portion of total income taxes that is applicable to operating profit only. Tax on operating profit is the total of taxes on taxable operating profit for a fiscal year that either have been paid

by installments or are payable within twelve months.

Tax on operating profit is likely to be different than the actual amount payable to the taxing authority, because the actual amount payable will include taxes on non-operating items. Consider the following reconciliation between the current tax provision and tax on operating profit:

Current provision for income taxes
– Tax on non–operating profit
+ Interest tax shield
Tax on operating profit

Note that for an interest-paying company, the cash tax on operating profit will be greater than the current tax provision by an amount equal to T multiplied I (less tax on non-operating profit), where T is the marginal tax rate and I is the firm's interest expense.

The tax rate on operating profit, or value driver "T%" is calculated as:

$$T = \frac{\text{Tax on OperatingProfit} \times 100}{\text{TaxableOperating Profit}}$$

Risk and Time Value of Money Cost of Capital (K)

Risk and the time value of money are embedded into the cost of capital. The cost of capital, or discount rate should be an average of the company's cost of debt (on an after-tax basis) and cost of equity weighted at a market-based capital structure. The Debt/Equity ratio used in the weighting should mirror the anticipated, or target capital structure as that is the mix of capital that will fund the forecasted cash flows.

Value Growth Duration (N)

With each value driver explained, now let us define the calculation of shareholder value as the following expression (readers may want to program the formula into a spreadsheet):[8]

Shareholder (Equity) Value =

$$\sum_{t=1}^{n} \frac{1}{k}[(sales_{t-1})(1 + G)(P)(1 - T)]$$
$$- [(sales_{t-1})(G)(F + W)]$$

$$+ \left[\frac{\dfrac{(sales_{t-1})(1 + g^n)(P)(1 - T)}{k}}{(1 + K)^n} \right]$$

+ non-operating investments − market value of debt

Note that sensitivity analysis can easily be performed using any of the key value drivers as the independent variable. But be careful in its application. For instance, by increasing sales growth, holding all other drivers constant, to test the value impact of Gem Furniture's anticipated plant expansion, one should notice an increase in value (as cash flow increases). However, by properly accessing the related impact on the necessary investment required for the expansion (tested through changes in value drivers F & W), or by the increase in salary expense necessary to operate the plant, for example, (value driver P), one can understand if the tradeoff between the anticipated cash inflow (growth in sales) and the cash outflow (incremental investment and expense) will have a positive impact on value (i.e., a positive NPV strategy).

Value driver analysis also makes for an efficient valuation technique in an acquisition analysis, where the estimation of value is done "on the back of an envelope" using value driver analysis as the screening tool when a number of targets are being considered as part of an acquisition strategy:

- Number of Forecast Periods
- Sales (Last Historical Period)
- Sales Growth Rate (G)
- Operating Profit Margin (P)
- Incremental Fixed Capital Investment (F)
- Incremental Working Capital Investment (W)
- Tax Rate on Operating Profit (Tc)
- Residual Value Income Tax Rate (Tr)
- Cost of Capital (K)
- Marketable Securities and Other Investments
- Number of Common Shares

The value of Gem Furniture is calculated using value driver analysis as follows.[9] Please note that Gem's financial statements, cash flow, and ratios are located at the end of this chapter.

3. Evaluate the Implications of Valuation Projections

The Scratchpad version (see Exhibit 15.1) indicates that the market value of Gem's equity is negative $22.7 million.

Sales Growth Gem's sales growth has averaged 6% compounded annually, in a market growing at a faster pace. While Gem developed an innovative product the

---

8   Reproduced with permission: The Alcar Group Inc.

9   Alcar's Value Planner and Scratchpad software used with permission. The Alcar Group is a leading provider of financial analysis software and data tools. Alcar's software incorporates the shareholder value methodology and other valuation approaches for strategic planning and mergers and acquisition analysis. In addition, its software databases help firms to estimate important value drivers such as cost of capital using the traditional Capital Asset Pricing Model (CAPM) and Arbitrage Pricing Theory (APT). Readers who would like additional information on Alcar's software tools may call Joy Murawski at (708)967-4200.

company was forced to scrap the project. Economic and industry-wide factors that the firm's banker expects will influence

The Scratchpad Version
Base Case for Gem Furniture Company

N—	Number of Periods in Forecast	5
S—	Sales (Last Historical Period)	586.9
G—	Sales Growth Rate (G) (%)	6.0
P—	Operating Profit Margin (P) (%)	2.6
F—	Increm. Fixed Capital Invest. (F) (%)	8.3
W—	Increm. Working Capital Invest. (W) (%)	27.1
T—	Tax Rate on Operating Profit (%)	34.0
R—	Residual Value Income Tax Rate (%)	34.0
K—	Cost of Capital (K) (%)	10.0
M—	Marketable Securities and Investments	0.0
D—	Market Value of Debt & Other Obligations	98.9
O—	Number of Common Shares: Year End	0.0

sales growth are disposable income and demand for wooden tables, which are expected to remain constant.

Operating Profit Margins have fallen from 11% in 1989 to 2% in 1991 and is pegged at only 2.6% in the projection period, below historical levels because of intensifying price competition combined with higher production and manufacturing costs.

Incremental Fixed Capital Investment With a very steady fixed asset turnover of around 12%, incremental fixed capital investment has averaged 8% of the increase in sales over the past few years. It may be possible that Gem could begin to realize some improvement on its existing fixed asset base. However, there are significant risks that some technological change and price competition could force Gem to invest heavily to update equipment and reduce manufacturing costs in the future. Several scenarios should be

Exhibit 15.1

Cash Flows and Shareholder Value
Base Case
Cost of Capital = 10.000%
(Scratchpad Version)

	Cash Flow	Present Value Cash Flow	Current PV Cash Flow	Present Value Residual Value	Current PV CF + PV Residual Value	Increase in Value
1	$(1.780)	$(1.618)	$(1.618)	$97.050	$95.432	$(5.280)
2	(1.886)	(1.559)	(3.177)	95.521	90.344	(5.080)
3	(2.000)	(1.582)	(4.679)	90.120	85.441	(4.903)
4	(2.320)	(1.448)	(6.127)	86.863	80.716	(4.725)
5	(2.247)	(1.395)	(7.522)	83.685	76.163	(4.553)
						(24.549)

	Mkt. Securities & Investments	0.000
	CORPORATE VALUE	76.163
	Less: Mkt. Value of All Obligations	98.900
	SHAREHOLDER VALUE	(22.737)

run to assess the valuation impact of the assumption that Gem will be able to reduce incremental fixed capital investment.

Incremental Working Capital Investment Seventeen cents of working capital was required by Gem to support every additional dollar of sales in 1991, the result of poor inventory control and slow receivables. Maybe Gem will be able to manage working capital better and potentially reduce investment accordingly. However, this assumes that competitive pressures will not force Gem to relax its credit policies further, or extend terms more than they have, which would increase working capital requirements.

We valued Gem Furniture (Exhibit 15.1A) using a discounted cash flow approach (DCF), which as we saw, attempts to determine the economic value of a company by discounting relevant future cash flows back to a present value at the cost of capital—or the minimum return demanded by debt and equity holders for their assumed risk. Consistent with the discounted cash flow approach, we now focus on Gem's value drivers or, more specifically, those variables that determine cash flow (sales growth, operating margins, fixed and working capital needs and the cash tax rate); the appropriate discount rate (weighted average cost of capital spelled out in appendix one); and the length of time it is expected to take for competitive forces to drive Gem's returns down to their cost of capital (VGD).

In the course of strategic planning and corporate valuation, and credit analysis, it is crucial to determine the value drivers making the most significant impact on shareholder value as illustrated in Exhibits 15.2, 15.3, and 15.4.

Exhibit 15.2, produced on Alcar's Value planner software, reveals the relative

significance of the key valuation variables based on how a change of 1% in each variable affects shareholder value. This information helps pinpoint the variables that have the greatest impact on shareholder value. Note that the "1% increase" represents a change in a variable from 10% to 10.1%, not to 11% (i.e., it represents a point elasticity for each item, assuming other items are held constant). We see that Gem Furniture shareholder value is very sensitive to the variable margin and cost of capital, with incremental working capital investment, a significant third factor as well (Exhibit 15.4).

Lenders and financial managers focusing on areas of the business most sensitive to value creation are able to concentrate energy and resources in these areas. For example, Exhibit 15.4, as we saw, reveals to Gem's bankers that the variable margin and cost of capital are a much more important determinant of value than sales growth. In this case management (and their bankers) will no doubt feel that less time should be spent developing new sales opportunities and more time developing strategies directed at holding down risk (cost of capital) and improving operating performance (margins).

Alcar developed the threshold margin and threshold spread, two important barometers of value creation.

■ ■ ■

The Threshold Margin is a single period measure of the minimum operating profit margin that is required for the company to earn the long-term required rate of return for an investment, given the following: 1) investment requirements (Fixed and Working Capital) for each additional dollar of sales; and 2) the Residual Value Income Tax Rate and Long-Term Cost of Capital. This "breakeven" margin offers managers a target of the minimum level of operating profit margin

Exhibit 15.1A

Cash Flows and Shareholder Value for Gem Furniture Company
Base Case (Full Version)
Average Cost of Capital (%) = 10.000 (In thousands of $)

Year	Cash Flow	Present Value Cash Flow	Cum. PV Cash Flow	Present Value Residual Vale	Cum. PV CF + PV Residual Value	Increase in Value
1992 F	($1,597)	(1,451)	(1,451)	103,536	102,085	16,087
1993 F	($1,491)	(1,232)	(2,684)	96,671	93,987	(8,098)
1994 F	($1,992)	(1,497)	(4,181)	90,064	85,884	(8,103)
1995 F	($2,563)	(1,750)	(5,931)	83,698	77,767	(8,117)
1996 F	($3,213)	(1,995)	(7,926)	77,577	69,651	(8,117)
						(16,347)

Cash	0.00
Invest. in Bonds and Stocks	0.00
CORPORATE VALUE	69,650.57
Less: Market Value of Debt	90,904.00
Less: Underfunded Pension Liabilities	0.00
Less: Mkt Value of other Obligations	0.00
SHAREHOLDER VALUE (PV)	(21,253)

Exhibit 15.2

Sensitivity of Shareholder Value for Gem Furniture Company Base Case

			Variable Margin (vP)		
			(1.00) **% points**	**0.00** **% points**	**1.00** **% points**
Increm. Fixed	(5.00)	% points	(63,353)	(13,812)	35,729
Cap. Invest.	0.00	% points	(70,794)	(21,253)	28,288
(F)	5.00	% points	(78,236)	(28,695)	20,846

Exhibit 15.3

Sensitivity of Shareholder Value for GEM Furniture Company Base Case
To Inc. Work. Cap. Inv. (W) (%)

Change In Variable	Value	Change In Value
(1.00)% points	(19,765)	1,488
(0.50)% points	(20,509)	744
(0.00)% points	(21,253)	0
(0.50)% points	(21,998)	(744)
(1.00)% points	(22,742)	(1,488)

Exhibit 15.4

Relative Impact of Key Variables on Shareholder Value for Gem Furniture Company
Base Case
(In thousands of $)

A 1% Increase In	Increases Shareholder Value by	% Increase
Sales Growth Rate (G)	$(296)	1.392
Variable Margin (vP)*	**1,227**	**(5.775)**
Fixed Costs (fC)	0	0.000
Inc. Fixed Cap. Inv. (F) (%)	(123)	0.579
Inc. Work. Cap. Inv. (W) (%)	(408)	**1.918**
Tax Rate on Operating Profit (T)	(233)	1.094
Residual Value Inc. Tax Rate	(400)	1.880
Cost of Capital (K)	**(1,093)**	**5.144**

* The Variable Margin reflects those costs which change with short-term changes in sales. It is calculated by adding fixed costs to taxable operating profit to get the margin attributable to variable costs.

that is necessary to create value for shareholders in a particular year.[10]

The Threshold Spread represents how much "spread" or difference, there is between the actual Operating Profit Margin on sales and the Threshold Margin (the minimum single period margin required in order to create value for shareholders). Whenever the Threshold Spread is greater than zero (as shown in the Profit Margins exhibit), then value is being created in that period. Similarly, a negative Threshold Spread would indicate that value would be declining in that period.[11]

■ ■ ■

Gem's threshold spread (Exhibit 15.5) is negative beginning in 1993. Gem needs an operating profit margin of 2.9% to create shareholder value for that year. The firm's margin is only 2.7%, which means that management's business strategies as reflected in the financial projections are destroying shareholder value.

4. Refine Strategies that Maximize Value

Understanding the Mission of the Business

Arnoldo Hax and Nicolas Majluf at the Massachusetts Institute of Technology[12]

have also made significant contributions to strategic planning. The mission of a business, they say, is a statement of the current and future expected product, market, and geographical scope; and a definition of the way to attain competitive leadership. For example, a company aiming to increase market share with existing products often requires a concentrated marketing effort in addition to improved operational efficiency at all functional levels. On the other hand, introducing new products in existing markets puts a heavy burden on R&D and engineering development efforts whenever new products are internally developed. What is most challenging is the work to be done when new products are intended to serve new markets. Often, such strategies can best be carried out via acquisitions.

Formulation of Business Strategy and Broad Action Programs

According to Hax and Majluf, a business strategy is a set of objectives supported by well-coordinated action programs aimed at establishing a long-term sustainable advantage over competitors. Managers interested in formulating a foundation for value maximization should develop broad action programs

Exhibit 15.5

Valuation Ratios

	1992	1993	1994	1995	1996
Oper. Profit Margin (P) (%)	2.774	2.688	2.598	2.506	2.410
Threshold Margin (%)	2.382	2.892	2.811	2.727	2.639
Threshold Spread (%)	0.392	(0.205)	(0.213)	(0.221)	(0.229)
Increm. Profit Margin (%)	12.001	1.251	1.12	0.963	0.817
Increm. Threshold Margin (%)	5.079	4.867	4.867	4.866	4.867

10 The Alcar Group, Inc.

11 Ibid.

12 *Strategic Management: An Intergrative Perspective*, Arnoldo C. Hax and Nicolas S. Majluf; Prentice Hall, 1984.

defined over a multi-year planning horizon. Business strategy is derived from:

- Corporate strategic thrusts and planning challenges
- The business mission
- Environment scan at the business level (the degree of attractiveness of the industry in which the business belongs)
- Internal scrutiny at the business level
- The internal scrutiny at the business level attempts to identify the firm's major strengths and weaknesses against its most relevant competitors and includes:[13]
  1. Identification of the most relevant competitors
  2. Determination of critical success factors, that is, those capabilities controllable by the firm, in which it has to excel in order to secure a long-term success over its competitors
  3. Assessment of the firm's strengths and weaknesses against each of the most relevant competitors

Consolidation of Business and Functional Strategies

This step requires the involvement of all the firm's key managers who share responsibility for shaping its strategic direction. The following issues need to be addressed:

- Resolving departmental conflicts for the good of the corporate entity
- Balancing the business portfolio of the firm concerning: (1) short-term profitability versus long-term development; (2) risks versus returns; (3) cash flow balance

- Defining the availability of strategic funds, the debt policy, and maximum sustainable growth
- Preliminary evaluation of proposed action programs and assignment of priorities for resource allocation to each business
- Defining a strategy for divestment decisions

Management's decision to divest a business unit can often be quantified by the spreads between cash flow value and liquidation value. Hax and Majluf are proponents of the Market Value/Liquidation Value ratio.[14]

They suggest that individual business units within an enterprise can subtract value from the entire enterprise if their profitability (cash flow) is low and sustained by resources that could be better served elsewhere. Business units of this sort are "cash traps" involving a permanent negative cash flow that diminishes the contribution of units with positive cash flows. Under such conditions, divestiture might be the most logical move. The central question is whether the liquidation alternative is better than holding onto that unprofitable unit. Gem's wholly owned subsidiary, Gem Junior Corporation is an example of how a divestment decision is made as illustrated in Exhibit 15.6.

If business units have underperformed and management has exhausted its abilities to improve them, a sale of such units becomes an attractive alternative. Management's goal is then to find another company or management team that can improve results via a better strategic fit in its organization or through better management practices. Business units that are perform-

---

13 Ibid.
14 Ibid.

ing well may also be divested. In these situations, other factors can be at work. Management may feel that a unit is distracting attention and that improving other operations of the company will require divestment of the unit. In short, Gem's management would be well advised to sell the subsidiary's value-draining Business Unit A.

Back to the Gem Furniture Loan Request

Gem's Average Collection Period

Recall that Gem relaxed credit standards to book more sales, contributing to a 19-day increase in the average collection period to 55 days. The bank, in an attempt to identify those variables critical to the success of any

strategy, prepared a pro forma cash flow statement that showed a 5-day improvement in the collection period translated into a 41% reduction in short-term bank exposure.

Had the average collection period approached the industry average, short-term debt would have been retired. The point is that a small improvement in Gem's average collection period, measurable in just a few days, can make a big dent in cash flow (Exhibit 15.7). Now we are ready to ask, how does the improvement affect shareholder value?

We see that shareholder value improved almost $10 million with an improvement of five days in the average collection period (Exhibit 15.8 and 15.8A). Yet, incremental working capital invest-

Exhibit 15.6

Gem Junior Corp. Summary of Business Units

	Cash Flow Value	Liquidation Value	Result	Decision
Business Unit A Office Furniture	$6,500	$2,500	Cash flow Value > Liquidation Value	Keep A
Business Unit B Patio Furniture	$1,000	$600	Cash flow Value > Liquidation Value	Keep B
Business Unit C Picnic Furniture	$400	$900	Cash flow Value < Liquidation Value	Divest C

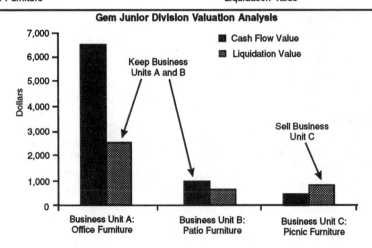

Gem Junior Division Valuation Analysis

Exhibit 15.7

GROSS OPERATING CASH FLOW	Improved	Original	Cash Flow
	8,085	8,085	
(Inc.)/Dec. Net A/R)	(16,471)	(32,685)	16,214
(Inc.)/Dec. Inventory	(40,889)	(40,889)	
Operating Cash Needs	(57,360)	(73,574)	

Applying cash generated by the improved collection period to debt repayments

ment was not the dominant value driver. Indeed, base case valuation pointed out that the margin attributable to variable costs – the variable margin (Taxable Op. Profit + Fixed Costs) / Sales was the most influential value driver. In turn, we know that if we decompose the variable margin, the gross profit margin stands out. Let's see how shareholder value is affected by a 1.5 percentage point increase in Gem's gross profit margin.

Gem's Gross Profit Margin

Is it possible to test the implications of alternate strategies to identify and develop strategies to optimize shareholder value? Recall from previous chapters that the gross profit margin shows if higher produc-

tion costs have been successfully passed on to consumers

Gross Profit Margin	1989	1990	1991
	20.8%	18.7%	14.8%

Industry Average
18.0%

Thus, a small improvement in the gross margin creates considerable shareholder value (Exhibits 15.9 and 15.9A).

The firm and its bankers now understand how management decisions—some "trivial," like shaving a few days off the average collection period, or trimming production costs (perhaps not trivial)—have affected shareholder value. And, at the very least—to concentrate Gem's resources on value-creating opportunities and acceptable lending risks.

Exhibit 15.8

	Base Case	Five Day Improvement: A.C.P.
Corporate Value	$69,651	$79,213
Market Value of Debt	90,904	90,904
Shareholder Value	($21,253)	($11,691)

Exhibit 15.9

	Base Case	Five Day Improvement: GPM
Corporate Value	$69,651	$157,372
Market Value of Debt	90,904	90,904
Shareholder Value	($21,253)	$66,468

Exhibit 15.8A

Cash Flows and Shareholder Value for Gem Furniture Company
Accounts Receivable Adjustment: 5 Days
Average Cost of Capital (%) = 10.000 (In thousands of $)

Year	Cash Flow	Present Value Cash Flow	Cum. PV Cash Flow	Present Value Residual Vale	Cum. PV CF + PV Residual Value	Increase In Value
1992 F	$7,121	6,474	6,474	103,536	110,010	24,012
1993 F	($967)	(800)	5,674	96,671	102,345	(7,665)
1994 F	($1,438)	(1,080)	4,594	90,064	945,658	(7,687)
1995 F	($1,975)	(1,349)	3,245	83,698	86,943	(7,715)
1996 F	($2,590)	(1,608)	1,636	77,577	79,213	(7,730)
						(6,785)

Cash	0.00
Invest. in Bonds and Stocks	0.00
CORPORATE VALUE	79,213.12
Less: Market Value of Debt	90,904.00
Less: Underfunded Pension Liabilities	0.00
Less: Mkt Value of other Obligation	0.00
SHAREHOLDER VALUE (PV)	(11,691)

Exhibit 15.9A

Cash Flows and Shareholder Value for Gem Furniture Company
Improve Gross Profit Margin 1.5 Percentage Points
Average Cost of Capital (%) = 10.000 (In thousands of $)

Year	Cash Flow	Present Value Cash Flow	Cum. PV Cash Flow	Present Value Residual Vale	Cum. PV CF + PV Residual Value	Increase In Value
1992 F	$7,735	7,031	7,031	159,523	166,555	80,557
1993 F	$8,401	6,943	13,974	150,626	164,600	(1,954)
1994 F	$8,493	6,381	20,355	142,056	162,411	(2,189)
1995 F	$8,552	5,841	26,196	133,801	159,997	(2,414)
1996 F	$8,568	5,320	31,516	125,856	157,372	(2,626)
						71,374

Cash	0.00
Invest. in Bonds and Stocks	0.00
CORPORATE VALUE	157,371.67
Less: Market Value of Debt	90,904.00
Less: Underfunded Pension Liabilities	0.00
Less: Mkt Value of other Obligations	0.00
SHAREHOLDER VALUE (PV)	66,467.67

Income Statement for Gem Furniture

Income Statement for Gem Furniture Company

Base Case

(in thousands of $)	1989 H	1990 H	1991 H	1992 F	1993 F	1994 F	1995 F	1996 F
Net Sales	$512,693	$553,675	$586,895	$622,109	$659,435	$699,001	$740,941	$785,398
Cost of Goods Sold	405,803	450,394	499,928	529,912	561,707	595,409	631,134	669,002
Depreciation Expense	4,781	4,973	6,120	7,006	7,995	9,098	10,329	11,701
Gross Profit	$102,109	$98,308	$80,847	$85,191	$89,733	$94,494	$99,478	$104,695
SG&A Expense	38,369	46,034	50,643	53,626	56,843	60,254	63,869	67,701
Miscellaneous Expenses	6,082	10,672	17,174	14,309	15,167	16,077	17,042	18,064
Net Operating Profit	$57,658	$41,602	$13,030	$17,256	$17,723	$18,163	$18,567	$18,930
Interest Expense	3,648	5,258	8,974	7,087	7,042	6,997	6,952	6,907
Pre-Tax Profit	$54,010	$36,344	$4,056	$10,169	$10,681	$11,166	$11,615	$12,023
Tax Expense	26,068	17,589	2,091	3,457	3,631	3,796	3,949	4,088
Net Income	$27,942	$18,755	$1,965	$6,712	$7,050	$7,370	$7,666	$7,935
Common Dividends	$0	$4,463	$266	$1,678	$1,762	$1,842	$1,917	$1,984

Balance Sheet for Gem Furniture Company

Balance Sheet for Gem Furniture Company

Base Case

(in thousands of $)	1989 H	1990 H	1991 H	1992 F	1993 F	1994 F	1995 F	1996 F
Cash	$15,445	$12,007	$11,717	$12,443	$13,190	$13,983	$14,820	$15,710
Accounts Receivable - Net	51,793	55,886	88,571	93,938	99,575	105,549	111,882	118,595
Inventory	56,801	99,087	139,976	148,684	157,605	167,061	177,085	187,710
Total Current Assets	$124,039	$166,980	$240,264	$255,065	$270,370	$286,593	$303,787	$322,015
Plant & Equipment	53,283	60,301	68,621	78,545	89,627	101,998	115,796	131,174
Less:Accum. Depreciation	8,989	13,961	20,082	27,088	35,083	44,181	54,510	66,211
Net Plant & Equipment	44,294	46,340	48,539	51,457	54,544	57,817	61,286	64,963
Total Assets	$168,333	$213,320	$288,803	$306,522	$324,914	$344,410	$365,073	$386,978
Accounts Payable	$20,292	$31,518	$59,995	$63,455	$67,262	$71,298	$75,576	$80,111
Current Portion Debt	500	500	500	500	500	500	500	500
Short Term Borrowings	9,562	15,300	54,698	54,698	54,698	54,698	54,698	54,698
Accruals	10,338	15,300	21,994	23,267	24,663	26,143	27,711	29,374
Total Current Liabilities	$40,682	$62,618	$137,187	$141,920	$147,123	$152,639	$158,485	$164,683
Senior Long Term Debt	27,731	36,491	35,706	35,206	34,706	34,206	33,706	33,206
L-T Debt: Excess	#N/A	#N/A	#N/A	8,452	16,853	25,805	35,373	45,639
Total L-T Debt	27,731	36,491	35,706	43,658	51,559	60,011	69,079	78,835
Total Liabilities	$68,413	$99,109	$172,893	$185,578	$198,682	$212,650	$227,564	$243,518
Common Stock	69,807	69,807	69,807	69,807	69,807	69,807	69,807	69,807
Retained Earnings	30,113	44,404	46,103	51,137	56,425	61,953	67,702	73,653
Total Owner's Equity	99,920	114,211	115,910	120,944	126,232	131,760	137,509	143,460
Total Liabilities and Equity	$168,333	$213,320	$288,803	$306,522	$324,914	$344,410	$365,073	$386,978

Financial Ratios for Gem Financial

Financial Ratios for Gem Furniture Company

Base Case

(in thousands of $)	1989 H	1990 H	1991 H	1992 F	1993 F	1994 F	1995 F	1996 F
Profit Performance Ratios								
Gross Profit Margin (%)	19.916	17.756	13.775	13.694	13.608	13.518	13.426	13.330
Change in Net Income (%)	N/A	(32.879)	(89.523)	241.578	5.036	4.539	4.016	3.509
Return on Sales (%)	5.450	3.387	0.335	1.079	1.069	1.054	1.035	1.010
Return on Equity (%)	27.964	16.421	1.695	5.550	5.585	5.594	5.575	5.531
Return on Assets or Inv. (%)	18.030	10.419	2.731	3.716	3.600	3.481	3.357	3.229
Return on Net Assets (%)	23.776	14.748	5.203	6.919	6.579	6.251	5.932	5.620
Leverage Ratios								
Debt/Equity Ratio (%)	37.823	45.785	78.426	81.737	84.572	87.439	90.377	93.429
Debt/Total Capital (%)	27.443	31.406	43.954	44.975	45.821	46.649	47.473	48.301
Equity Ratio (%)	59.359	53.540	40.135	39.457	38.851	38.257	37.666	37.072
Times Interest Earned	15.805	7.912	1.452	2.435	2.517	2.596	2.671	2.741
Activity Ratios								
Days in Receivables	36.873	36.842	55.084	55.115	55.115	55.115	55.115	55.115
Days in Receivables (avg.)	N/A	35.493	44.920	53.540	53.555	53.555	53.555	53.555
Days in Payables	18.039	35.263	43.273	43.137	43.094	43.050	43.004	42.956
Days in Payables (avg.)	N/A	20.764	33.003	41.961	41.874	41.831	41.787	41.740
Inventory Turnover	7.228	4.596	3.615	3.611	3.615	3.618	3.622	3.626
Inventory Turnover (avg.)	N/A	5.842	4.234	3.720	3.720	3.724	3.728	3.732
Fixed Asset Turnover	N/A	11.948	12.091	12.090	12.090	12.090	12.090	12.090
Total Asset Turnover	N/A	2.596	2.032	2.030	2.030	2.030	2.030	2.030
Liquidity Ratios								
Quick Ratio	1.653	1.084	0.731	0.750	0.766	0.783	0.799	0.816
Current Ratio	3.049	2.667	1.751	1.797	1.838	1.878	1.917	1.955
Per-Share Data								
Valuation Ratios								
Oper. Profit Margin (P) (%)	11.246	7.514	2.220	2.774	2.688	2.598	2.506	2.410
Threshold Margin (%)	N/A	11.326	8.096	2.382	2.892	2.811	2.727	2.639
Threshold Spread (%)	N/A	(3.812)	(5.875)	0.392	(0.205)	(0.213)	(0.221)	(0.229)
Increm. Profit Margin (%)	N/A	(39.176)	(86.008)	12.001	1.251	1.112	0.963	0.817
Increm. Threshold Margin (%)	N/A	12.327	17.791	5.079	4.867	4.867	4.866	4.867
Increm. Threshold Spread (%)	N/A	(51.505)	(103.800)	6.922	(3.616)	(3.755)	(3.903)	(4.050)
Value Drivers								
Sales Growth Rate (G) (%)	N/A	7.993	6.000	6.000	6.000	6.000	6.000	6.000
Variable Margin (vP)	11.246	7.514	2.220	2.774	2.688	2.598	2.506	2.410
Inc. Fixed Cap. Inv. (F) (%)	N/A	4.992	6.620	8.286	8.270	8.272	8.271	8.271
Inc. Work. Cap. Inv. (W) (%)	N/A	65.255	114.723	28.591	27.064	27.061	27.058	27.060
Tax Rate on Operating Profit	N/A	46.576	39.464	33.997	33.997	33.998	33.999	34.001
Discount Rates								
Average Cost of Capital (%)	10.000	10.000	10.000	10.000	10.000	10.000	10.000	10.000
Long-Term Cost of Capital	10.000	10.000	10.000	10.000	10.000	10.000	10.000	10.000
Internal Rate of Return (%)	5.623	5.623	5.623	5.623	5.623	5.623	5.623	5.623

FAS95 Cash Flow for Gem Furniture Company

FAS 95 Cash Flow for Gem Furniture Company

Base Case

(In thousands of $)	1990 H	1991 H	1992 F	1993 F	1994 F	1995 F	1996 F
OPERATING ACTIVITIES:							
Net Sales	$553,675	$586,895	$622,109	$559,435	$699,001	$740,941	$785,398
Cost of Goods Sold	450,394	499,928	529,912	561,707	595,409	631,134	669,002
Depreciation Expense	4,973	6,120	7,006	7,995	9,098	10,329	11,701
Gross Profit	$98,308	$80,847	$85,191	$89,733	$94,494	$99,478	$104,695
SG&A Expense	$46,034	$50,643	$53,626	$56,843	$60,254	$63,869	$67,701
Miscellaneous Expenses	10,672	17,174	14,309	15,167	16,077	17,042	18,064
Interest Expense	$5,258	$8,974	$7,087	$7,042	$6,997	$6,952	$6,907
Operating Profit (after Int)	$36,344	$4,056	$10,169	$10,681	$11,166	$11,615	$12,023
Tax. Oper. Profit (aft Int.)	$36,344	$4,056	$10,169	$10,681	$11,166	$11,615	$12,023
Depreciation Expense: Funds	$4,973	$6,120	$7,006	$7,995	$9,098	$10,329	$11,701
Incr. in Accounts Payable	11,226	28,477	3,460	3,807	4,036	4,278	4,535
Incr. in Other Curr Liabs.	4,972	6,694	1,273	1,396	1,480	1,568	1,663
Incr. in Accts Receivable	4,093	32,685	5,367	5,637	5,974	6,333	6,713
Incr. in Inventories	42,386	40,889	8,708	8,921	9,456	10,024	10,625
Net Cash from Operations	($6,453)	($30,318)	$4,376	$5,690	$6,554	$7,484	$8,496
INVESTING ACTIVITIES:							
Fixed Capital Investment	$7,019	$8,319	$9,924	$11,082	$12,371	$13,798	$15,378
Net Cash Used in Investing	$7,019	$8,319	$9,924	$11,082	$12,371	$13,798	$15,378
FINANCING ACTIVITIES:							
Incr. in Notes Payable	5,738	39,398	0	0	0	0	0
Incr. in Sr. L-T Debt	8,760	(785)	(500)	(500)	(500)	(500)	(500)
Incr. in Debt: Excess	#N/A	#N/A	8,452	8,401	8,952	9,568	10,256
Common Dividends	4,463	266	1,678	1,762	1,842	1,917	1,984
Net Cash Prov. by Financing	$10,035	$38,347	$6,274	$6,139	$6,610	$7,151	$7,772
Incr. in Cash & Cash Equiv.	($3,438)	($290)	$726	$747	$793	$837	$890
Cash & Cash Equiv. (beg.)	15,445	12,007	11,717	12,443	13,190	13,983	14,820
Cash & Cash Equiv. (end)	12,007	11,717	12,443	13,190	13,983	14,820	15,710

Financial Ratios for Gem Financial (continued)

Profitability

Total Gross Profit/Sales	19.916	17.756	13.775	13.694	13.608	13.518	13.426	13.330
Gross Profit excl Depr/Sales	20.849	18.654	14.818	14.820	14.820	14.820	14.820	14.820
Selling & Admin. Exp./Sales	7.484	8.314	8.629	8.620	8.620	8.620	8.620	8.620
Operating Expenses/Sales	8.670	10.242	11.555	10.920	10.920	10.920	10.920	10.920
Operating Profit/Sales	11.246	7.514	2.220	2.774	2.688	2.598	2.506	2.410
Net Margin	5.450	3.387	0.335	1.079	1.069	1.054	1.035	1.010
Net Income/Sales	5.450	3.387	0.680	1.079	1.069	1.054	1.035	1.010
Return on Total Assets	16.599	8.792	0.680	2.190	2.170	2.140	2.100	2.051
Return on Total Owner Equity	27.964	16.421	1.695	5.550	5.585	5.594	5.575	5.531
Return on Avg. Total Assets	33.198	9.828	0.778	2.255	2.233	2.202	2.161	2.110
Return on Avg. Owner Equity	55.929	17.517	1.708	5.668	5.704	5.713	5.694	5.648
Effective Tax Rate	48.265	48.396	51.553	33.995	33.995	33.996	33.999	34.001

Growth (%)

Sales	#N/A	7.993	6.000	6.000	6.000	6.000	6.000	6.000
Total Gross Profit	#N/A	(3.722)	(17.762)	5.373	5.332	5.306	5.274	5.244
Net Operating Profit	#N/A	(27.847)	(68.679)	32.433	2.706	2.483	2.224	1.955
Pre-Tax Earnings/Loss	#N/A	(32.709)	(88.840)	150.715	5.035	4.541	4.021	3.513
After Tax Earnings/Loss	#N/A	(32.879)	(89.523)	241.578	5.036	4.539	4.016	3.509
Total Net Income/Loss	#N/A	(32.879)	(89.523)	241.578	5.036	4.539	4.016	3.509

Activity Ratios

Inventory Turnover-COGS	7.144	4.545	3.572	3.564	3.564	3.564	3.564	3.564
Inventory Turnover-Sales	9.026	5.588	4.193	4.184	4.184	4.184	4.184	4.184
Inventory Holding Period	51.090	80.300	102.197	102.413	102.413	102.412	102.413	102.412
Accounts Receivable Turnover	9.899	9.907	6.626	6.623	6.622	6.623	6.623	6.623
Average Collection Period	36.873	36.842	55.084	55.115	55.115	55.115	55.115	55.115
Fixed Asset Turnover	11.575	11.948	12.091	12.090	12.090	12.090	12.090	12.090
Accounts Payable Turnover	19.998	14.290	8.333	8.351	8.351	8.351	8.351	8.351
Average Settlement Period	18.252	25.542	43.803	43.707	43.707	43.707	43.707	43.708
Working Capital Turnover	6.151	5.305	5.694	5.498	5.351	5.218	5.099	4.992
Owner Equity Turnover	5.131	4.848	5.063	5.144	5.224	5.305	5.388	5.475

Leverage

Total Liab./Owner Equity	0.685	0.868	1.492	1.534	1.574	1.614	1.655	1.697
Total Liab./Tang. Net Worth	0.685	0.868	1.492	1.534	1.574	1.614	1.655	1.697
Total Liab./Total Assets	0.406	0.465	0.599	0.605	0.611	0.617	0.623	0.629

Liquidity/Coverage

Current Ratio	3.049	2.667	1.751	1.797	1.838	1.878	1.917	1.955
Quick Ratio	1.653	1.084	0.731	0.750	0.766	0.783	0.799	0.816
Interest Expense Coverage	15.805	7.912	1.452	2.435	2.517	2.596	2.671	2.741

Measuring the Cost of Capital

The Importance of Cost of Capital in the Valuation Process

The proper discount rate (weighted average cost of capital) is a highly significant value driver because the present value of cash flow changes inversely with increases in the discount rate. Thus, it is critical to assess the company's cost of capital, its consistency with the overall valuation approach and the riskiness of the firm's operating and financial strategies.

To be consistent with the cash flow approach to valuation, the cost of capital must:

1. Comprise the weighted cost of all sources of capital (primarily debt and equity) since (operating) cash flow represents cash available to all providers of capital.

2. Be computed after tax since cash flow is stated after tax.

3. Employ market, not book rates, for each financing element because the market reflects the true economic claims of each type of financing instrument outstanding. Book value does not address this issue.

4. Perceived as subject to change across the forecast period because of expected changes in inflation, systematic risk, or capital structure. However, in most cases, the cost of capital assigned to the first projection period is left unchanged.

Definitions Commonly Used to Describe Risk

- **Marginal cost of capital.** The cost of one additional unit. The marginal cost of capital is the cost of an additional dollar of new funds.

- **Discount rate.** The interest rate used in the discounting process. Sometimes called the capitalization rate. For example, risk-free returns are capitalized using the risk-free rate. Risky returns, on the other hand, are discounted back to present value using risk-adjusted rates. The discount rate includes a default risk premium which is most relevant for corporate long-term debt where bankruptcy could become a reality. The usual method for determining default risk is to refer to bond ratings and credit grade.

■ **Systematic risk.** This is known as market risk including factors that affect all firms simultaneously. Systematic risk is also referred to as covariant risk, which is the sensitivity of security price changes in general economic conditions. The Capital Asset Pricing Model and Arbitrage Pricing Model are powerful tools to measure covariant risk.

■ **Hurdle rate.** The minimum accepted rate of return on a project. If the expected return is below the hurdle rate, the project is not accepted. If the expected return of an acquisition candidate is below the hurdle rate, the acquisition is not accepted.

■ **Market risk premium.** The spread between market returns and the risk-free rate.

■ **Required rate of return.** The rate of return stockholders expect to receive on common stock investments.

■ **Capital components.** These are the items on the right hand side of the balance sheet: various types of debt, preferred stock, and common equity. Any net increase in assets must be financed by an increase in one or more capital components.

The costs associated with both debt and equity financing are primarily a function of risk. Lenders and investors require compensation in proportion to the risks they bear in providing financing. Addition-

ally, the liquidity of the financing instrument (i.e., the relative ease of converting the instrument or assets underlying the instrument into cash) will also affect its cost. All else being equal, higher liquidity entails a lower cost of financing.

The cost of debt and the cost of equity differ primarily in two ways:

■ The annual cost of debt is known (whether the interest rate is fixed or adjustable, it is explicit), whereas the cost of equity is never explicit and, thus, must be estimated.

■ Because providing equity capital is riskier than providing debt, it costs more. Although equity does not require fixed payments, its cost is inherent in the return on investment provided through dividends and stock price appreciation necessary to entice investors to provide initial equity capital, and to be willing to leave that capital in the business.

Senior debt is the least risky and the least expensive form of financing since it has priority over all other debt. Secured senior debt holds liens against specific assets such as inventory, receivables, and fixed assets and, therefore, is generally less costly than unsecured debt. However, administration costs, in some cases, may raise rates over unsecured debt. Commercial banks and finance companies are the principal providers of secured debt. Commercial finance companies generally have higher costs than commercial banks to obtain funds, evaluate collateral, and administer portfolios. Interest rates for both groups are generally based on a "spread" above the "prime rate" charged by commercial banks.

Subordinated debt is below senior debt in liquidation priority. Because of its higher risk, providers of subordinated debt demand higher yields than those charged on senior debt. These lenders, such as insurance companies and pension funds, utilize these higher yield investments, in combination with other investments (e.g., real estate, equity, etc.) to satisfy rate of return objectives dictated by the liabilities their funds seek to offset. Additionally, commercial banks and thrift institutions are entering the market of subordinated lending.

The interest rate required for some subordinated loans is so high that a portion of the required yield may be satisfied with an equity "kicker," usually in the form of warrants.

Preferred and common equities are subordinate to all debt financing. Their economic costs are higher than that of debt financing because the investor will require a higher return on the investment to compensate for the higher inherent risk caused by a lower claim on the assets of the company. This investment return comprises two components: dividends and appreciated value.

The cost of preferred equity is generally lower than that of common equity, because its dividend rate is generally higher and is accrued at fixed periods and is paid before common dividends. Common equity, the riskiest form of capital, is more expensive than preferred equity because investors require a combined return from dividends and investment appreciation to reflect the risks assumed (lack of any claim on assets and lack of a specified periodic return, such as preferred dividends or interest).

If the company does not meet the investor's expectations, it may not be able to raise new capital through the issuance of common stock. Venture capital firms, for example, that specialize in high-risk situations and have the highest rate of return requirements for their investments, almost always obtain an equity interest when they participate.

Finally, every firm has an optimal capital structure representing the mix of debt, preferred stock and common equity that causes its stock price to be maximized. A value-maximizing firm will establish its optimal or target capital structure and raise new capital that will keep the capital structure on target over the projection horizon to satisfy its goals of value maximization.

Cost of Capital Components

Debt:
- Defined as short-term interest-bearing debt plus current portion of long-term debt, plus non-current debt.
- Does not include non-interest bearing liabilities such as accounts payable and accruals since they are netted against current assets in determining working capital requirements.

Equity linked/hybrid financing:
- In addition to fixed income obligations, firms raise funds by using instruments (warrants or convertibles) linked to all or part of their businesses.
- Minority interest: Claims by outside shareholders on a portion of a firm's business. Minority interest usually arises after acquisitions when the acquiring firm does not purchase all of the target firm's shares.
- Preferred stock: Long-term equity security paying a fixed dividend.

Common stock:
- Perpetuity ownership.

Cost of Debt: Bond Yields

The yield is the return desired by the buyer or the "real value." Because the face value of the bond and dollar amount of the coupon payment are fixed, the selling price, or present value, of the bond is adjusted to arrive at the current yield. Thus a bond sells at a premium when its coupon rate exceeds the market yield, while a bond sells at a discount if its coupon rate is below the market yield. The yield (desired by an investor) is a function of many factors: the issuer's bond rating, the state of the economy, and the amount of bonds purchased, to name a few.

What price would you pay on June 2, 1988 for a 10% corporate bond that matures on April 1, 1999, if you want a yield of 12.5%? For calculations on the HP19B, assume that you normally express dates in the month-day-year format.

FIN BOND CLEAR DATA TYPE A/A SEMI EXIT 6.021988 SETT 4.011999 MAT 10 CPN% MORE 12.5 YLD% PRICE

Calculator answer is 85.34

The market is quoting $86 for the bond described in the preceding example. What yield will that provide?

86 PRICE YLD%

Calculator answer is 12.375

The component cost of debt used to calculate the weighted average cost of capital is the interest rate on debt, Kb, multiplied by $(1 - t)$ where t is the firm's tax rate.

If a company borrows $100,000 for one year at 10% interest, it must pay the investors who purchase the debt a total of $10,000 annual interest on their investment:

Kb = Before tax cost of debt = Interest/Principal = $10,000/$100,000 = 10%

Assume, for now, that the firm pays no corporate taxes. Under this assumption, the firm's interest cost is $10,000, and its percentage cost of debt is 10%. Assume the tax rate is 40%. The cost of debt then becomes:

$Kb(1-t)$ = Before tax cost of debt $(1 - $ tax rate$) = 10\%(1 - .40) = 6\%$.

Cost of Preferred Stock

Preferred stock is a hybrid between debt and common stock. Like debt, preferred stock carries a fixed commitment by the corporation to make periodic payments. In liquidation the claims of the preferred stockholders take precedence over those of common stockholders.

From the firm's standpoint preferred stock is somewhat riskier than common stock but less risky than bonds. To the investor preferred is less risky than common but more risky than bonds.

The component cost of preferred stock used to calculate the weighted cost of capital (Kp) is the preferred dividend (Dp) divided by the net issuing price (P) or the price the firm receives after deducting flotation costs:

Component cost of preferred stock = $Kp = Dp/P$

Assume the preferred issue is a perpetuity that sells for $75 a share and pays an $8 annual dividend. Its yield is calculated as follows:

Preferred yield = Preferred dividend/Price = $8/$75 = 10.67%

If the firm receives less than the market price, the price should be adjusted for flotation cost. Assume the flotation cost is $3 per share (flotation percentage is $3/$75 or 4%). The new cost of preferred stock becomes:

Kps = Cost of preferred = Preferred yield/(1—f)

where f = flotation percentage, or

10.67%/(1−.04) = 11.11%.

Stock Valuation

The Capital Asset Pricing Model

The Capital Asset Pricing Model (CAPM) and, more recently, the Arbitrage Pricing Theory (APT) are generally accepted by the financial community as the techniques for estimating an equity investor's required return and hence a company's cost of equity capital. Essentially, each model suggests that the required return demanded by shareholders is equal to a risk-free return (as measured by a thirty-year treasury security) plus some additional risk premium to compensate the investor for market risk. This infers that all investors have alternative investment opportunities and will bid on investments yielding the highest return for a given risk profile.

The riskiness of a portfolio of assets (whether it be stocks or a "basket" of capital expansion projects), has direct implications for the required rate of return on a given security. Since investors generally hold portfolios of securities, it is reasonable to consider the riskiness of a security in terms of its contribution to the riskiness of the portfolio rather than in terms of its riskiness if held in isolation.

CAPM Equation:

$Rj = Rf + (Rm - Rf) \beta j$
Where:
Rj is the required return the investor demands for investing in the individual stock.

Rf is the risk free rate.

Rm is the required rate of return on a market portfolio.

βj is the "beta" measure of risk of an asset or security relative to the market portfolio. If beta equals one, the stock is no more or less volatile than the market. If beta is greater than one, the stock is more volatile; less than one, less volatile.

Examples: (1) Assume twenty-year Treasury bonds currently yield 9%. The market returns 12% on a portfolio while the historical long-term average yield on Treasury bonds is 3.1%. Beta estimate for Detroit Edison is .55. What is Detroit Edison's cost of equity?

$Rj = Rf + (Rm - Rf)\beta$
$13.9\% = 9\% + (12\% - 3.1\%).55$

To Develop the Weighted Average Cost of Capital:

1. Establish target market value weights for capital structure. Future financing levels could be different from current or past levels. Estimate the current market value capital structure of the company. Review capital structure of comparable companies. Review management's approach to financing the business.

2. Estimate cost of non-equity financing.

3. Exclude non-interest bearing liabilities such as accounts payable from the calculation of the weighted average cost of capital to avoid inconsistencies and simplify the valuation process. Non-interest bearing liabilities have a cost of capital like other forms of debt, but this cost is implied in the price paid for goods, and thus is recorded in operating costs and free cash flows.

4. Include short-term debt, current-portion of long-term debt, long-term debt and preferred stock.

5. Estimate cost of equity financing. If a market exists, the calculation is stock price × outstanding shares. The current market capitalization is more appropriate than book value as that is representative of the returns current equity holders are demanding.

Cost of capital components:

Cost of equity × percent equity to total capital = product

Cost of debt × percent of debt to total capital = product

Weighted average cost of capital = sum

To better understand this methodology, let's introduce Pillsbury into the picture. The information in Exhibit A1.1 is drawn from Pillsbury's annual report, since bankers use this document as a resource tool for analysis. The following criteria are assumed:

1. Short-term debt book value is close to market value because of the diminutive maturity date.

2. Long-term debt is converted to market value.

3. Equity cost of capital is calculated using the Capital Asset Pricing Model.

4. The tax rate is 40%.

When the cost of equity is determined, the required rates of return on equity and the after tax cost debt are then weighted in order to arrive at the weighted of average cost capital. In Pillsbury's case: 11.4%

Exhibit A1.1

Cost of Captial: Pillsbury 1988

	Capitalization Weights	Pillsbury Cost of Capital	Percentage
Market value of debt:			
Short-term debt BV = MV		$41,900	1.01%
LTD including C/P		$946,100	22.75%
Equity Value:			
Shares outstanding 1988	88,089		
Less shares in treasury	(2,702)		
Total	85,387		
Share market value at fiscal	$37.13		
= Market value of equity		$3,170,419	76.24%
Total market capitalization		$4,158,419	100.00%

Cost of Capital Calculation

Instrument	Before taxes	After taxes	Percent	Product
Short-term debt	9.80%	5.94%	1.01%	0.06%
Long-term debt	10.50%	6.30%	22.75%	1.43%
Equity (CAPM)	13.00%	13.00%	76.24%	9.91%
Weighted cost of capital				11.40%

APPENDIX *II*

Capital Budgeting

A major determinant of a firm's success is the investments it makes. In well-managed firms, this process starts when senior management determines how and in which businesses the company will compete.

Operating managers then translate these strategic goals into concrete action plans for specific investment proposals. This involves employing capital budgeting as a key evaluation process.

In simple terms, the outlay of money today is expected to result in future cash flow. It is important to decide whether the anticipated future cash flow is large enough, given certain risks, to justify the initial outlay. Also, the proposed investment should be the most cost-effective way to achieve strategic objectives. So, it is necessary to:

A. Identify relevant cash flows

B. Estimate the appropriate discount rate (risk adjusted)

C. Calculate the present value of the cash flows, where:

$$NPV = \sum_{t=0}^{n} \frac{F_t}{(1+k)^t}$$

where:

NPV = Net Present Value
Ft = Cash flow in each period
k = cost of capital

Net Present Value Defined

1. Investment is defined as the immediate outlay of funds.

2. Gross Present Value (GPV) or Discounted Cash Flow is the present value of all cash flows after the initial investment.

3. Net Present Value (NPV) is the present value of all cash flows, including the initial investment.

4. NPV is synonymous with the term "value added." If the NPV of a stock or project is positive, the present value of the expected proceeds is greater than the required investment. The implication is that the investor is earning a "value added" return.

273

5. If NPV is positive, the implication is that the investment is earning a rate of return greater than its cost of capital.

Example

Investment of $1,000,000 that earns annual cash flows of $200,000 for 10 years. The appropriate discount rate (or cost of capital) is 12%. What is the NPV? Using a HP 19BII financial calculator:

FIN CFLO 1000000 +/− INPUT 200000 INPUT 10 INPUT CALC 12 I% NPV

Calculator answer is 130044

The project is considered since the NPV > 0.

Internal Rate of Return (IRR)

The internal rate of return (IRR)—or the yield on the project—is the discount rate that equates the present value of the expected future cash flows, or receipts, to the initial cost of the project. The equation for calculating this rate is:

$$0 = \text{NPV} = \sum_{t=0}^{n} \frac{F_t}{(1+r)^t}$$

where r represents the internal rate of return.

We can find the rate of return on a bond purchased and held as an investment. This rate of return is called the yield-to-maturity (YTM), and if a bond's YTM exceeds its required rate of return, then it represents a good investment. Exactly the same concepts are employed in capital budgeting when the internal rate of return method is used.

Example

Consider an investment of $1,000,000 that earns annual cash flows of $200,000 for 10 years. What is the IRR? The cost of capital (k) is 12%.

FIN CFLO 1000000 +/− INPUT 200000 INPUT 10 INPUT CALC 12 I% IRR%

Calculator answer is 15.10

The project is considered since the IRR > k.

Section V

Regional Bank and Community Bank Lending: Issues and Techniques

CHAPTER *Sixteen*

Entrepreneurship Lending: Small Businesses[1]

According to the U.S. Commerce Department, the failure rate of independent start-ups the first year is 40%.

This would indicate that failure is the rule, not the exception. But entrepreneurship lending continues to be a growing, profitable, and largely untapped business source for banks. Furthermore, it presents an opportunity for banks to establish long-term relationships as trusted advisors.

True, entrepreneurs are risk takers. But, they are also innovative and creative visionaries seeking to build long-term value, identifying opportunities and capitalizing on change.

Small businesses should not be viewed as short-term propositions, but serious long-term prospects. Successful pioneers such as Sam Walton, Steven Jobs and Ray Kroc were all entrepreneurs who harnessed small ideas and converted them into large, profitable corporations. Today's adventurers will be tomorrow's leaders.

Before lending to an entrepreneur, bankers must be sure to have satisfactory answers to the following questions:

1. Is the entrepreneurial goal viable in the marketplace?

2. Can the company capitalize on the opportunity with the resources reasonably available?

3. What is the company's structure? Can it work, given its direction and available resources?

4. Does the company have a comprehensive business plan in place? If

---

1 This chapter was written in collaboration with my Fordham G.B.A. student research team: Peter Tirschwell, Beulah Brown, Guy Ferrara, and John Vaccarelli.

so, is it feasible? No business plan, no loan.

5. Can the company eventually compete in the global market?

6. How good is the company's leadership? This is important because there is a definite distinction between leadership and management qualities. Leaders direct the concept, focus and vision to attain a goal. Management's goals stem from necessity rather than ambition. Leaders are proactive instead of reactive, breeding ideas rather than responding to them.

7. What phase of the business cycle is the company in? This is important to consider if, for example, the borrower is in the "survival" stage versus the "takeoff" stage.

8. What loan product is right for the borrower? (See the next chapter for detailed suggestions.)

With these questions in mind, let's review some loan guidelines as they pertain to such entrepreneurial ventures as franchises, Sub S corporation or family-owned businesses.

A Few Pointers on Franchises

The growing presence of franchises underscores their strength as a business idea. The sales and number of franchise establishments in the U.S. have grown approximately 5% annually over the past decade, accounting for an estimated 34% of the $1.5 trillion U.S. retail market. It is conceivable that market share could climb to 60% or better by the year 2001.

These numbers imply strong and steady growth, broadly paralleling the emergence of the service sector as the dominant segment of the U.S economy. Why? Franchising has a decided edge over its competition due to its highly sophisticated retailing approach, which gives franchises more adaptability to changing consumer demands and purchasing habits. The "mom and pop" or small chain competition simply cannot keep pace with this level of competition.

Despite their impressive stats, franchises have mainly relied on financial resources other than banks. For instance, financial institutions such as the ITT Small Business Finance Corporation and the Money Store of Union, N.J., have become prominent lenders to franchises.

Franchisers have also become heavily involved in direct financing of their own franchisee outlets. According to *Entrepreneur Magazine*, 25% of the "Franchise 500" provides direct financing to franchisees. For example, Wicks N' Sticks, a Houston-based franchiser of candle shops will finance the remaining start-up fees if the franchisee produces 25–30% of the initial $150,000–200,000 investment.

In general, banks' reluctance to finance franchising relates to a lack of understanding of, and consequent discomfort with, the franchise concept. The success of franchising relates to several factors, the most important being the ongoing relationship between franchiser and franchisee. This affiliation between franchiser and franchisee pledges a commitment to pass on expertise in areas such as marketing, production, and distribution. In addition, the franchisee may be the beneficiary of a host of supporting services such as personnel training, initial location analysis, facility construction assistance, store design, cash flow projections, and strategically timed new-product introductions. Verifying which franchises offer which services is not very difficult.

The credit analysis of a franchise deal is a double-edged sword covering both the national and the local partnership. This means that the credentials and personal finances of the perspective franchisee are carefully scrutinized, and that the franchiser is subject to an equally, if not more, thorough investigation.

The in-depth analysis of the prospective franchisee includes a detailed financial history and chronicle of attributable skills brought to the business. Banks should be comfortable with the applicant's personal credit rating, management ability, education, track record in other businesses, community reputation, and personal net worth. Since any extension of credit will likely be secured by collateral, the bank will also have an interest in the applicant's assets, including real estate holdings. The applicant's liquid assets are particularly important because franchises are rarely profitable in the initial stage, often requiring periodic cash infusions over the course of the loan.

The second dimension of franchise credit analysis involves the nature and viability of the product or service of the franchiser. In other words, the franchiser's track record. As mentioned earlier, what separates the franchisee loan application from an ordinary business start-up is the ongoing relationship between franchisee and franchiser. Therefore, it is the quality of the prospective relationship that must be confirmed. Creditors should carefully evaluate the commitment the franchiser gives to its franchisees.

Franchisers will always say they are committed to the success of their franchisees but talk is cheap. For example, the typical pitch, "If you don't succeed, we won't either!" may not always be true. A typical red flag is if the bulk of the franchiser's revenues are from the sale of franchises or royalties, rather than ongoing sales of underlying goods or services.

If the franchiser is really in the business of selling franchises and collecting fees, little support will be given beyond the initial sale. An analyst would be well advised to read the financials to resolve the origin and distribution of revenues. In addition, the ratio of initial fees to ongoing fees, and of franchiser-owned and operated outlets to franchised outlets should be identified. This will give the bank a stronger indication of how the operation is really run. Although the trend has been to convert company-owned outlets to franchises, a healthy involvement at the local level is a plus. There is ample reference material available to shed light on this point.

Beyond those aspects of the franchiser/franchisee relationship (personnel training, etc.) other issues need to be appraised. They include the existence and conditions of repurchase agreements, equitable and legally binding contracts that protect all parties, and the franchiser's willingness to intervene in a troubled situation. Even the number of rejected franchise applications provides a measure of the quality of the franchising organization.

Bankers should ask:

1. How many franchised outlets make up the network?

2. How rapidly has that number grown?

3. What is the average age of a franchise?

Bankers should watch for:

1. Unusually high levels of debt

2. Shaky cash flow or questionable trends

And, they should remember that if the franchiser fails, the franchisee will not be far behind.

Highlights of Subchapter S Corporations

Some entrepreneurs elect to take on Subchapter S status. S corporation status is an elective provision permitting certain small business corporations and their shareholders to be handled in accordance with the operating rules of Sections 1363–1379 of the Internal Revenue Code for income tax purposes. S corporations are now widely used by very substantial, highly profitable, closely held corporations. However, these corporations are limited as to the number of stockholders they may have.

Before a corporation can elect to be treated as an S corporation, it must satisfy certain requirements, the most important of which are that:

■ The corporation is a domestic corporation

■ The corporation has at most 35 shareholders.

■ The corporation has as its shareholders only individuals, estates, and certain trusts

■ No nonresident aliens are permitted as stockholders

■ The corporation may issue only one class of stock

Probably the most notable difference between an S corporation and a regular C corporation is that the S corporation is gen-

erally not subject to federal income tax. Its net taxable income is reported by the stockholders of the S corporation on a pro rata basis and added to their other income or losses on their personal federal income tax returns.

Before the Tax Reform Act of 1986, the maximum income tax rate for individuals had always been higher than the maximum rate for corporate taxpayers. Given the same level of taxable income, the overall tax obligation would have been higher for an S corporation than for a regular taxable C corporation. The Act brought the individual income tax rate down to a level lower than that of the corporation. This is why many substantial, closely held businesses deemed it worthwhile to elect S corporation status.

Another benefit of electing to be taxed as an S corporation is that profits can be distributed tax-free. This feature would most likely attract the attention of the lenders. A C corporation pays tax on its profits, and its shareholders pay a second tax when the corporation distributes the dividends. Shareholders of S corporations pay tax on the corporation's income and can receive dividends without paying another tax. Many businesses consider this feature when deciding on whether or not to elect S status.

Some of the disadvantages of S corporations are that they cannot deduct expenses unless or until actually paid to stockholders and they are limited in their ability to deduct certain fringe benefits of shareholders (e.g., health insurance). Also, income is taxed to top shareholders even if it is not distributed.

There are certain provisions which lenders should include in their loan agreements with S corporations to reduce credit risk. Information about corporate distributions is *very* important, i.e., "How much?" and "When?" Information on who authorizes distribution as well as any distribution limitations should be contained in the loan agreement. The agreement should also contain information on whether or not the S corporation allocates funds to former stockholders so they could pay taxes on S corporation earnings.

Virtual Corporations

Another viable business sector banks should recognize is the virtual corporation: A temporary alliance of independent companies such as suppliers, customers, and rival businesses who share skills, profits, and expenses introducing new goods and services to the marketplace. A virtual corporation can exist without a central office, hierarchy, or vertical integration. The key to its success is simply the formation of a partnership.

Virtual corporations exist mainly for two reasons: (1) the majority of existing companies have the inability to introduce products quickly enough in ever changing global markets, and (2) startups usually lack the capital or desire to build an organization from the ground up. Two well-known corporations, Apple and Compaq have thrived on this concept for years at the expense of their competitors. Smaller companies take advantage of outsourcing to maintain flexibility, cash flow, and low overhead.

The bottom line is it can be a very profitable way of doing business for all parties concerned. Banks involved in virtual corporations not only benefit from its success, they also build relationships with all the players involved. This can have a multiplier effect on future business as old virtual corporations are disbanded and new ones established. From the banks' perspec-

tive, the key is prudent credit judgment on all partners involved.

The Family-Owned Small Business

Family-controlled businesses typically represent a market segment in which financial service needs are great and profit margins are large. Small to middle market businesses provide bankers with an opportunity to offer advice on expansion, estate planning, financial asset management and consulting. This can result not only in maintaining operating accounts for the business, but also personal accounts for family members. This improves the bank's operating balances for the current period, as well as the present value of all future balances.

In the past, family business management was automatically handed down to the eldest son. Now management control tends to be more "up for grabs" and business owners are generally more willing to seek help in making these choices. Just how influential are family businesses? In the United States alone family-controlled small business produces half the GNP and employs half the nation's work force. As further evidence of increasing awareness of family businesses, nearly 20 colleges (including The Wharton School of Business) now offer family business programs.

Typical middle market, family-run businesses are more prone to financial crises than comparable firms run by non-family management. This is particularly evident in transitional phases from one generation to the next. Typically, family businesses lack definitive direction due to having ill-prepared succession management and to having family members work together. This often results in a failure to recognize or admit that financial problems exist early enough to solve them.

However, in 8 of 10 cases, management fails to properly train the heir apparent. In many cases, the chief executive places far too many expectations on his or her successor, yet resists training the offspring and/or bringing in competent management from the outside. In one commonly experienced scenario, the successor is shielded from the day-to-day operating activities (the "nuts and bolts" of the organization). When management responsibility is suddenly thrust upon this person, inexperience leads to gross mismanagement. For example, drastic changes are sometimes implemented (i.e., dropping or adding product lines, moving plant facilities). While some of these changes may be theoretically sound, they often fail because the business simply can't tolerate their pace or unexpectedness.

But these problems present opportunities to the alert banker. The owner/manager of a family-run business relies heavily on the lending officer who can offer good advice on a wide range of issues. Here, for instance, are some useful alternatives to merely handing the reins over to one heir:

Executive Committees

With the executive committee, two or more family members are chosen to jointly manage the company. Each member takes a turn as president, with terms running one or two years. This allows for better decision making due to the increased input although accountability could become a problem. However, accountability is not as important as identifying errors and taking preventive steps to avoid repetition.

Dividing the Company

This succession strategy involves splitting the company into several divisions with an heir heading up each division or group of divisions. This can be used prior to retirement to test management and leadership ability before selecting one person to run the entire operation. Alternatively, this strategy can be set up as a permanent arrangement. Naturally it is not appropriate for certain businesses—such as restaurants—which are not large enough to allow for a separation of duties.

Expanding the Company

When a business can't be split up, some families add new businesses for the heirs to manage. It is important, however, that the new businesses fit in with the company's core business and that the family does not spread itself too thin.

Family-run small businesses commonly run afoul of other problems such as the transformation from a "big-small" company to a "small-big company." The trouble here is not necessarily revenue or sales growth, but the resultant change in the company's structure. These changes often occur quickly in response to the needs of various areas of the company such as operations, finance, and marketing. Other transitions include accountability by function and strategic planning. The most important transition of all is the change in mentality from entrepreneurial to professional management. In the small but growing family business, delegation of authority becomes a strategic necessity. The owner/manager must be able to rely on a team of managers to solve problems throughout the firm. It is of key importance that these managers (family or other) are able to operate efficiently and effectively together.

The lender must stand ready to advise the small business as these potentially troublesome situations arise. To reduce risk and to be a good counsellor the banker should heed warning signals and take proper action. The following "red flags" should lead quickly to advice and corrective action:

- **A decline in operating margins and/or a loss of working capital.** Review the company's current asset management polices. If not addressed immediately, a short-term cash shortfall could turn into a severe liquidity crisis. If sales remain constant or even increase, where is the breakdown in the conversion cycle and what is the quality of current assets?

- **Overly optimistic sales forecasts.** Often small family businesses will project strong performance in an attempt to hide financial distress signals. Review the guidelines set forth in the projections chapter for immediate application to this scenario.

- **Failure to keep pace with changing trends.** This includes customer preferences, new technologies, government regulations and stiffer competition as the industry matures.

- **Inability to submit financial statements in a timely manner.** Typically the date on the accountant's opinion letter should not be more than 30 days past the fiscal year-end.

- **Problems associated with work-in-process.** This revolves around the failure to properly maintain existing equipment or replace obsolete equipment.

The most severe financial problems in family-run businesses occur within a year of the first cash-flow problem. A review of key ratios will confirm any suspicions of neglect. It is important that the loan officer be decisive and aggressive in alerting management to trouble signs.

It is also the loan officer's responsibility to tailor the right type of loan product to the needs of the small business and to make the small business owner aware of financing alternatives, a topic covered in detail in the next chapter.

CHAPTER Seventeen

Small-Business Loan Products and Agreement Structure

Small businesses often lack the expertise to select, or even recognize, the wide variety of financing opportunities open to them. The alert banker sees this as an opportunity to create loan activity mutually beneficial to both the bank and its small-business clientele.

This chapter reviews a comprehensive range of short-term and intermediate-term loans most appropriate to the small business owner's needs. It concludes with a detailed discussion of loan structure guidelines, particularly as they relate to intermediate-term loans.

SHORT-TERM FINANCING

The types of loans reviewed in the short-term category include:

- Own paper borrowing
- Lines of credit
- Check or business credit
- Letters of credit

Own paper borrowing implies that lenders evaluate each request on its own merit. Typically this represents short-term unsecured borrowings not falling under a line of credit.

Lines of Credit

Unlike own paper borrowings, credit lines are usually established with a bank letter stating the approved advances and maximum amount. Working capital or seasonal loans providing temporary capital are perfect examples of how lines of credit are initiated. At the end of a seasonal cycle, debt is repaid through the firm's conversion cycle. Although these loans are frequently unsecured, lenders will secure accounts receivable and/or inventory if conditions make it necessary. The amount borrowed may be repaid and reborrowed up to line. While banks are not legally obligated to honor loan requests against lines of credit, arbitrarily canceling lines is the fastest way to alienate customers and lose business. Hence, lines are generally limited to high-quality customers with little chance of failing. Lines of credit offer considerable advantages to banks and borrowers alike:

Advantages to Bank:

1. Lines of credit tend to solidify relationships with customers. Firms seldom switch banks with which they have established lines.

2. Banks are able to forecast future needs for available funds. By identifying the amount their business customers are likely to borrow, banks may invest their funds more productively.

3. Yields are often higher when lines are structured with compensating balances or fees in lieu of balances.

4. Time spent analyzing credits is less than on individual loans.

Advantages to Borrower:

1. Receipt of advance bank support to finance maximum seasonal requirements helps management plan its operation more efficiently.

2. Bank lines serve to reinforce management's judgment that projected seasonal activities are realistic.

3. If the bank reduces its commitment or cancels a line, management, whose capital often underwrites seasonal risk, will be duly warned to change proposed modes of operation.

4. Knowing a firm operates under lines of credit means suppliers and other creditors are more apt to pre-approve credit.

When a bank grants a *joint line,* the parent, together with each of its subsidiaries, may borrow singly, or collectively, so that the aggregate amount of loans outstanding does not exceed the confirmed line. Conversely, a parent may wish to borrow against the line and downstream funds to subsidiaries. On the other hand, it may prefer to allow a subsidiary to draw funds and upstream to the parent.

An *overline* is a line of credit granted to a correspondent bank's customer. Typically, smaller banks can call upon large regional or money center correspondents to advance a line to customers when the aggregate amount required surpasses the small bank's lending limit. Borrowings are done on a LIFO basis (Last In First Out), whereby the large bank's line is drawn down when the smaller correspondent has fully utilized its own line. Repayments are made to the bigger bank first.

When funds are used sporadically, *guidance lines* may be established to redeem maturing commercial paper should the borrower experience a liquidity squeeze.

Check or Business Credit

Check credit services are provided by three basic methods: overdraft, cash reserve, and special draft.

Most common is the overdraft system where a transfer is made from a pre-established line of credit to a customer's deposit account when an overdraft occurs. Transfers are normally made in stated increments up to a maximum line of credit approved by the bank with the customer always being notified of the transfer.

In a cash reserve system, the customer must request the bank to transfer funds from the pre-established line of credit to the deposit account before negotiating a check against them.

A special draft system has the customer negotiating a special check drawn directly against a pre-established line of credit. With this method, deposit accounts are not affected.

In all three systems, the bank periodically provides its customers with a statement of account activity. Required minimum payments are computed as a fraction of the account balance (on the cycle date) and may be made by automatic charges to the deposit account.

The Federal Reserve suggests that delinquencies often are experienced when an account is at or near the maximum credit line. Accordingly, account reports should be generated and reviewed regularly and frequently. These reports should contain schedules of:

1. Delinquent accounts (aged)

2. Accounts where payments are made by drawing on reserves

3. Accounts with steady usage

Banks extending check credit to small businesses have found it advisable to control them stringently. Because such loans are basically unsecured lines of credit, loan approvals and review should be held to the same standards exercised in approving unsecured commercial loans.

Letters of Credit

There are several ways for firms to finance international trade, including cash, open terms (pre-arranged between importer and exporter), and consignment. However, letters of credit are the most widely used instruments in financing foreign transactions.

Customers using letters of credit include high-volume manufacturers, retailers, and trading companies. An electrical goods maker, particularly one that imports many low-technology sub-assemblies from Asia, is a good example of an L/C-intensive business. Shoe or apparel wholesalers may also have profitable volumes of L/C business for the bank. Large retail chains may do a significant volume of their own importing, in apparel, housewares, or ceramics. Commodity middlemen such as fuel distributors are often L/C customers.[1]

L/Cs are beneficial because the customer knows that the bank will refuse payment to the seller unless the seller's documents conform to the terms and conditions of the Letter of Credit. Thus examination of the documents backing up a letter of credit is perhaps the most important function of the issuing bank. Care in examination of documents facilitate the accuracy, speed and ease of handling letters of credit. More important, since the bank is in the middle between importer and exporter, it protects itself and all other parties by honoring documents if and only if they conform to the terms and conditions of the credit, the condition of the merchandise not withstanding.

The two major types of letters of credit are the commercial documentary letter of credit and the standby letter of credit,

---

1   From an interview with a Citicorp executive. N.A. Credit Products.

both of which will be discussed in this chapter.

The issuance and negotiation of letters of credit on the part of the bank are governed by the Uniform Commercial Code and the Uniform Customs and Practice for Documentary Credits. Both are published by the International Chamber of Commerce. All letters of credit must be issued:

1. In favor of a definite beneficiary

2. For a specific amount of money

3. In a form clearly stating how payment to the beneficiary is to be made and under what conditions

4. With a definite expiration date

Exhibit 17.1 illustrates how a commercial documentary letter of credit transaction is conducted.

1. American buyer and Korean seller agree on price, quantity, delivery, and method of payment of goods.

2. Importer applies to his bank for a letter of credit in favor of the seller.

3. Letter of credit is sent to the exporter's advising bank.

4. Advising bank informs beneficiary. If the credit is to be confirmed, the advisory bank adds its name to the obligation and there exists an irrevocable and confirmed letter of credit.

5. When shipment is ready, the draft and documents are sent to the advising bank or directly to the importer's issuing (or paying) bank.

6. The draft and documents are examined for compliance with credit terms and if all is in order, the exporter's draft is honored.

7. Merchandise and documentation are sent to the carrier. Goods are shipped. Shipping documents are given to the importer by the issuing bank when goods arrive. Importer picks up merchandise in exchange for shipping documents.

8. Payment is made by the importer and in turn by the issuing bank.

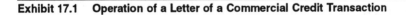

Exhibit 17.1   Operation of a Letter of a Commercial Credit Transaction

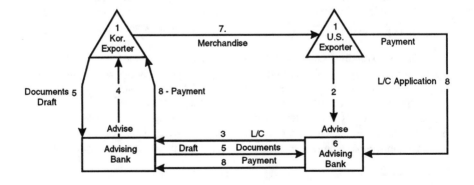

The procedure for commercial documentary letters of credit is outlined as follows:

Drafts:

1. Must be drawn properly by the beneficiary of the credit.

2. The amount should not exceed the remaining balance of the credit.

3. Endorsement of the draft should be proper.

4. The amount identified in words must correspond to the amount in figures.

Invoices:

1. Description of the merchandise with respect to conditions, terms and prices conform exactly to the credit.

2. The merchandise must be invoiced in the name of the party in whose account the credit was opened.

3. Merchandise must be free of charges not pertaining to same.

4. Invoice should not exceed the amount of the credit or remaining balance.

5. Invoices should stipulate identification marks identical to those on other documents.

Insurance:

1. Insurance should cover the risks for at least the actual value of the invoice.

2. The document should be in negotiable form, properly counter-signed by the designated party.

3. The shipment date and dates appearing on bills of lading should not be before the date of the insurance document.

4. Insurance should be issued in the currency of the credit.

Bills of Lading:

1. Document should be marked *on board* with notation dated and signed by the steamship company or its agents.

2. Merchandise described in the invoice should be covered by bills of lading, and such documents should yield marks and group terms.

3. The document should be presented within a reasonable time, and not stale dated. Freight prepaid should be stamped on the document where required. Destination, shipment port, shipment date, the consignee and notifying party should be in agreement with those criteria indicated in the credit.

If the seller is willing, the buyer can also arrange for a Letter of Credit which is payable at a future date, for example, from sight to 180 days after presenting conforming documents. If the draft is drawn at sight, the bank will effect payment upon presentation of the draft provided the terms of the credit have been met. If the draft is drawn on a time basis, the bank will accept the draft (by stamping "Accepted" on the face of the draft), which then can be held by the seller or the bank until maturity.

By accepting the draft, the bank signifies its commitment to pay the face amount at maturity to anyone who presents it for payment at that time. This way, the bank provides its name and credit, which enables its customer (who pays a commission to the accepting bank for this accommodation) to secure financing readily and at a reasonable interest cost.

Keep in mind that rarely can payment under a letter of credit be made to coincide with sale of the purchased goods, conversion to accounts receivable and the ultimate collection of the receivable associated with the original transaction period of interim financing.

Revocable versus Irrevocable

Usually the customer (importer/buyer) with the prior agreement of the (exporter/seller) beneficiary, instructs its bank to issue the letter of credit in either a revocable or irrevocable form.

A revocable letter of credit may be amended or canceled by the issuing bank at any time with or without prior notice to, or agreement of, the beneficiary. Therefore, the beneficiary should not depend on a revocable letter of credit for financial protection. But the revocable letter of credit is not truly a bank letter of credit. Rather, it is a mechanism which provides the buyer and the seller with a means of settling payments for shipments. If a revocable letter of credit designates a bank other than the issuing bank as the paying bank, the paying bank will not pay under the letter of credit should it receive a notice of revocation from the issuing bank. The exporter (beneficiary) must have faith that the importer (customer) will abide by the underlying sales contract or other agreement, and will not instruct the issuing bank to revoke its letter of credit.

An irrevocable letter of credit cannot be amended or canceled without the agreement of all parties concerned. An irrevocable letter of credit is a definite commitment by the issuing bank to pay, provided the beneficiary complies with the terms and conditions in the letter of credit. The terms and conditions cannot be amended or canceled without the consent of the bank.

Confirmed versus Unconfirmed

Some beneficiaries (sellers), particularly those not familiar with the issuing bank, request the buyer to have the irrevocable credit issued in the buyer's country and "confirmed" by a bank in the seller's country.

Confirmed letters of credit are evidenced by the confirming bank's notation: "We undertake that all drafts drawn . . . will be honored by us" or similar words. The beneficiary of a confirmed credit has a definite commitment to pay from a bank in his or her country and does not need to be concerned with the willingness or ability of the issuing bank to pay. One bank may play more than one role. For example, an advising bank may add its confirmation and be designated in the letter as the paying bank.

Other Conditions, Properties and Terms Universally Used in Documentary Commercial Letters of Credit

1. **Tenor:** draft of the beneficiary drawn on the paying bank. Tenor is presented along with documents.

2. **Expiration date:** beneficiary is required to present the draft and documents on or before the expiration date.

3. **Negotiable bill of lading:** this instrument, endorsed in blank, is a receipt for goods, a contract of carriage and evidence of title to property. Possession of the bill of lading is required for delivery of the merchandise, and will be withheld

by the bank until the drawee pays or accepts the draft associated with the shipment.

4. **Marine insurance certificate:** protects the parties against marine perils.

5. **Commercial invoice:** relates to the shipment in terms of types, prices and terms.

6. **Sight draft:** A draft payable on presentation.

7. **Time draft:** Drafts payable either at a specified future date, or at a certain period after sight.

8. **Clean draft:** These drafts are drawn by an exporter to collect an amount due from an importer for a shipment of goods. This type of draft is not accompanied by documents, and is used when the exporter has complete confidence in the integrity and creditworthiness of the importer.

9. **Documentary drafts:** accompanied by documents conveying title to the goods. A documentary draft may take two forms: documents against payment, whereby the exporter turns over to his bank the draft, together with documents with instructions not to release the documents to the importer until the draft is paid, or documents against acceptance, whereby the bank is ordered to withhold documents until the importer has accepted the draft. The accepted draft is called a *trade acceptance.*

10. **Red clause letters of credit:** This type of instrument provides funds for the beneficiary before the merchandise is ready for shipment. The bank, thus, finances on the basis of the letter of credit acting as collateral, since shipping documents would not be available for inspection. This financing instrument is normally used only when a close relationship exists between buyer and seller. Red clause credits contain an element of risk and banks should exercise caution in their negotiation.

Processing of L/Cs is time consuming and paper intensive. As a result, Citibank offices in Asia have been encouraging customers (importers) to open letters of credit with Citibank's Electronic Letters of Credit (Electronic L/C). This will put them in direct contact with Citibank locations all over the globe. More important, electronic letters of credit have reduced customers' costs and turnaround time, while increasing control.

Standby Letters of Credit

A standby letter of credit by the issuing bank guarantees payment to the beneficiary in the event of default or nonperformance by the account party (the bank's customer). Although a standby letter of credit may arise from a commercial transaction, it is not linked directly to the shipment of goods from seller to buyer. It may cover performance of a construction contract, serve as an assurance to a bank that the seller will honor his or her obligations under warranties, or relate to the performance of a purely monetary obligation. A good example is when the credit is used to guarantee payment of commercial paper at maturity. The role of the bank in issuing standby letters of credit differs from that used in issuing commercial letters of credit.

Under all letters of credit, the banker expects the customer to be financially able to meet his or her commitments. A banker's payment under a commercial credit for the customer's account is usually reimbursed immediately by the customer and does not become a loan. However, the bank only makes payment on a standby letter of credit when the customer, having defaulted on his or her primary obligation, will probably be unable to reimburse it. Thus, a standby letter of credit transaction involves a higher potential risk for the issuing bank than does a commercial documentary letter of credit.

Unless the transaction is fully secured, the issuer of a standby letter of credit retains nothing of value to protect it against loss, whereas a commercial documentary letter of credit provides the bank with title to the goods being shipped. To reduce the risk of a standby letter of credit, the issuing bank's credit analysis of the account party should be equivalent to that applicable to a borrower in an ordinary loan situation.

One of the most common uses for a Standby L/C involves the rental of property. Landlords may require that their tenants provide them with Letters of Credit to assure rent payment and protect the landlords' income stream and avoid costly and time-consuming eviction. Other situations which do not involve documents but do involve guaranteed payment to a party are payments of principal and/or interest on bonds, promissory notes, salaries payable abroad and intercompany payments. In these contracts, the beneficiary of the payment likes the comfort of knowing that the integrity of the company with which he is dealing is also backed by a bank's promise to pay.

Intermediate Term Loans

Unlike confirmed lines of credit, Revolving Credits (R/Cs) and Term Loans (T/Ls) involve a *legal commitment* on the part of the issuing bank. The loans (commitments) are made under a written loan agreement which sets down the terms and conditions of advances. Commitment fees are computed on the average daily unused portion of line, generally 1/4 to 1/2%. Commitments require a loan agreement containing restrictive covenants.

Revolving Commitments known as Revolving Credits or R/Cs authorize discretionary borrowing up to a specific amount for periods of at least one year. R/Cs typically convert into term loans at the end of a specific period, as specified in the agreement. Revolving credits are useful financing vehicles for new projects not expected to produce immediate cash flows. The expiration of revolving credits (and conversion to a term loan) can be timed to coincide with the project's expected cash flow, matching cash inflows and outflows.

Term loans are non-revolving commitments with maturities beyond one year. These loans generally contain periodic (annual, semiannual or quarterly) amortization provisions. Term loans involve greater risk than do short-term advances, because of the length of time the credit is outstanding. Because of the greater risk factor, term loans are sometimes secured loans. Agreements on such credits normally contain restrictive covenants during the life of the loan. These loans have assumed increasing importance in recent years. Term loans generally finance capital expenditures needed to maintain low production costs and improve competitive superiority. Term loans also finance new ventures and acquisitions such as new product procurement or vertical/ horizontal mergers.

Construction Loans

The purpose of construction lending is to allocate funds for construction projects for a designated time. Repayment of the loan is contingent upon the borrower obtaining permanent financing or finding a buyer with sufficient funds to retire the debt. As a result, the risk factor associated with construction loans can be quite high. Risk is emanated because the borrower is committed to finish the project within the limits of cost and time constraints. Serious problems can transpire if the project's completion or cost overruns exceed the takeout dates. This may void sale prices or permanent funding commitments. Lenders may also find out—all too late—that the finished project will be an economic failure. Other major risks include diversion of progress payments resulting in nonpayment of material bills or sub-contractors and the financial breakdown of contractors before completion. Also imperiling the project— bankruptcy of a key supplier or subcontractor, strikes, higher material or labor costs, or an act of God.

Construction lending is categorized as unsecured front money, land development, commercial construction or residential construction loans. Unsecured front money loans are working capital advances to borrowers intended for use in a new and unproven venture.

Front money loans are often used as pre-construction funding to start a project. The funds may be used to acquire or develop a building site, eliminate title impediments, pay the architect, standby fees, and/or meet minimum working capital requirements established by construction lenders.

Because repayment often comes from the first draw against construction financing, many construction loan agreements define the purposes for which the first advance may be used. Advances are usually secured by a first mortgage or deed of trust and backed by a purchase or takeout agreement from a permanent lender, such as a savings bank.

Disbursements are predetermined in advance based upon either a standard payment plan or a progress payment plan. The standard payment plan is normally used for residential and smaller commercial construction loans. This utilizes a pre-established schedule for fixed payments at the end of each specified stage of construction. The most common is a five-payment, equal installment plan. The first four disbursements are made when construction has reached agreed upon stages verified by actual inspection of the property. The final payment is made after the legally stipulated lien period has lapsed.

The progress payment plan is normally used for larger, more complex, building projects. Basically, this plan dictates monthly disbursements totaling 90 percent of the value with 10 percent held back until the project is completed. Completion of the project is verified by either an architect's certification or by evidence of labor and material costs approved by the owner. In both cases, a percentage of the loan proceeds are usually retained until a notice of completion has been filed, and the stipulated period under which liens may be filed has lapsed.

Banks considering construction loans must study documentation relating to reputation, work and credit experience and, of course, audited financial statements (three years at least). Other lenders and trade creditors should be contacted to determine the financial histories of the builders and permanent lender.

Loans financing commercial construction projects are usually collateralized, and such collateral is generally identical to that for real estate loans. Supporting documentation of such collateral would include:[2]

1. A recorded mortgage or deed of trust which can be used to foreclose and to obtain title to the collateral.

2. A title insurance binder or policy, usually issued by a recognized title insurance company or, in some states, an attorney's opinion. That information should be updated with each advance of funds, if such additional protection is available.

3. Insurance: builders' risk policies with evidence of payment of premiums, fire and extended coverage, vandalism and malicious mischief, etc.

4. An appraisal showing the value of the land and improvements to date or, possibly, a total appraisal based on specifications. In the absence of an appraisal, the write-up of specifications showing total costs should be reviewed and the credit file should indicate the borrower's initial equity.

5. Evidence that taxes have been paid to date.

Once the project has commenced, inspection reports must be maintained, keeping the bank abreast of the borrower's progress in order to monitor the loan. The person or firm engaged to inspect the project should be qualified and should have no business association with either the obligor or the contractor. The fact that the project is not proceeding as anticipated should be shown in the inspection reports.

Loan Structure: Structuring Loan Agreements

Loan agreements offer a considerable amount of protection for banks involved in intermediate term lending by providing periodic review and renewal of a credit.

Protection for the lender is based on two perceptions: (1) the longer a borrower has the money, the more likely a downturn in the business or economic environment will occur, (2) the plans on which the borrower based its financial plan will change. The loan agreement is normally prepared by the bank's legal counsel and reviewed by the borrower's attorney. A loan agreement defines the conditions under which lenders have the right to review the bank's credit decision. This should be at a point and on a level where the customer's condition has not slipped beyond retrieval. In other words, the lender can still step in while the borrower has enough flexibility left to solve problems not anticipated in the original projections.

The provisions of term loan agreements are tailored to each specific situation, but usually contain provisions under each of the following headings:

1. Preamble

2. Amount and term of the loan

3. Representations and warranties

4. Conditions of lending

5. Default Provisions

6. Description of collateral

7. Covenants of the borrower

8. Miscellaneous

---

2   Board of Governors of the Federal Reserve System. *Federal Reserve Examination Manual,* June 1985. Real Estate Construction Loans Introduction.

Preamble and Description

The preamble sometimes does little more than name lenders and borrowers, stating that an agreement has been entered into. A statement of purpose may be included, as well as commitment fees, interest rates, prepayment rights and a definition of terms used in the agreement.

Amount and Term of the Loan

As implied, this portion of the agreement sets forth the amount of the loan, the manner in which the borrower may draw down amounts, the interest rate, fees, maturity dates, and the provisions relating to prepayments. If the commitment agreement supports a term loan, it will call for periodic equal payments. However, provisions are sometimes made for a balloon payment or "bullet payment" at maturity. Balloon payments require periodic equal payments made with a larger lump sum payment due at the end of the term loan. Similar to a balloon payment, a "bullet payment" sometimes includes a provision requiring cash flows from operations or asset sales above a predetermined amount to be earmarked for loan amortization to reduce the balloon or bullet portion of the loan. Banks do not generally impose a fee for the prepayment of an installment or for the early retirement of the entire loan if the funds are derived from current operations, from funding the debt, or from the sale of assets. However, if prepayment is the result of loans from another bank, a penalty is prescribed.

In cases where the loan is a revolving credit with provision for changing the credit into a term loan, a commitment fee can be charged. The bank is permitted to assess a fee for unused but committed funds since they must be readily available for the borrower's use. The bank will not feel free to invest these funds in high earning assets such as other loans of intermediate maturities.

Representations and Warranties

Generally this section of the agreement refers to the possession of adequate licenses, patents, copyrights, trademarks, and trade names to conduct business in addition to the economic, financial, and legal circumstances prevailing at the time the original credit decision was made. The representations and warranties specify the borrower is:

1. Legally incorporated.

2. In good standing.

3. Empowered to make the agreement, execute the notes and perform.

4. Submitting financial statements that are correct and reflect the borrower's true financial condition.

5. Permitted to borrow under the borrower's charter and bylaws, governmental regulation, and other agreements as authorized by the board of directors.

This section may also include statements that the business and properties of the company have not in any way been materially or adversely affected since its latest audit, and that the firm has no federal income tax liability in excess of the amount shown on its balance sheet.

Finally, the representations and warranties should include a paragraph dealing with any material pending litigation. This will ensure that the outcome of such litigation will not materially impair the ability of the borrower to perform under the agreement.

Conditions of Lending

This article of the agreement is concerned with the conditions that must exist and the representations that must be delivered to the lender in order to make the commitment binding. Before disbursing any monies under the loan, legal counsel must be satisfied with the documents submitted by the borrower including:

- Charter and bylaws.
- Resolutions adopted by the company's board of directors authorizing the contemplated transaction, together with any other required resolutions (for example, authorizing hypothecation of collateral, insurance, or guarantees).
- Certificates of good standing from those jurisdictions where the major properties of the borrower are located or a substantial portion of the borrower's business is transacted.
- Copies of all consents and approvals which might have had to be obtained.
- Copies of other debt instruments to which the borrower might be subject.

A review of all the required documentation should enable legal counsel for the lender to determine if everything is legally acceptable. In most instances, corporate affairs of borrowers are far from simple, so counsel for the lender should not be expected to become familiar with all the ramifications of the business of the borrower, guarantor, or any other party to the agreement. For that reason, opinions should be obtained from the borrower's counsel (preferably independent) stating that all necessary legal actions have been

taken and that no provisions of charter, bylaws, or other applicable agreements have been violated.

It should also be noted that the loan agreement and any notes to be issued in connection with it are valid and binding obligations of the borrower. That way they will be enforceable in accordance with the terms of the loan. It should further be determined that all other instruments (guarantees, for example) are similarly valid and enforceable.

On the financial side of the conditions precedent, it is obvious that the lender should have obtained a signed copy of the loan agreement and note(s) to be issued. In those instances where collateral is to be pledged, appropriate instruments should have been executed and, if applicable, the collateral should be in the hands of the lender. A similar consideration evolves around the execution and delivery of guarantees.

Certifications should also be obtained when a contemplated loan is part of a larger financing program involving the raising of additional capital funds, the discharge of other indebtedness, or the prior investment of the borrower's own funds in a venture to be financed partly by the contemplated loan.

Finally, as a condition precedent, the lender will require two additional documents:

1. An incumbency certificate listing the names and signatures of the officers (with their respective titles) having the power to act for the borrower.

2. A certification by a responsible officer that the representations and warranties contained in the agreement are true and correct as of the closing date.

Default Provisions

All term loans have default provisions under which the long-term lender has the right to accelerate the payment of the loan. This is mandated with an acceleration clause stating that if certain conditions are not met, the total loan is immediately due, or at the very least, that the bank has the right to renegotiate the terms. If such a clause is excluded from the agreement, the bank is obliged to wait until each installment is due before legal action can be taken against the borrower. The fact that the right exists does not mean that it is always used, but it does give lenders maneuverability when they need it.

Several default provisions are ordinarily included in term loan agreements. Probably the most important act of default relates to bankruptcy, reorganization, and nonpayment of indebtedness. Lenders must have the right to call in their outstanding loans or be relieved of any obligation to make further loans in the case of voluntary bankruptcy or reorganization proceedings. If lenders have not reserved the right to accelerate under the foregoing conditions, the lender might be in the awkward position of not having matured claims to present to the bankruptcy trustee. This, in turn, might stop them from proving their claims and/or recovering claims in full.

Another act of default is the misrepresentation of financial information presented in financial statements. This not only indicates financial trouble, it also raises the question of management's moral integrity. Since financial statements are one of the principal means by which management is measured, misrepresentation is a clear indication that the borrower is not of high moral character. In this instance, it would be best for all parties concerned to dissolve the relationship. The failure to perform or observe any of the terms of the agreement is also a default.

The argument against acceleration is that it could precipitate bankruptcy. This, however, might or might not be the case and the holder of other unpaid indebtedness might rewrite the obligation so that it is repaid over the near term (just keeping the debtor out of bankruptcy) or the creditor might take security to protect its interests. To what extent these possibilities are serious threats depends to a large degree on the strength of the covenants. Certainly in any lending arrangement where term loans are made with only a few covenants, the acceleration of other indebtedness should cross-accelerate the subject loan.

The Next Group of Defaults

These relate to such things as material falsity or representation and warranties, default under negative covenants, or default under covenants contained in other debt instruments. Certainly if a representation on which a lender has based its decision should prove to be false in a material respect, the lender should have the right to review its decision. At times this can protect the lender from serious problems, especially if the contemplated loan is in violation of other agreements or statutory regulation.

Loan Covenants

This is a very important part of the loan agreement. The covenants of a loan agreement lay the framework for the financial plan jointly agreed upon by the borrower and the lender. The number and detail of the covenants will largely depend on the financial strength of the enterprise, management's aptitude, and the length of the proposed loan. For example, if the borrower is financially solid and has strong management, the number of covenants will be less than for a borrower who is only moderately strong. Some of the largest, best managed companies borrow term money without restrictive covenants and with only certain basic Events of Default. With smaller companies in the prime commercial group, lenders are often content to set broad covenants limiting debt to an overall ratio of tangible net worth, prohibiting secured debt, and providing for the maintenance of a certain minimum working capital.

In actuality, the basic covenants in every term loan agreement should he constructed around these three principles:

1. Limitation of other indebtedness.

2. Prohibition of secured obligations or of obligations ranking ahead of the commercial term loan.

3. A provision for the maintenance of a certain minimum working capital.

4. Furnishing financial statements.

Covenants can also be viewed as being negative or affirmative, primary, secondary, or tertiary.

Affirmative Covenants

Affirmative covenants are good general business practices that management may not have control over. However, they remain obligations imposed on management. One of the most common affirmative covenants is the requirement that the bank be furnished with financial statements periodically with any other relevant information as requested. This alerts the bank to any potential financial deterioration. It is common practice to require unaudited statements for the first three quarters of the borrower's fiscal year, in addition to audited statements at year end. Term loan agreements generally require, also, that the borrower carry insurance to reduce risks.

Many term loan agreements require the borrower to maintain working capital at or above a stated amount. Some bankers consider this one of the most important provisions since it requires the borrower to maintain a specific amount of liquidity. For obvious reasons, it also provides a measure of protection for other creditors as well.

However, this provision may not provide as much protection as some people think. Why? It would be possible for a business to maintain the working capital requirements while carrying large investments in inventory and accounts receivable.

To say the least, a company in this situation is not very liquid. Therefore, a close check must be kept on the quality of current assets and current liabilities. Nevertheless, the working capital requirement is influential because it gives the bank the right to declare the borrower in default should the working capital drop below the agreed level.

In some instances, an affirmative covenant incorporated in term loan agreements may require management that is satisfactory to the bank. This means that if the management should change due to resignation, death, or other causes, the bank must give its blessing before new personnel is hired. Banks often require that *keyman* or *keywoman* insurance be carried on those people in responsible positions who cannot be readily replaced.

Description of Collateral

When the loan is secured, the agreement sets forth a detailed description of the collateral and how it is to be handled. If the collateral consists of securities, the agreement normally specifies who is to receive the interest or dividends, who is to have the right to vote the stock, under what conditions the securities are to be sold, and if sold, who is to receive the proceeds from the sale.

Negative Covenants

The objective of negative covenants is to prevent a dissipation of assets that would weaken the firm's financial strength, and the assumption of obligations (definite or contingent) that might reduce the borrower's ability to repay the loan. Negative covenants are particular things the borrower agrees *not to do* during the life of the loan without prior consent from the lending bank. This is usually satisfied with an amendment to the term loan agreement or by letter.

Some negative covenants are those that take a definite management decision to violate. For example, if a borrower agrees not to pay dividends, it cannot happen by accident that dividends are paid. Financial ratios are usually treated as negative covenants even though conscious management decisions are not always required to break them. For instance, losses caused by adverse trading conditions may lead to the breach of the working capital minimum, or even a specified debt/equity ratio, despite management effort to the contrary.

In negotiation, certain exceptions will be agreed upon including, for instance, that overseas subsidiaries may pledge their assets to support their own borrowing, that prior existing secured debt is excluded, or that certain minimal monetary amounts can be raised on a secured basis annually without the lender's specific approval. In limiting indebtedness, lenders should include limitations on leases and contingent liabilities other than normal product warranties.

A common negative covenant is the negative pledge clause usually found in unsecured loans where the borrower agrees not to pledge assets as security to other lenders, and not to sell receivables. Even though this clause may be included if the loan is secured, its importance is probably lessened since other lenders would be reluctant to loan sizable amounts to a firm that has already pledged most of its assets. Such a covenant assures the bank that other lenders will not be placed in a more favorable position than it occupies.

Prohibitions regarding merger and consolidation, except with the approval of the bank, are also generally included for the bank's protection. To assure that the productive ability of the concern remains intact, a prohibition is usually included against the sale or lease of substantially all of the borrower's assets. Term loan borrowers also usually agree not to make loans to others or to guarantee, endorse, or become surety for others. Such a prohibition reduces the possibility of cash withdrawals, a weakened financial position, and the assumption of contingent liabilities which can become a heavy responsibility.

Restrictive Clauses and/or Secondary Covenants

Restrictive clauses and/or secondary covenants seem similar to negative covenants but are basically different. Negative covenants in general prohibit certain acts of management, while restrictive clauses permit certain acts but restrict their latitude. For example, a negative covenant may prohibit a term loan borrower from mortgaging plant and equipment during the life of the loan, while a restrictive clause may limit the amount of dividends the borrower is permitted to pay. These clauses may be required even if the primary covenants are tight. This is because a lender does not want all earnings in excess of debt requirements and fixed asset maintenance expenditures to be diverted into unknown or unspecified uses. The further out in time a loan runs, the more questionable it becomes that the original credit and financial tests will adequately protect the lender. These covenants include:

1. Prohibition of the sale, discount, or other disposition of accounts receivable with or without recourse.

2. Prohibition of changes in other debt instruments.

3. Limitation of prepayment or redemption of other long-term debt. The purpose of such a provision is to prevent the bank from being the last to be repaid. It also prevents the firm from using the bank's funds to pay off some other lender. If a borrower owes long-term debts to others, a limitation may be placed on the amount that may be retired annually without also retiring a portion of the term debt owed to the bank.

4. Prohibitions on mergers or consolidations, asset sales, and acquisitions.

5. Prohibitions on investments in other enterprises.

6. Limitations on capital expenditures. The purpose of this is to prevent the firm from overextending itself. The amount that can be invested will vary considerably but may be limited to the company's annual depreciation charges.

7. Limitations may also be placed on salaries, bonuses, and advances to officers and employees, as well as to others. The limitation on salaries and bonuses is a way of forcing a borrower to "tighten the belt" until adequate capital funds are in hand.

8. Limitations on dividends. This may be in terms of a certain percentage of *cumulative* earnings, or it may specify that dividends not be allowed to reduce retained earnings below a certain level.

9. Limitations on treasury stock purchases to prevent a weakening of the firm's financial strength.

10. Restrictions on the purchase of securities, with the usual exception of United States government obligations. This limitation is designed to prohibit speculation in securities.

The Miscellaneous Section

The final agreement section sets forth any matter to be specified that does not logically fall in one of the previous sections. It includes where notices to borrowers or lenders shall be sent, what law governs the agreement, the duties of the agent bank in syndicated loans, and the borrower's agreement to pay certain expenses.

In summary, as necessary as it is for bankers to discover means of financing their growing small-business clientele, it is just as necessary to structure loan agreements so that they provide adequate protection for the lending institution.

■■■
Section VI
■■■
When Things Go Wrong
■■■

CHAPTER *Eighteen*

Financial Distress: Predictive Modeling

A survey of credit practices at the country's 100 largest banks shows that most of them are not using statistical financial distress models to evaluate credit, decide appropriate pricing, and monitor loan loss reserves.

To date, the most widespread use of these models has been in the screening of consumer loan applications. However, as banking evolves, statistics will become more popular in reinforcing traditional credit techniques and distress prediction will emerge as an important tool for the '90s and beyond.

This all demands a comprehensive understanding of the theory and practice of predictive distress modeling which, of course, is provided in this chapter.

We'll start with the history of distress prediction models which first gained widespread recognition thanks to the work of Edward Altman. Altman developed his classic Z-Score equation in 1968, using discriminant analysis to establish a model for predicting bankruptcy.

His sample comprised 33 financially distressed manufacturing firms and a control group of 33 healthy companies. From their financial statements one period prior to bankruptcy, Altman obtained 22 financial ratios, of which 5 were found to contribute most to the prediction model. The discriminant function Z was found to be:

$$Z = 1.2x_1 + 1.4x_2 + 3.3x_3 + .6x_4 + .999x_5$$

where

x_1 = Working capital/Total assets
x_2 = Retained earnings/Total assets
x_3 = EBIT/Total assets
x_4 = Market value of equity/Book value of debt
x_5 = Sales/Total assets

Z > 2.99: classified as healthy entities. The higher the Z score, the healthier the firm and the lower the probability of failure.

Z < 1.81: classified as financially distressed or bankrupt.

1.81 > Z< 299: classified as grey area firms.

By applying the discriminant function to data obtained two to five years before bankruptcy, it was found that the model correctly classified 72 percent of the initial sample two years before failure. A trend analysis shows that all five observed ratios $x_1 \ldots x_5$ deteriorated as bankruptcy approached and that the most serious change in most of these ratios occurred among the third and second years before failure.

The income statement and balance sheet for NS Group, a manufacturer of specialty steel products, traded on the NYSE, is presented for the year ending September 1992. These abbreviated financial statements provide the data needed to use the discriminant Z function.

The NS Group Income Statement and Balance Sheet September 26, 1992

Net Sales	281,242
Cost of Sales	261,130
Operating Income	20,112
Other Income	980
Total Income	21,092
Depr. & Amor.	18,711
Interest Exp.	21,797
Taxes (Credit)	6,058
Net Loss	(15,900)
Dividends	808

Assets

Cash	8,514
Investments	3,865
Accounts Rec.	37,141
Tax Refund	4,825
Inventories	42,597
Other C/A	17,159
Current Assets	114,101
Net Property	186,468
Other Assets	18,510
Total Assets	319,079

Liabilities and Equity

Notes Payable	20,681
Current debt	8,892
Accounts Pay.	27,342
Accruals	16,359
Income Taxes	151
Current Liab.	73,425
Long-Term Debt	164,180
Deferred Taxes	12,900
Common Stock	47,353
Warrants	100
Retained Earnings	21,121
Total	319,079

Using the data on the NS Group Inc., the five key financial ratios required for function Z can be calculated. The Z value for the NS Group as of fiscal 1992 is:

x_1 = Working capital/Total assets = 40,676/319,079 = .1275

Working Capital = Current Assets − Current Liabilities

Current Assets	$114,101
Current Liabilities	$73,425
Working Capital	$40,676
Total Assets	$319,079

x_2 = Retained earnings/Total assets = 21121/319079 = .0662

x_3 = EBIT/Total assets = 20112/319,079 = .0630

x_4 = Market value of equity/Book value of debt (all liabilties) = 78,504/250,505 = .313

Average price per share in 1992 was approximately $5.80.

Shares Outstanding	13,505
Average Price Per Share	5.813
Market Value Of Equity	78,504
Book Value of Debt	250,505

x_5 = Sales/Total assets = 281,242/319,079

Z = 1.2(.1275) + 1.4(.0662) + 3.3(.0630) + .6(.3133) + .999(.8814) = 1.53

The resulting Z value is 1.53. Recall the critical Z value is 1.81. NS Group's 1.53 Z-Score falls below 1.81, placing it in the category of firms likely to go bankrupt. However, the firm's situation might not be as bad as the model suggests. According to Value Line, the firm is likely to cut losses by 65% in fiscal 1993 due to higher sales and improved capacity. Here, the improvements in operations should go a long way toward improving cash flows, reducing interest costs and strengthening assets.

There has been a general deterioration in the average Z score for U.S. manufacturing companies since the recent recession. Therefore, why not combine Z-score with traditional credit analysis and loan review?

One reason is the obvious lack of industry-to-industry homogeneity. Altman's **original** (Z-Score not Zeta, the newer version) model examined distressed firms in only one industry—manufacturing. Industries outside the industrial sector—financial institutions, utilities, and transportations—cannot fit the old model.

Also, James A. Hoeven's study of Z ratings suggests Z-scores are not very useful in determining the quality of small business loans.[1] Hoeven questioned the dependability of small business firms' financial statements, noting that differences between successful and troubled small businesses are not as pronounced as the differences found in Altman's study of large corporations.

Hoeven says that the weak financial condition of a small, closely held firm may not reveal other financial resources possessed by its owners that can become quickly available. This may have dissuaded many banks, particularly those serving lower to middle markets, from investigating the merits of such a decision tool actively.[2] Hoeven suggests that the key element in the analytical process continues to be the loan officer. *"While discriminate decision models are useful because they form a totally objective view of financial information, models will never relieve the loan officer of the ultimate decision or responsibility."* A majority of bankers obviously agree. Further, two researchers, Moses and Liao suggest that *individual ratios included in the model may be highly correlated with each other. They suggest this poses a problem with the discriminate approach:* [3]

■ ■ ■

"Individual ratios included in the model may be highly correlated with each other. This causes three problems. First, the relationship between individual ratios and the dependent variable (failure status) may be distorted. Second, correlation between predictor ratios may differ in other samples making results developed on one sample applicable only to that specific sample. Third, individual coefficients are not meaningful so conclusions concerning the importance of any individual ratio in explaining failure are not possible, making the model difficult to interpret. In fact the standard approach may assign coefficients with signs that are counterintuitive."

■ ■ ■

Yet, in spite of these arguments, I believe that, a brilliant fabric of logic un-

---

1 James A. Hoeven, "Predicting Default of Small Business Loans." *The Journal of Commercial Bank Lending,* April 1979.

2 Ibid.

3 Douglas Moses and Shu S. Liao, "On Developing Models for Failure Prediction." The Journal of Commercial Bank Lending, March 1987.

derlies Altman's original Z-score model. Let's assume that while the model's "logic" is buried within the regression formula, we're able to pry from it two invaluable lessons lying near the core of strategic planning. But before I share secrets, step into my Credit Management class for a moment:

M.G.   Class, look at the Z-score equation again. What variable do you think is the most important?

$$Z = 1.2x_1 + 1.4x_2 + 3.3x_3 + .6x_4 + .999x_5$$
x_1 = Working capital/Total assets
x_2 = Retained earnings/Total assets
x_3 = EBIT/Total assets
x_4 = Market value of equity/Book value of debt
x_5 = Sales/Total assets

Student # 1   That's easy, x_3 (EBIT/Total assets) because the x_3 coefficient carries the largest weight. Besides, EBIT launches cash flow, and without strong cash flow, the borrower's financial condition will weaken.

M.G.   True, except x_3 is not the critical Z-score variable. Try again.

Student # 2   Absolutely no question about it. The firm caves in if x_1 (Working capital/Total assets) crashes. Losses do not directly lead to bankruptcy; companies fail because they lose all their working capital—then liquidity.

M.G .   (Long pause). I see everyone writing. Take out the eraser, x_3 is not the critical variable.

Student # 3   It has to be x_4 (Market value of equity/Book value of debt). The 33 firms that bellied up probably had top-heavy capital structures. x_4 is a leverage ratio—the benchmark of unsystematic risk. Look at the denominator of leverage. If the firm does poorly, the stock price crashes, right? This will cause market leverage to skyrocket causing investors—suppliers, lenders as well, to lose confidence.

M.G.   Right on all counts . . . except, unfortunately, you picked the wrong variable, x_4.

Student # 4   Well here goes . . . a 50% probability of being right; it's x_2 (Retained earnings/Total assets). Retained earnings capture the bottom line, not EBIT. Wait! No, it's x_5 (Sales/Total assets). If sales plummet, other variables are triggered in a multiplier effect.

M.G.   Indeed! Let's call this disastrous sales malady the firm's "domino-multiplier syndrome."

Firms with high operating leverage are very sensitive to changes in sales. Modest sales increases can result in sizable jumps in operating income. This is well and good if investments in fixed assets lead to strong sales and healthy returns. But what happens if industrial firms lose markets?

Now, class, let's answer the question with a quick deal analysis. Suppose a firm applies for a bank loan to expand operating facilities. The financial manager tells the loan officer that he wants to take advantage of the low cost of capital in the marketplace. The proposed project increases the firm's fixed assets (raising operating leverage), and the breakeven or cost-volume-profit point. Subsequently, of the three pro forma projections submitted to the bank, only the best-case scenario shows a profit. If the company's "best-case" scenario is the only sales forecast that meets or surpasses the B/E point, the show is over. Why? Sales are not sufficient to justify immoderate fixed asset investments.

Lesson #1: Domino-Multiplier Syndrome

The Axiom:

Sales reductions trigger a Z-score domino effect, accentuated by large capital expenditures followed by failed sales. Therefore don't lend to provide excessive operating leverage until you are convinced healthy projected sales end up healthy actual sales. Develop worse case projections to establish that borrowers can safely withstand recessions and/or sharp sales reductions.

Proof of the Pudding: Lesson #1:

Sale reductions force down the Z-score. Sale declines also drive down x_3 (EBIT/Assets) due to the negative effects of operating leverage.

A drop in x_3 (EBIT/Assets) knocks over a domino by driving down x_2 (Retained earnings/Total Assets) as losses flow through.

Retained earnings is a component of working capital (along with increases in long-term obligations and reductions in fixed assets). Thus, x_2 (Retained earnings/Total assets) links to x_1 (Working capital/Total assets).

And what effect will our dominos have on x_4 (Market value of equity/Book value of debt)? Investors start dumping shares in panic selling fearing that the firm's weak liquidity (caused by operating losses) makes it difficult or nigh impossible to reduce debt.

Lesson #2: Low Asset Productivity: A Key to Failure

The Axiom:

Companies can go bankrupt because assets like inventory, receivables and equipment are out of control. Financially distressed companies break the cardinal rule of strategic planning: keep assets at minimum levels consistent with maintaining strong sales and profits. It's the planning that counts!

Proof of the Pudding: Lesson #2:

Note that four out of five Z-score variables carry total assets in the denominator.

$$Z = 1.2x_1 + 1.4x_2 + 3.3x_3 + .6x_4 + .999x_5$$

x_1 = Working capital/Total **assets**

x_2 = Retained earnings/Total **assets**

x_3 = EBIT/Total **assets**

x_4 = Market value of equity/Book value of debt

x_5 = Sales/Total **assets**

Zeta will drop like a lead balloon if management loses its hold on assets. Management should keep assets in check, ensure assets reach optimal efficiency, develop goods and services that produce healthy profits, and watch over the firm's equity base and capital structure—making sure it strengthens along with the industry. While still on the subject of assets, let's do something perhaps historic and connect (in mathematical terms) the sustainable growth model with Altman's Z-model. Recall, from the chapter dealing with sustainable growth, the sustainable growth rate measures a company's growth rate compared to the targeted growth rate to find out if the company is growing prudently or is straining its capital structure. The sustainable growth equation is:

$$g^* = \frac{P\,(1-d)\,(1+L)}{A/S - P\,(1-d)\,(1+L)}$$

As implied from the equation, if assets increase, the variable A/S increases causing a decline in the sustainable growth rate. If this decline falls below the targeted growth rate, the company may be placing an excessive strain on its capital structure.

The assets to sales ratio is an important component of the sustainable growth model. It is positioned in the equation to represent the base (before profit retention) on which an appropriate and sustainable growth rate is calculated. If this rate exceeds tolerance, we know that leverage will increase rapidly. The assets to sales ratio is largely decided by management, as their policies give rise to asset expansion.

Again, look at what is the leading variable in the financial needs equation:

$$F = \frac{A}{S}\,(\Delta S) - \frac{L_1}{S}\,(\Delta S) - P\,(S)(1 - d)$$

The net effect of low asset productivity—increased assets without a strong corresponding increase in sales—leads to excessive borrowing. This scenario translates into a high debt to equity ratio that may strain the capital structure. Thus, cash flow, financial needs, sustainable growth and Altman's financial distress equation are members of the same family. What is particularly important: the models prove the connection between the capital output ratio (A/S) and **financial** performance. With due respect to Moses and Liao, correlation indeed exists in Z-score, but that's hardly a negative.

ZETA: Altman Updated

But Altman's original model did lack cross-industry capabilities. A new version, called Zeta and marketed by Zeta Services, Inc., of New Jersey, does go cross-industry and adds several highly useful variables to the model mix:

x_1 **Return on Assets** is measured by earnings before interest and taxes/total assets. This variable has proven significant in evaluating firm performance in several past multivariate analyses.

x_2 **Earnings Stability.** Zeta measures risk by using a normalized measure of the standard error of estimate around a 10-year trend. It's no surprise that this variable is important since earnings volatility and risk not only drive market returns but significantly influence bond ratings.

x_3 **Debt Service** represents the traditional interest coverage ratio.

x_4 **Cumulative Profitability** is measured by the firm's retained earnings/total assets. This ratio, which incorporates factors such as the firm's age, dividends and profit accumulation was found to be quite helpful in past studies.

x_5 **Current Ratio.** The famous current assets/current liabilities ratio which tests liquidity, was found to be more informative in identifying failures.

x_6 **Capitalization.** The common equity/total capitalization ratio. The updated model measures capitalization ratio using a five-year average of market (not book) value. In addition preferred stock is included at liquidation value.

x_7 **Size of the Business.** The firm's total tangible assets is the criteria used to measure this variable. Old established businesses will generally be larger than new ventures, having built up their assets over extended periods of time. Statistically, newer businesses fail more rapidly than old established ones.

Altman has tested the updated ZETA model with the earlier (1968) model:

■ ■ ■

'First, we compare the five-year accuracy of each model, using the particular sample of firms of each study. The newer ZETA model is far more accurate in bankruptcy classification in Years 2 through 5 with the initial year's accuracy about equal. The older model showed slightly more accurate non-bankruptcy classification in the two years when direct comparison is possible . . . the new seven variable model is, in some years, only slightly more accurate than the 'old' five variable model when the data are comparable, that is, adjusted for more meaningful evaluation."[4]

■ ■ ■

Zeta analysis is available on a subscription basis from Zeta Services which downloads from *Compustat* data banks and provides histories of up to ten years for firms in every conceivable industry.

Expected Default Efficiency

Default risk monitoring systems improve loan portfolios and risk rating systems by providing better estimates of the expected probability or default in each risk grade. San Francisco-based KMV Corporation developed a superb risk monitoring system. KMV's *Credit Monitor* measures default probabilities by tracking the level and volatility of equity prices. Credit Monitor provides two programs: The *Implicit Debenture Rating (IDR)* and the *Expected Default Frequency (EDF)*.

The IDR, an econometric analog of S&P ratings, simulates how a borrower's senior debt would be rated by S&P. It is also a credit measure in its own right and can be interpreted as a measure of balance sheet strength.

---

4 Ibid.

The EDF, KMV's primary credit measure, is the percentage probability of default occurring within a specified time horizon. Default is defined as the failure to make scheduled debt payments in a timely manner. EDF works differently from IDR in that it extrapolates the default information contained in the company's stock price. The lower the credit quality of the firm, the higher the probability of default. As a default predictor, EDF has been extensively validated and currently overshadows agency ratings such as S&P.

Why? Established companies such as S&P focus their attention primarily on financial statement analysis, whereas KMV utilizes market measures.

It is this distinction that makes the difference in identifying credit risk variances. While the traditional methods are only efficient in identifying credit risk variances in low credit risk firms, EDF displays superiority in distinguishing between low-risk companies and high-risk companies.

The EDF model (presented in an appendix at the end of this chapter) also provides a method for evaluating credit risks of nonpublic firms, thereby allowing banks to supplement their credit analysis of borrowers in a major way.

KMV's Firm Valuation Model springs from powerful financial theory, particularly the implementation of option pricing. The FV model weighs causal relationships that may lead to default. EDF works by using a tracking system that measures data indigenous to a firm's stock price. In turn, these data are positioned into a default risk measure; EDF links logical relationships between: (1) the market value of a firm's equity and its assets, (2) the risk and value of its assets, and (3) the default risk of liabilities. In other words, what the model identifies as the asset coverage of a firm's liabilities is in terms of market value.

Let's stop and think about this for a moment. Liabilities and equity are considered claims on a firm's assets. For companies with publicly traded stock, the market value of equity can be directly measured and used to infer the market value of debt. If the market value of a firm's assets is derived as a result of its liabilities and equity, then the market value of its assets must equal the market value of its liabilities and equity (assets = liabilities + equity).

Therefore, the market value of the assets equals the equity and debt values, including current liabilities at par. But what about calculating the market value of assets by other means? This is also possible since value of all claims is theoretically equivalent to the market value of all assets.

It is also important to note that the relationship between the market value of debt and equity also depends on the stability of a firm's asset value. Let's take a look at the two extremes. In a stable market, the value of a firm's assets imply higher value debt, whereas, in an unstable or volatile environment, the value of a firm's assets implies lower debt value. The variability of the assets is directly related, through the leverage ratio, to fluctuations in the market value of equity. As a result, asset variability can be inferred from the variability of the stock price.

Once the current market value of the firm's assets and the variability of those assets is estimated, likely future ranges for the asset value can be constructed. When will a firm default? The model assumes that the firm will continue to meet its obligations so long as the market value of assets exceeds those obligations. If this is true, XYZ firm has the ability to sell assets, borrow, or even issue equity to meet its obligations.

This brings us back to the heart of option pricing. Remember in the chapter on loan pricing, we found that equity in a firm with debt can be regarded as a call option. When creditors extend credit, shareholders receive cash by selling assets to creditors plus a call option. At maturity, if the firm's value exceeds the value of debt, stockholders exercise their call by paying creditors. *However, if operating strategies cause the firm to fail, shareholders will not exercise their options. They will walk away as if the options were purchased in the market and the stock declined below the exercise price. Banks end up with assets, which will be valued below the face amount of debt.* Likewise, if the market value of the firm's assets dips below that line within a year, then the firm is "in default" from the perspective of the model.

If the goal is to avoid defaults at all costs, then there is a perfect credit granting criterion: don't lend. Setting high credit standards is similar. It excludes most defaults, but it also excludes many profitable lending opportunities. The same point can be made about credit measures. A measure can err by not identifying a high risk firm as low risk; it can also err by not identifying a low risk firm as high risk. The incidence of one type of error can be reduced at the cost of increasing the other type.

The model provides real-time estimates of changing default potentials and has been proved to signal credit difficulties on an average of one to three years before they are recognized by the rating agencies. It also provides a means of determining the variance of losses from their expected magnitudes, enabling banks to allocate capital to loans in proportion to the risk of unexpected loss.

KMV has another model that establishes the default potential of private middle market borrowers based on financial statement data, account behavior information, and sectional economic data. Though by no means as accurate as the methodology used for public corporations, this automated tool has been found superior to other evaluation methods currently relied upon by leading banks. Therefore, it provides a sounder foundation for the estimation of default likelihood and risk charges.

We need more than quantitative tools—as essential as they are—to track credit risk and extinguish the fire before the barn burns down. But, sometimes the barn does burn down. And, that is exactly what we deal with in our next chapter, a case study centered on the Holly & Jenks Corporation.

APPENDIX

KMV Corporation: The Expected Default Frequency Model (EDF)[1]

How does the EDF work? The EDF is designed to "translate" the information contained in a firm's stock price into a measure of default risk. This "translation" is accomplished using a logical model of the relationship (i) between the market value of a firm's equity and the market value of its assets, and (ii) between the risk and value of the assets, and the default risk of the firm's liabilities. In essence, the model determines the asset coverage, in market value of the firm's liabilities.

The market value of the firm's economic assets is determined by noting that the firm's liabilities, including equity, form an exhaustive set of claims on the firm's assets. Thus the market value of the assets must be the same as the market value of the liabilities. For companies with publicly traded stock, the market value of the equity can be directly observed. This information is used to infer a market value for the firm's debt. The market value of assets is obtained by adding the equity and debt values, including current liabilities at par.

The relationship between the market value of the debt and the market value of the equity depends greatly on the stability of the firm's asset value. A stable market value for the firm's assets implies higher valued debt; more volatile assets imply lower debt value. The variability of the assets is not observed, but can be obtained from the variability of the equity value, which is determined from the fluctuations of the stock price.

---

1   Abstracted from KMV Corporation Credit Monitor Overview. Reprinted with permission. Readers who want additional information can contact KMV Corporation, 1620 Montgomery St., San Francisco, California, 94111; (415) 292-9669.

Once the current market value of the firm's assets and the variability of those assets is estimated, likely future ranges for the asset value can be constructed.

This process is illustrated below. The graph shows two possible price paths for the asset value. The vertical scale represents the market value of the assets; the horizontal scale represents time. Over time, the asset value will change. The actual path will look similar to the firm's stock price path.

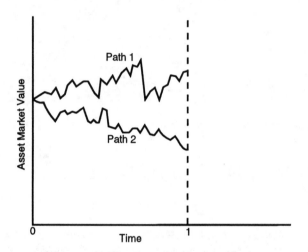

In one year's time, there will be a range of possible values for the firm's assets. It is possible to represent the likely frequency of each outcome in the graph by letting the horizontal axis beyond one year represent frequencies of outcome. The distribution of possible values is centered around the most likely value; higher and lower values become progressively less likely. Approximately 2/3 of the time, the path will lie within the dotted lines.

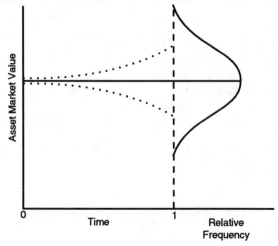

When will a firm default? The model assumes that the firm will continue to meet its obligations as long as the market value of assets exceeds those obligations. As long as that is true, the firm can either sell assets, borrow, or even issue equity to meet its obligations. The horizontal line labeled "Current Obligations" represents the level of obligations which the firm must pay within one year. If the market value of the firm's assets dips below that line within a year, then the firm is "default" from the perspective of the model.

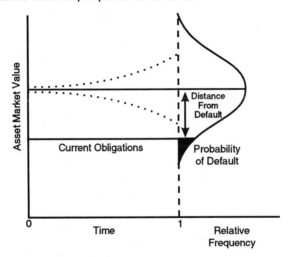

Knowing the variability of the assets allows us in theory to construct the probability distribution of the market value of the assets at the end of the year. The likelihood of the asset value falling to the point that the firm cannot cover the obligations (the darkened region) measures the credit quality.

In practice, we do not know either the exact frequencies for the market value of assets in one year, nor do we know exactly the point at which a firm will actually default. These problems are dealt with in the following fashion. The distance between the expected asset value in one year and the default point, measured in units of the asset variability, is expressed as a standardized distance: the "distance from default." All firms with the same distance from default are determined suing the actual default experience of publicly traded firms over the last decade. Using the horizon of one year as depicted in the graphs, the resulting number is the Expected Default Frequency, or EDF.

CHAPTER *Nineteen*

The Turnaround

The successful turnaround of a financially distressed company depends on the ability of the workout team to analyze and evaluate the full picture. This includes investigating the potential and limitations of management, the basis of projections and the quality of financial data presented.

While no two turnaround situations are exactly alike, it is highly instructive to follow the thinking and procedure of a company teetering on the brink of disaster.

The following case study, based on the misfortunes of Holly & Jenks, Inc., is divided into three parts: an introductory background, a precis of a bankers meeting and an analysis of the situation provided by Morton Scheer and Co. Inc., a highly respected consulting firm specializing in turnarounds. Morton shared his expertise with us in commenting on the case.

■ ■ ■

Part One: Holly & Jenks, Inc. Case Study[1]

This case builds on sequential credit and restructuring decisions as events trigger the rapid deterioration of Holly & Jenks, Inc., an apparel manufacturer.

Bankers participating in the Holly & Jenks credit will have to decide how far the bank group should go in supplying credit to the firm. A broad range of issues faces the bank group a month after the fiscal books close. The bank meeting, with Money Center Bank in a leadership role, must focus on the nature of the credit issues, the relationship between the bankers, the broader contextual factors, and how these variables will influence the group's decisions to either see the credit restructured or liquidated.

At the meeting, account officers from participating banks will be faced with all the facts, opinions, and prejudices which shape bankers' decisions. While a certain amount of financial analysis within the PRISM framework will be factored into the decision making, discussions leading to credit decisions are frequently grounded upon stubborn facts that bankers face in real life situations.

As the leader of the lending team handling the H & J account and as lead bank (Money Center Bank), you must prepare a presentation to the bank group on how to proceed. Read the case, noting clues along the way. After completing the case study, prepare what you consider a short (no more than one page) presentation on the "state of affairs" concerning Holly & Jenks before reading the "actual" analysis.

Your presentation should focus on PRISM elements, Repayment, Safety, and Perspective along these lines:

1. Major areas of weakness in the credit

2. The bank's bank losses if it does not continue to finance the company's need

3. How covenants could be amended

4. The feasibility of engaging a turnaround specialist

5. Liquidation versus restructuring analysis

Liquidation versus restructuring analysis involves detailing each alternative with the operating and financial strategies required. For the restructuring route to make sense, the firm's core business must remain dominant. For example, if the core business, Youthwear, represents only three percent of the total business of the troubled company, you might want to forgo the restructuring approach and liquidate.

---

1   The author wishes to thank R. Scott Graham and David J. Stone for their help in analyzing this case.

On the other hand, if the core business dominates the firm's activities, it might be better to sell off the businesses that are causing the firm problems and restructure so that the firm's remaining ongoing value exceeds its liquidation value.

The technique for determining whether to restructure is as follows:

■ The core business must be analyzed separately from the total business to determine what its cash flow would have been if the other businesses hadn't drained it.

■ The cash flow of the core business should be carried forward several years (or whatever amount of time it takes for a reasonable forecast horizon) at an appropriate growth rate and then discounted to its present value.

■ For the period beyond the forecast horizon, the growth rate should be taken to perpetuity by dividing the final year's operating cash flow by the cost of capital. By adding the present values of the future cash flows (forecast horizon and residual period) and the net of anticipated investments in working capital and in fixed assets, one can determine the value of the firm.

■ Then, subtract the current debt. The result represents what an investor would pay for the restructured business (i.e., its market value). If the market value of the restructured business is $17 million, and the liquidation value of the total business is only $4 million, it might make sense to restructure the business. (Obviously, if the bank's loan is only $2 million, liquidation may be the preferable route. This analysis would only apply if the bank loan exceeds the collateral value.)

■ The key to the valuation analysis is using the correct discount rate. This rate, at which cash flows are discounted to their present value, should be representative of the firm's overall cost of equity capital, given its risk. To be conservative, the analyst should set the discount rate high because there is no guarantee that the restructuring will be successful.

The Case

Holly & Jenks Industries, Inc., is a mid-sized clothing manufacturer and distributor. Founded in 1958 primarily as a children's wear manufacturer, H & J currently operates three business units: Youthwear, Designer Sportswear for men and women, and Playeasy for toddlers. Manufacturing and distribution operations for the Youthwear and Designer Sportswear divisions are located in New Jersey. The toddlers' line is manufactured in the Dominican Republic under a licensing agreement. Operating designs for all clothing lines are contracted out, with approximately 35% of the product manufactured by outside contractors.

Since inception, Youthwear has been the core business with peak season in May and June. This popular and profitable "back-to-school line" accounts for approximately 60% of volume, with sales to 9,000 department stores and specialty stores nationwide. Designer Sportswear, an off-price clothing line for men and women was established in 1989. Initial speculation, based on five and ten year strategic projections concluded that Designer Sportswear would be an up-and-coming line for the future. Designer Sportswear has yet to come close to meeting management's expectations. Due to this unit's poor sales performance and the severity of inventory write-downs, the liquidity position of Holly & Jenks has been significantly eroded. Designer Sportswear currently operates 10 regional outlet stores located primarily in the Northeast. Although the current retailing trend indicates a move toward specialty stores for designer clothing, this market segment has tightened due to heavy competition. The most unprofitable outlets may be closed to cut overhead costs. Initial contingency plans indicate sales must be shifted to department stores, chain stores, and mail order houses to boost sagging sales revenue.

The Playeasy line, which is responsible for 13% of the company's sales was first introduced in 1990. This unit specializes in clothing for distribution to Playeasy specialty store franchises, which carry a full array of Playeasy apparel, jewelry, music and watches. Playeasy apparel is manufactured in the Dominican Republic under a licensing agreement, and in terms of sales and profits, Playeasy has been a very successful venture for Holly & Jenks.

Company policy mandates payments are to be made by all customers within 30 days of receiving new merchandise. However, as of December 20, 1992, Calo, Inc., a financially troubled retailer located in Portland, Maine owed Holly & Jenks $4,291,000 with $1,239,000 or 29% past due over ninety days. Calo, Inc., accounted for 15% of sales in 1992. Since Calo has no rating from D & B, its receivables are uninsured. Holly & Jenks decided to terminate its business relationship with Calo, Inc.

Recently, management disclosed plans to expand and diversify operations by entering into a joint venture agreement with a bottler to manufacture glass and plastic containers. Sales will be targeted at food, beverage, chemical, and pharmaceutical companies.

Management is comprised of three key players: Bill Holly, Herb Gold, and Mary Tyler.

Bill Holly, sixty years of age, is Chairman and one of the original founders of the company. To date, he owns 40% of the firm's publicly traded stock.

Herb Gold, President, has been with Holly & Jenks for 17 years. His area of expertise is in the production department where he has spent most of his career. As president, Herb has now taken on various functions new to him which has turned his focus away from the production end of the business. It is a likely that Herb may be spreading himself too thin.

Mary Tyler, the Vice President of Finance, was hired by H & J in September 1992. Surprisingly, she is the third executive to hold this title in the past eighteen months.

Alexanders & Co. is the accounting firm responsible for auditing the fiscal statements. At this time, the accountants are considering qualifying their opinion because of the term loan covenant violations and potential write-off of Calo's receivables.

In 1980, Holly & Jenks opened its account with Money Center Bank. H & J's debt is secured by a blanket lien on accounts receivables shared by the lenders under a collateral-sharing agreement. The bank group recently filed a lien on fixed assets. Finally, inventory financed by letters of credit (approximately 13% of total inventory value) are also collateralized.

Bank Debt
(000's Omitted)

	Line	Term Loan (A)	Term Loan (B)	L/C Line
Money Center Bank	$7,360	$3,910	$1,208	$2,100
National Bank	4,320	2,295	709	2,100
Windy Bank	3,040	1,615	498	800
Local Bank	1,280	680	210	0
Total	$16,000	$8,500	$2,625	$5,000

The first layer of debt is comprised of the $16 million credit line from the four-bank consortium, the $8,500,000 Term Loan (A), and the $4,061,000 of insurance debt. Any excess collateral remaining after the first level of debt is used to cover Term Loan (B) and a U.S. Government Direct Loan of $1,000,000 obtained in 1991. The U.S. Government will guarantee 90% of repayment on Term Loan (B) since its proceeds were used to build a plant and create new jobs in an economically depressed area.

Playeasy Inc. has threatened to revoke its licensing agreement because Letters of Credit are always arranged late. If this comes to pass, the combined loss in sales from Calo and Playeasy will account for at least 28% of total sales. Holly & Jenks is also being squeezed from the other end of its business. Suppliers are steadily decreasing trade support, threatening to put purchases on COD. Combining these pitfalls with layers of debt, the loss in fiscal 1992, and a debt-to-equity ratio of 4.7, Holly & Jenks finds itself in a precarious financial situation.

Situation: It is late November 1992, and you have just received the preliminary 10/2/92 fiscal statements. During 1992 sales fell as a result of a significant decrease in volume in the company's Designer Sportswear division. The bottom line has been seriously eroded by inventory markdowns and the operating loss for the year was $12,553M. H & J's projections from October had indicated that net income would be in excess of $4,000M fiscal 1993, but Ms. Tyler has stressed that at the time she prepared the budget she was not completely familiar with the company and that it may have to be revised downward after the first quarter results are available.

The firm has $6,750M outstanding under its $16,000M line. *Total Outstandings* are as follows:

Line of credit	$6,750M
Term Loan (A)	8,500
Term Loan (B)	2,625
L/Cs	3,000
Total Bank Debt	20,875
Insurance Co. Debt	4,061
Financial Institution Debt	$24,936M

Income Statement	9/27/89	9/27/90	9/26/91	10/2/92
Net Sales	82,351	92,469	111,437	100,507
Cost of Goods Sold	(61,698)	(68,524)	(77,702)	(81,384)
Gross Profit	20,653	23,945	33,735	19,123
Operating Expenses	(19,047)	(22,490)	(29,147)	(31,065)
Other Income (Expenses)	386	1,142	306	(611)
Net Income before Taxes	1,992	2,597	4,894	(12,553)
Taxes	(571)	(772)	(1,967)	3,669
Net Income	1,421	1,825	2,927	(8,884)

Balance Sheet	9/27/89	9/27/90	9/26/91	10/2/92
Cash	2,073	2,993	3,105	362
Accounts Receivable	14,742	17,598	19,713	19,549
Inventory	17,398	21,627	27,660	20,414
Other	127	46	95	95
Prepaid Expenses	392	1,048	1,334	1,683
Taxes Receivable				3,541
Current Assets	34,732	43,312	51,907	45,644
PP&E	7,815	7,314	6,782	6,471
Leasehold Improve	1,016	575	939	515
Other	204	674	864	811
Goodwill	1,422	1,378	1,334	1,290
Noncurrent Assets	10,457	9,941	9,919	9,087
Total Assets	45,189	53,253	61,826	54,731
Note Pay—Banks	4,550	5,000	2,500	12,500
Accounts Payable	5,872	5,551	7,343	4,472
Accruals	3,548	4,979	6,607	5,013
Taxes	255	187	1,478	
Current Portion LTD	1,680	877	2,076	3,159
Deferred Taxes	271	336	355	
Current Liabilities	16,176	16,930	20,359	25,144
Long-Term Notes Payable	13,704	19,045	20,965	17,872
Other	218			790
Deferred Taxes		394	555	
Liabilities	30,098	36,369	41,879	43,806
Treasury Stock	(20)	(20)	(20)	(150)
Add'l Paid-in Capital	7,238	8,021	9,314	11,189
Preferred Stock	1,769	1,790	1,472	1,416
Common Stock	158	176	205	231
Retained Earnings	5,946	6,916	8,914	(1,761)
Stockholders' Equity	15,091	16,883	19,885	10,925
Liabilities and Equity	45,189	53,252	61,764	54,731

Projected Balance Sheet Fiscal 1993

	1Q	2Q	3Q	4Q
Current Assets				
Cash	0	0	0	1,491
Accounts Receivable	14,142	17,448	24,916	18,927
Inventory	24,684	29,829	31,117	23,734
Other Receivables	500	500	500	500
Prepaid Expenses	1,600	1,600	1,600	1,600
Taxes Receivable	2,500	0	0	0
Current Assets	43,426	49,377	58,133	46,252
PP&E	6,799	6,598	6,397	6,196
Other	1,786	1,672	1,558	1,444
Total Assets	52,011	57,647	66,088	53,892
Notes Pay—Banks	7,000	10,000	16,000	5,000
Accounts Payable and Accrs	12,797	15,714	17,403	14,577
Current Portion LTD	3,146	3,146	3,146	3,146
Current Liabilities	22,943	28,860	36,549	22,723
Noncurrent Liabilities	17,099	15,995	15,357	14,666
Total Liabilities	40,042	44,855	51,906	37,389
Paid-in Capital and R/E	10,519	11,342	12,732	15,053
Preferred Stock	1,450	1,450	1,450	1,450
Total Stockholders' Equity	11,969	12,792	14,182	16,503
Total Liabilities & Equity	52,011	57,647	66,088	53,892

Accounts Receivable Detail

Customer	to 89 days	over 90	Totals	% Total
Calo, Inc.	3,052	1,239	4,291	23.0%
Federated Stores	1,006		1,006	5.4%
RH Macy	533		533	2.9%
May Company	526		526	2.8%
USAAF Exchange	502	4	506	2.7%
Jages of Mayfair	458		458	2.5%
WS Wormser Company	357	80	437	2.3%
Associated Dry Goods	316		316	1.7%
Gimbels	297		297	1.6%
Limited Stores, Inc.	297		297	1.6%
Others	8,752	1,652	10,404	55.7%
Credits	xxx	xxx	(395)	−2.1%
Total	16,096	2,975	18,676	100.0%
Percent of Total	86.2%	15.9%	100.0%	

	9/27/89	9/27/90	9/26/91	10/2/92
Liquidity Ratios				
Current ratio	2.15	2.56	2.55	1.82
Quick ratio	1.07	1.28	1.19	1.00
Activity Ratios				
Inventory TO	3.55	3.17	2.81	3.99
Working capital TO	4.44	3.51	3.53	4.90
Fixed asset TO	10.54	12.64	16.43	15.53
ACP	65.3	69.5	64.6	71.0
Leverage Ratios				
LT Debt/net worth	0.91	1.13	1.05	1.64
Profitability Ratios				
Net profit margin	1.7%	2.0%	2.6%	-8.8%
GP margin	25.1%	25.9%	30.3%	19.0%
Oper exps/Sales	23.1%	24.3%	26.2%	30.9%
ROE—before tax	13.2%	15.4%	24.6%	-114.9%

Financial Covenants

1. Cleanup: The Company and its operating units will be free of all short-term bank indebtedness for not less than 30 days during each 15-month period from January 1 of each year to March 31 of the succeeding year.

2. Ratio of Quick Assets to bank indebtedness (not including gov't. guaranteed loan) may not be less than 1.0 to 1.0 at the end of the first, second, and fourth quarters and not less than .9 to 1.0 at the end of the third quarter.

3. Working Capital may not be less than:

1992	$28,500M
1993	29,000M
1994	29,500M
1995	30,000M
1996	30,500M
1997	31,000M
1998 and thereafter	31,500M

4. Tangible Net Worth may not be less than:

1992	$15,750M
1993	16,500M
1994	17,250M
1995	18,000M
1996	18,750M
1997	19,500M
1998 and thereafter	20,250M

5. Consolidated Indebtedness to Consolidated Tangible Net Worth may not exceed the following:

6/30/92	275%
9/30/92	240%
6/30/93	250%
9/30/93	225%
6/30/94	225%
9/30/94	210%
6/30/95	210%
9/30/95	195%
6/30/96	195%
9/30/96	180%
6/30/97	180%
9/30/97	175%
6/30/98	175%
9/30/98	170%

Holly & Jenks Interim Consolidated Cash Budget: Jan.–Sept. 1993

	Jan	Feb	Mar	Apr	May	June	July	Aug	Sept
Projected Cash Receipts–Accounts Receivable	6,505	5,421	9,632	11,167	4,570	5,557	10,465	15,915	15,150
Tax Refund		2,500							
Retail	163	146	128	175	105	127	136	221	138
Total Projected Available Cash	6,668	8,067	9,760	11,342	4,675	5,684	10,601	16,136	15,288
Piece Goods	1,571	346	1,946	1,906	390	378	1,713	3,450	1,535
Freight In	91	91	86	86	56	48	72	54	47
Trim	402	320	283	420	319	336	405	331	242
O/S Production	4,025	3,406	2,249	2,516	3,840	4,554	3,684	1,674	2,269
Direct Labor	1,130	904	868	1,142	877	914	1,096	914	868
Factor O/H	930	832	840	921	831	830	927	832	842
Operating Expenses	2,318	2,131	1,689	1,890	1,899	2,316	2,960	2,031	1,936
Timing Differences	(78)	(354)	(331)	13	(76)	(668)	(442)	(436)	(313)
Principal Payments	762	21	321	596	21	21	597	23	71
Interest Payments	846	28	132	868	28	55	995	27	55
Total Disbursements	11,997	7,725	8,083	10,358	8,185	8,784	12,007	8,900	7,552
Net Cash Inflow (Outflow)	(5,329)	342	1,677	984	(3,510)	(3,100)	(1,406)	7,236	7,736
Cumulative	(5,329)	(4,987)	(3,310)	(2,326)	(5,836)	8,936	(10,342)	(3,106)	4,630
Net Cash Inflow (Outflow)	(5,329)	342	1,677	984	(3,510)	(3,100)	(1,406)	7,236	7,736
Cash Balance Available Beginning of Month	(1,139)	(468)	(1,126)	(1,449)	(1,465)	(1,975)	(1,075)	(2,481)	(1,245)
Total Cash Available before financing	(6,468)	(126)	551	(465)	(4,975)	(5,075)	(2,481)	4,755	6,491
Short-Term Loan (Beginning of Period)	7,000	13,000	12,000	10,000	9,000	12,000	16,000	16,000	10,000
Advances–(Payments Short-Term Loan)	6,000	(1,000)	(2,000)	(1,000)	3,000	4,000	0	(6,000)	(5,000)
Short-Term Loan—End of Period	13,000	12,000	10,000	9,000	12,000	16,000	16,000	10,000	5,000

H & J Interim Collateral Worksheet

	Jan	Feb	Mar	Apr	May	June	July	Aug	Sept
Estimated Average Sales	7,333	7,333	7,333	8,434	8,434	8,434	9,723	9,723	9,723
Accounts Receivable	15,942	21,405	14,448	11,426	16,344	24,916	30,605	26,120	18,927
Inventory	26,684	24,684	29,829	29,829	29,829	31,117	31,117	31,117	23,734
Net Fixed Assets	6,799	6,799	6,598	6,598	6,598	6,397	6,397	6,196	6,196
Short-Term Loan—End of Period	13,000	12,000	10,000	9,000	12,000	16,000	16,000	10,000	5,000
Term Loan (A)	8,000	8,000	8,000	7,500	7,500	7,500	7,000	7,000	7,000
Insurance Co. Debt	3,894	3,894	3,594	3,594	3,594	3,594	3,594	3,594	3,594
10% Term Loan (B)	263	263	263	263	263	263	263	263	263
Letter of Credit	3,115	3,543	4,705	4,731	4,803	3,444	2,507	3,031	3,855
Total Exposure	28,272	27,700	26,562	25,088	28,163	30,801	29,364	23,888	19,712
Assumptions									
% imported inventory (Disney)	0.13	0.13	0.13	0.13	0.13	0.13	0.13	0.13	0.13
% collectible-imported inventory	0.6	0.6	0.6	0.6	0.6	0.6	0.6	0.6	0.6
% collectible-receivable	0.75	0.75	0.75	0.75	0.75	0.75	0.75	0.75	0.75
% collectible-PP&E	0.5	0.5	0.5	0.5	0.5	0.5	0.5	0.5	0.5
Total Inventory	24,684	24,684	29,829	29,829	29,829	31,117	31,117	31,117	23,734
Imported Inventory	3,209	3,209	3,209	3,878	3,878	4,045	4,045	4,045	3,085
Collectible Inventory	1,925	1,925	2,327	2,327	2,327	2,427	2,427	2,427	1,851
Total Receivables	15,942	21,405	17,448	11,426	16,344	24,916	30,605	26,120	18,927
Collectible-Receivables	11,957	16,054	13,086	8,570	12,258	18,687	22,954	19,590	14,195
Net PP&E	6,799	6,799	6,598	6,598	6,598	6,397	6,397	6,196	6,196
Collectible-PP&E	3,400	3,400	3,299	3,299	3,299	3,199	3,199	3,098	3,098
Total Collectible	17,281	21,379	18,712	14,195	17,884	24,313	28,579	25,115	19,145
Exposure	28,272	27,700	26,562	25,088	28,163	30,801	29,364	23,888	19,712

H & J Valuation	1993	1994	1995	1996	1997	1998	1999	2000	Residual
Enter Post Restructuring	$2,000								
Enter Profit Growth	*****	5.00%	6.00%	12.00%	17.00%	17.00%	17.00%	17.00%	
Post Restructuring Profit	$2,000	$2,100	$2,226	$2,493	$2,917	$3,413	$3,993	$4,672	
GOCF as % Net Profit(a)	110.00%	110.00%	110.00%	110.00%	110.00%	110.00%	110.00%	110.00%	
Gross Operating Cash Flow	$2,200	$2,310	$2,449	$2,742	$3,209	$3,754	$4,392	$5,139	$5,447
Enter Cost of Equity	20.00%	20.00%	20.00%	20.00%	20.00%	20.00%	20.00%	20.00%	20.00%
Term	1	2	3	4	5	6	7	8	9
Present Value C/F Operations	1,833	1,604	1,417	1,323	1,289	1,257	1,226	1,195	5,279
Cummulative PV/CF Operations	1,833	3,438	4,855	6,177	7,467	8,724	9,950	11,145	16,423
Excess Assets Value over BK	0								
Value of Restructured Business	16,423								

(a) Assumes depreciation expense matches capital expenditures.

Part Two: H & J Bank Meeting, December 16, 1992

Presentations were first made by members of the bank group voicing concern about H & J's rapid deterioration. The following are highlights of a presentation made by Money Center Bank:

The arguments raised so far deal with the condition of the financial statements and the ability of the bank group to continue financing. Holly & Jenks' business is seasonal, which means the primary source of payment originates from the balance sheet. Focusing on current asset quality, we note the precipitous decrease in cash. A total of $362,000 cash to pay $25.1 million current liabilities at the seasonal low points to a disaster. During the low point, cash should increase dramatically to cover current liabilities. The fact that H & J is now carrying bank debt makes it improbable that we'll see reductions soon. And with 25% of past due receivables tied up in Calo, payments to suppliers and other creditors are in jeopardy. Holly & Jenks' belated decision to terminate its business with Calo, Inc. also forces it to find another viable customer or customers who can make up the 15% sales generated by Calo last year.

The cash budget reveals that $5.3 million will be required in January. An additional $3.5 million will be required in May and another $3.1 million in June. The core of the problem is painfully obvious: we have to put more money in (to support the firm's next season) to get our other money out. This means $25.1 million current debt sitting on the fiscal statement is going to remain there for some time. Retained Earnings also went into the red for the first time since the company's inception in 1958. We don't know how many suppliers and buyers will stick around after they review the fiscals. Without their support the firm may have trouble surviving.

A covenant requiring quick assets to bank debt to be sustained at certain levels will be violated in both the first and second quarters. Given the company's receivable collection problems and the likelihood of net losses in 1993, it is reasonable to assume that it will violate this covenant for at least the first three quarters of the year.

Although Mary Tyler projects that H & J will be in compliance with the tangible net worth covenant at the end of 1993, a more realistic income statement will put it in violation of this one as well. The tangible net worth covenant requires a net worth of $16.5 million.

To summarize:

■ Designer Sportswear needs a major overhaul if it is to succeed.

■ The loss of future sales and bad debt write-off of Calo receivables could prove to be an irreversible blow to the company. There is a very good chance that based on the current condition of H & J company, no alternate company would be willing to give that much business and take on such risk. This one factor alone could force Holly & Jenks into liquidation.

■ Current debt-to-equity, already at around 400%, will deteriorate further if cash flow doesn't improve.

■ Pressures from creditors and suppliers must be relieved while the bank restructures the company so production can continue smoothly.

Liquidation Analysis points to an $11 million loss to the bank group if the company is forced to liquidate. That's the difference between the $25 million exposure forecast in April, 1993 and $14 million anticipated collateral coverage.

Based on the negative returns associated with the Designer Sportswear business, I don't think there's enough expertise or financial support to make the unit profitable. It might be advantageous to Holly & Jenks to solicit offers for licensing the Designer Sportswear line. By doing this, Holly & Jenks will be able to focus attention on Youthwear and the expansion of Playeasy's line. As far as the bottling joint venture is concerned—no way!

Reorganization, if we all agree to go that route, needs to be effected through the counsel of a qualified consultant. The firm will have to make that decision on its own, choosing the consulting firm it elects to work with. The right goals and strategies must be established, and guidelines toward reaching these goals should be implemented by key personnel. The power of decision making by Bill Holly is in question given his recent "absentee management" performance and preoccupation with non-business matters.

Our files are on the way to workout and legal. After consulting with them, we'll set up an agenda for the next meeting, which should be scheduled no later than two weeks hence.

Part Three: The Consultant's Report

Board of Directors/
Holly & Jenks Inc.
10 Seventh Avenue
New York City, N.Y. 10000

At your request Morton H. Scheer & Co., Inc. has completed a preliminary analysis on Holly & Jenks, Inc. The most obvious problem we see is lack of effective senior management in day-to-day operations.

The most common complaint lodged by staff personnel we interviewed was senior management's lack of decision making or concern over the direction of the company.

It was most evident that a nonchalant, negative, "who cares" attitude permeates the entire company. This is the major contributing factor to morale problems. Some long-term employees said of Bill, "At one time, he was a tiger totally committed to the business—always on top of every aspect of the operations. Bill was demanding in a positive way—*He was the boss!* Bill Holly led by example, and we followed his lead."

The designer sportswear debacle began around the time Bill started losing interest in the business. Bill founded Holly & Jenks thirty-five years ago with nothing and built it into a superb youthwear operation. He's credited with having the raw talent and ability to design and merchandise clothing lines and motivate and direct people. We believe that he still possesses these talents and can turn around the firm. The all-important question is, does he still have the desire, passion and fire?

Herb Gold, president, should refocus on production and design where he was a standout for many years. Middle management told us that Herb is a very energetic executive who may have too many outside interests. This has caused Herb to lose touch with the business. It is possible that his redirected priorities have been the result of following Bill Holly's lead. Although Herb has maintained the image of a caring and loyal employer (many see him as a friend), he has instilled fear in his employees, the result of numerous temper tantrums. There is nothing wrong with being demanding, but Herb can insist on high performance without antagonizing and publicly humiliating his managers.

Management by fear and intimidation is unprofessional and retards the creativity and motivation needed to run a company.

We feel that Edith Braun, vice president-merchandising, may have lost the pulse of the markets. She buys from the heart, without a budget or "open to buy" positions; there is little accountability and almost no cost awareness on her part. Travelling on the Concord, staying in suites at some of the most expensive hotels, and flying buyers first class to the Dominican Republic to get a glimpse of "what we're all about" is not only impractical, but unnecessary during these lean times.

In today's economy, expenses such as these are no longer feasible regardless of how well a company is doing.

Sales drive this business. Fred Simpson, vice president-sales, is a good salesman, but lacks the drive and aggressiveness we would expect in this responsible position. Not to have the knowledge of major customers in major territories is shocking to say the least. Merchandisers indicate they get little input from Mr. Simpson.

Another negative reflection on Fred Simpson is the sales staff turnover rate. Sales have been adversely affected by a salesperson turnover of 17% in Designer Sportswear. Turnover rates of 10% or more are costly and disrupts, ordering routines and customer sales support. We are told that many of H & J's sales personnel see "unreasonable" quotas and excessive paper work. Unattainable quotas hinder performance and boost turnover.

Mary Tyler, vice president-finance, is inexperienced in the apparel industry. Hiring her was a poor decision since she is the third V.P. of Finance in the past year and a half. While she is literate in finance, hiring her solely on a Harvard MBA without any hands-on experience was a gamble. She must be brought up to speed within the next month if the firm is to send positive signals to its creditors.

Lines of communication between the firm's various departments, divisions and subsidiaries need to be opened and made more cohesive. We found no evidence of regular management meetings to foster the interchange of ideas.

These should take place once a week to share departmental problems, projects and predicaments.

Inventory is handled "loosely" on a manual system rather than with computers. For example, there is no standard cost system or cutting registers available to calculate real cost. By maintaining this outdated system, tracking and balancing inventories is almost impossible. Another inherent problem involving inventory is the current warehousing arrangements. Unless a Youthwear warehouse can be found to segregate it from the Designer Sportswear, we believe additional problems controlling inventory will arise. Since the Designer Sportswear division is a picking operation and Youthwear division has prepackaged boxes only requiring labelling, foul-ups are frequent.

Overbuying and misdirected buying has generated substantial inventory in both Designer Sportswear warehouse and outlet stores. Overbuying resulted in a large position of dated piece goods: 52% at fiscal, the highest in four years. We need to liquidate redundant piece goods, and look to see what is not usable or exchangeable. Purchasing of raw materials should conform strictly to production schedules—hard to track since the company does not have a breakdown of inventory by season readily available. A good tracking system keeps inventory at proper levels and allows the company to make better use of its purchasing power. If an analysis of purchases and subsequent competitive quotes from various vendors were done, significant savings would result.

While credit terms are net 30 days, the average collection period has increased to 71 days. In total, 16% or roughly $3.0 million in collections are over 90 days. The Calo receivable needs more clout behind collection efforts; we'll recommend a collection agency that a den full of lions would fear. Holly & Jenks can do better than a $150 dBase software package to control receivables. A computerized A/R system and a prudent collection policy are a must.

The 1988 acquisition of a manufacturing and warehouse facility was unfortunate. It is an old, out of date building with poor insulation and inefficient heating. As a warehouse, the building is long and low with limited stacking capacity, thereby causing storage to be spread over thousands of square feet. The warehouse should be in one building equipped with shelving and a hi-lo. To have all inventory on ground level and not use the building's height to its maximum advantage is a total waste. The company should consider selling the building, leasing space elsewhere.

The production department lacks procedures and controls. The first problem plaguing production is the manner in which orders are positioned during the season high point. Production schedules needlessly cater to large volume orders during the last month of the quarter, resulting in more assembly line workers and overtime charges. By creating an even stream of production, the high cost of last minute orders disappear.

Since a large percentage of production is done by outside contractors, strict controls must be established. A designated production coordinator must visit contractors to inspect merchandise (quality control) and confirm delivery dates. The production coordinator, not the contractor, will also be responsible for setting sewing costs. To allow contractors the freedom to set sewing costs and accept those costs as long as they achieve the desired gross profit is a bad business decision. Operating designs must be sent to several contractors for a quote. Whatever price the lowest contractor quotes on a particular garment is accepted and not questioned. In some cases the contractor is told the selling price of the garment, so that he/she can quote a cost to meet the selling price.

Last year, one individual visited contractors throughout the world, inspected their plants, authorized the opening of Letters of Credit and watched production, all without management's supervision. The result was usually a huge amount of orders not delivered because contractors never made good. Certain orders placed with contractors were never accepted by those contractors. L/Cs were opened for no reason, and no one in senior management seemed aware of problems. Lines of credit were utilized and L/Cs costs created for no reason.

The Designer Sportswear and Youthwear outlet stores must be reevaluated with the thought of closing some of them. In reviewing the outlet store numbers, gross profits ranging between 8–12% translate into operating losses. We think that those stores are not properly merchandised, so either bring in a good retailer, or close the stores. Since the specialty store market is shrinking, new merchandising and marketing plans must immediately be instituted. Department store chains and mail order business must be developed quickly.

In a real sense, any major distribution decision can affect every cost in the business and each cost is related to all the others. Stockouts, excessive delivery time or variability of delivery time results in lost sales. If you are to compete successfully with the leaders in sportswear fashions, you can't rest on your laurels when it comes to distribution. Any change in the distribution system will hurt customer service and cost you sales. These effects, while difficult to measure (at least initially), must be considered part of the real cost of distribution. We anticipate that by rearranging H & J's distribution pattern and making appropriate shifts in production and warehousing loads, it will be possible to increase company profits without any increase in facilities. The largest ingredient in this improvement would come from reduced materials and warehousing costs, direct labor saving and plant overhead.

Not to have an agent overseas, as an importer, is asking for trouble. In your current situation, having to dump sportswear because of poor quality is uncalled for. A qualified agent would have inspected those goods before they left the overseas manufacturer, preventing the dumping of merchandise, and the losses incurred. Your letters of credit should require inspection before shipment.

The firm's Dominican plant requires constant supervision and controls that will guarantee whatever enters the operation returns. This is necessary because its production lead time and raw material needs are much greater than the domestic operations. Raw material requirements must be one month on the ocean, one month backup, and one month work-in-process. Since you must pay salaries if work is completed or not, the Dominican operation could lose its cost advantage without the ability to maintain inventory requirements. We believe that properly handled, the Dominican operations will be a tremendous asset to the company. Supervision must be redirected with the proper people overseeing your contractors on-site. Once this is accomplished, the next step is to prepack customer shipments to reduce shipping costs.

Over the long run we will need to establish a business plan that helps formulate policies and strategies that will return the company to profitability. Customer demographics must be better defined, warehouse operation streamlined, and overhead reductions put into effect. The next step is to prepare and monitor cash flow and projections on a monthly basis to evaluate performance. It is important that sales and expense budgets be compared to profit and loss statements on a monthly or quarterly basis. As part of the annual budgetary planning process we hope to establish at least six major objectives:

1. Motivate management to achieve company goals and objectives.
2. Prepare management to effectively deal with problems and opportunities as they arise.
3. Continuously remind management of the actions they elected to pursue.
4. Make managers realize that the future is just as important as the present, maybe more important.
5. Institute guidelines for control reporting.
6. Show bankers, suppliers and buyers that we mean business.

Each of the firm's middle managers should be responsible for submitting budget proposals to senior management. Senior management then must decide whether to approve the proposals as they stand, modify them in some way, or return them for revision and resubmission. Isolating the poorly performing sportswear operation for a moment, management will need to examine the proposals from four points of view:

- Do the anticipated benefits of proposed expenditures justify the costs?
- Are estimates realistic?
- Are the proposals consistent with the company's strategic plans that Mort Scheer & Co. Inc. and management will work out?
- Are budgets feasible in light of the company's financial, marketing, and production capacities?

Budgets are part of the planning process while planning is the process of deciding on a course of action—finding and choosing among the alternatives available and includes:

1. Strategic projections—Bill Holly and the rest of senior management must determine the direction the organization should take.

2. Project and situation planning—final decisions involve optimal allocation of resources.

3. Long-range planning—translating strategic plans into maximum shareholder value.

In conclusion the following changes should be addressed **immediately:**

1. Weekly management meetings must be held to make everyone aware of the various departmental problems, so that a team effort will help provide solutions. These meetings cannot be permitted to become gripe sessions.

2. Create a well-planned fixed asset and warehouse procurement process to alleviate fixed asset strain, improve the quality of inventory, reduce returns and allowances and reduce the need for markdowns.

3. Accounts receivable and inventory must be brought under control.

4. Put certain slow-paying customers on a C.O.D. basis and do more timely credit checks on all customers.

5. If sportswear lines do not improve in three quarters we will consider dropping them altogether.

6. Smooth relations with the owner of the Playeasy name. Reassure Playeasy that you are the right company to help represent their name.

We will seek a revision to most loan agreement Covenants. We're going to ask the bank group to package debt long-term to give us some breathing room. The situation we are confronted with at the banks is that H & J is currently at the low point in its seasonal cycle. Under normal circumstances, short-term borrowing zeros out and current liabilities are at absolute minimum levels. No wonder creditors are in a state of panic. You can be sure that the lead bank's workout officer needs to be convinced that the business—particularly Sportswear—is a viable operation, guided by realistic goals and strategies.

Morton H. Scheer & Co., Inc. is prepared to assist the firm as follows:

■ Implementation of a standard cost system, and perpetual inventory control with the aid of the company's outside accountants.

■ Determine whether or not to continue or change the present computer installation.

■ Line up agents overseas to insure quality.

■ Control the Dominican Republic operation.

■ Reduce overhead through people and cost reductions.

■ Determine whether or not to consolidate some of its operations and plants.

- Put necessary controls on outside contractors in place.
- Hold its weekly management meetings to promote good communications within the company.
- Set up an effective quality control system.
- Assist the company in its organizational restructuring.
- Reduce and dispose of old inventories.
- Assist management in production scheduling to reduce the large markdown problems.
- Set a direction for the company, and make sure of its implementation.
- Determine what lines should or should not be dropped.

Probably the most important function we will serve is to make management do the things it knows should be done, but won't or can't do. We will serve as the catalyst to get things done.

We wish to thank you and your staff for their cooperation.

Very truly yours,

Morton H. Scheer
President

■ ■ ■

Postscript: Morton H. Scheer and Co. Inc., was the key factor in turning the company around. Designer Sportswear was liquidated and the remaining business units are thriving. The credit facilities were restructured allowing time for the turnaround to take hold.

APPENDIX

An Overview of U.S. Lender Liability Litigation[1]

There is no scarcity of scholarly and legal writings on the subject of lender liability.[2]

This appendix, rather than adding new research to the already vast quantity of materials, will attempt only to provide an overview of the legal basis for the proliferation of law suits against lenders in the United States.

Lender liability claims have arisen as a part of a "new, growing consumerism against banks"[3] that manifests itself in a conflict between the interests of the lender and those of the borrower and its owner.[4]

The increase in the number of law suits brought against lenders has been traced to a fragile economy, favorable verdicts and large monetary judgments.[5] A weak economy, for example, has the effect of prompting banks to protect their own financial position by calling in loans and refusing to extend credit to marginal borrowers, and causing those same marginal borrowers to sue the banks when the loans are called or credit not advanced.[6]

---

1   The author owes a special debt of gratitude to Bertram G. Kaminski, a litigation attorney at Kroll & Tract, who researched and prepared this appendix.

2   Readers can find cases and commentaries by reference to computer search facilities at law libraries.

3   Davis, "The Case Against Juries in Lender Liability", *ABA Journal* at 184 (Oct. 1987).

4   *Id.* One commentator has stated that "in almost all the situations I have seen, the lender had nearly always the right to do what it did. The issue was in the manner in which it exercised its rights." Cocheo & Clark, "Lenders, Better Watch Your Backs", *ABA Banking Journal*, at 31–32 (Nov. 1986).

5   Thierbach, *Lender Liability: Should Lenders Be Required to Continue to Advance Credit to Marginal Borrowers?* 15 West. St. U. L. Rev. 631, 633 (1988).

6   *Id.* at 633–34.

Although borrowers have won only one case in nine against lenders,[7] those that have been won tend to result in large jury verdicts against lenders.[8] Additionally, a review of lender liability cases demonstrates that borrowers are not only being released from their obligations to the lenders, but are also being awarded, by judge and jury alike, both compensatory and punitive damages.

Generally, lender liability litigation arises from the conduct of lenders in negotiating and administering loans, rather than from mistakes contained in the loan documents themselves.[9]

The conduct of lenders commonly serves as a factual basis for legal action when: (a) lenders become highly involved in the management and operations of the borrowers' businesses;[10] (b) lenders fail to honor loan commitments or impose new terms;[11] (c) lenders commence litigation against borrowers for nonmonetary defaults;[12] (d) lenders improperly accelerate demand notes;[13] (e) lenders substitute a stronger borrower for a weaker one in connection with a loan for a failing business or property;[14] and (f) lenders are perceived to have broken promises or made untrue statements.[15]

Borrowers most often assert lender liability claims as counterclaims in response to collection actions brought by lenders.[16]

As a legal cause of action, however, the term "lender liability" does not denote any particular theory of liability.[17] Rather, claimants against lenders employ traditional legal theories in a new fashion in an attempt to redress perceived injustices in the lending relationship. The legal theories under which borrowers commence litiga-

---

7   Blogdgett, *"Lender Liability Still Lurking: Borrowers Win Only One in Nine Cases But Banks Worry,"* 74 *ABA Journal* 42(1) (May 1, 1988). It must be noted, however, that most lender liability actions are dismissed or settled prior to trial. J. Hubbell, Defending Lender Liability Suits, 19 Colorado Lawyer 2409 (Dec.1990).

8   *See, e.g., State Nat'l Bank v. Farah Manufacturing Co.,* 678 S.W.2d 661 (Tex. Ct. App. 1984) (holding the lender liable for $18,947,348.77 in damages); *K.M.C. Co., Inc. v. Irving Trust Co.,* 757 F.2d 752 (6th Cir. 1985) (holding the lender liable for $7.5 million); *Landes Constr. Co., Inc. v. Royal Bank of Canada,* 833 F. 2d 1365 (9th Cir. 1987)(verdict awarding $18.5 million). Recently, however, courts have limited the circumstances under which borrowers may recover for claims against lenders. *See, e.g., Penthouse Int'l Inc. v. Dominion Federal Savings & Loan Ass'n,* 855 F. 2d 963 (2d Cir. 1988), *cert. denied,* 490 U.S. 1005 (1989) (reversing $128.7 million judgment against lender) 17; *Kruse v. Bank of America,* 202 Cal. App. 3d 38, 248 Cal. Rptr 17. (1988), *cert. denied,* 488 U.S. 1043 (1989) (reversing $37.5 million judgment against lender).

9   D. Shuller, *Techniques to Reduce Lender Liability Risk,* 6 Probate & Property 16 (May/June 1992).

10 *Farah Manufacturing Co., Inc. v. State Nat'l Bank,* 678 S.W.2d 661 (Tex. Ct. App. 1984).

11 *999 v. C.I.T. Corp.,* 776 F.2d 866 (9th Cir. 1985).

12 *See Universal C.I.T. Credit Corp. v. Shepler,* 164 Ind. App. 516, 329 N.E.2d 620 (1975).

13 *K.M.C. Co. Inc. v. Irving Trust Co.,* 757 F.2d 752 (6th Cir. 1985).

14 J. Hubbell, *Defending Lender Liability Suits,* 19 Colorado Lawyer 2409, 2410 (Dec. 1990).

15 *Id.*

16 J. Hubbell, *Defending Lender Liability Suits,* 19 Colorado Lawyer 2409 (Dec. 1990).

17 For example, in the case of *Sanchez-Corea v. Bank of America,* 38 Cal. 3d 892, 701 P.2d 826, 215 Cal. Rptr. 679 (1985), bank customers brought an action against their bank under the legal theories of breach of contract, fraud, breach of implied covenant of good faith and fair dealing, disparagement of credit, interference with prospective economic advantage, promissory interference with prospective economic advantage, promissory estoppel, negligence, and intentional infliction of emotional distress.

tion include various common law causes of action (including fraud, misrepresentation, economic duress, breach of contract, and tortious interference) and several statutory prescriptions (including environmental, antitrust, racketeering, and banking statutes).[18]

A key element in many of these theories is the concept of the lender's undue or unlawful "control" over a borrower.[19] Although it is virtually impossible to drawn a clear line between permissible and unlawful control,[20] lenders are often sued as a result of the power they exert over borrowers' disbursements, income, sales or equity.[21] It has been held that in order to be found liable for such undue control, a lender must exercise sufficient authority over a borrower so as to dictate the borrower's corporate policy and dispossession of assets.[22]

Common Law Causes of Action

Lenders have been held liable to borrowers under a variety of common law causes of action. Among these, claimants have successfully proceeded under the theories of fraud and misrepresentation.[23] To commence an action based on fraud, a borrower must allege that the lender made a material misrepresentation that, when made, the lender was aware that it was false, or recklessly made it as a positive assertion without any knowledge of its validity. Moreover, the borrower must allege that the lender made the representation with the intention that it be acted upon by the borrower, and that the borrower acted in reliance upon it to its detriment.[24]

An action for misrepresentation will lie when a lender with knowledge superior to that of the borrower (or a means of knowledge not open to the borrower) is silent,[25] or where the lender knows that the

---

18 The "flawed" application of these theories to lender liability cases has, according to one commentator, "occasionally resulted in both disaster and confusion." Granoff, *Emerging Theories of Lender Liability: Flawed Application of Old Concepts*, 104 Bank. L. Journ. 492, 493 (1987).

19 For example, in the case *A. Gay Jenson Farms Co. v. Cargill, Inc.*, 309 N.W.2d 285 (Minn. 1981), a lender was held liable for the debts of a borrower when it was determined that the lender was an "active participant in [the borrower's] operations rather than simply a financier." *Id.* at 292.

20 A. Cappello & F. Komoroske, *Lender Liability Based on Undue Control over a Borrower*, 28 Trial 18, 19 (Dec. 1992).

21 More specifically, lenders are subject to liability upon findings that they maintained a security interest over most of a borrower's assets; placed their own employees in the borrower's business; subjected a borrower's decision-making to lender approval; participated in the daily business operations of the borrower; made the borrower's personnel decision; and conducted regular audits and visits of the borrower. *See* A. Cappello & F. Komoroske, *Lender Liability Based on Undue Control over a Borrower*, 28 Trial 18, 19–20 (Dec. 1992).

22 *In re Aluminum Mills Corp.*, 132 B.R. 869, 895 (N.D. Ill. 1991). *See also Creditor Liabilities Resulting from Improper Interference with the Management of a Financially Troubled Debtor*, 31 Bus. Law. 343 (1975).

23 *See Danca v. Taunton Sav. Bank*, 385 Mass. 1, 429 N.E.2d 1129 (1982); *Stirling v. Chemical Bank*, 382 F. Supp. 1146 (S.D.N.Y. 1974), *aff'd*, 516 F.2d 1396 (2d Cir. 1975).

24 *Custom Leasing, Inc. v. Texas Bank & Trust Co. of Dallas*, 516 S.W. 2d 138, 142-43 (Tex. 1974); *see also* Restatement (Second) of Torts § 527 (1977).

25 *Mullin v. Bank of America*, 199 Cal. App. 3d 448, 245 Cal. Rptr. 66 (1988); *Noved Realty Corp. v. A.A.P. Co, Inc*, 250 A.D. 1, 5, 293 N.Y.S. 336, 340 (1st Dep't 1937).

borrower is acting under a mistake of material fact and fails to correct the error,[26] or if lender's disclosure to the borrower is only partial.[27] Thus, lenders have been found liable under this tort for creating a false impression regarding the lender's decision (or lack of decision) to declare a default,[28] and by making representations that, although the lender has in fact decided not to extend further loans, promise further financing if the accounts receivable are assigned,[29] and by the creation of the false impression to a third party of the borrower's financial soundness.[30]

A lender was held liable for the tortious nondisclosure of material facts when it undertook to provide information about a customer's financial position but failed to disclose acts suggesting the instability of that position.[31]

Borrowers have prevailed against lenders on the theory of constructive fraud as well.[32] In one case, a bank was held liable when a bank officer had failed to inform a loan customer of the officer's involvement in the purchase of the customer's ranch, and failed to consider the customer's best interest. The court determined that a fiduciary relationship existed between the bank and the loan customer, on the bases that the customer had dealt with the lender for 24 years and the bank officer had acted as a financial advisor to the customer.[33]

A lender has also incurred liability under the theory of negligent misrepresentation when it failed to exercise reasonable care in making promise that it would loan money on a corporation's purchase order. The court noted that the lender had "permitted the corporation to solicit orders, establish production lines, commence the manufacture of products, and exhaust its cash reserve in the process thereof, without once issuing a word of warning or caution that the known necessary financing would not be forthcoming .... These defendants were led down a primrose path of promised financing and were impaled on the thorns

---

26 *Aaron Ferrer & Sons, Ltd. v. Chase Manhattan Bank, N.A.*, 731 F.2d 112, 123 (2d Cir. 1984); *Beth Israel Medical Center v. Smith*, 576 F. Supp. 1061, 1071 (S.D.N.Y. 1983); *Fund of Funds, Ltd. v. Arthur Andersen & Co.*, 545 F. Supp. 1314, 1359-60 (S.D.N.Y. 1982).

27 *Southeastern Financial Corp. v. United Merchants & Manufacturers, Inc.*, 701 F.2d 565, 567 (5th Cir. 1983); *Sheridan Drivein, Inc. v. State*, 16 A.D.2d 400, 228 N.Y.S.2d 576, 585 (4th Dep't 1962).

28 *State Nat'l Bank v. Farah Manufacturing Co.*, 678 S.W.2d 661 (Tex. Ct. App. 1984).

29 *Sanchez-Corea v. Bank of America*, 38 Cal. 3d 892, 701 P.2d 826, 215 Cal. Rptr. 679 (1985).

30 *General Motors Acceptance Corp. v. Central Nat'l Bank*, 773 F.2d 771, 780 (7th Cir. 1985).

31 *Central State Stamping v. Terminal Equip. Co.*, 727 F.2d 1405, 1409 (6th Cir. 1984). In the case of *Richfield Bank & Trust Co. v. Sjogren*, 244 N.W.2d 648 (Minn. 1976), the court held that it is the "moral duty of banks to the community in which they do business to use reasonable care in seeing that their depositors are not committing a fraud on the public." *Id.* at 651.

32 Constructive fraud arises from a breach of a legal or equitable duty, trust, or confidence resulting in damages to another. *Barrett v. Bank of America, N.T. and S.A.*, 183 Cal. App. 3d 1362, 1368-69, 229 Cal. Rptr. 16, 20 (1986).

33 *Deist v. Wachholz* 108 Mont. 208 678 P.2d 188 (1984). *See also Whitney v. Citibank, N.A.*, 782 F.2d 1106, 1116 (2d Cir. 1986).

of improvident investments and personal guarantees en route".[34]

Borrowers have successfully proceeded against lenders under the theory of "tortious interference," both in connection with contractual relationships and economic advantage.[35] This theory is based on a line that the law has draw beyond which it prohibits members of the community to intentionally intermeddle with the business affairs of others.[36] Interference is considered unlawful unless justified or privileged in some way,[37]but is actionable only if such interference is motivated by legal "malice".[38] A lender was held liable for interference in the contractual relations of a borrower when it violated a nonencumberance provision in an asset sale agreement between the borrower and the seller of assets by taking a security interest in such assets.[39] A lender was found to have inter-

fered in a borrower's business when it imposed a thirteen point program to help "salvage whatever is possible from the debtor's situation," which included the reduction of the salary of borrower's president, the replacement of the borrower's accountant with one chosen by the lender, and having all of the borrower's disbursements approved by the lender.[40] In another case, however, a lender was held not to have tortiously interfered when it sent letters to a borrower's customers requesting that they send the money they owed the borrower directly to the lender.[41]

Courts have held that once a lender undertakes to process a loan application, it has a duty to do so with the exercise of reasonable care, or be liable in tort for negligence.[42]

One court held a lender liable for negligence on the basis that the lender

---

34 *Banker's Trust Co. v. Steenburn*, 95 Misc. 2d 967, 409 N.Y.S.2d 51, 66 (Sup. Ct. 1978). Interestingly, the court in *First City Bank v. Global Auctioneers, Inc.*, 708 S.W.2d 12 (Tex. 1986), upheld an award of actual and punitive damages against a lender for inducing the transfer of funds through misrepresentations about the financial soundness of the transferee, even though the jury concluded that the plaintiff could have discovered the falsity through a reasonable investigation. The court's reasoning was grounded on the proposition that a person committing fraud cannot avoid liability by proving that the other party could have uncovered the fraud through reasonable diligence.

35 *Leonard Duckworth Inc. v. Michael L. Field & Co.*, 516 F.2d 952 (5th Cir. 1975); *Nordic Bank PLC v. Trend Group Ltd*, 619 F. Supp. 542 (S.D.N.Y. 1985); *Black Lake Pipe Line Co. v. Union Constr. Co.*, 538 S.W.2d 80 (Tex. 1976); *Delcon Group v. Northern Trust Corporation*, 135 Ill. Dec. 212, 543 N.E.2d 595, 187 Ill. App. 3d 635 *app.den.*, 139 Ill. Dec. 511, 548 N.E.2d 1067, 128 Ill.2d 672 (1989); *State Nat'l Bank of El Paso v. Farah Manufacturing Co.*, 678 S.W.2d 661 (Tex. Ct. App. 1984).

36 45 Am. Jur. 2d *Interference* § 1 (1969).

37 *State Nat'l Bank v. Farah Manufacturing Co.*, 678 S.W.2d 661 (Tex. Ct. App. 1984). *See Frank Colson, Inc. v. Buick v. General Motors Corp.*, 488 F.2d 202, 206 (5th Cir. 1974) (holding that even where there a justifiable business interest exists for the lender to so interfere, there is no absolute privilege for a lender to interfere with a borrower's contractual relationships with others.

38 Restatement (Second) of Torts, Introductory Note to Chapter 37 (1979).

39 *First Wyoming Bank, Casper v. Mudge*, 748 P.2d 713 (Wyo. 1988).

40 *Melamed v. Lake Country Nat'l Bank*, 727 F.2d 1399, 1403–04 (6th Cir. 1984).

41 *Delcon Group v. Northern Trust Corporation*, 135 Ill. Dec. 212, 543 N.E.2d 595, 187 Ill. App. 3d 635, *app. den.*, 139 Ill. Dec. 511, 548 N.E.2d 1067, 128 Ill.2d 672 (1989).

42 *Jacques v. First Nat'l Bank*, 307 Md. 527, 515 A.2d 756 (1986); *First Federal Sav. & Loan Ass'n v. Caudle*, 425 So.2d 1050 (Ala. 1983).

"failed in its responsibility to exercise reasonable care and diligence" after several of its officers made conflicting statements to the borrower (that were, however, not severe enough to constitute fraud).[43] Lenders have also been held liable on the basis that they intentionally sought to inflict emotional distress on borrowers,[44] and under prima facie (or general) tort principles.[45]

The theory of "economic duress" has also been employed by borrowers in response to collection actions instituted by lenders.[46] Under this theory, a borrower claims that a lender is threatening it with costly situations, including bankruptcy or loss of credit rating.[47]

Borrowers seek to be relieved from an obligation assumed from the lender.[48] Borrowers must show more, however, than mere "pressure of business circumstances,

financial embarrassment or economic necessity."[49]

Liability under economic duress has been imposed on a lender where such lender, in bad faith, threatened to declare a default, bankrupt the borrower and "padlock his doors,"[50] and where it refused to provide financing to a mortgagor and would not transfer its financing commitment to another lender unless the mortgagor paid a $12,000 debt of the lender.[51]

As opposed to actions sounding in tort, breach of contract claims have afforded many borrowers recovery against lenders for both oral and written contracts.[52] Lenders have been found liable under this theory for a failure of a lender to finance the purchase of farm animals despite a prior agreement,[53] the failure of a lender to disclose funds under an irrevocable line of credit,[54] and for the lender's

---

43 *Champion Int'l Corp. v. First Nat'l Bank of Jackson,* 642 F. Supp. 237, 242 (S.D. Miss. 1986). In the case of *United States & Carnegie Pension Fund, Inc. v. Orenstein,* 557 F.2d 343 (2d Cir. 1977), however, a lender was held not to be liable for furnishing incorrect information to the borrower when the lender had acted in good faith and expressly disclaimed any intent to give investment advice. *Id.* at 345–46.

44 See *Sanchez-Corea v. Bank of America,* 38 Cal. 3d 892, 701 P.2d 826, 215 Cal Rptr. 679 (1985).

45 See *State Bank of Commerce v. Demco of Louisiana, Inc.,* 483 So. 2d 1119 (La. 1986).

46 *Federal Deposit Ins. Co. v. Linn,* 671 F. Supp. 547, 556 (N.D. Ill. 1987); *Nordic Bank PLC v. Trend Group, Ltd.,* 619 F. Supp. 542, 560 (S.D.N.Y. 1985); *Citibank, N.A. v. Real Coffee Trading Co.,* 566 F. Supp. 1158, 1162 (S.D.N.Y. 1983); *Union State Bank v. Weaver,* 526 F. Supp. 29, 33 (S.D.N.Y. 1981); *805 Third Ave. Co. v. M.W. Realty Assoc.,* 58 N.Y.2d 450, 448 N. E. 2d 15, 461 N.Y.S.2d 778 (1983); *First Texas Sav. Ass'n v. Dicker Center Inc.,* 631 S.W.2d 179 (Tex. App. 1982)

47 *See* Restatement (Second) of Torts § 871 comment F (1977).

48 *State Nat'l Bank v. Farah Manufacturing Co.,* 678 S.W.2d 661, 683 (Tex. Ct. App. 1984).

49 *First Texas Sav. Ass'n v. Dicker Center, Inc.,* 631 S.W.2d 179, 186 (Tex. App. 1982).

50 *State Nat'l Bank v. Farah Manufacturing Co,* 678 S.W.2d 661 (Tex. Ct. App. 1984).

51 *Pecos Constr. Co. v. Mortgage Investment Co.,* 80 N.M. 680, 459 P.2d 842 (1969).

52 *Landes Constr. Co., Inc. v. Royal Bank of Canada,* 833 F.2d 1365, 1371 (9th Cir. 1987). The advantage, however, of using a tort theory, rather than one in contract, against a lender is that a plaintiff recovers all damages by the lender's conduct, instead of those merely foreseeable at the time the contract was entered into. Proximately-caused damages are generally both easier to prove and produce higher recoveries *Sanchez, Symposium: Lender Liability Introduction,* 15 West. St. U. L. Rev. 177 (1988).

53 *National Farmers Organization, Inc. v. Kinsley Bank,* 731 F.2d 1464 (10th Cir. 1984).

54 *Shaughnessey v. Mark Twain State Bank,* 715 S.W.2d 944 (Mo. App. 1986).

breach of an implied obligation of good faith where it discounted the borrower's financing without prior notice.[55]

Statutory Causes of Action

In addition to the application of common law theories of liability, borrowers have managed to forge myriad federal statutes into powerful liability weapons against lenders. In recent times, the Federal Comprehensive Environmental Response, Compensation and Liability Act[56] (a.k.a. "CERCLA" or "Superfund") has become one of the most potent federal statutory weapons asserted against lenders. Under CERCLA, lenders have been held liable to share in damages and environmental cleanup costs where hazardous or toxic materials are discovered on mortgagors' property.[57] CERCLA assigns liability for clean-up costs: (1) to the current owners or operators of a contaminated facility; (2) to those who were owners or operators at the time of the waste disposal; (3) to the transporters of the hazardous waste; and, (4) to the generators of the hazardous waste.[58]

It is generally alleged that lenders fall within the categories of "owners or operators." For example, a lender may be considered to be an "owner" of a contaminated facility if it foreclosed on a security interest and took title to such a property. A lender may be considered an "operator" if its involvement with the borrower's business goes beyond what is regarded as necessary to protect its security interest. The CERCLA law holds responsible parties strictly liable for all costs and damages,[59] and will apportion all such damages and cleanup costs jointly and severally if allocation cannot be made among individual responsible parties.[60]

As a result of government's failure to articulate a clear national environmental policy balancing economic interests and environmental concerns, legal precedent applying CERCLA to claim against lenders is unstable and frequently inconsistent.[61] Recently, for example, developing case law had provided that, prior to foreclosure, a secured lender was exempt from CERCLA liability so long as it did not participate in

---

55 *K.M.C. Co. Inc. v. Irving Trust Co.*, 757 F.2d 752 (6th Cir. 1985). *See also Brown v. Aveco Inv. Corp.*, 603 F.2d 1367 (9th Cir. 1979); *First Nat'l Bank in Libby v. Twombley*, 213 Mont. 66, 689 P.2d 1226 (1984).

56 Pub. L. No. 96-510, 94 Stat. 2767, (codified as amended at 42 U.S.C. §§ 9601-9675 (1988). CERCLA was amended by the Superfund Amendments and Reauthorization Act of 1986 (SARA), Pub. L. No. 99-499, 100 Stat. 1613.

57 *See United States v. Maryland Bank & Trust Co.*, 632 F. Supp. 573 (D. Md. 1986).

58 42 U.S.C. § 9607(a)(1)-(4).

59 *See County Line Inv. Co. v. Tinney*, 933 F.2d 1508, 1515 (10th Cir. 1991); *United States v. Monsanto Co.*, 858 F.2d 160, 167 & n.11 (4th Cir. 1988), *cert. denied*, 490 U.S. 1106 (1989).

60 *County Line Inv. Co. v. Tinney*, 933 F.2d at 1515 & n.11 (10th Cir. 1991). In other words, if a reasonable basis cannot be found to apportion costs and damages, any one defendant could become liable for the entire harm. This will tend to result in a lender having to bear a larger percentage of the cleanup costs than its proportionate contribution to the environmental harm. N. Tolume & D. Cloud, *The Fleet Factors Case: A Wrong Turn for Lender Lliability Under Superfund*, 26 Wake Forest L. Rev. 127, 129 (1991).

61 G. Wolf, *Lender Liability Under the Federal Superfund Program*, 23 Ariz. St. L. J. 531 (1991). *See R. Mayes, Secured Creditors and Superfund: Avoiding the Liability Net*, 20 Env't Rep. (BNA) 609 (Jul. 28, 1989 ("The liability net created by CERCLA is like a mile-long net behind a modern fishing trawler: it is wide,m deep, and dangerous to anything that gets caught up in it.")

the day-to-day management of a borrower's operations.[62]

In 1991, however, a federal appeals put this rule into doubt, holding that a lender could be held liable under CERCLA if the lender had the "capacity to influence" hazardous substance disposal decisions through its participation in the facility's financial management, regardless of whether the lender had actually ever exercised that capacity.[63]

That decision had caused a wave of panic among lenders, who petitioned Congress for legislative action to clarify lenders' exposure under Superfund.[64] In April 1992, the U.S. Environmental Protection Agency ("EPA") ended the "nightmare"[65] for lenders as presented by CERCLA liability, by issuing a regulation which de-

fined the parameters of the security interest exemption set forth in the CERCLA statute.[66] Under the EPA regulation, lenders can be held liable only if they participate in and exercise decision-making control over the management and operations of borrowers.

Borrowers have asserted claims against lenders under myriad other federal statutes as well. For example, lenders have been held responsible for a borrower's unpaid withholding taxes under the Internal Revenue Code,[67] or liable as a "controlling person" or "aider and abettor" of borrower under federal securities laws.[68] Moreover, under the Federal Bankruptcy Code, a lender's claims could be equitably subordinated to a debtor's other claimants on the basis that the lender was in control of the

---

62 *See* N. Toulme & D. Cloud, *The Fleet Factors Case: A Wrong Turn for Lender Liability Under Superfund,* 26 Wake Forest L. Rev. at 133.

63 *United States v. Fleet Factors Corp.,* 901 F.2d 1550, 1557-58 (11th Cir. 1990), *cert. denied,* 111 S. Ct. 752 (1991). *But see In re Bergsoe Metal Corp.,* 910 F.2d 668, 672 (9th Cir. 1990) (opining that "some actual management of the facility" is required before a lender loses the secured creditor exemption).

64 N. Toulme & D. Cloud, *The Fleet Factors Case: A Wrong Turn for Lender Liability Under Superfund,* 26 Wake Forest L. Rev. at 128.

65 A. Cappello & F. Komoroske, *Lender Liability Based on Undue Control over a Borrower,* 28 Trial 18, 21 (Dec. 1992).

66 57 Fed. Reg. 18344 (1992) (codified at 40 C.F.R. § 300.1100). *See* P. Quentel, *EPA Issues Long-Awaited Lender Liability Rule,* 22 E.L.R. 10637 (Oct. 1992).

67 26 U.S.C. §§ 3505, 6672 (1988). Section 6672 of the Internal Revue Code provides that: [a]ny person required to collect, truthfully account for, and pay over any tax imposed by this title [employment witholding taxes] who willfully fails to collect such tax, or truthfully account for and pay over such tax, or willfully attempts in any manner to evade or defeat any such tax or the payment thereof, shall . . . be liable to a penalty equal to the total amount of the tax evaded. . . .

   26 U.S.C. § 6672 (a). *See United States v. First Nat'l Bank of Circle,* 652 F.2d 882 (9th Cir. 1981); *United States v. McMulllen,* 516 F2d. 917 (7th Cir.), *cert. denied,* 423 U.S. 915 (1975); *Mueller v. Nixon,* 470 F.2d 1348 (6th Cir. 1972), *cert. denied,* 412 U.S. 949 (1973). Lenders can be liable for a borrower's withholding taxes simply on the knowledge that the borrower was unable to pay such taxes.

68 *Metge v. Baehler* 762 F.2d 621 (8th Cir. 1985), *cert. denied sub. nom., Metge v. Bankers Trust Co.,* 474 U.S. 1057 (1986); *Technology Exch. Corp. of Am. v. Grant County State Bank,* 646 F. Supp. 179 (D. Colo. 1986).

debtor, and should be treated as an "insider" who owes a fiduciary duty to such other claimants.[69]

In addition, the Racketeer Influenced Corrupt Organizations Act ("RICO")[70] has been interpreted to permit private borrowers to hold lenders liable for treble damages in connection with loans received from lenders. Borrowers have asserted RICO-based liability claims on the bases of fraudulent interest charges,[71] fraudulent efforts by lenders to protect existing loans,[72] *refusals by lenders to extend promised financing,*[73] *and unlawful attempts by lenders to acquire control of the borrower's assets, customers or operations.*[74]

Borrowers have asserted lender liability actions under federal antitrust statutes, primarily under the authority of the Sherman Antitrust Act[75] and the Clayton Antitrust Act.[76]

Lender liability actions under these statutes have not increased materially in recent years, however, predominately due to the heavy burden of proof imposed on the plaintiff,[77] and because the scope of such laws has been declining. Consequently, there have been relatively few plaintiff victories utilizing antitrust laws, and include cases primarily where a lender's decision to terminate a borrower's credit was sudden and unsubstantiated,[78] where there was evidence of a conspiracy to drive a borrower out of business,[79] and where several banks conspired in an unlawful combination to illegally fix a high prime rate.[80]

---

69 *United States v. Kayser-Roth Corp., Inc.*, 910 F.2d 24, 27 (1st Cir. 1990), *cert denied*, 111 s ct. 957 (1991); A lender's new status of "insider" may result in the subordination of its claim through the doctrine of equitable subordination. 11 U.S.C. § 510(c) (1988). The mere ability to exercise control is, however, insufficient to invoke this doctrine. The lender must have exercised control in such a way as to result in actual injury to the borrower. *Porter v. Yukon Nat'l Bank*, 866 F.2d 3 (10th Cir. 1989). *See In re Clark Pipe & Supply Co.*, 87 B. R. 21, 23–24 (E. D. La. 1988) *mod'f* 893 F.2d 693 (5th Cir. 1990) (bank considered to be insider as a result of its sole control of a borrower's accounts receivable and disbursement of operating funds).

70 RICO, 18 U.S.C. §§ 1961 *et seq.* The RICO statute prohibits a "person" from furthering an "enterprise," or his interests in such an enterprise, through a "pattern" of "racketeering activity."

71 *Wilcox v. First Interstate Bank of Oregon, N.A.*, 815 F.2d 522 (9th Cir. 1987); *NCNB National Bank of North Carolina v. Tiller, 814 F.2d 931, 936 (4th Cir.)* petition denied 484 U.S. 974 (1987); *Atkinson v. Anadarko Bank and Trust Co.*, 808 F.2d 438 (5th Cir. 1987), *cert. denied*, 483 U.S. 1032 (1987).

72 Lawaetz v. Bank of Nova Scotia, 653 F. Supp. 1278 (D.V.I. 1987); Hatherley v. Palos Bank and Trust Co., 650 F. Supp. 832 (N.D. Ill. 1986); Heritage Insurance Company of America v. First National Bank of Cicero, 629 F. Supp. 1412 (N.D. Ill. 1986).

73 Runnemede Owners, Inc. v. Crest Mortgage Corp., 861 F.2d 1053 (7th Cir. 1988); Dunham v. Independence Bank of Chicago, 629 F. Supp. 983 (N.D. Ill. 1986); LSC Assoc. v. Lomas & Nettleton Financial Corp., 629 F. Supp. 979 (E.D. Pa. 1986).

74 Citibank v. Data Lease Financial Corp., 828 F.2d 686 (llth Cir.), *cert. denied*, 484 U.S. 1062 (1987).

75 15 U.S.C. §§ 1 and 2.

76 15 U.S.C. §§ 14 and 15.

77 A complainant must, *inter alia*, furnish proof that the lender's actions have had an anticompetitive effect, and must produce evidence establishing a conspiracy or monopoly.

78 *Neel v. Waldrop*, 639 F.2d 1080 (4th Cir. 1981).

79 *Id.*

80 *Michaels Building Co. v. Ameritrust Co., N.A.*, 848 F.2d 674 (6th Cir. 1988).

The Bank Holding Company Act[81] has also been applied against lenders. This act prohibits improper and anticompetitive tying arrangements[82] by lenders,[83] and entitles borrowers who have been injured by an unlawful tying arrangement to maintain a private cause of action permitting the recovery of both general and treble damages. Unlike antitrust laws, the Bank Holding Company Act does not require proof of market power or impact on competition.[84]

Conclusion

The litigious nature of American society, coupled with the tenuous condition of many sectors of the country's economy, have resulted in a plethora of liability suits against lenders. As shown, these suits find their basis in imaginative uses of traditional state common law and federal statutory law. There are, of course, many defenses available to lenders also within this same body of law.[85] Nevertheless, there is no substitute, legal or otherwise, for ordinary prudence and discretion on the part of lenders to avoid litigation in the first place.

Lenders could avert lawsuits, or mitigate their effects, if they follow a few basic, precautionary steps. Lenders should avoid any types of oral understandings with borrowers that are not set forth within the loan documentation. Lenders should avoid intruding into the day-to-day operation of a borrower's business, and avoid any type of conduct that might lend support to a legal claim of malice or ill will. Borrowers should be afforded as much advance written notice as possible should lenders decide to terminate a loan or refuse further credit.[86]

In addition, potential lender liability exposure can be reduced through the inclusion of contractual provisions in the loan documentation that seek to avoid jury trials. [87]

---

81 *See* 12 U.S.C. §§ 1971 *et. seq.* The purpose of the Bank Holding Company Act is to prohibit anticompetitive banking practices which borrowers accept or provide some other service or product or refrain from dealing with other parties in order to obtain the bank product or service that they desire. *Lancianese v. Bank of Mount Hope,* 783 F.2d 467, (4th Cir. 1986).

82 A tying arrangement is one in which a supplier of a given product conditions the sale of the product on the purchase of a different (less desirable) product, or requires that the purchaser not buy the product from any other supplier.

83 *Sharkey v. Security Bank & Trust Co.,* 651 F. Supp. 1231 (D. Minn. 1987); *Nordic Bank PLC v. Trend Group, Ltd.,* 619 F. Supp. 542 (S.D.N.Y. 1985).

84 *Bruce v. First Federal Sav. & Loans Ass'n of Conroe, Inc.,* 837 F.2d 712 (5th Cir. 1988).

85 For example, lenders may assert a waiver or estoppel defense if it can be shown that the borrower requested the lender to control the business or failed to object when the lender did. *Citibank v. Data Lease Financial Corp.,* 828 F.2d 686 (11th Cir.), *cert. denied,* 484 U.S. 1062 (1987). Lenders may also assert the defenses of justification or privilege, where lenders have the right to intermeddle in the borrower's business if the lender's financial interests are at stake. *Riquelme Valdes v. Leisure Resource Group, Inc.,* 810 F2d 1345 (5th Cir. 1987.

86 Granoff, *Emerging Theories of Lender Liability: Flawed Applications of Old Concepts,* 104 Bank. L. Journ. 492, 51315 (1987).

87 It is believed that in connection with lender liability litigation, juries are more likely than judges to err in favor of borrowers in finding lenders liable and in determining the amount of damages. *See* D. Shuller, *Techniques to Reduce Lender Liability Risk,* 6 Probate & Property 16 (May/June 1992).

To insure against sharing in potentially crushing environmental cleanup costs, lenders should require borrowers to complete an environmental questionnaire or conduct their own due diligence assessment. Loan documentation should cover present and potential environmental matters, and should specifically leave control of all such environmental matters to borrowers.[88]

The proliferation of actions against lenders only underscores the importance of lenders to use guidelines such as these, and to follow the basic precepts of caution and common sense in their lending and workout policies.

---

88 G. Wolf, *Lender Liability Under the Federal Superfund Program*, 23 Ariz. St. L. J. 531, 551-52 (1991).

■■■
Section VII

■■■

Credit Quality

■■■

CHAPTER Twenty

Credit Quality and Portfolio Management

Section One: Arguments for Loan Portfolio Management

Bank reform legislation and Federal Reserve audit guidelines unmistakably identify the impact loan and investment diversification has on portfolio-related risk and profit volatility.

This new awareness will move lenders to investigate mathematical and statistical models of evaluating portfolio risk. This should stimulate a shift toward less risky, more efficient bank assets. Banks realizing the validity of portfolio diversification will lower risk by offsetting the specific risk of one asset (loan) with another. In this way only undiversifiable market risk remains. Thus, a diversified portfolio minimizes risk and profit volatility without sacrificing returns.[1]

The goal of loan portfolio management is to spread loans among dissimilar business lines to prevent homogenous firms from borrowing excessive amounts. Instituting this policy will safeguard depositors, maximize diversifiable market risk, and reduce profit volatility.

Although it is perceived that diversified loan portfolios reduce exposure to credit risk, distinguishing between a truly diversified and moderately diversified portfolio is convoluted. Systematizing an efficient loan portfolio and getting it to work is no less challenging. This leads us to reviewing the issues of portfolio risk, or better yet, what portfolio risk is all about.

The Federal Reserve Examination Manual for Commercial Banks includes various types of concentrations, defining concentrations as "direct, indirect or contingent obligations exceeding 25 percent of

---

1 Jean LeGrand, *The Bankers Magazine*, March–April 1993.

the bank's capital structure."[2] Included are the aggregate of:

- overdrafts
- cash items
- securities purchased outright or under resale agreements
- sale of federal funds
- suspense assets
- leases
- acceptances
- letters of credit
- placements
- loans endorsed, guaranteed or subject to repurchase agreements and any other actual or contingent liability
- concentrations involving one borrower, an affiliated group of borrowers, or borrowers engaged in or dependent on one industry

■ ■ ■

"In recognizing a concentration, it is important to determine the key factors germane to credits within the loan portfolio. Loans concentrated in one borrower are, to a large degree, centered in and predicated on the financial capability and character of that individual or entity. Loans centered in an affiliated group are susceptible to a domino effect if financial problems are experienced by one or a few members of the group. Concentrations within or dependent on an industry are subject to the additional risk factors of external economic conditions and market acceptance which might affect all members of the group."[3]

"An easily recognizable concentration of credit is advances single to a borrower under exceptions to the legal lending limits. Because of exceptions within such statutes, senior management may become complacent in approving additional credit to the borrowers. As in any credit advance, an element of risk is present and potential for loss should remain the major concern. Prudent banking would dictate certain restrictions not imposed by statute. Every loan proposal sheet submitted to the board of directors or its committee should include a listing of the borrower's outstanding loans as well as any outstanding obligations to affiliated interests. In reviewing concentrations within the portfolio, those sheets should be used and the amount of liability updated as of the examination date."[4]

■ ■ ■

Generally, money center banks reduce portfolio risk by advancing funds to a large variety of industries, spreading risk among a broad client base. These banks, aware of concentration risk, usually operate within industry thresholds limiting credit exposure to achieve the best mix of individual and portfolio safety. While most bankers believe that loan portfolio concentration in similar industries should be avoided, others suggest specialization may promote high-caliber loans by concentrating expertise in a few industries. Some banks do assign loans to officers by industry (media, defense, health care, real estate, etc.), allowing them to become experts in all facets of specific industries. This strategy often pays off handsomely, as teams of expert loan originators solicit, analyze and sell off portions of industry portfolios they don't want.

Although loans in a concentration may be sound and profitable, periodic reviews should be made on industry trends

---

2   Board of Governors, The Federal Reserve System Commercial Bank Examination Manual Supplement No. 6, September 1992, Section 205.

3   Ibid.

4   Ibid.

and the credits' susceptibility to external factors. Historically, outside forces—mainly cyclical economic forces and changes occurring in industry life cycles—have been manifest in transportation, real estate, defense, and electronic data processing. When industry problems do surface, banks are awakened quickly by unreported concentrations that were allowed to develop.

Banks located in farming, dairying or livestock areas may grant most loans to individuals or concerns engaged in and dependent on that industry. Concentration is prevalent and normal—even necessary if the bank is to follow its charter. Bankers operating in this environment are close to borrowers and have expertise relating to economic and industry concerns within markets they serve. Unforeseen events are not exceptional, and therefore portfolio positions should be maintained, breaking up and categorizing loans into portfolios decided by economic and market sensitivities. This strategy tells bank managers what percentage of the loan portfolio is affected by the successful harvesting and marketing of a specific crop or on the sale of a type of livestock. That information provides a useful tool in deciding adjustments that might be made to reduce exogenous loan risk.

To that end, Glenn D. Pederson studied the effectiveness of asset allocation models in refining the portfolio management of rural, agricultural banks.[5] Pederson examined decision factors involved in finding the optimum mix of loan assets and securities that achieved targeted portfolio profits within acceptable risk levels. An asset allocation model quantified how rural banks managed their portfolios under conditions of rising interest rates and credit risks. The study suggested that (1) rural banks shifted assets to securities and reduced the volume of agricultural loans when loan default rates increased, and (2) agricultural credit crunches had a spillover effect to the nonagricultural loan sector.

Another type of concentration involves credit extensions to foreign governments, governmental agencies, and majority-owned or majority-controlled entities. Portfolio selection focuses on the economy's performance and structure, profitability of export markets, the ability to service debt and the debtor country's ability to develop natural resources.

An important variable deals with economic growth, particularly the question of broad-based growth versus growth concentrated in certain sectors. Deciding the dimensions of governmental influence on the economy is a matter of fiscal policy—specifically policies influencing savings and investment. The current revenue base may be insufficient to support expenditures impeding savings and investment. The diversity of the export sector is another important indication of the volatility of export earnings.

For example, Chemical Banking Corporation, one of the most prominent banks in the country, points out economic concerns across borders:

■ ■ ■

"Because multinational companies and private domestic companies are often sensitive to changes in national policy environments and because they can often portend shifts in a country's creditworthiness, shifts in foreign direct investment patterns and patterns of non-government long-term capital flows

5   Glenn D. Pederson, *American Journal of Agricultural Economics*, August 1992, v74, n3 9672.

deserve close attention. Similarly, short-term capital outflows on the part of domestic residents, which are often sensitive to the domestic outlook may also be important indicators of changes in a country's creditworthiness."

■ ■ ■

Finally, the nature and composition of debt by maturity and lender helps: (1) to validate a country's ability to repay and/or borrow sums abroad, (2) to refinance existing debt, (3) to maturate resilience to shifts in interest rate, and (4) to change the availability of credit.

The Federal Reserve points to another class of loan concentration that may not manifest itself—clusters of borrowers who "handle the same manufacturer's product." For example, the bank may finance a large concentration of dealers' floor planning of a particular brand of recreation vehicle along with discounting customers' conditional sales contracts. Any one dealer could form a concentration when direct obligations are combined with the indirect paper. Furthermore, additional concentration may surface when product defects are discovered and generate adverse publicity. Sales and profits may decline if governmental agencies impose restrictions until the product defects are corrected. In turn, customers whose paper was discounted by the bank may halt payments until they are personally satisfied. The problem may be only temporary, but a large portion of the portfolio may be of questionable collectibility or in outright default.

Banks may grant most of their loans to firms (and employees) that are the dominant business establishment in a small city or town. It may be seen as the bank's civic duty, so to speak, since the repercussions of a dominant business closing down in a small town will affect suppliers, unemployment levels and the town's economic well-being.

■ ■ ■

"The bank should code all loans to employees of a single company and maintain continuing controls on the outstanding debt. It is difficult to evaluate the further effects of such a situation on other merchants borrowing at the bank who are heavily dependent on such companies. To determine the concentration, it is not only necessary to include loans directly to the company involved, but also loans to its employees and any supplier whose business is dependent on the company."[6]

■ ■ ■

Summary: Concentration of Credit Examination Procedures[7]

Review the bank's internal controls, policies, practices, and procedures relating to concentration of credit. The bank's system should be documented in a complete and concise manner and should include, where appropriate, narrative descriptions, copies of forms used, and other pertinent information.

Concentration of Credit Policies

- Has a policy been adopted which specifically addresses concentrations of credits?
- Does the policy include deposits and other financial transactions with financial institutions?

---

6 Ibid.

7 Credit Examination Procedures; *Federal Reserve Commercial Bank Examination Manual.*

- Have controls been instituted to monitor the following types of concentrations:
  - Loans and other obligations of one borrower?
  - Loan predicated on the collateral support afforded by a debt or equity issue of a corporation?
  - Loans to a company dominant in the local economy, its employees and major suppliers?
  - Loans dependent upon one crop or herd?
  - Loans dependent upon one industry group?
  - Loans considered out of normal territory?
- Are periodic reports of concentrations required to be submitted to the board or its committee for review?
- Are the periodic reports checked for accuracy by someone other than the preparer before being submitted to the board or its committee?
- When concentrations exist predicated upon a particular crop or herd of livestock, does the bank attempt to diversify the inherent potential risk by means of:
  - Participations?
  - Arrangements with governmental agencies such as:
    - Guarantees?
    - Lending arrangements?
- When concentrations exist predicated upon a particular industry, does the bank make a periodic review of industry trends?

Now that the Federal Reserve ground rules have been outlined, what is the next step in portfolio risk management? For one thing, a qualitative approach alone won't help lenders improve their loan portfolios.

What is needed is a basic understanding of the quantitative techniques used to estimate portfolio risk. Let's start by surveying the evolution of modern portfolio theory.

Section Two: Development of Modern Portfolio Theory

The Basics of Modern Portfolio Theory

Modern Portfolio Theory (MPT) began with Harry Markowitz 35 years ago, who suggested that investors cannot select investment portfolios based simply on returns alone; this approach ignores volatility of returns. Markowitz showed that returns failed to insulate investors from levels of risk associated with individual investments.

From here portfolio theory evolved into the nucleus of modern finance—from merchant and commercial banking, to foreign exchange trading.

MPT mathematically creates efficient equity portfolios designed to provide investors with maximum returns for different risk levels. Theoretically, efficient investment portfolios benefit investors because risk incorporated in a portfolio is less than the risk of any single instrument. Also consider that uncertainty intrinsic in single asset (loans) in portfolios differs from the uncertainty of that same asset held alone. Portfolios are composed of a diverse array of investments that, from a standpoint of risk, tend to cancel each other. How diversification is accomplished varies from investor to investor. Banks diversify loan portfolios by lending across industries to firms with dissimilar economic sensitivities and borrowers in demographically diverse areas.

Let's set up MPT with an example. Food Products Co. Inc., a beef producer, has asked the bank to help finance the acquisition of Poultry Farms Corp., a poultry producer. Assume the $30 million five-year term loan will be matched by $30 million new equity, thus keeping the debt to equity ratio unchanged. The question the banker asks from a portfolio point of view is how will the bank's risk exposure be affected by the acquisition?

First, we'll compare the expected returns of both firms by calculating the mean and standard deviation of both firms' probability distributions (see Exhibit 20.1). Let's start by considering Food Products Co. Inc. As a point of reference, we consider FPCO a cyclical business since more people tend to eat beef during good times (economic expansion).

In this particular exercise, the economy is composed of three categories. For instance, in a recession (17% probability) FPCO suffers a negative 19% return due to a decline in aggregate demand for beef. However, if economic expansion takes place, returns jump 51% as consumers purchase more beef. Conversely, Poultry Farms Corp., a cyclical business that counters Food Products Co. Inc., enjoys a 51% return in a down economy, but suffers a negative 19% return in good times.

If we study the charted probability P(s) and return associated with investment (Ra) for both companies in an average economy, they are both equal. For example, given a 50% probability of an average economy both firms are expected to generate an 18% return.

While the example seems somewhat exaggerated, it is not by any means far fetched. Finance companies tend to do better in a downturn, when people need to borrow money. Also, the returns from gold mining companies have historically tended to move inversely with the general pattern of business activity.

Moving along, let's look at the expected returns of the two firms. Food Prod-

---

Exhibit 20.1

Calculations of the *Mean* and *Standard Deviation* for Food Products Co. Inc.

State of Economy	Ps	Ra	PsRa²	(Ra-Ra)	(Ra-Ra)²	Ps(Ra-Ra)²
Down	0.17	-0.19	-0.0323	-0.4160	0.1731	0.0294
Average	0.50	0.18	0.0900	-0.460	0.0021	0.0011
Up	0.33	0.51	0.1683	0.2840	0.0807	0.0266
_Ra =_	0.2260	Food Products Co. Inc = a			S²a =	0.0571
					Sa =	0.2389

Calculations of the *Mean* and *Standard Deviation* for Poultry Farms Corp.:

State of Economy	Ps	Rb	PsRb²	(Rb-Rb)	(Rb-Rb)²	Ps(Rb-Rb)²
Down	0.17	0.51	0.0867	0.3960	0.1568	0.0267
Average	0.50	0.18	0.0900	0.0660	0.0044	0.0022
Up	0.33	-0.19	-0.0627	-0.3040	0.0924	0.0305
_Rb =_	0.1140	Poultry Farms Corp = b			S²b =	0.0593
					Sb.=	0.2436

ucts Co. Inc.'s expected return is $\underline{Ra}$ = 22.6%, while Poultry Farms Corp. expected return is $\underline{Rb}$ is 11.4%. $\underline{Ra}$ and $\underline{Rb}$ are the sum of each return multiplied by its respective probability.

To better illustrate this concept, let's go to a casino to bet on a coin toss. On the first toss, someone offers you a $1,000 payoff if the coin turns up heads, nothing if it turns up tails. The expected payoff on the first coin toss is 50% heads ($1,000) plus 50% tails (zero) or $500.

However, let's say before the first toss is made, the same individual offers you $300 if you agreed to take the money and run. In this instance, the $300 payoff represents a riskless return since no action is required. If a bank financing this hypothetical transaction lends the funds at the risk-free rate, the difference between the riskier expected return of $500 and the assured return of $300 is known as the risk premium. As the risk taker, the risk premium is what causes you to flip the coin. But the process is far from this simple.

Because $\underline{Ra}$, the riskier expected return, fails to measure earnings variability, the standard deviation must be examined once again. The standard deviations for Food Products Co. Inc. and Poultry Farms' Corp. are .2389 and .2436, respectively. Poultry Farms' variance, of .0593 is slightly more risky than FPCO since its return deviates further from the mean. However, the variance causes problems of distance from the mean (expected return) because deviations from the mean are squared, causing statistical inflation. Statistical inflation is adjusted with the standard deviation. For any normal distribution, the probability of an outcome falling within plus or minus one standard devia-

tion from the mean is 68.26% (34.13% × 2.0). If the outcome falls within two standard deviations of the mean, the probability of an occurrence within this range is 95.46%, and 99.74% of all outcomes will fall within three standard deviations.

While the standard deviation provides helpful information to the user, its value as a risk measurement and loan portfolio tool is limited. Why? Because assets (loans) are held jointly with other assets and not isolated independently. Thus, the riskiness of an asset can be influenced by the interaction of the pattern of its return with the patterns of return of the other assets held in combination. This leads directly to portfolio risk—covariance— the standard measure of how returns relate to each other.

The covariance of returns of Food Products Co. Inc. with returns of Poultry Farms Corp. is:

Ps	(Ra-Ra) (Rb-Rb)	Ps(Ra-Ra) (Rb-Rb)
0.17	-0.164736	-0.028005
0.05	-0.003036	0.001518
0.33	-0.086336	-0.028491
Cov(Ra,Rb) =		**-0.058014**

The covariance of Food Products Co. Inc.'s return with Poultry Farms Corp. is −.058. This suggests that the returns of the two firms move in opposite directions given cyclical and counter cyclical economic sensitivities. But, the expected return, standard deviation and covariance cannot be analyzed in isolation either, so we incorporate these statistics into aggrandized measures that establish the portfolio value of the merger. Let's assume each firm will contribute equal amounts to consolidated assets and sales. The expected return on this two-investment portfolio is:

1. $Rp = WaRa + WbRb,$

Where Wa is the investment weight of Food Products Co. Inc. (50%) and Wb represents the investment weight of Poultry Farms Corp. (50%). The weighted returns to investors of the combined entity becomes:

$Rp = 0.5(.2260) + 0.5(0.1140) = .170$

Recall earlier that Food Products Co. investors realized a pre-merger expected return of 22.6%. Post-merger return drops 5.6% to 17%. It is a strong possibility that FPCO stockholders will resist a merger with Poultry Farms Corp. unless their objective is to lower macroeconomic risk. In other words, FPCO shareholders may be willing to forgo high profits (or losses) in return for long-term stability. Let's carry this notion further.

The standard deviation of a two-investment portfolio is:

2. $\sigma p = [Wa^2\sigma a^2 + Wb^2\sigma b^2 + 2WaWb\ Cova,b]^{1/2}$

$\sigma p = [(.5^2)(.2389^2) + (.5^2)(.2436^2) + 2(.5)(.5)(-.058014)]^{1/2} = 0.010$

With a standard deviation of only 1%, the portfolio's risk has been reduced to near zero. Let's summarize the results:

	Stand Alone Return	Merged Return	Stand Alone Risk	Merged Risk
Food Products Co. Inc.	22.6%	17%	23.89%	1%
Poultry Farms Corp.	11.4%	17%	24.36%	1%

Poultry Farms Corp. shareholders are clear winners since the firm's increased returns are also accompanied by reduced risk. The banker is off and running, toasting the town as well, since a non-cyclical loan (Food Products along with its new acquisitions) has replaced a cyclical loan in his/her portfolio.

The correlation coefficient tidies up the covariance by translating it from absolute values to relative terms. That is, the correlation coefficient standardizes the covariance of Food Products' returns with Poultry Farms Corp. by dividing the covariance by the product of the two standard deviations, Food Products' and Poultry Farms Corp. The range of the correlation coefficient is + 1 and –1:

3. $Cov(Ra,Rb) = \rho ab\sigma a\sigma b$

Solving for the correlation coefficient:

4. $\rho ab = Cov(Ra,Rb)/\sigma a\sigma b$

In our example: Food Products Co. Inc. and Poultry Farms Corp.:

$\rho ab = -.058014/(.2389)(.2436) = -.997$

A correlation coefficient near + 1 suggests strong positive ties between two data points. A correlation coefficient close to –1 shows a strong negative relationship between the returns of Food Products Co. Inc. and Poultry Farms Corp. A correlation factor in and around zero means that there is little or no relationship between two sets of data. Note that $\rho ab = -.997$; the merger of the two companies nullifies the business cycle, reducing risk to zero. Notice—the correlation coefficient and the standard deviation of a two-investment portfolio give us identical answers.

But this exercise is not over just yet; additional challenges lie ahead. The reason for introducing the standard deviation, covariance, etc., is that we need them to grasp the Capital Asset Pricing Model (CAPM). But what does CAPM have to do with loan portfolio management? Doesn't CAPM provide equity investors with expected risk-return tradeoffs for individual securities? And for that matter, aren't banks and equity investors like two ships passing in the dark, since banks can only experience downside risk? The answers to these questions are: more than you think, yes and yes. CAPM opens the door to the Arbitrage Pricing Theory (APT).

APT measures sensitivities of investment portfolios to macroeconomic factors—identical constituents of loan portfolio management. Picture this: the sharp reduction in oil price (and capacity) affecting stockholders who invested their life savings in oil stocks also affects the bank whose entire loan portfolio is in Texas oil wells. A fundamental insight into the behavior of investors suggests that risk and return are intimately related. Financial markets exhibit risk aversion with investors demanding greater rates of return when they assume greater risk is involved, and vice versa. Therefore, to know what is an appropriate rate of return to demand on an investment, one must know its risk.

Financial theory defines risk as the uncertainty of the future returns of an investment. For example, a Treasury Bill held to maturity has little or no risk because there is virtually no chance of receiving anything other than the promised payout. By contrast, the stock of a high-technology firm is quite risky as the range of possible returns is expansive. Financial theory has also provided a variety of models of risk measurement, many of which are based on

statistical reasoning. Among these are models using the coefficient of variation and standard deviation of Net Present Value, which is measured directly or through a simulation process.

Back to the Capital Asset Pricing Model. The CAPM, the most popular risk model in a lifetime of financial models, argues that investments are held in portfolios, and therefore, the risk of an investment is its marginal risk impact on a well-diversified portfolio. Only part of the investment's total risk is relevant to the variability of the portfolio: the volatility of the investment with respect to the general economy. This portion, the systematic risk, is captured by the parameter "beta." The CAPM concludes that the appropriate rate of return on a security is the sum of the rate available on a riskless investment plus a premium for risk calculated as a function of the investment's beta. That is to say, in a competitive marketplace, investors require risk premium (Rj − Rf) in direct proportion to beta. This means investments people make fall along a sloping line called the Security Market Line (SML) (See Exhibit 20.2).

For example, an investment with a beta of .5 will generate half the expected risk premium, while investments having a beta of 2 will produce twice the expected risk premium. In a two-investment world, the covariance of the returns two securities generate is found. What we want to know is how two securities move with or against each other. If two securities move together, risk increases, as we would realize quite quickly if we put two eggs in a basket and then dropped the basket.

After calculating the covariance and correlation coefficient, we can derive the CAPM. The development of the CAPM begins with the relationship.

Exhibit 20.2

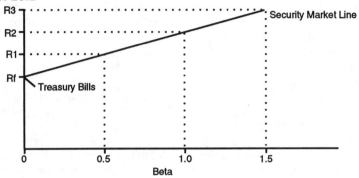

5. $Rj = Rf + \gamma\, Cov(Rj,Rm)$ where Rj = the rate of return demanded by investors of security j and Rf = the risk free or Treasury bill rate.

6. $\beta j = \dfrac{Cov(Rj,Rm)}{\sigma^2_m}$

Equation (6) tells us that the beta of asset j represents the covariance with market returns divided by a normalization factor: variance of market returns. Beta, one of the most important stats in business, measures systematic risk or the sensitivity to future market movements. There is now enough information to complete the derivation of the capital asset pricing model (CAPM):

7. $Rj = Rf + \gamma\, Cov(Rj,Rm)$, as before

where $\gamma = \dfrac{(Rm - Rf)}{\sigma^2_m}$

Substituting for γ in equation (5):

8. $Rj = Rf + (Rj - Rm)\, \dfrac{Cov(Rj\,Rm)}{\sigma^2_m}$

9. $Rj = Rf + (Rm - Rf)\beta j$

The Capital Asset Pricing Model (equation 9) suggests that the rate of return (Rj) on any common stock (from dividends and stock price appreciation), is less certain (i.e., riskier) than the relatively predictable returns available from U.S. government bonds (Rf). As compensation for the higher risk involved in owning common stock, investors demand a rate of return on stocks that is greater than the Risk Free Rate (Rf). Therefore, the rate of return on any stock is equal to the Risk Free Rate plus a "risk premium," $Rf + (Rm - Rf)\beta j$ for holding that stock rather than holding U.S. government bonds.[8] Betas listed in *Value Line Stock* have reports on file in most local libraries.

One factor systematic risk of stock "j" regressed with the market

$\beta = 1$: Stock "j" no more, no less volatile than market

$\beta > 1$: Stock "j" more volatile than market

$\beta < 1$: Stock "j" less volatile than market

---

8   The Alcar Group, Inc.

Example:

Determine the cost of equity capital (shareholders' required return) for the NS Group, traded on the NYSE:

- *Value Line* published a beta (βj) of .90 for NS Group with 1.00 = Market.
- Rf = .06 which is the current rate on 30-year government bonds.

Most analysts recommend using the current rate on long-term government bonds for the risk free rate. The Treasury bill rate is not generally used because the rate incorporates short-term expectations of less than 90 days. Long-term risk free rates factor in investors' expectations for inflation and interest rate fluctuations.

- The Market Risk Premium (Rm – Rf) is .068.

The market risk premium is the additional rate of return that must be paid over the risk-free rate to persuade investors to hold investments with systematic risk equal to the market portfolio.

The market risk premium is calculated by subtracting the expected long-term risk free rate from the expected market return. These figures should approximate future market conditions as closely as possible. There are two basic approaches to accomplish this goal:[9]

1. "Historical" or "ex-post" risk premium approach, which claims that past market returns are the best estimator of future market returns.

2. "Forecast" or "ex-ante" risk premium approach, which claims that current market information can be used to improve the accuracy of historically based estimates.[10]

The historical approach suggests that the market risk premium is stable over the long term and uses an arithmetic average of historical risk premiums—the difference between market returns and the returns on 20-year government bonds from 1926 until the present.

The other, more widespread approach, modifies historical estimates with present expectations of future stock market trends. The current yield curve is a valuable source of information about forecasted risk.

Thus, NS Group shareholders require a 12.1% return:

Rf = .06
(Rm-Rf) = .068.
(βj) of .90
$Rj = Rf + (Rm - Rf)\beta j = .06 + (.068).90 = .1212$

Now that CAPM has been examined, it's time to move on to Arbitrage Pricing Theory (APT).

Section Three: Portfolio Management: Economic (Systematic Risk) Analysis

Arbitrage Pricing Theory

While the CAPM is useful in analyzing a portfolio of securities, it has limited value in predicting the risk premium investors

---

9 Ibid.
10 Ibid.

will require of an individual firm not viewed in the context of a portfolio. This has created problems for financial managers and analysts who evaluate individual firms. A perfect example of such a scenario is a commercial banker completing a credit analysis.

Unable to apply modern finance theory, the banker must rely on more traditional methods of analysis. In practice, individual firms are measured by: (1) analyzing cash flow patterns, (2) financial ratios, and (3) pro forma financial statements. Cash flow patterns are a strong indicator of the firm's ability to generate and spend the money needed to run the business. Ratios are trended and compared to industry standards to get a sense of a firm's liquidity, financial leverage, and ability to use assets to generate sales and profits. Lastly, pro forma statements permit the analyst to gauge possible future paths and needs of the firm and to test the firm's sensitivity to assumptions about its economic and managerial environment. If only because of the availability and compelling logic of these analyses, it is unlikely that their use will diminish or be replaced by a CAPM based analysis.

Furthermore the CAPM has been criticized as being too simplistic. Prominent researchers have asserted that the CAPM is not testable because it requires a market index that is mean variance efficient. Such an index would have to include all assets, and therefore, its returns cannot be measured. In one well-known test of the CAPM performed by Fama and MacBeth in 1973, all NYSE stocks were grouped into 20 portfolios, plotting estimated betas of each portfolio. The resulting errors reduced CAPM's glitter as a predictive power tool:

$Rj = Rf + (Rm − Rf)βj + ej$ where ej represents errors in returns shareholders should be receiving

While actual returns in the Fama and MacBeth portfolios plot adjacent to the Security Market Line, returns do not plot exactly *on the line* (Exhibit 20.3)—and that's the key to the whole test! The implication is the CAPM provides investors with only a rough approximation of real markets.

In a well-known study of beta activity, Levy and Blume demonstrated that betas of individual stocks are unstable.

Exhibit 20.3

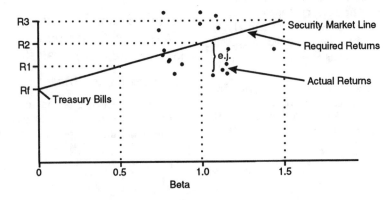

Hence, past betas are not necessarily good indicators of future risk. However, the betas of ten or more randomly selected stocks are more stable than individual betas because errors above the security market line tend to cancel errors below the line. Thus, in a portfolio context, while the capital asset pricing model is useful, it is only a one-factor model. Remember that beta is driven by one statistic: the volatility of the stock returns against the volatility of the market.

The Arbitrage Pricing Theory (APT) was developed by Richard Roll in 1976 and propagated from CAPM. APT assimilates a number of fundamental factors common to all securities, not just one (beta) to explain stock returns. Current APT research concentrates on multivariate statistical techniques such as factor analysis to decompose an investment's total return into separate pieces explainable by exogenous factors, each of which explains a unique amount of the variance of the investment's total returns. The fundamental factors are macroeconomic and include—but are not restricted to:

1. Industrial production (or the market portfolio)

2. Changes in a default risk premium (measured by the differences in promised yields to maturity on AAA versus Baa corporate bonds)

3. Twists in the yield curve (measured by the differences in promised yields to maturity on long- and short-term government bonds)

4. Unanticipated inflation

5. Changes in the real rate (measured by the Treasury bill rate minus the consumer price index)

The underlying variables of economic logic make sense. For instance, common stock prices represent the present value of discounted cash flows or how industrial production relates to profits. Other APT variables relate to the discount rate.

Because APT partitions economic factors, portfolios having disparate sensitivities to these systematic factors can be constructed. For example, a portfolio consisting of rental properties would be downside sensitive to unanticipated inflation, since rents can't be raised overnight to compensate for an unanticipated jump in oil prices. Choosing investments with upside sensitivities to unanticipated inflation would conceivably reduce the portfolio's risk. Thus, returns of securities are influenced by several principal factors that affect economy. Consider also:

■ Changes in these factors affect stock returns in several ways depending on how sensitive the stock's return is to each of these factors.

■ The sensitivity of a stock's return to a factor, i.e., interest rates, is the factor's beta. If three factors affect stock returns, there will be three factor sensitivities or factor betas.

■ In addition to these systematic factors, asset returns are affected by factors unique to the firm in question (unsystematic risk). However, if large portfolios are constructed, these risks cancel out through the process of diversification.

■ Multivariate statistical techniques such as factor analysis decompose an asset's total return into separate pieces, which explains a unique amount of the variance of the asset's total return.

The formula for the Arbitrage Pricing Model is:

$E(Rj) = Rf + \beta j_1 [E(R^1) - Rf] + \beta j^2 [E(R^2) - Rf] + \beta j_3 [E(R_3) - Rf]$

where:

$E(Rj)$ = Expected return on stock j

Rf = Risk free rate

βj_1 βj_2 βj_3 = sensitivities of stock j to factors 1, 2, 3

Factor 1 might be the stock's sensitivity to industrial production; factor 2 could easily represent sensitivity to changes in the default risk premium; while factor 3 may measure the stock's reaction to unanticipated inflation or twists in the yield curve.

$E(R_1)$ $E(R_2)$ $E(R_3)$ = Average returns on factors 1, 2, 3

Example:

Let's assume APT factor sensitivities on a particular security, stock k, are 1.3, 0.9 and -1.2 with factors 1, 2, and 3, respectively. Thus, $\beta k_1 = 1.3$; $\beta k_2 = 0.9$ and $\beta k_3 = -1.2$. Assume the average response to factors 1, 2, and 3 marketwide is 11%, 7%, and 3%, respectively. We can set $E(R_1) = 11\%$, $E(R_2) = 7\%$, $E(R_3) = 3\%$. Lastly let's set the long-term government bond rate Rf. = 6%. The expected return on stock k E(Rk) is:

$E(Rk) = .06 + 1.3 (.11 - .06) + 0.9 (.07 - .06) - 1.2 (.03 - .06) = 17.0\%$

Shareholders demand a return of 17.0%. But what return is "right" for banks electing to finance this business?

A Little Philosophy

While pricing issues are addressed in the loan pricing chapter, loan pricing in the context of portfolio management has never really been approached. Is modern portfolio theory even applicable to loan portfolio management? Good question. Although some bankers still argue in favor of time honored methods, more and more bankers think otherwise, working long hours to spark the metamorphosis in loan risk management.

Indeed, the academic work that underpinned Modern Portfolio Theory, the Capital Asset Pricing Theory and Arbitrage Pricing Theory was not readily accepted by the investment community for years. Many equity portfolio managers still resist strategies based on finance theory and quantitative analysis, perceiving a threat to their position in the decision making process. However, the continued popularity of index funds by institutions and mutual funds by individual investors is indicative of the declining value of "active" fund management. Does the situation in the banking industry parallel that of equity fund management ten years ago? If so, are the quantitative techniques described in this book transferable to the banking industry? Without a doubt the answer is yes, but the major barriers are not so much the technical challenges as they are the managerial challenges. Applications of advanced portfolio management techniques in the banking industry will require major changes in the role of key decision makers, such as calling officers and loan committee members.

Risk Analysis and Management of Bank Loan Portfolios[11]

A bank portfolio manager faces a higher magnitude of different risk/reward decisions than his counterpart in the equity markets. For example, most bank loans provide a fixed return to the lender over a fixed period that is dependent on interest rates and the borrower's ability to pay. A good loan will be repaid on time and in full. It's hoped that the bank's cost of funds will be low and permit attractive returns. If the borrower's business excels, the bank will not participate in upside growth (except for a vicarious pleasure in the firm's success.) However, if business failures result in loan defaults, the lender shares much, perhaps most of the pain. Limited upside risk and unlimited downside risk of bank lending were the cause of innumerable problems in the late 1980s.

One solution is to price "riskier" loans differently from "safe" loans. However, recurring overcapacity in the banking industry has made this difficult or nearly impossible, as we saw in the pricing chapter. Alas, if a bank wants to add to its book, it must be willing to compete with the low- bid banker who usually has the least understanding of risk. There is an inevitable organizational bias toward optimism. Unlike the stock market, few banks "bottom fish" by loaning to troubled companies—with the exception of Debtor in Possession (DIP) financing.

Traditional credit analysis has always focused on the borrower's financial risk more than the firm's sensitivity to macroeconomic events. The result is that

compensating for pricing is difficult and perhaps unrealistic. A perverse problem arises when a bank acquires superior origination skills in a particular region or industry. As a bank builds expertise, it usually increases exposure to that area in its loan portfolio. A portfolio of loans to various non-oil drilling companies in Oklahoma in the early 1980s suffered because these businesses depended on the dominant industry in the state. Likewise, a lender developing a niche in the motion picture industry will be vulnerable to cycles affecting that business. To sum it up, the lender is vulnerable to two disadvantages: pricing that does not compensate for risk and overconcentration in a region or industry. Portfolio management techniques can ameliorate some of these problems.

As we saw, Modern Portfolio Theory states that investors will be rewarded only for nondiversifiable risk. A portfolio composed of 100% ABC stock will be risky but the investor should only expect rewards that would accrue to a diversified ABC investor. Finance theory states that prices in the equity market are set by the diversified investor, not by the one who puts all the eggs in one basket. CAPM and APT postulate that the investor will be compensated only for the systematic risk that remains in his/her diversified portfolio. Given that an ABC position adds to a portfolio's exposure, if the economy surges, the investor can expect to outperform the market. A bank loan portfolio manager quickly realizes that there is *no reward for taking diversifiable risk.*

APT suggests that investors will be rewarded for accurately forecasting eco-

---

11 The author wishes to thank Andrew C. Robertson, president of Atlantic Systems, Inc., New York, for his invaluable assistance in developing the section on equity portfolio management.

nomic (systematic) events and positioning their equity portfolios accordingly. In the best scenario, the bank portfolio manager creates a portfolio with high spreads, low cost of funds and minimal defaults. In the worst case, the portfolio and the bank are under water. As the 1980s demonstrated, the worst case was often the most likely scenario. But clearly, banks took risks that were not priced appropriately. Even loans supported by superior credit analysis often defaulted because of damaging macroeconomic events and pricing pressure caused by overcapacity. Given that loans cannot be priced to adequately compensate for risk, it is appropriate to minimize risk through diversification. APT and related techniques can help bank managers identify those risks.

Risk Diversification

As we saw earlier, the principal benefit of advances in investment theory for bank management is risk reduction. This implies a commitment to diversification and risk measurement. Data from the equity markets can be used within APT-style models to quickly and accurately gauge concentrations of industry, geographic and systematic risk. Provided with the appropriate mandate, a portfolio manager can structure his or her bank's loans to diversify away as much risk as possible.

However, risk analysis of commercial loans can be quite difficult because there is little or no public information on the past or future economic sensitivities of most privately held companies. Therefore, it is usually necessary to use proxy companies from the bank's existing loan portfolio or the public equity markets to

calculate a company's risk profile. Below are steps that can be taken to calculate the systematic risk of individual companies and ultimately a bank's loan portfolio.[12]

Calculate Company Systematic Risk

1. If the company has publicly traded equity or debt, the price history should be analyzed using APT modeling techniques such as those explored by firms like Portex, a division of Piper Capital. Portex provides risk factors for several thousand firms in its data base. If the company's securities are lightly traded or closely held it may be necessary to calculate APT factors on a case by case basis. Several firms, such as Atlantic Systems, can assist the bank in this area.

2. In many cases, firms that were publicly traded before a leveraged transaction have price histories. These data may be helpful in understanding the company's reaction to past economic shocks such as the oil crisis of the 1970s. In most cases, it will be necessary to choose a proxy company or industry to estimate APT factors. For example, Mars Candy Bars can be expected to have economic sensitivities similar to those of Hershey or Nestle. We can use either company's APT risk factors or an average of all candy manufacturers.

3. Geographic concentration is rarely an issue that affects equity risks (exception: the effect of Hurricane Andrew on Florida companies in 1992). However, the location of a small company's operations can be

---

12 Atlantic Systems, Inc., New York, New York, published with permission.

critically important and should be considered as a systematic risk.

Aggregate Systematic Risk at the Portfolio Level

4. The end result of this exercise should be factored sensitivities for each company that can be applied to various APT risks outlined previously in Richard Ross' original model and more. Besides sensitivities to interest rates, inflation, and economic growth, macroeconomic factors may also include influences such as oil prices, investor confidence and geography. Certain regional banks may wish to calculate specific systematic risks pertinent to their market areas, e.g., peso devaluation in South Texas or earthquakes in California. These APT and specific systematic risk factors should be calculated or estimated for every current and prospective loan in the portfolio.

5. The weighted risk contribution of each loan should then be calculated. This requires an understanding of the company's capital structure and the position of the loan in the hierarchy of debt obligations. A simple way to weight these risks is to use the Debt to Equity ratio. For example, the APT risks of a loan to a

company with 95% debt and 5% equity should be valued at .95. In fact, the bank should consider this loan to be quasi equity. The risk contribution of a senior debenture to an established company with a strong balance sheet is much less than that of a bridge loan to a new highly leveraged company. Of course, the risks should also be weighted by absolute size as well.

6. A matrix showing the various factor risks, capital structures and loan sizes should be constructed using standard financial software such as Javelin. The total portfolio risk can be calculated using a weighted approach such as that outlined in Exhibit 20.4.

In the example, the portfolio consists of three loans to companies with widely varying risks and capital structures. While Sunshine Company is the most highly leveraged, its risk factors are below 1 or less than average. Acme and Zero are each particularly sensitive to a risk factor but because they represent smaller parts of the portfolio and their capital structures give the bank more protection, they contribute less risk to the overall portfolio. The loan portfolio's adjusted factors are below 1 or the market average as can be expected. This means the diver-

Exhibit 20.4

	Int. Rate Risk	Inflation Risk	Debt/Equity	Pct. of Portfolio	Adj. Int. Rate Risk	Adj. Inflation
Acme	1.2	2	50–50	10	.060	.100
Sunshine	.75	.8	90–10	60	.405	.432
Zero	2.0	.85	10–90	30	.060	.0255
Portfolio					**.525**	**.5575**

sified portfolio has no particular exposure to any single risk factor.

Eliminate Unwanted Factor Risk

7. Once the loan portfolio's risks have been identified, the banker should determine whether there are any factor risks that are over or under represented. A diversified portfolio should have equal risk exposure to all factor risks. If the factor risks approach 1 or the equity market average, the manager should realize that the portfolio is as risky as that of an equivalent stock portfolio. As noted previously, it is unlikely that the returns will compensate for the risk. The next task is to eliminate unwanted factor risks and to reduce the overall level of the risk. Reviewing individual loans applying simple sorting techniques will quickly flag the loans that contribute the most risk to the portfolio. This risk could be the result of high factor sensitivity or thin balance sheet protection. In either case, the manager should proceed to divest the most risky loans. Clearly, this implies a liquid market for the loans under question. If there is difficulty selling off these loans in the secondary market, another warning signal has been raised. Conversely, the manager should attempt to purchase loans in the secondary markets that have risk characteristics that are under represented in his portfolio.

8. APT tools can be used to quickly and accurately (as accurately as the current technology permits) diversify away systematic risk. APT data bases such as Portex's can be reviewed to identify firms or industries with factor risks opposite to those in the current portfolio. A more direct approach uses equity price data to spot companies that move counter to those in a portfolio. Exhibit 20.5 shows the performance of the big three automakers relative to the stock market between 1987 and 1992. It is obvious that the markets perceived problems for the auto makers well in advance of the 1990 recession. In addition, the markets also picked up the turn in the industrial economy in late 1991. Atlantic Systems uses customized APT technology to identify companies that are negatively correlated with auto stocks. Companies in the drug, food, cosmetics and apparel industries are typically least affected by recessions. The analysis also identified companies in the auto parts, paper and publishing industries that share the same risks as the auto industry.

The portfolio manager with a large exposure to the auto industry will avoid loans to companies in industries with risks that are highly correlated with autos and add loans to negatively correlated industries. However, he or she should be aware that risks change over time as do company's sensitivities to particular risks. The auto industry's problems in the late 1980s reflected sensitivity to GNP shocks, i.e., recession. However, the industry is also sensitive to interest rates and oil prices. If those economic factors become prevalent, a different set of industries must be identified to hedge unwanted macroeconomic risk.

If this process is successful, the resulting loan portfolio will have no particular exposure to any systematic risk and the overall risk will be low. Note that the projected profitability of a loan is not considered. We know that even a well-structured

Exhibit 20.5

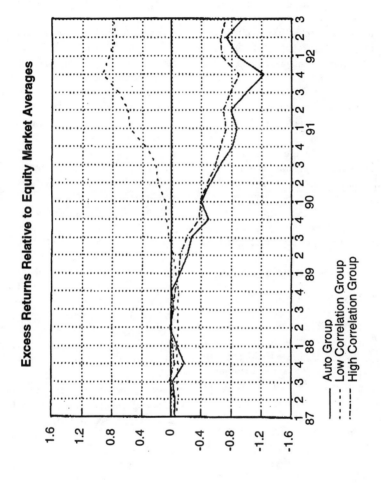

Excess Returns Relative to Equity Market Averages

loan can provide unwanted systematic risk. But if it is good paper, it should be easily and profitably sold in the secondary market. The portfolio management process also implies other changes in traditional lending practice. Most important, the functions of the portfolio manager and the loan officer should be separate to avoid obvious conflicts. Although applications of standard portfolio management techniques will require organizational change, the rewards will outweigh the risks.

Now that economic considerations in loan portfolio management have been addressed, the scope narrows further to industry analysis. Looking at industries, how does Chemical Banking Corporation use the resources of its industry specialists to reduce portfolio risk? Let's find out.

Section Four: Industry Analysis

An industry comprises companies with similar risk characteristics shaped by the nature of shared or closely related economic function. The economic function influences the industry life cycle, the rapidity of change, and the degree of capital intensity. Generally, competition within the industry greatly determines the success or failure of firms. Changes in the environment can have an impact on a broad range of companies within an industry. An industry's sensitivity to environmental or "systematic" factors, such as change in demand, regulations, taxation, and the cost of key inputs, periodically contributes to surges in business failures. Successful companies adapt their capital structure to suit the challenges of their industry and manage the uncertainty of future profitability. The industry of an obligor represents an important determinant of the credit risk.

Chemical Banking Corporation has established mechanisms to measure industry risk and to track industry concentrations. Industry Specialist/Market Intelligence Group, a unit of Risk Policy, focuses on industry risks within CBC's portfolio. Industry specialists are experienced in the industry they follow. They analyze all aspects of business conditions within their industry to develop a well-balanced perspective on success criteria. Industry specialists work closely with the line to shape the industry portfolio by originating attractive business. They also advise senior management on the prospective performance of the existing portfolio—key to reducing overall risk exposure.

Industry specialists' analysis of the future outlook in an industry is reflected in the Industry Grade. Industries are broken down into *portfolio categories for risk analysis*. Common SIC codes are grouped to create industry subsegments which roll into major Macro Industry grouping. Different industry subsegments have different risk/reward characteristics. Industry grades are assigned on a medium-term basis (five years) and range from one to ten. An industry grade of one is reserved for industries with clearly outstanding performance while grades seven through ten represent industries with significant to severe long-term problems.

The assessments by industry specialists play an important role in individual company risk grading. Account officers should evaluate the financial performance of a customer or prospect within the context of its peer or industry group. This evaluation must reflect industry risk. The industry grade, provided by the industry specialists, combined with an assessment of the obligor's competitive tier, provides a reference point for risk grading. Finally industry and macroeconomic factors coalesce in loan portfolio administration.[13]

Industry Characteristics

Emerging Phase

Key Words: Technology and Production

Product: New products with a technological edge. Product significantly improves customer's situation by reducing labor or other input costs or improving standard of living. Emphasis is on developing the production capabilities that bring the technology to market in volume and at a price that makes it viable.

Management: Very technologically- or engineering- or detail-oriented. Hands on management with a very centralized reporting structure.

Financing: Initially from management resources or venture capital. Later in this phase, some banks and stock underwriters enter the picture. Critical bottleneck.

Distribution: Limited by production capabilities. Tend to use outside distributors.

Regulation: Incidental or generic to general legislation.

M & A: Some astute large firms acquire firms operating in this phase to gain access to patent or technology skills.

Growth Phase

Key Words: Marketing and Distribution

Product: Emphasis is now on adding bells and whistles to the basic product in order to enhance market appeal and to distinguish the product from an increasing number of imitators, and to reach into new markets.

Management: Focus shifts from technological, entrepreneurial qualities of the founding fathers to the executives (probably outside hires) with marketing and financial skills.

Financing: At this phase, internal capital growth rates are good, ROE is good, outside funds can be acquired from stock markets and/or banks. But, outside lenders place a financial reporting discipline on these companies.

Distribution: Emphasis shifts from outside distributors to internally controlled sales and distribution organizations.

Regulation: As these companies get more into the public realm, SEC regulations come into play. Also a body of case law emerges which has a quasi-regulatory influence. Oftentimes, specific legislation regulating or governing the product begins to emerge.

M & A: M & A picks up, particularly on a horizontal basis, as companies seek distribution capability (market share). Occasionally vertical acquisitions to protect availability or price of raw materials or components.

Mature Phase

Key Words: Price Competition and Cost Cutting

---

13 Provided by Chemical Bank. Reprinted with permission.

Product: Technologically well established, markets saturated, long-term growth in line with general economy. Companies compete for market share on price basis

Management: Old management reflects hereditary culture, usually clubby in nature by now. Difficult to do cost cutting necessary to maintain at least average ROE. In the emerging phase; production was the management goal, in the growth phase; distribution was the goal, in the mature phase; management of the corporation itself becomes the goal.

Financing: Price earnings ratio is down; therefore, the equity market is less attractive to the company. Because of increased size and long-term operating records, debt markets are still open. Generally, reduced need for financing.

Distribution: Smart management is trying to add-on related products with higher margins to utilize distribution network.

Regulation: Nuisance level. Regulatory cultures change even more slowly than corporate cultures.

M & A: M & A activity takes place with a view to (1) reduce administrative costs (2) more fully utilize production and distribution capacity and/or (3) acquire emerging companies.

Industry Grades

General Comments

■ Factor grades should be assigned based on long-term industry trends.

Historical results should include at least one full business cycle and, where possible, the outlook should cover four to seven years.

■ Grades for factors are assigned on a one to ten scale in the same manner as credit grades. In assigning grades, the industry should be compared to the typical or average industry, which would be graded four. Grade one is reserved for outstanding performance on a given factor, and grades seven through ten represent significant to severe long-term problems.

■ The comments section explains the indicators used (e.g., asset growth versus revenue growth), or articulates issues relating to a particular factor. If an industry segment performs differently on many factors compared with the broader industry definition, it should be graded separately.

Definitions and Guidelines for Using the Industry Grade Worksheet

■ **Market growth rate** may be measured using any indicator relevant to the industry, including revenues, units shipped or produced, and assets. Appropriate benchmarks include real GNP growth, PCE (consumer spending), and S&P 500 growth. Long-term growth trend equal to the benchmark would indicate a grade of four. Long-term shrinkage should be graded seven through ten.

■ **Cyclicality** should be compared to a benchmark consistent with that used above, such as real GNP growth, and should consider both industry-specific cycles and economic cycles.

■ **Entry barriers** include economies of scale and other cost advantages, capital requirements/intensity, product differentiation, access to distribution channels, and regulations.

■ **Competitor rivalry** includes several factors:

• **Competitor mix**, or homogeneity versus diversity. Competition is generally high among companies with the same structure or strategic stakes, and it is generally lower when competitors have a different structure or focus. However, similarities among competitors may allow them to better understand and anticipate competitors' strategies, reducing the likelihood of retaliatory moves.

• **Competitor number.** A concentrated industry generally enjoys reduced competitor rivalry through price leadership and/or pricing stability.

• **Production Differention** reduces pricing volatility and increases profits.

• **Market share stability** occurs in more mature markets' volatility is most intense following deregulation.

• **Changes in the nature of geographic competition** tend to destabilize an industry and increase competition. Industries that are in the process of globalizing generally become more competitive. Note, however, industries that are already global may be stable and are not necessarily more competitive than regional industries.

• **Pricing volatility** may result from extreme reactions to overcapacity. These reactions are often seen in industries with high fixed costs or high exit barriers.

■ **Substitution threat** considers alternative products and the threat of product obsolescence.

■ **Buyer power** is high (a poor factor grade) if the industry's customers are concentrated (i.e., less numerous more homogeneous, or larger) relative to firms in the industry, or if customers' purchase volume is high. Price sensitivity measures the industry's ability to pass along price changes.

■ **Supplier power** is the opposite of buyer power, and the same factors should be considered. This should be defined as suppliers of raw materials, capital, and labor. Availability should also be considered as a key factor.

Industry Tier Position

Tiering in an industry/industry segment is specific to the industry and should reflect a company's medium to long-term competitive position relative to its peers. The factors used to determine tier position may be quantitative or qualitative. Among the factors which could be used to evaluate a company's tier position are:

■ Market share (dominant share)
■ Pricing
  • Price leadership
  • Product differentiation/premium pricing
■ Cost Structure
  • labor cost
  • material cost
  • capital intensity
  • economies of scale
  • technological advantages/disadvantages
  • operating leverage
■ Managerial Skills
  • Industry reputation, expertise
  • Marketing ability
  • Long-term strategic focus

■ Financial
  • Cash flow measures
  • Debt levels, coverages
  • Profitability measures
  • Other industry-specific perform-
    ance ratios
■ Miscellaneous
  • Diversification/Concentration
  • Divestiture/Acquisitions
  • Contingent liabilities and other off-
    balance sheet obligations

Section Five: Implementing Portfolio Management: Loan Sales and Securitization

Conventional Loan Sales

Until recently, banks expanded by making loans and keeping them on their books until borrowers paid them off. Now they are reversing course and getting loans off their books by selling them.

Loan sales provide a valuable risk management tool, particularly in minimizing portfolio risk through diversification. From the standpoint of smaller banks, buying portions of loans made by larger banks has two advantages: (1) it improves portfolio diversification, and (2) earns a higher rate of return than could be obtained on the sale of federal funds, investing in commercial paper or government securities with comparable maturities. Loan sales also allow management to control the overall size of the bank. Other advantages include:

■ Loan sales provide increased return on assets by reducing assets on the bank's balance sheet and providing more fee-generated income.

■ Capital/Asset ratios are examined closely as banks are limited by asset growth and legal lending limits.

■ As a form of risk management, loan sales allow banks to originate large commitments and sell them down to end with relatively small commitments.

■ As a fee generator, loan sales provide greater than proportional up-front fees on the bank's net commitment.

■ Loan sales enable banks to tap a wider investment base.

While loan sales have not changed that much over the past few years, there have been some significant modifications in the nature of many of the credits being sold. Particular emphasis has been placed on approving loans to quality borrowers for very short or relatively long maturities with the clear intent of selling all, or virtually all, of these loans in the marketplace.

Short-term investments consist of under 90 day paper executed by investment grade or high-quality, non-rated borrowers, or "strips" of revolving credits to this same class of borrower. Yields are thin, usually a small basis point spread between these investments and government securities.

Medium-term investments are referred to as loan sales involving underlying transactions greater than one year with both investment grade and non-investment grade transactions. These investments generally require a fully documented credit facility. Medium term loan sales usually carry an attractive rate of interest. These types of loan participations are referred to by the investment bankers as "story paper," since the loans do not carry a national credit rating and must be "reviewed" prior to purchase. Bankers who buy paper with only a story attached are playing the game at their own risk. Clearly, the responsibility of analysis and credit investigation rests upon the investor. The loan sale mechanism includes:

Syndication: Investors commit to a primary position in a transaction prior to closing. Syndication may represent distribution of either a "best effort" syndication amount or an underwritten syndication amount. The deal sponsor provides the structure and runs his/her own analysis. The syndication process may include the following arrangement:

Suppose the borrower wants to raise $100 million with Bank A as agent (See Exhibit 20.6).

In the example, Bank A will negotiate the documents with the borrower and then solicit a group of investors offering them pieces of the $100 million loan, $20 million each.

The key issues from the borrower's perspective:

- Speed and simplicity
- The participating banks negotiate one document, not four
- The lead bank acts as agent/intermediary with the other banks
- Pricing tends to be more aggressive
- The arrangement eliminates market risk

The key issues from the agent bank's perspective:

- Bank A continues to maintain a senior relationship with the borrower
- The bank has its points represented in all of the loan documentation
- The bank is rewarded with an upfront fee

Novation. (Exhibit 20.7) Novation involves an assignment by the seller (originating bank) to the buyer, whereby the borrower has consented, of all seller rights and responsibilities to the borrower. The seller is released from its responsibilities

---

Exhibit 20.6

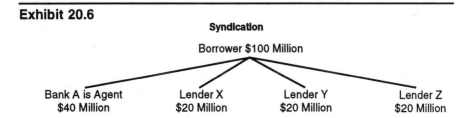

Syndication

Borrower $100 Million

| Bank A is Agent | Lender X | Lender Y | Lender Z |
| $40 Million | $20 Million | $20 Million | $20 Million |

Stated Terms
　Lien on assets or negative pledge
　Financial performance to be met
　Pricing: LIBOR or Prime or CD plus spread
　Up front fee
　Description of syndication process
　Underwriting fee

Exhibit 20.7

Novation

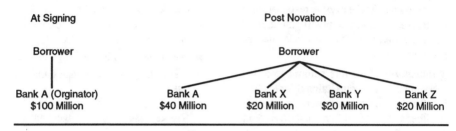

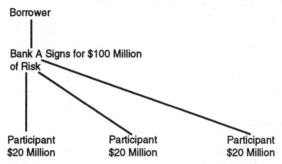

and the buyer (investor) is situated as if it were an original signing party to the loan agreement. Overseas, a novation is commonly accomplished through a Transferable Loan Certificate.

Participation. An agreement whereby a selling bank transfers to investors the right to receive a pro rata share of the payments from the borrower. Generally, a participation imposes limitations on the rights of a seller to agree, without buyer approval, to changes in principal, interest, payment schedule, collateral, guarantors, and possibly advance rate formula. Such an arrangement, which does not transfer voting rights, is generally completed without the borrower's direct approval.

Up-front fees. Originating banks receive higher than proportional up-front fees illustrated by the following example (Exhibit 20.8).

Assume the deal called for a $500 million exposure carrying 1% up-front fee. If the bank kept the loan in portfolio, it

Exhibit 20.8

Up-Front Fees
(In Millions)

Banks	Amount	Total	Fee	Fee Income
Six Banks	$50,000	$300,000	1%	$3,000
Six Banks	$25,000	$150,000	3/4%	$1,125
Bank A (Hold)	$50,000	$50,000	1.75%	$875
Total		$500,000		$5,000

would earn $5 million: $500 million (1%) = $5 million. Selling parts of the loan will reduce the bank's investment. However, generated income will increase to 1.75%.

Definitions

Following are common definitions encountered in loan sale activities:

- **Underwritten Amount:** The amount which the bank formally "commits" to a transaction. This is the amount for which the bank is at economic risk and for which it must sign if syndication is not completed.

- **Downstream Correspondent Bank:** Usually refers to small or medium size banks that purchase loan participations from larger regional banks.

- **Best Efforts Syndication Amount:** The difference, if any, between the total facility amount and the selling bank commitment amount. Generally, risks with respect to syndication amount relate to reputation risk and/or arrangement/syndication fees. The seller performance is on a best efforts basis.

- **Repo Clause:** An agreement in which the seller of a participation promises to repurchase the participation at a higher price on a specific date.

- **Resyndication:** Process undertaken when one or more banks underwrite an entire loan and then syndicate to a group of primary lenders.

- **Underwriting Liability:** The general reference to any seller liability to the buyer arising before, during, or slightly after the completion of a loan sale transaction. Risks generally relate to misrepresentation and/or non-disclosure of information.

- **Latent Liability:** The general reference to any ongoing seller liability to the buyer arising from either underwriting liability or from ongoing seller responsibilities to the buyer.

- **Bid Loan:** A loan to a borrower for a particular maturity date and generally for an absolute interest rate.

- **Loan Part:** The commonly used term in the investor marketplace for the economic transaction in which an investor purchases a participation in a bid note or a grid bid note.

- **Skim/Scalp:** The part of a loan's yield that sellers of participations retain for their own profit.

- **Competitive Bid Option:** When a borrowing company wishes to draw all or part of its funds under an existing loan, it puts that piece of the credit up for bid among the primary syndicate members. The bank bidding lowest wins the right to finance that piece.

- **Drop Dead Fee:** A fee paid by a borrower to compensate lenders for committing funds to finance a takeover bid that never takes place.

- **Upstream Correspondent Bank:** Refers to money centers and other major banks that sell loan participations to regional banks.

- **Signing Amount:** The amount for which the originator or seller bank intends to sign. The amount may be no more than the originator bank commitment amount nor less than the portfolio hold amount and is most often between those amounts.

- **Strips:** The sale to investors of specific rollovers under a committed credit facility, the duration of which is longer than the specific rollover (e.g., a 30 advance under a 3 year revolving credit).

Securitization

Securitization is a prominent form of loan sale in which securities are backed by pools of mortgage loans, auto loans, credit card balances, boat loans, computer equipment leases, airplane leases, high yield bonds, life insurance policy loans, and commercial real estate loans, among other types of collateral. The key to securitization is finding assets on a company's books that generate a predictable cash flow stream—like loans.

The securitized loans are relatively homogenous as to rates, terms, and collateral. A commercial bank, or its subsidiary, would book car loans and sell the loans to another entity, which would form them into a loan pool. The pool retains the loans as collateral for its own obligations which, in turn, would be sold to the third-party buyers. Typically, an investment banker would structure the deal and the originating bank, or its subsidiary, would continue to service the loans.

Most asset-backed securities are not issued by banks, but by limited purpose entities (such as trusts or single-purpose corporations) created by the banks. The bank sells the loans to the issuing entity, the issuer sells securities backed by the pool of loans to investors and pays the bank for the purchased loans with the proceeds from the sales of the securities. The bank usually retains the right to service the loans for the issuer of the securities—for a fee. If the transactions pass certain legal and accounting tests, they are considered to be a true sale of assets from the originator of the loans to the issuer of the securities.

Originators of asset-backed securities usually want to sell loans without recourse. Thus, three methods generally protect investors: overcollateralization, senior/subordinated structures and, credit enhancement. Overcollateralization simply involves collateral whereby scheduled cash flow exceeds the cash flow needed to pay principal and interest on the securities. As long as the actual losses in the collateral pool are less than the excess cash flow built into the collateral pool, there should be enough cash flow to make all required payments to investors.

In the senior/subordinated structure, the issuer of a passthrough security sells two distinct classes of certificates, both of which are secured by the single pool of collateral. The senior certificates are offered to investors, whereas the subordinated certificates are usually purchased by the originator. At the time the senior and subordinated certificates are issued, the scheduled cash flow from the collateral pool must be enough to support the scheduled principal and interest on both the senior and junior certificates. However, the cash flow from the collateral is allocated first to pay principal and interest to the owners of the senior certificates. The holders of the subordinated certificates only receive payments from cash flow above and beyond that needed to pay the senior certificate holders. As long as actual losses in the collateral pool do not exceed the scheduled payments on the subordinated certificates, there should be enough cash flow to pay the senior certificate holders. The larger the subordinated class relative to the total issue, the greater the protection for the senior class holders.

Asset-backed securities can be enhanced by a letter of credit which the issuing entity draws upon to cover losses in the collateral. The letter of credit is obtained from a bank (other than the originating bank) or insurance company. Typically, credit enhancement covers a certain percentage of first loss on the total pool. This is at a level comparable to historical losses, plus a margin. Banks receive fees for providing a letter of credit (as long as they are not the originator) which adds to the bank's income.

Below are key reasons why securitization can (1) improve a bank's loan portfolio and (2) produce additional fee-based income.

Liquidity Traditional credit produces illiquid assets. There is presently no secondary market for most commercial loans, and banks can do little to adjust their portfolios to changing interest rates or market conditions. Securitization provides the necessary liquidity for such adjustments.

Credit Risk The traditional credit system concentrates credit risk both geographically and within weak institutions. Banks can geographically diversify their portfolios by purchasing securitized credit from all parts of the nation. In a properly structured securitized credit transaction, credit risk is spread among the originator, a credit enhancer (either another commercial bank, foreign bank, or insurance company) and the investor.

Interest Risk Commercial banks are highly sensitive to interest rate risk. Securitization places that risk with investors more willing and able to take such risk, such as pension funds, insurance companies, and mutual funds. A securitized credit system allows banks to offer fixed rate loans and to choose whether to take the interest risk.

Money Velocity and Earnings Banks can improve their profitability through the increased velocity of money flowing through the bank:

- Banks earn fees from issuing entities for servicing
- Securitized loans and issuing letters of credit
- Reduced costs and thorough management of a smaller and more diversified loan portfolio

Developments

As part of President Clinton's program for spurring lending to low-income communities, the Senate Banking Committee included provisions drafted by Senator Alfonse D'Amato of New York to create a secondary market in which small business loans can be bundled and resold similar to the way home mortgages are treated. The conviction is that banks will be more consenting to small business loans if they can sell some of the loans to investors thereby improving asset productivity, profitability, and diversifying credit risk.

Reflections

Portfolio risk management is new to some in the banking industry and it's continuously evolving and may never be perfect. But there is little doubt that stepping beyond timeworn loan analytics is a priority issue if lenders are to revitalize the industry and survive. In the words of Wall Street legend Henry Kaufman, "Change is always very difficult to accept, but change is the essence of life."

CHAPTER *Twenty-One*

Credit Risk Grading

Risk grading systems generally fall into one of four structural categories: Dual System Strategies, Highly Decentralized, Au Fond Decentralized and Centralized. These are defined as follows:

Dual System Strategies: This is a dual approval structure which acts as the backbone of the credit process. DSS segregates the loan administration operations from the origination function. By doing so, there can be a dual credit structure in each unit separate from origination. Each business unit has senior credit officers, a credit department, and industry specialists who authorize and monitor the relationship. A tightly controlled credit process, DSS involves both line and credit groups in credit evaluation and monitoring and is propelled by the credit staff.

Highly Decentralized: This type of structure entrusts line officers with lending authority and assumes that sound credit policies and procedures are firmly entrenched. Line officers are required to follow policy and must have expertise in the

process and corroboration of risk grading. Highly decentralized institutions are sensitive to market opportunities and encourage judicious risk taking. As loan amounts increase in size, higher levels of approval are a prerequisite. In highly decentralized structures, the line, not the credit staff, drives the bank.

Au Fond Decentralized: This structure runs parallel to a highly decentralized structure with the exception that some banks may include an additional structure whose responsibility is to administer policy guidelines from the underwriting process to the end of the loan. Au fond decentralized structures assign a senior credit policy officer to each lending unit.

Centralized: More commonly found in regional banks, lending authority is delegated to a loan committee. Account officers do not have approval limits in a centralized structure. Other attributes include a low level of procedures and controls and underwriting standards. The tendency with centralized structures may be in the direction of safe, low-margin loans.

It is important to note that the current trend is away from the centralized structure. And, no matter what the structure, credit risk grading should follow a systematic process.

The Risk Grading Process[1]

A risk rating system evaluates and tracks risk on individual transactions and relationships on a continuous basis. More important, it also enables the bank to track and manage risk within the portfolio as a whole.

The principles underlying a risk rating system are as follows:

■ A common framework for assessing risk

■ Uniformity throughout the bank's units, divisions, and affiliates

■ Compatibility to regulatory definitions, which distinguish various levels of "Poor" credit risk

■ The ability to distinguish various levels of "Satisfactory" credit risk

■ Common training through expanded definitions and risk-rating guides

■ Initiation and maintenance of ratings on a continuous basis

■ Review of these ratings by the bank's credit audit department to test for accuracy, consistency, and timeliness

A bank's risk rating system is, critically, a judgmental one. The skill and experience of the lending personnel and credit people are vital to accurately assessing risk.

The rating system will also be helpful in setting rates and/or fees commensurate with the risk level, as well as in determining the degree of lending officer service and monitoring required. Ratings indicating a high level of risk will drive managerial and accounting actions.

Credit Risk-Grading: Risk Defined

Webster defines risk as the "possibility of loss or injury." For credit purposes, RISK is defined as the degree of possibility that a loss will be sustained in a loan or investment. A commercial loan exposes the bank to two types of risk: Creditworthiness or Borrower Risks and Activity or Transaction Risks. Borrower Risk stems from *industry economic risks, industry structure risks, customer-specific risks, and the ever-present operating risks* inherent in the lending business. Transaction Risks are risks inherent in an *instrument or facility.*

Borrower Risk

■ **Industry Economic Risk** refers to the level of high energy inflation risk or foreign exchange risk present in the environment in which a company operates. If a bank feels these risk levels are unacceptable, it might sell the loans or acquire other loans that are less exposed to these forces, thus reducing the risk of the portfolio.

■ **Industry Structure Risk** is the risk inherent in a company's business environment. These risks have unique characteristics such as concentration ratios, exit or entry barriers, the power of suppliers or customers, the

1   The remainder of this chapter was written by the author and Jeffrey J. Bottari, vice president of First Fidelity Bancorporation, Lawrenceville, New Jersey. The author wishes to thank First Fidelity Bancorporation for the exhibits the bank kindly furnished. The Risk Grading Exhibits are the property of First Fidelity Bancorporation, Lawrenceville, New Jersey.

impact of technology, regulation, taxes, and capital intensity.

- **Customer Specific Risk** refers to the PRISM components of credit previously discussed at the beginning of this book.

- **Operating Risk** refers to a borrower possibly becoming insolvent and being unable to repay his loan. Other considerations are the chances of error and fraud. In middle market lending, some of these risks, once identified, should not change. Others are highly recast-dependent and must be closely watched.

Transaction Risks

- Instrument/Facility Risk refers to the risks inherent in an individual facility (commitment or loan). This includes the risk inherent in the credit product itself, the tenor/maturity (long versus short) of the facility, terms and agreements, and collateral and support. For example, fixed rate term loans expose the bank to a very real basic risk should interest rates change and the bank be mismatched. Revolving credits expose a bank's balance sheet to implicit call options for which a bank is rarely compensated.

STEPS OF RISK RATING

Conceptually, the rating system begins with the risk of the BORROWER itself, then adds the risks of the particular transaction variables which would increase or decrease the risk such as collateral, guarantees, terms, or tenor. The risk rating is the "key" rating, as it is the risk of the facility or transaction. A single borrower would have only one borrower rating but might have several different facilities with different Risk Ratings, depending on

terms, collateral, etc. See Exhibit 21.1 at the end of this chapter for an example of the flow from Borrower Rating to Risk Rating.

The Borrower Rating

The borrower rating is a measure of risk based on the historical, current and especially anticipated financial characteristics of the borrower. in arriving at the Borrower Rating, consideration should be given to:

a. **Industry and Operating Environment**
  - Does the borrower operate in a strong and growing industry?
  - Is the borrower a significant factor in the industry or market?
  - Are legal or regulatory climates favorable?

b. **Earnings and Operating Cash Flow**
  - Are earnings stable, growing, and of high quality?
  - Are margins solid?
  - Is operating cash flow strong in relation to present and anticipated debt?

c. **Asset and Liability Structure**
  - Are assets solid and fairly valued?
  - Does the liability structure match the asset structure?
  - Are there few or no intangibles?
  - Are we lending where the assets are and do we have access to them?
  - Are we avoiding holding companies or effectively subordinated positions?

d. **Debt Capacity**
  - Is leverage low?
  - What alternative sources of debt and capital exist?

e. **Management and Controls**
 * Is management capable, now and for the foreseeable future?
 * Are strong operating and financial controls in place?

f. **Financial Controls**
 * Is an audit regularly done by a reputable firm?
 * Are financial reports promptly issued?
 * Are they accurate and complete?

Many large commercial banks use a scale of 1 through 10 when assessing borrower risk. A Borrower Rating of 1 is "Substantially Risk Free," while a Borrower Rating of 10 is a "Loss." See Exhibit 21.2 at the end of the chapter for definitions of risk levels.

Risk Rating

The Risk Rating is an index of risk intended to reflect the collectability of a specific credit extension in accordance with its terms. Thus, each facility extended to a customer will carry its own risk rating. It is the risk of the particular facility or transaction to a particular borrower. It attaches to the facility (commitment or loan) and all drawdowns under the facility carry the same risk rating.

The facility Risk Rating may be better or worse than the Borrower Rating due to the existence of collateral, guarantees, unusual terms, etc. For example, if a loan is unsecured, the collectability of the loan is primarily a function of the factors considered in assigning the Borrower Rating, and most often the Risk Rating will be the same as the Borrower Rating.

Situations will arise, however, where there are other positive or negative factors of sufficient significance to materially im-

pact on the risk and collectability of the loan and, accordingly, are reflected in the Risk Rating. In such situations, these factors "adjust" the "risk" represented by the Borrower Rating. The Borrower Rating, however, is not affected by these factors and therefore is not changed.

Not too wide a spread should exist between the borrower rating and the risk rating. There may be exceptions. The risk rating is directly impacted by the borrower rating. While the collateral pledged probably improves one's ability to obtain cash to repay the loan from liquidation, we are still looking to the borrower to repay us from operating cash flow. Exceptions exist and a two-level spread may provide the bank with comfort and control in case of liquidation.

There are possible positive and negative variables that could impact a particular loan or credit facility. Some of the more common factors are collateral, ownership, guarantees or support, unusual terms or tenor, subordinated position, and country risk.

COLLATERAL

Collateral is property pledged as security for the satisfaction of a debt or other obligation.

The Risk Rating assigned to secured loans will depend upon the degree of coverage, the economic life cycle of the collateral versus the term of the loan, possible constraints of liquidating the collateral, and the lender's ability to skillfully and economically monitor and liquidate the collateral.

With collateral, three basic issues must be evaluated:

1. What is its value compared to credit exposure?

2. What is its liquidity, or how quickly may its value be realized and with what certainty?

3. What demonstrated legal right does the bank have to the collateral?

Strong collateral support is dependent upon all three.

Example: Hitech Corporation is a manufacturer of high-capacity disk drives. The bank extends a $15 million line of credit secured by accounts receivable, inventory, and equipment. The company has suffered substantial losses over the last three years due to price reductions from its major competitors. The company is leveraged 2.5 times, meaning the debt to equity ratio is 250%. Due to losses, extreme competition in the industry, and its leverage position, a borrower rating of 9 is warranted.

Our line, secured by accounts receivable, equipment, and inventory is on a controlled basis. Advances are made based on 70% of eligible downstream receivables, 40% of foreign receivables, and 70% against the knockdown value of the equipment. Collections are controlled by lock box, and agings are received monthly with on site audits at least three times a year. Turnover of receivables is 55 days.

Due to advances being on a controlled basis, a risk rating of 6 is warranted.

Ownership

The Risk Rating to be given as a result of ownership is subject to many factors. If the borrower is a 100% owned subsidiary and an integral part of a prime name, the investment by the parent is substantial in relation to the borrower's debt. This would have a positive effect on the Risk Rating, if the bank is confident that the parent company will support the subsidiary.

Example: Johnson Securities is a regional broker/dealer which is a wholly owned subsidiary of National Mutual Life Insurance Company. Although Johnson Securities is a profitable, sound broker/dealer, the industry has shown signs of weakening. The bank extends a $10 million secured broker's line and a $5 million unsecured short-term line of credit.

Johnson is well capitalized and continues to maintain capital above SEC requirements. For the nine-month period ending 12/31/89, Johnson had excess net capital of $39 million. Net income for the nine-month period ending 12/31/89 totaled $11.7 million compared to $11.0 million in the prior period and $11.4 million for FYE 3/31/89. Revenues of $179 million are up 18% from the previous period.

National Mutual has over $4 billion in assets and carries an A+ rating from Best, signifying solid financial condition. Additionally, National Mutual has the capacity to provide additional financial resources, if necessary.

The facilities are short term in nature and although unsecured, our risk is minimized by the collateral that Johnson holds as a result of their strict margin requirements. Based on this, borrower and risk ratings are as follows:

Secured Line:
    Suggested Borrower Rating 5
    Suggested Risk Rating 4

Unsecured Line:
    Suggested Borrower Rating 5
    Suggested Risk Rating 6

Guarantees or Support

A **Guaranty** is a written contract, agreement, or undertaking involving three parties. The first party, the **guarantor**, agrees to see that the performance of the second party, the **guarantee**, is fulfilled according to the terms of the contract, agreement, or undertaking. The third party is the **creditor**, or the party to benefit by the performance. For example: Party B makes a loan through his bank. The bank desires a guarantor for this loan in case of default by B. B asks A to act as guarantor. A agrees and signs a Guaranty Agreement. A is the Guarantor, B is the Guarantee, and the bank is the creditor.

The Risk Rating assigned to loans supported by third-party undertakings will lie somewhere between the Borrower Rating and the Borrower Rating which would be assigned to the party issuing the undertaking were this party the borrower. The "where" will depend upon the nature of the undertaking. Unconditional guarantees of payment will have considerably more impact than will a non-guarantee such as comfort letters or "verbal assurances."

Example: The bank issued a $5 million unsecured term loan to Wilson and Smith to refinance long-term notes issued by Olive Baking Company in conjunction with Wilson and Smith's 1987 acquisition of Southern Type and Supply Company.

Wilson and Smith, a wholly owned subsidiary of the Olive Baking Company since 1965, is a wholesale distributor of graphic art supplies, equipment, and chemicals to the printing industry. For Year End 1988, Wilson and Smith contributed 47% of Olive's consolidated revenues and 22% of its net income. For the nine-month period ended 9/30/89, Wilson and Smith's sales increased 6.7% from the prior period to $98.9 million. The higher sales volume combined with consistent gross margins and continued control of operating expenses resulted in net income of $2.3 million compared to $1.4 million at 9/30/89. These trends were expected to continue

given the company's emphasis on maintaining margins and improving profitability.

Olive Baking Company was incorporated in 1914 as a baking company specializing in single portion pies, cakes and cookies. Olive purchased Wilson and Smith in 1965 for diversification purposes. On a consolidated basis, total revenues and net income for FY 1988 were $246 million and $9.5 million, respectively. For the nine-month interim ended 9/30/89, consolidated revenues were $204 million and net income was $7.4 million, up 5% and 9% respectively when compared to the similar period during FY 1988.

While both companies have performed consistently, Olive Baking remains the stronger of the two, both on a balance sheet and profit and loss basis. On a consolidated basis, the company displays strong interest coverage, adequate debt service capacity and a satisfactory leverage position. In addition, the $5 million unsecured term loan to Wilson and Smith is guaranteed by Olive Baking Company. Historically, Olive has generated sufficient cash flow to meet current maturities and payments of dividends. Cash flow from operations coupled with short-term borrowings are used to fund capital expenditures.

Suggested Borrower Rating 5
Suggested Parent Rating 4
Suggested Risk Rating 4

Unusual Terms or Tenor

For various reasons, a bank may extend credit on terms or for a tenor (time period/maturity) that for a given borrower subjects the bank to a greater level of risk than indicated by the Borrower Rating. The incremental risk should be reflected in a higher risk rating. For example, an unsecured line of credit to a company with a Borrower Rating of 4 (absent other considerations), would not usually warrant a change in Risk Rating. However, a term loan of longer than usual tenor or with a bullet maturity or a weak loan agreement, may warrant a 5 or worse Risk Rating. On the other hand, the same loan to a 2-rated borrower may not represent sufficient incremental risk to warrant reflection in the Risk Rating. Generally, term loans that amortize with equal installments up to three years will carry the same rating as the borrower. Bullet and balloon term loans of the same tenor would usually be one grade lower.

In addition, terms of the credit documentation may influence the risk of the transaction. For instance, term loans with few or weak covenants may represent additional risk, whereas usually tight or restrictive agreements may represent less.

Example: The bank has a $1.4 million unsecured term loan (original amount = $1.5 million) used to finance the construction of an addition to Quickbuy's tobacco and candy warehouse. The repayment schedule for this unsecured facility consists of fixed quarterly principal and interest payments over a ten-year period based upon a fifteen-year amortization.

Founded as a dairy in 1954, Quickbuy entered the convenience store business in 1964 and currently operates 450 convenience stores in the northeastern region of the United States. Quickbuy has demonstrated consistent earnings, strong and stable cash flow, liquidity, and capitalization. For the fiscal year ended 12/31/88, Quickbuy generated $251 million in revenues and posted a net profit of $3.3 million.

Quickbuy has consistently generated more than sufficient cash flow from operations to cover current maturities and dividends. Its market position in the Middle Atlantic Region remains quite strong. The company ranks number one in sales and profitability per store. Quickbuy also maintains a debt/capitalization ratio of .59 which is lower than many of its competitors.

Due to the length of the term of an unsecured basis, the suggested ratings are as follows:

Suggested Borrower Rating 4
Suggested Risk Rating 6

Subordinated Position

A **Subordinated Position** occurs when more than one "legal entity" has an interest or claim upon the assets of a prospective borrower. A bank may require that the other interested parties sign "Subordination Agreements" before a loan will be granted. These are agreements in which another interested party grants the bank a priority claim or preference to the assets of the borrower ahead of any claim that he may have. However, if the bank is placed in a subordinated position to other creditors, a poorer Risk Rating should be considered in those instances where the bank has a subordinated loan or an unsecured loan to a borrower which has pledged a major portion of its assets to other lenders.

Country Risk

Country Risk is the risk to the bank that the servicing of its loans to a foreign borrower may be abridged, frozen, or denied by acts of, or conditions in, the nation where the borrower is located. This risk is unrelated to the actual borrower's capacity to repay; rather it refers to the risk that a borrower within a country cannot repay its obligation because of political or general economic factors, such as a lack of foreign currency exchange.

The domicile of the borrower or guarantor must be considered in determining Risk Rating. Given the same quality of borrower, the country of location will be a major factor in determining Risk Rating. As a general rule, except for local currency indigenous loans, the Risk Rating assigned would probably be less than or equal to the Country Rating.

A Risk Rating might be better than that of the country of the borrower's domicile if its assets and earning capability are materially outside that domicile/jurisdiction.

DEVELOPING A RISK GRADING WORKSHEET

The Borrower and Risk Rating Criteria found on the Risk Grading Worksheets should be used by lending officers to help arrive at appropriate Borrower and Risk Ratings. The worksheets give short descriptions of the characteristics of a Borrower at various levels of risk. Lending personnel would match characteristics with their borrowers to arrive at a risk rating. Refer to Exhibit 21.3 at the end of the chapter for an example of a Borrower Rating Worksheet, based on our familiar example Gem Furniture.

Borrowers are unlikely to exhibit characteristics uniformly at a single level across the grid. For instance, a Borrower might be in a Class 3 industry, with a Class 5 position in that industry, have Class 4 cash flow trends and assets, and Class 3 management controls.

The Risk Grading Worksheets drive lending personnel through the analytical process and break down a large subjective judgment into smaller, more focused ones. The worksheets may also be used to highlight areas of disagreement between different lenders in evaluating a credit and focus the discussion, for instance, onto differing views of debt capacity. This should aid in resolving different evaluations, and also aid in training.

Risk Grading Gem Furniture Company

Earlier in this chapter, we talked about Risk Grading Worksheets and how to use them to grade the risk of a borrower and eventually the risk of the borrower's individual transactions. Keep in mind that the worksheets are only guides for the banker to follow. The actual ratings are the result of the officer's judgment, skill, and expertise in evaluating the borrower.

To grade Gem Furniture, we will use the Borrower Grade Worksheet and Risk Grading Worksheets in Exhibits 21.1 and 21.3 respectively. We will take a column-by-column approach to assigning a borrower rating to Gem and carry this rating through to Gem's line of credit.

Take a look at the Borrower Grade Worksheet under the columns titled "Industry/Industry Segment" and "Position Within the Industry." Traditional Line Furniture Manufacturing as an industry is not in serious financial decline but is fairly cyclical and subject to unfavorable changes in the economy. This simply means that when the economy is in a downswing, consumers tend to forego the purchase of non-vital items such as new furniture and automobiles. Because of the characteristics of the furniture industry, we will assign Gem an industry rating of 5. Gem, however, is in a class-7 position within the industry due to its poor performance relative to its peers. If you look at the Borrower Grading worksheet for Gem in Exhibit 21.1, you will see that these sections have been highlighted on the worksheets themselves.

Next we look at Gem's earnings and cash flow trends. As you may recall, Gem's operating cash flow in year 1990 was $23.7 million and its new debt financing totaled $14.5 million. By 1991, gross operating cash flow had dropped to $8.1 million and new financing had increased to $39.4 million. Now lets play "You Make the Call . . . "

If this trend continues, will the company:

1. Double its size due to excessive cash flow from operations?

2. Become insolvent because leverage will reach the level at which the company would require new debt just to pay interest on existing debt?

3. Eventually become an acquisition target because of its strong cash position?

Of course, you chose 2 as the correct response. If not, review Chapter 1 and start all over again. If Gem's earnings and cash flow from operations continue on this trend, the company cannot possibly remain viable. Now review Exhibit 21.3 once more and scan down the column labeled "Earnings/Operating Cash Flow." You will see that the box in the row with a borrower grade 8 has been highlighted to reflect Gem's earnings and cash flow position on the grid.

The new bank debt Gem acquired was partly used to make up the operation shortfalls the company experienced during its asset conversion cycle. This is the correct use of this type of financing. The remainder of this new short-term debt,

however, was used to finance capital expenditures. This is traditionally a mismatching of funds since long-term assets such as plant and equipment should be financed with long-term debt, not short-term financing. If you look at the worksheet under Asset/Liability Values, you will see that this places Gem in a class-7 position in this section of the grid.

Next, let's look at Gem's financial flexibility and debt capacity. Gem is currently requesting an increase in its Line from Second City of $10 million. With Gem's current financial position, the bank would be hesitant to continue providing the existing line let alone increase the line $10 million. Other banks would also be hesitant about lending to a company in this position. On the worksheet in Exhibit 21.1, under the column labeled "Financial Flexibility/Debt Capacity," this places Gem in a 6 to 7 position on the grid. Taking a conservative approach, we place Gem in the 7 position.

Another key element in determining a company's borrower grade is management and controls. In other words, we look at how well the company is being managed. One of Gem's major weaknesses is its lack of financial planning and management's "fire fighting" approach to the firm's operations in recent years. Gem has typically taken a reactive approach to management rather than a proactive approach. This has contributed significantly to the deterioration of Gem's financial position. Once again, on the borrower grade worksheet we can find the spot on the grid under the column labeled "Management and Controls" that best describes Gem's management. Again this places Gem in a class-7 position in this category.

Finally, let's look at Gem's financial reporting. Gem has always provided the bank with detailed quarterly statements from a reputable accounting firm. In addition, Gem has always received a clean audit with qualifications of nominal impact. From a financial reporting perspective, Gem represents average risk and is in a class-5 position on the worksheet under the column labeled "Financial Reporting."

Now that we have completed each category on the grid in Exhibit 21.3, let's summarize our analysis of Gem:

Category	Borrower Grade
Industry/Industry Segment	5
Position Within the Industry	7
Earnings/Operating Cash Flow	8
Asset/Liability Values	7
Financial Flexibility/Debt Capacity	7
Management and Controls	7
Financial Reporting	5

As the table shows, not all categories received the same grade, as they seldom do. This is where the process becomes reliant on the officer's skill, expertise, and knowledge of the borrower. The officer must decide which factors weigh most heavily in assigning a grade to the borrower. In our analysis, we will weight each category equally and assign Gem a borrower grade of 7. This borrower grade places the company in a category call "Criticized" which signals management to pay additional attention. In addition, if Gem's condition continues to deteriorate, its borrower grade will be downgraded and a recommendation made to place Gem on "non-performing" status.

Assigning a Risk Grade to Gem's Line of Credit

As stated earlier, the borrower rating is, in effect, the risk of an unsecured line of credit to the borrower. Looking at the Risk Grading grid in Exhibit 21.2, we see that the determinants of the Risk Grade from the borrower grade are all neutral. Therefore, we assign Gem's line of credit a Risk Grade of 7, the same as the borrower grade. If other conditions had existed, such as a guarantee or unusually long tenor on the note, we would have adjusted the Risk Grade up or down accordingly.

First Fidelity Bancorporation Borrower Rating Guide

Borrower: Gem Furniture Company

Date:

Borrower Rating Decision:

Lending Officer:

Borrower Rating	Industry/Business Outlook	Position Within Industry	Operating Trends/Earnings & Cash Flow	Asset Quality/Values	Financial Flexibility/Debt Capacity	Management	Financial/Accounting
1. ELITE/ MINIMAL RISK	GOVERNMENTS OF MAJOR INDUSTRIALIZED COUNTRIES, TOP WORLD CLASS BANKS, AND MAJOR MULTINATIONALS						
2. MINIMAL RISK	MINIMAL INDUSTRY CYCLICALITY AND VULNERABILITY TO SUDDEN ECONOMIC OR TECHNOLOGICAL CHANGE. CAPITAL INTENSIVENESS AND DEGREE OF OPERATING LEVERAGE MODEST. HIGHLY FAVORABLE REGULATORY, LEGAL AND LABOR ENVIRONMENTS AND LONG TERM OUTLOOK	LEADER WITH DOMINANT SHARE IN STABLE INDUSTRY. PRICING LEADER AND LOW COST PRODUCER. PERFORMANCE RATIOS AMONG BEST IN INDUSTRY. RANKS IN TOP TIER OF INDUSTRY	VERY STRONG EARNINGS TREND CONTINUING SUBSTANTIAL EXCESS CASH FLOW AND INTEREST COVERAGE	HIGHEST QUALITY ASSETS. MINIMAL OR INSIGNIFICANT INTANGIBLES. LEVERAGE EXTREMELY LOW. LIABILITY TYPE AND TENOR FIT ASSET STRUCTURE EXTREMELY WELL	SUBSTANTIAL DEBT CAPACITY WITH ACCESS TO GLOBAL CAPITAL MARKETS VIRTUALLY ASSURED AT ALL TIMES. LONG TERM DEBT RATED AAA, AA OR EQUIVALENT	WORLD CLASS ORGANIZATION. HIGHLY EXPERIENCED MANAGEMENT TEAM WITH CONTINUITY AND DEPTH. MODERN / HIGHLY EFFICIENT FACILITIES AND EXCELLENT INTERNAL CONTROLS	CLEAN AUDIT WITH NO QUALIFICATIONS. MAJOR ACCOUNTING FIRM
3. MODEST RISK	INDUSTRY NOT OVERLY CYCLICAL OR VULNERABLE TO SUDDEN ECONOMIC OR TECHNOLOGICAL CHANGE. CAPITAL INTENSIVENESS AND OPERATING LEVERAGE MODEST. FAVORABLE REGULATORY, LEGAL AND LABOR ENVIRONMENTS AND LONG-TERM OUTLOOK	NEAR TOP IN INDUSTRY WITH VERY STRONG MARKET SHARE. INFLUENCES INDUSTRY PRICING. PERFORMANCE RATIOS SUBSTANTIALLY BETTER THAN PEERS. RANKS IN TOP TIER OF INDUSTRY	CONSISTENTLY GENERATES EXCESS CASH FLOW AND INTEREST COVERAGE	ASSETS OF VERY HIGH QUALITY. NO RELIANCE ON THE VALUE OF INTANGIBLES. LEVERAGE VERY LOW. LIABILITY TYPE AND TENOR PROVIDE A GOOD MATCH FOR THE ASSET STRUCTURE	HAS ACCESS TO NATIONAL CAPITAL MARKETS. AMPLE DEBT CAPACITY. LONG TERM DEBT RATED A, BBB OR EQUIVALENT	BROAD INDUSTRY EXPERIENCE WITH GOOD CONTINUITY AND DEPTH IN MOST POSITIONS. RELATIVELY EFFICIENT OPERATIONS AND A HIGH LEVEL OF INTERNAL CONTROLS	
4. BELOW AVERAGE RISK	MODERATE LINKAGE TO BUSINESS CYCLE. MAY BE SOME VULNERABILITY TO SUDDEN ECONOMIC OR TECHNOLOGICAL CHANGE. NEUTRAL LEGAL, LABOR AND REGULATORY ENVIRONMENTS AND LONG-TERM OUTLOOK	OBLIGOR IS WELL KNOWN IN DOMESTIC/REGIONAL MARKETS. MEANINGFUL MARKET SHARE IN INDUSTRY. PERFORMANCE RATIOS GENERALLY BETTER THAN PEERS. RANKS IN SECOND TIER OF INDUSTRY	POSITIVE EARNINGS TREND WITH EXCESS CASH FLOW AND INTEREST COVERAGE. GOOD TRACK RECORD	ASSETS OF ABOVE AVERAGE QUALITY. LITTLE RELIANCE ON THE VALUE OF INTANGIBLES. LEVERAGE BELOW AVERAGE. LIABILITY TYPE AND TENOR PROVIDE A GOOD MATCH FOR THE ASSET STRUCTURE	REASONABLE ACCESS TO CAPITAL MARKETS OR OTHER LARGE BANKS BUT MAY BE LIMITED DURING DIFFICULT ECONOMIC PERIODS. LONG TERM DEBT RATED BB OR EQUIVALENT REASONABLE DEBT CAPACITY	MODERATE INDUSTRY EXPERIENCE IN MOST AREAS. SOME DEPTH. AVERAGE OPERATING EFFICIENCY. AVERAGE FACILITIES AND INTERNAL CONTROLS	
5. AVERAGE RISK	MAY BE SUSCEPTIBLE TO UNFAVORABLE CHANGES IN THE ECONOMY BUT GENERALLY PROTECTED FROM A DETERIORATION IN INDUSTRY FUNDAMENTALS. FAIRLY HIGH CYCLICALITY. NEUTRAL LEGAL, LABOR AND REGULATORY ENVIRONMENTS AND LONG-TERM OUTLOOK	TENDS TO BE PRICE FOLLOWER. AVERAGE MARKET SHARE. PERFORMANCE RATIOS WILL BE AROUND PEER GROUP AVERAGE. RANKS IN SECOND OR THIRD TIER OF INDUSTRY	EARNINGS AND CASH FLOW TRENDS ARE POSITIVE BUT MAY NOT BE CONSISTENTLY STABLE	ASSETS OF AVERAGE QUALITY. THERE MAY BE SOME RELIANCE ON THE VALUE OF INTANGIBLES. LEVERAGE AVERAGE. LIABILITY TYPE AND TENOR PROVIDE AN AVERAGE MATCH FOR THE ASSET STRUCTURE	WILL USUALLY HAVE ACCESS TO LARGE BANKS BUT MAY BE DIFFICULT DURING ECONOMIC DOWNTURN. LONG TERM DEBT RATED B OR EQUIVALENT AVERAGE DEBT CAPACITY	REASONABLE INDUSTRY EXPERIENCE WITH A MODEST AMOUNT OF DEPTH IN KEY POSITIONS. FACILITIES MAY BE GENERALLY OLDER AND LESS EFFICIENT THAN AVERAGE. INTERNAL CONTROLS MAY BE AT OR SLIGHTLY BELOW AVERAGE QUALITY	CLEAN AUDIT/GRANT WITH QUALIFICATION OF MINIMAL IMPACT. ACCOUNTING FIRM OF REPUTABLE OR OF HIGHEST CALIBRE

Exhibit 21.1 (continued)

First Fidelity Bancorporation Borrower Rating Guide

	Industry	Market Share / Performance	Earnings & Cash Flow	Assets / Leverage	Access to Banks	Management / Facilities	Audit
6: MANAGEMENT ATTENTION RISK	INDUSTRY MAY BE INTENSELY COMPETITIVE AND SUBJECT TO WIDE CYCLICAL SWINGS OR SUDDEN DETERIORATION DUE TO TECHNOLOGICAL OR ECONOMIC FACTORS. LEGAL, LABOR OR REGULATORY ENVIRONMENT MAY BE A PROBLEM. OUTLOOK MAY BE UNFAVORABLE	BELOW AVERAGE MARKET SHARE. PERFORMANCE RATIOS BELOW PEER GROUP AVERAGES. RANKS IN THIRD TIER OF INDUSTRY	EARNINGS AND CASH FLOW SOMEWHAT STRAINED AND SUBJECT TO VOLATILITY.	ASSETS OF BELOW AVERAGE QUALITY. SIGNIFICANT INTANGIBLES MAY EXIST. LEVERAGE ABOVE AVERAGE. LIABILITY TYPE AND TENOR MAY NOT PROVIDE A GOOD MATCH FOR THE ASSET STRUCTURE.	LIMITED ACCESS TO LARGE BANKS. STRONG RELIANCE ON DEBT FINANCING WITH MULTIPLE SOURCES	LIMITED INDUSTRY EXPERIENCE WITH LITTLE OR NO DEPTH. FACILITIES OUTDATED AND GENERALLY MUCH LESS EFFICIENT THAN AVERAGE. INTERNAL CONTROLS GENERALLY WEAK.	AUDIT CONTAINS QUALIFICATIONS THAT POTENTIALLY HAVE A NEGATIVE IMPACT. UNAUDITED STATEMENTS MAY NOT BE RELIABLE. CREDIBILITY OF THE ACCOUNTING FIRM MAY BE QUESTIONED
7: SPECIAL MENTION	INDUSTRY MAY BE START UP OR DECLINE PHASE WITH POSSIBLE SIGNIFICANT EXPOSURE TO ECONOMIC OR TECHNOLOGICAL CHANGE. LEGAL, LABOR OR REGULATORY ENVIRONMENT MAY ALSO BE A PROBLEM. OUTLOOK MAY BE UNFAVORABLE	MARKET SHARE AND PERFORMANCE RATIOS ARE WELL BELOW INDUSTRY AVERAGES AND RANKING. FIRM MAY BE IN A MIDDLE OR DECLINING INDUSTRY. RANKS IN THIRD TIER OF INDUSTRY OR LOWER	EARNINGS AND CASH FLOW ARE SIGNIFICANTLY STRAINED AND SUBJECT TO SIGNIFICANT VOLATILITY	ASSET QUALITY IS WELL BELOW AVERAGE. MAY BE VERY DELAYED OR INTANGIBLE. LEVERAGE IS WELL ABOVE AVERAGE. LIABILITY TYPE AND TENOR ARE SOMEWHAT MISMATCHED WITH THE ASSET STRUCTURE	WITHOUT NO PRESENT ACCESS TO LARGE BANKS AND WILL RELY ON HEAVY/EXCESSIVE DEBT CAPITAL	LIMITED INDUSTRY EXPERIENCE WITH NO DEPTH. FACILITIES OUTDATED AND OUTMODED... INTERNAL CONTROLS ARE WEAK	AUDIT CONTAINS SIGNIFICANT DISCLAIMERS OR AN ADVERSE OPINION. TIMELINESS IS AN ISSUE. ACCOUNTING FIRM RESPONSIBLE FOR THE AUDIT IS SUSPECT
8: SUB-STANDARD	INDUSTRY HAS SIGNIFICANT PROBLEMS WHICH ADVERSELY AFFECT A LARGE PERCENTAGE OF PARTICIPANTS. PROBLEMS MAY BE CYCLICAL OR LONGER TERM IN NATURE. OBLIGOR RANKS IN BOTTOM TIER OF INDUSTRY		EARNINGS AND CASH FLOW MAY NOT COVER FIXED CHARGES	LOWEST QUALITY ASSETS. VALUE MAY BE PREDOMINANTLY INTANGIBLE. LEVERAGE EXTREMELY HIGH. LIABILITY TYPE AND TENOR ARE GREATLY MISMATCHED WITH ASSET STRUCTURE.	NO PRESENT ACCESS TO LARGER BANKS WITH STRICT AND HEAVY RELIANCE ON DEBT FINANCING	HIGH MANAGEMENT TURNOVER OR INEXPERIENCED MANAGEMENT MAY CREATE FURTHER RISKS. VERY WEAK INTERNAL CONTROLS.	
9: DOUBTFUL	INDUSTRY HAS MAJOR LONGER TERM PROBLEMS WHICH ADVERSELY AFFECT THE MAJORITY OF PARTICIPANTS. OBLIGOR RANKS IN BOTTOM TIER OF INDUSTRY	EXCESSIVE DEGREE OF RISK. FINANCIAL AND MANAGEMENT DEFICIENCIES ARE WELL DEFINED AND MAKE IMPROBABLE THE OBLIGOR'S ABILITY TO PAY OUT FROM ANTICIPATED SOURCES UNDER EXISTING TERMS AND CONDITIONS. COLLECTION IN FULL IS HIGHLY IMPROBABLE, BUT THE TIMING OF A LOSS IS UNCERTAIN.					UNACCEPTABLE FINANCIAL REPORTING
10: LOSS	SEVERE PERMANENT INDUSTRY PROBLEMS EXIST WHICH ADVERSELY AFFECT VIRTUALLY ALL PARTICIPANTS. OBLIGOR RANKS IN BOTTOM TIER OF INDUSTRY	DUE TO SEVERE DEFICIENCIES AND EXCESSIVE RISK, UNSECURED DEBTS TO THIS BORROWER ARE CONSIDERED UNCOLLECTIBLE AND SHOULD NOT BE CONTINUED AS ACTIVE ASSETS OF THE BANK.					

Exhibit 21.2

First Fidelity Bancorporation Risk Rating Definitions

RISK RATING	RISK RATING DEFINITIONS
1: SUBSTANTIALLY RISK FREE	BORROWERS OF UNQUESTIONED CREDIT STANDING AT THE PINNACLE OF CREDIT QUALITY. BASICALLY, GOVERNMENTS OF MAJOR INDUSTRIALIZED COUNTRIES, A FEW MAJOR WORLD CLASS BANKS AND A FEW MULTINATIONAL CORPORATIONS.
2: MINIMAL RISK	BORROWERS OF THE HIGHEST QUALITY. ALMOST NO RISK IN LENDING TO THIS CLASS. CASH FLOWS OVER AT LEAST 5 YEARS DEMONSTRATE EXCEPTIONALLY LARGE AND/OR STABLE MARGINS OF PROTECTION AND BALANCE SHEETS ARE VERY CONSERVATIVE, STRONG AND LIQUID. PROJECTED CASH FLOWS (INCLUDING ANTICIPATED CREDIT EXTENSIONS) WILL CONTINUE A STRONG TREND. AND PROVIDE CONTINUED WIDE MARGINS OF PROTECTION, LIQUIDITY AND DEBT MANAGEMENT SERVICE COVERAGE. EXCELLENT ASSET QUALITY AND MANAGEMENT. TYPICALLY LARGE NATIONAL CORPORATIONS.
3: MODEST RISK	BORROWERS IN THE LOWER END OF THE HIGH QUALITY RANGE. VERY GOOD ASSET QUALITY AND LIQUIDITY; STRONG DEBT CAPACITY AND COVERAGE; VERY GOOD MANAGEMENT. THE CREDIT EXTENSION IS CONSIDERED DEFINITELY SOUND. HOWEVER, ELEMENTS MAY BE PRESENT WHICH SUGGEST THE BORROWER MAY NOT BE FREE FROM TEMPORARY IMPAIRMENTS SOMETIME IN THE FUTURE. TYPICALLY LARGER REGIONAL OR NATIONAL CORPORATIONS.
4: BELOW AVERAGE RISK	THE HIGH END OF THE MEDIUM RANGE BETWEEN THE DEFINITELY SOUND AND THOSE SITUATIONS WHERE RISK CHARACTERISTICS BEGIN TO APPEAR. THE MARGINS OF PROTECTION ARE SATISFACTORY. BUT SUSCEPTIBLE TO MORE RAPID DETERIORATION THAN CLASS 3 NAMES. SOME ELEMENTS OF REDUCED STRENGTH ARE PRESENT IN SUCH AREAS AS LIQUIDITY, STABILITY OF MARGINS AND CASH FLOWS, CONCENTRATION OF ASSETS, DEPENDENCE UPON ONE TYPE OF BUSINESS, CYCLICAL TRENDS, ETC., WHICH MAY ADVERSELY AFFECT THE BORROWER. TYPICALLY GOOD REGIONAL COMPANIES OR EXCELLENT LOCAL COMPANIES. CLASS 4 BORROWERS AND BETTER USUALLY BORROW UNSECURED.
5: AVERAGE RISK	BORROWERS WITH SMALLER MARGINS OF DEBT SERVICE COVERAGE AND WHERE DEFINITE ELEMENTS OF REDUCED STRENGTH EXIST. SATISFACTORY ASSET QUALITY AND LIQUIDITY; GOOD DEBT CAPACITY AND COVERAGE AND GOOD MANAGEMENT IN ALL CRITICAL POSITIONS. THESE NAMES HAVE SUFFICIENT MARGINS OF PROTECTION AND WILL QUALIFY AS ACCEPTABLE BORROWERS; HOWEVER, HISTORIC EARNINGS AND / OR CASH FLOW PATTERNS MAY BE SOMETIMES UNSTABLE. A LOSS YEAR OR A DECLINING EARNINGS TREND MAY NOT BE UNCOMMON. TYPICALLY SOLID LOCAL COMPANIES MAY OR MAY NOT REQUIRE COLLATERAL IN THE COURSE OF NORMAL CREDIT EXTENSIONS.

Exhibit 21.2 (continued)

First Fidelity Bancorporation Risk Rating Definitions

6: MANAGEMENT ATTENTION RISK	BORROWERS WHICH ARE BEGINNING TO DEMONSTRATE ABOVE AVERAGE RISK THROUGH DECLINING EARNINGS TRENDS, STRAINED CASH FLOW, INCREASING LEVERAGE AND/OR WEAKENING MARKET FUNDAMENTALS. ALSO, BORROWERS WHICH ARE CURRENTLY PERFORMING AS AGREED BUT COULD BE ADVERSELY IMPACTED BY DEVELOPING FACTORS SUCH AS, BUT NOT LIMITED TO: DETERIORATING INDUSTRY CONDITIONS, OPERATING PROBLEMS, PENDING LITIGATION OF A SIGNIFICANT NATURE, OR DECLINING COLLATERAL QUALITY / ADEQUACY. SUCH BORROWERS OR WEAKER TYPICALLY REQUIRE COLLATERAL IN NORMAL CREDIT EXTENSIONS.
7: SPECIAL MENTION	A SPECIAL MENTION BORROWER EXHIBITS POTENTIAL CREDIT WEAKNESS OR A DOWNWARD TREND WHICH, IF NOT CHECKED OR CORRECTED, WILL WEAKEN THE ASSET OR INADEQUATELY PROTECT THE BANK'S POSITION. WHILE POTENTIALLY WEAK, THE BORROWER IS CURRENTLY MARGINALLY ACCEPTABLE. NO LOSS OF PRINCIPAL OR INTEREST IS ENVISIONED. INCLUDED COULD BE TURNAROUND SITUATIONS, AS WELL AS THOSE PREVIOUSLY RATED 8 OR 5 NAMES THAT HAVE SHOWN DETERIORATION, FOR WHATEVER REASON, INDICATING A DOWNGRADING FROM THE BETTER CATEGORIES. THESE ARE NAMES THAT HAVE BEEN OR WOULD NORMALLY BE CRITICIZED "SPECIAL MENTION" BY REGULATORY AUTHORITIES.
8: SUB-STANDARD	A BORROWER WITH A WELL DEFINED WEAKNESS OR WEAKNESSES THAT JEOPARDIZE THE ORDERLY LIQUIDATION OF THE DEBT. BORROWERS THAT HAVE BEEN OR WOULD NORMALLY BE CLASSIFIED "SUBSTANDARD" BY REGULATORY AUTHORITIES. A SUBSTANDARD LOAN IS INADEQUATELY PROTECTED BY THE CURRENT SOUND WORTH AND PAYING CAPACITY OF THE OBLIGOR. NORMAL REPAYMENT FROM THIS BORROWER IS IN JEOPARDY, ALTHOUGH NO LOSS OF PRINCIPAL IS ENVISIONED. THERE IS A DISTINCT POSSIBILITY THAT A PARTIAL LOSS OF INTEREST AND / OR PRINCIPAL WILL OCCUR IF THE DEFICIENCIES ARE NOT CORRECTED.
9: DOUBTFUL	A BORROWER CLASSIFIED DOUBTFUL HAS ALL WEAKNESSES INHERENT IN ONE CLASSIFIED SUBSTANDARD WITH THE ADDED PROVISION THAT THE WEAKNESSES MAKE COLLECTION OF DEBT IN FULL, ON THE BASIS OF CURRENTLY EXISTING FACTS, CONDITIONS, AND VALUES, HIGHLY QUESTIONABLE AND IMPROBABLE. SERIOUS PROBLEMS EXIST TO THE POINT WHERE A PARTIAL LOSS OF PRINCIPAL IS LIKELY. THE POSSIBILITY OF LOSS IS EXTREMELY HIGH, BUT BECAUSE OF CERTAIN IMPORTANT, REASONABLY SPECIFIC PENDING FACTORS WHICH MAY WORK TO THE ADVANTAGE AND STRENGTHENING OF THE ASSET, ITS CLASSIFICATION AS AN ESTIMATED LOSS IS DEFERRED UNTIL ITS MORE EXACT STATUS MAY BE DETERMINED. PENDING FACTORS INCLUDE PROPOSED MERGER, ACQUISITION, OR LIQUIDATION PROCEDURES, CAPITAL INJECTION, PERFECTING LIENS ON ADDITIONAL COLLATERAL, AND REFINANCING PLANS.
10: LOSS	BORROWERS DEEMED INCAPABLE OF REPAYMENT OF UNSECURED DEBT. LOANS TO SUCH BORROWERS ARE CONSIDERED UNCOLLECTABLE AND OF SUCH LITTLE VALUE THAT THEIR CONTINUANCE AS ACTIVE ASSETS OF THE BANK IS NOT WARRANTED. THIS CLASSIFICATION DOES NOT MEAN THAT THE LOAN HAS ABSOLUTELY NO RECOVERY OR SALVAGE VALUE, BUT RATHER IT IS NOT PRACTICAL OR DESIRABLE TO DEFER WRITING OFF THIS BASICALLY WORTHLESS ASSET EVEN THOUGH PARTIAL RECOVERY MAY BE EFFECTED IN THE FUTURE.

Exhibit 21.3

First Fidelity Bancorporation Risk Rating Worksheet

IMPACT ON BORROWER GRADE *	DETERMINANTS			
	TERMS/ DOCUMENTATION	TENOR	COLLATERAL	GUARANTY / THIRD PARTY SUPPORT
STRONGLY IMPROVES	TERMS BEST TO EFFECTIVELY REDUCE THE TENOR OF THE LOAN.	OVERNIGHT LOANS	CASH, CASH EQUIVALENTS, GOVERNMENT SECURITIES, OR PROPERLY MARGINED, WIDELY DIVERSIFIED READILY MARKETABLE SECURITIES TRADED ON MAJOR EXCHANGES, HELD BY BANK IN VAULT. HIGHEST QUALITY OR HIGHLY DIVERSIFIED ACCOUNTS RECEIVABLE. HIGHLY COMFORTABLE MULTI-USE FIXED ASSETS.	GUARANTOR RATING SIGNIFICANTLY BETTER THAN BORROWER GRADE. UNCONDITIONAL COVERAGE IN FULL FOR ANY AND ALL OF OBLIGOR'S INDEBTEDNESS. COVERS ALL ECONOMIC AND POLITICAL RISKS IF APPLICABLE. **
IMPROVES	COVENANTS EXIST IN DOCUMENTATION TO TRIGGER POTENTIAL PROBLEMS.	SHORT TERM LOANS OF 2 - 30 DAYS	VALUE IS ACCEPTABLE WITH MODERATE VOLATILITY, AND PROVIDES A MARGIN OVER THE SUPPORTED OBLIGATION. COLLATERAL IS OF AVERAGE LIQUIDITY. ACCOUNTS RECEIVABLE WITH GOOD TURNOVER AND MODEST CONCENTRATIONS. RAW MATERIALS OR FINISHED INVENTORY WITH AVERAGE LIQUIDATION VALUE. ATTRACTIVELY LOCATED REAL ESTATE WITH MULTIPLE USES. USEFUL LIFE OF COLLATERAL, SEASONABLE AND WELL MATCHED TO TENOR OF BORROWINGS. FUNDS ARE MADE ON SPECIFIC ASSETS. **	GUARANTOR RATING BETTER THAN BORROWER GRADE. COVERAGE MAY INCLUDE A FEW CONDITIONS YET IS INTENDED TO COVER ANY AND ALL OF OBLIGOR'S INDEBTEDNESS UNDER ALL ECONOMIC AND POLITICAL RISKS. **
NEUTRAL	ALL NEEDED DOCUMENTS ARE OBTAINABLE, PERFECTED, AND UNCOUNTERABLE. LOAN AGREEMENT IS WORKABLE AND COVENANTS ARE APPROPRIATE. REASONABLE COVENANTS EXIST FOR ADVANCE NOTICE OF POTENTIAL PROBLEMS.	NO IMPACT ON BORROWER GRADE FOR LOANS UP TO MAXIMUM TENOR AS FOLLOWS: BORROWER GRADE / MAXIMUM AMORTIZING TENOR 1 / 6 YRS 2 / 5 YRS 3-4 / 4 YRS 5 / 3 YRS 6 / 2 YRS 7-10 / 1 YR	VALUE IS IS HIGHLY DIFFICULT TO ASCERTAIN OR HIGHLY VOLATILE. VALUE PROVIDES A MINIMAL MARGIN OVER SUPPORTED OBLIGATION. COLLATERAL WITH POOR LIQUIDITY WHERE LIQUIDATION WILL ERODE VALUE. REAL ESTATE WITH SPECIALIZED USE OR POOR LOCATION. USEFUL LIFE OF COLLATERAL ONLY PARTIALLY MATCHED TO TENOR OF SECURED BORROWINGS.	GUARANTOR RATING SAME OR WORSE THAN BORROWER GRADE. COVERAGE IS VERY CONDITIONAL AND DOES NOT COVER ALL OF OBLIGOR'S INDEBTEDNESS OR ALL ECONOMIC AND POLITICAL RISKS. GUARANTOR VULNERABLE TO A DECLINE IN PERFORMANCE.
DETRACTS	WEAK LOAN AGREEMENTS WITHOUT PROPER COVENANTS OR TRIGGERS. SIGNIFICANT ASSETS PLEDGED TO OTHER CREDITORS EFFECTIVELY SUBORDINATE THE BANK'S POSITION.	TRANSACTIONS WHICH SLIGHTLY EXCEED ABOVE LIMITS OR TRANSACTIONS WHICH HAVE BULLET MATURITIES	COLLATERAL DOES NOT DETRACT FROM THE BORROWER GRADE	GUARANTY/THIRD PARTY SUPPORT DOES NOT DETRACT FROM THE BORROWER GRADE
STRONGLY DETRACTS	BANK IS SUBORDINATE TO OTHER CREDITOR CLAIMS. HIGHLY GENERALIZED DOCUMENTS MAKE PERFECTION, QUALITY AND SUITABILITY OF BANK'S CLAIMS HIGHLY QUESTIONABLE.	TRANSACTION WITH SIGNIFICANT TENOR BEYOND BORROWER GRADE LIMITS. LONG TERM TRANSACTION WITH NO AMORTIZATION.	COLLATERAL DOES NOT DETRACT FROM THE BORROWER GRADE	GUARANTY/THIRD PARTY SUPPORT DOES NOT DETRACT FROM THE BORROWER GRADE

BORROWER GRADE → RISK RATING **

* THE SPREAD BETWEEN THE BORROWER GRADE AND RISK RATING IS NOT LIMITED TO ONE LEVEL, AND DEPENDS ON THE QUALITY OF THE DETERMINANT.

** RISK RATINGS OF "6" WHICH ARE BETTER THAN THE BORROWER GRADE DUE TO VULNERABLE COLLATERAL OR GUARANTORS ARE DENOTED "6V".

Exhibit 21.4

First Fidelity Bancorporation Risk Rating Guide

Borrower: _____ Risk Rating Decision: _____

Date: _____

Lending Officer: _____

RISK RATING	VALUE / MARGIN	COLLATERAL — LIQUIDITY	SUPPORT — DOCUMENTATION & CONTROL	GUARANTEES — RAGE / CONDITI OCUMENTATIO	TERMS
1: SUBSTAN-TIALLY RISK FREE	VALUE IS HIGHLY STABLE & READILY ASCERTAINABLE. IF VOLATILE, VALUE IS WELL IN EXCESS OF SUP-PORTED OBLIGATION. VALUE UNDENIABLY SUPPORTS OBLIGATION UNDER ALL FORESEEABLE CONDITIONS.	COLLATERAL OF HIGHEST LIQUIDITY, i.e., - CASH/CD IN BANK POSSESSION - GOVERNMENT SECURITIES - WIDELY HELD NYSE STOCK IN BANK POSSESSION	FILINGS ARE MADE ON SPECIFIC ASSETS. ALL NEEDED DOCUMENTS ARE SUSTAINABLE AND PERFECTED ALL MONITORING AND CONTROL IS UNDER BANK'S DOMINION, i.e., FIELD WAREHOUSING OR IN BANK'S VAULT.		6 MONTHS OR LESS
2: MINIMAL RISK	VALUE IS STABLE & ASCERTAINABLE. SOME VOLATILITY IN VALUE MAY EXIST YET VALUE PROVIDES A HIGH MARGIN OVER THE SUP-PORTED OBLIGATION.	COLLATERAL OF HIGH LIQUIDITY, i.e., - LESS ACTIVELY TRADED STOCKS - HIGHEST QUALITY OR HIGHLY DIVERSIFIED ACCOUNTS RECEIVABLE - HIGHLY PORTABLE, MULTI-PURPOSE FIXED ASSETS	DOCUMENTATION AS ABOVE. THE MONITORING & CONTROL IS UNDER BANK'S DOMINION. COLLATERAL IS MONITORED DAILY. LOCK BOX OR SIMILAR COLLECTION CONTROLS IN PLACE. BANK AUDITS ARE DONE AT LEAST QUARTERLY.	UNCONDITIONAL COVERAGE IN FULL FOR ANY OR ALL OF 1 YEAR OR LESS OBLIGOR'S INDEBTEDNESS. COVERS ALL ECONOMIC AND POLITICAL RISKS IF APPLICABLE. ALL NECESSARY DOCUMENTATION EXISTS,	1 YEAR OR LESS
3: MODEST RISK	VALUE IS ASCERTAINABLE. HAS RELATIVELY LOW VOLATILITY AND/OR PROVIDES A RELATIVELY GOOD MARGIN OVER THE SUPPORTED OBLIGATION.	COLLATERAL OF ABOVE AVERAGE LIQUIDITY, i.e., - QUALITY & DIVERSIFIED ACCOUNTS RECEIVABLE - MULTI-PURPOSE & HIGHLY MARKETABLE INVENTORY OF RAW MATERIALS OF FINISHED GOODS - THINLY TRADED STOCKS	DOCUMENTATION AS ABOVE. THE BANK HAS DOMINION OVER THE MONITORING AND CONTROL. COLLATERAL IS MONITORED RELATIVELY FREQUENTLY (BUT AT LEAST WEEKLY). LOCK BOX OR SIMILAR COLLECTION CONTROLS IN PLACE TO MONITOR COLLECTION. BANKS AUDITS ARE DONE 3 TIMES A YEAR OR MORE FREQUENTLY.	IS PERFECTED AND UNCONTESTABLE	1-3 YEAR MATURITIES VERY STRONG LOAN AGREEMENT
4: BELOW AVERAGE RISK	VALUE IS ASCERTAINABLE. HAS MODERATELY MORE VOLATILITY AND/OR PROVIDES A MARGIN OVER THE SUPPORTED OBLIGATION.	COLLATERAL OF AVERAGE LIQUIDITY, i.e., - ACCOUNTS RECEIVABLE (WITH GOOD TURNOVER) ALTHOUGH SOME MODEST CONCENTRATIONS MAY EXIST - INVENTORY OF RAW MATERIALS OR FINISHED GOODS WHERE TURNOVER IS	DOCUMENTATION AS ABOVE. THE BANK HAS DOMINION OVER MOST OF THE MONITORING & CONTROL FUNCTIONS. COLLATERAL IS MONITORED ON A REGULAR BASIS BUT NO LESS THAN MONTHLY. BANK AUDITS DONE 3 TIMES A YEAR.	COVERAGE MAY INCLUDE A FEW CONDITIONS YET IS INTENDED TO COVER ANY OR ALL OF OBLIGORS INDEBTEDNESS UNDER ALL ECONOMIC AND POLITICAL RISKS.	

First Fidelity Bancorporation Risk Rating Guide

Borrower: _____ Risk Rating Decision: _____

Date: _____ Lending Officer: _____

RISK RATING	COLLATERAL — VALUE / MARGIN	COLLATERAL — LIQUIDITY	SUPPORT — DOCUMENTATION & CONTROL	GUARANTEES — RAGE / CONDITI OCUMENTATIO	GUARANTEES — TERMS
5: AVERAGE RISK	VALUE IS ASCERTAINABLE PERHAPS WITH SOME EFFORT. HAS AVERAGE VOLATILITY AND/OR PROVIDES A REASONABLE MARGIN OVER SUPPORTED OBLIGATION.	COLLATERAL OF AVERAGE LIQUIDITY, i.e., - ACCOUNTS RECEIVABLE WITH ADEQUATE TURNOVER WITH NO CONCENTRATION GREATER THAN 10% - INVENTORY OF RAW MATERIALS OR FINISHED GOODS WHICH MAY REFLECT SOME SPECIALIZATION BUT TURNOVER IS WITHIN INDUSTRY AVERAGES. - ATTRACTIVELY LOCATED REAL ESTATE WITH MULTIPLE USES	DOCUMENTATION AS ABOVE. THE BANK MONITORS THE COLLATERAL THROUGH CROSS-CHECKING BORROWING BASE CERTIFICATES AND RECEIVES AT LEAST MONTHLY RECEIVABLE, INVENTORY AND PAYABLE AGINGS.	COVERAGE I ALL NECESSARY SEVERAL C DOCUMENTATION EXISTS AND NOT COVER IS PERFECTED. HOWEVER, INDEBTEDN THE DOCUMENTATION MAY DOES NOT C BE QUESTIONED. ECONOMIC AND POLITICAL RISKS.	NORMAL AMORTIZATION
6: MANAGEMEN ATTENTION RISK	VALUE MAY NOT BE EASILY DETERMINED OR MONITORED. HAS ABOVE AVERAGE VOLATILITY BUT PROVIDES A MODERATE MARGIN OVER THE SUPPORTED OBLIGATION.	COLLATERAL OF BELOW AVERAGE LIQUIDITY, i.e., - STATIONARY FIXED ASSETS OF SPECIALIZED NATURE - ACCOUNTS RECEIVABLE HIGHLY CONCENTRATED AND/OR LOW QUALITY CUSTOMERS - REAL ESTATE WITH SPECIALIZED USE OR POOR LOCATION	ALL NEEDED DOCUMENTS ARE SUSTAINABLE & PERFECTED. THE NATURE OF THE AGREEMENTS DUE TO OTHER LIENS OR MODIFICATIONS, MAY LIMIT THE BANK'S ABILITY TO PURSUE COLLECTION AGGRESSIVELY. THE BANK IS NOT MONITORING COLLATERAL ON A REGULAR BASIS BUT IS DEPENDENT ON GENERAL UCC FILINGS.		
7: SPECIAL MENTION	VALUE MAY BE HIGHLY DIFFICULT TO DETERMINE OR IS HIGHLY VOLATILE. VALUE MAY ALSO PROVIDE MINIMAL MARGIN OVER OBLIGATION SUPPORTED.	COLLATERAL WITH POOR LIQUIDITY, i.e., - ASSETS WHERE LIQUIDATION DUE TO ASSEMBLY OF ASSETS, SPECIALIZED IN NATURE, ENVIRONMENTAL ISSUES WHERE FORECLOSURE MAY NOT BE WARRANTED, ETC., WILL ERODE COLLATERAL VALUE.	PERFECTION IS QUESTIONABLE OR DOCUMENTS ARE HIGHLY GENERALIZED WHICH MAKES THE QUALITY AND SUBSTAINABILITY HIGHLY QUESTIONABLE. BANK HAS NO DOMINION OVER MONITORING/CONTROLLING COLLATERAL.	COVERAGE IS VERY CONDITIONA ALL NECESSARY COVER ALL DOCUMENTATI 7 YEAR MATURITIES INDEBTEDN IS PERFECTED OR MORE ECONOMIC CLEARLY LACKS STRENGTH. RISKS.	BULLET LOANS OR LARGE BALLOON PAYMENTS VERY WEAK LOAN AGREEMENTS SUBORDINATED DEBT SIGNIFICANT ASSETS PLEDGED TO OTHER CRE
8: SUB-STANDARD	COLLATERAL WEAKNESS IS PRONOUNCED. DISORDERLY MARKET HAS NEGATI EFFECTS ON LIQUIDATION VALUE. CONTROL OVER COLLATERAL MAY BE POOR DUE TO INADEQUATE DOCUMENTA N PROCEDURES.				

Exhibit 21.4

First Fidelity Bancorporation Risk Rating Guide

Borrower: _____ Risk Rating Decision: _____

Date: _____ Lending Officer: _____

RISK RATING	COLLATERAL		SUPPORT	GUARANTEES	
	VALUE / MARGIN	LIQUIDITY	DOCUMENTATION & CONTROL	RAGE / CONDITI	OCUMENTATIO	TERMS
9: DOUBTFUL	COLLATERAL WEAKNESSES ARE SEVERE AND LIQUIDITY IS POOR. VALUE DOES OT COVER CREDIT AMOUNT. CONTROL OVER COLLATERAL MAY BE MINIMAL.			NO VALUE	
10: LOSS	COLLATERAL HAS NO SIGNIFICANT VALUE.				

Index